FORENSIC PSYCHOLOGY

FORENSIC PSYCHOLOGY

EDITED BY

Graham Davies

Clive Hollin

Ray Bull

University of Leicester, United Kingdom

WITH CONTRIBUTIONS BY

Julie Blackwell-Young
Charles J. Brainerd
Brian R. Clifford
Pär Anders Granhag
Maria Hartwig
Ruth Hatcher
Robyn E. Holliday
Ulf Holmberg
Joanna Jamel
Ola Kronkvis
James McGuire
Emma J. Palmer
Valerie F. Reyna
Tim Valentine
Helen L. Westcott
Jacqueline M. Wheatcroft

John Wiley & Sons, Ltd

Other Wiley Editorial Offices

John Wiley & Sons Inc., 111 River Street, Hoboken, NJ 07030, USA

Jossey-Bass, 989 Market Street, San Francisco, CA 94103-1741, USA

Wiley-VCH Verlag GmbH, Boschstr. 12, D-69469 Weinheim, Germany

John Wiley & Sons Australia Ltd, 42 McDougall Street, Milton, Queensland 4064, Australia

John Wiley & Sons (Asia) Pte Ltd, 2 Clementi Loop #02-01, Jin Xing Distripark, Singapore 129809

John Wiley & Sons Canada Ltd, 6045 Freemont Blvd. Mississauga, Ontario, L5R 4J3, Canada

Library of Congress Cataloging-in-Publication Data

Forensic psychology / edited by Graham Davies, Clive Hollin, Ray Bull.
     p. cm.
   Includes bibliographical references and index.
1. Forensic psychology. I. Davies, Graham, 1943- II. Hollin, Clive R.
III. Bull, Ray.
   RA1148.F5565 2008
   614'.15–dc22

                                                            2008004319

ISBN 978-0-470-05832-9 (H/B)
ISBN 978-0-470-05833-6 (P/B)

Typeset in India by Thomson Digital
Printed and bound in Great Britain by CPI Antony Rowe, Chippenham, Wiltshire

This book is dedicated to all our students over the years who have asked difficult questions and kept us on our toes!

CONTENTS

PREFACE

Nationally and internationally, forensic psychology is one of the fastest growing areas of applied psychology. Yet, there are few textbooks which cover the full range of forensic work: not just forensic work with offenders but also the psychology of investigative practice and court procedures. Most take the American legal justice system as their implicit or explicit model, which differs significantly from that of other countries. At Leicester, the happy coincidence of three professors of psychology, all seasoned practitioners and researchers in the forensic area, offered the prospect of an informed and authoritative text for advanced undergraduate and postgraduate students studying courses at the interface of psychology and law.

Our initial thought was to write the whole of the book ourselves, given our complementary interests, but a glance at our diaries and commitments suggested that this was an impractical proposal. Likewise we rejected the idea of a straightforward edited book, which given the idiosyncratic interests of contributors, would inevitably omit aspects of forensic work which we considered important. Instead we settled on a hybrid ('the third way'). We each took responsibility for a different facet of the discipline and produced a template of the topics concerning that facet which we would expect to find in a good textbook of forensic psychology. We divided our text into four parts: *Part 1* covering the nature of crime and psychological theories of crime and *Part 4* dealing with the consequences for the offender were edited by Clive Hollin. *Part 2* concerned with criminal investigation was the responsibility of Ray Bull, while Graham Davies looked after *Part 3* concerned with the trial process. Once we had agreed on the overall shape of the book (and some worthy topics had to be excluded to keep the book to a manageable size), each of the editors then approached authors to write the individual chapters covering the topics identified.

We sought a range of contributors, from different countries, at different stages of their careers and working in different settings — some were in senior research positions, while others were particularly experienced in lecturing and energizing a student audience. The authors also had features in common: all were prepared to write to a template and all were experienced at communicating with readers not immersed in the topic. Modern textbooks need to be much more than just text: today's student expects a dedicated website and links to other relevant sites; recommendations for further reading; case studies and essay topics. Lecturers look for exam questions and PowerPoint material. We are grateful to our authors for coping cheerfully with these additional requirements and we hope that students and lecturers alike will benefit from them.

Our publishers at John Wiley & Sons have greatly assisted us in realizing the challenge that we set ourselves three years ago. Vivien Ward, Publisher, first encouraged us to embark on the project and has been a source of support throughout. Mark Styles, Development Editor, provided invaluable author and editorial information as well as smoothing out contractual details. Deborah Egleton took over responsibility for the project from Mark and has seen it through to the end with just the right mixture of flattery and menace. We are grateful to them all and to those who first excited our interest in forensic matters.

The Editors

ABOUT THE EDITORS

Graham M. Davies is Professor Emeritus of Psychology at the University of Leicester, UK and holds honorary professorships at the universities of Birmingham and Coventry. His most recent book, edited with Mark Kebbell, is *Practical Psychology for Forensic Investigations and Prosecutions* (2006, John Wiley & Sons). He is editor of the journal *Applied Cognitive Psychology*. He has published extensively on eyewitness testimony in children and adults and the support of vulnerable witnesses at court and appears regularly as an expert witness. He is a former president of the Society for Applied Research in Memory and Cognition and of the European Association for Psychology and Law and he also sits as a Magistrate on the Melton, Belvoir and Rutland bench.

Clive R. Hollin is Professor of Criminological Psychology in the School of Psychology at the University of Leicester, UK. He wrote the best-selling textbook *Psychology and Crime: An Introduction to Criminological Psychology* (1989, Routledge). His most recent book, edited with Emma Palmer, is *Offending Behaviour Programmes: Development, Application and Controversies* (2006, John Wiley & Sons). He is co-editor of the journal *Psychology, Crime & Law*. Alongside his various university appointments, he has worked as a psychologist in prisons, special hospitals, and regional secure units. In 1998 he received the Senior Award for Distinguished Contribution to the Field of Legal, Criminological and Forensic Psychology from the British Psychological Society.

Ray Bull is Professor of Forensic Psychology at the University of Leicester. His most recent book, which he co-wrote with colleagues from the Forensic Group at Leicester, is *Criminal Psychology: A Beginners' Guide* (2007, One World). His main research interest lies in investigative interviewing, on which he has published extensively and presented invited lectures in many parts of the world and acts regularly as an expert witness. In 2005, he received the rare honour (for a civilian) of a Commendation from the Metropolitan Police Service for "Innovation and professionalism whilst assisting a complex rape investigation which supported a successful prosecution". In 2006, Ray was invited by the Association of Chief Police Officers of England and Wales to be a member of the Approval Panel for selecting regional interview advisors: experienced police officers who advise others on how to conduct interviews in serious cases.

INTRODUCTION

Graham Davies
Clive Hollin & Ray Bull

THE NATURE OF FORENSIC PSYCHOLOGY

It is often said that forensic psychology is a broad church, embracing a variety of studies at the interface of psychology and the law. However, to pursue the analogy a little further, it is a church with two main aisles: *legal psychology* covering the application of psychological knowledge and methods to the process of law and *criminological psychology* dealing with the application of psychological theory and method to the understanding (and reduction) of criminal behaviour. In a nutshell, legal psychology deals with evidence, witnesses and the courts while criminological psychology focuses on crime and criminals. In fact the use of the umbrella term *forensic psychology* to embrace both streams of research and application is a relative recent – and contentious – development. As Blackburn (1996) emphasized, the word 'forensic' refers strictly to the courts of law, but in the absence of a more appropriate term, forensic psychology is now used in its wider application, symbolized by the decision of the British Psychological Society in 1999 to re-christen its Division of Legal and Criminological Psychology, the Division of Forensic Psychology.

SOME HISTORY

To understand how forensic psychology emerged as the high profile science it is today, it is useful to look briefly in turn at the roots of criminological and legal psychology, referring where necessary to relevant sections of the text which highlight contemporary research.

CRIMINOLOGICAL PSYCHOLOGY

Common law has long recognized the important link between psychology and criminal behaviour. It is embodied in the legal principal of *mens rea* or 'guilty mind': an individual cannot be guilty of a crime unless he or she carries out the act wilfully and intentionally. Early theories of criminal behaviour emphasized the hereditability of criminal behaviour, reflected in the work of the Italian criminologist *Cesare Lombroso* (1835–1909). Lombroso also drew on ideas from physiognomy (the idea that human traits are reflected in the structure of the face) to argue that criminals were born to offend and that this was reflected in their particular facial characteristics and build, which he believed were present among habitual criminals. The general public continues to have clear conceptions as to what they believe a rapist or a murderer should look like (Goldstein, Chance & Gilbert, 1984), but there is little evidence that these stereotypes have any reality. As early as 1913, the English physician *Charles Goring* (1880–1917) found no systematic differences in physiognomy between a large sample of criminals and a comparison group of soldiers. As for genetics, the idea of a 'criminal gene' continues to intrigue researchers (Johnson, 1998), but the pessimistic view that criminals are born not made has been consistently challenged by psychologists and psychiatrists from the beginning of the twentieth century.

The application of the psycho-dynamic ideas of Sigmund Freud and his successors had a significant influence on conceptions of many aspects of everyday life, including crime. The English psychiatrist *John Bowlby* (1907–1990) argued that separation of mother and child during the second sixth months of life had permanent, damaging consequences for a child's later development and well-being. In his book *Forty-Four Juvenile Thieves* (Bowlby, 1946), Bowlby argued that in all cases he described, the cause of the delinquency could be traced to a period of 'maternal deprivation' in early childhood. The importance that Bowlby laid on this early bond is reflected in contemporary attachment theory (O'Connor & Zeenah, 2003), but his view that the damage was irreversible has not been supported by subsequent research (Rutter, 1981), nor that separation alone can explain which child develops into a criminal.

The behaviourist school in psychology placed a general emphasis upon the role of learning in shaping all human behaviour, whether normal or abnormal, through the mechanism of conditioning. In this context there are two broad lines of thought: Pavlov and classical conditioning, and Skinner and operant learning. The latter eventually mutates into Bandura's social learning theory. *Hans Eysenck* (1916–1997) used the principles of conditioning described by *Ivan Pavlov* (1849–1936) to develop a general theory linking crime with personality. Eysenck (1977) incorporated biological and social factors into his theory, bringing them together as factors that determined an individual's personality. According to Eysenck, an individual's personality determines, in large part, their ability to learn from (or condition to) other people in their social environment. Thus, personality plays a fundamental role in the process of the child's socialization, with certain configurations of personality more or less likely to behave in a manner that is antisocial or criminal.

According to Eysenck, the likelihood of an individual developing into a criminal will be determined by their levels of the personality dimensions of extraversion and neuroticism. Eysenck suggests a biological basis for extraversion and neuroticism linked to the functioning of an individual's cortical and autonomic nervous systems. High levels of both extraversion and neuroticism lead to poor conditionability, so that neurotic extraverts, the personality type the least easy to condition, will be the least well socialized. In turn, low socialization increases the likelihood of criminal behaviour and so it would be predicted that neurotic-extraverts would be disproportionately represented in the criminal population. Eysenck's theories encouraged psychological research with offenders, which found some support for his theory, but it was widely condemned by contemporary criminologists as overly mechanistic, biological, and deterministic (Taylor, Walton & Young, 1973). Although criminology and psychology, particularly forensic psychology, may have a common interest, the history of the interaction between the two disciplines is punctuated by periods of antipathy (Hollin, 2007).

While an important landmark in the application of psychological theories to explain criminal behaviour, Eysenck's theory did not have a large impact with respect to the rehabilitation and treatment of offenders. The American psychologist, B.F. Skinner (1904–1990), advanced Pavlovian theory with the development of the notion of *operant learning*. Simply, Skinner suggested that an individual's behaviour acts (or *operates*) on the environment, so producing consequences for the individual. Behaviour that produces consequences (social or material) that the person finds rewarding is likely to be repeated, in which case Skinner would say that the behaviour is being *reinforced*; if the behaviour produces consequences that people find aversive then they are less likely to repeat that behaviour, in which case Skinner would say that the behaviour is being *punished*. Skinner's notion of operant conditioning was taken and applied to explain criminal behaviour (Jeffery, 1965). Further, Skinner's operant learning was put to work, with some success, in working with offenders to reduce the likelihood that they would reoffend (Milan, 2001).

In the late twentieth century, the emergence of cognitive psychology encouraged the integration of 'internal' processes, such as thoughts and emotions, into learning theory. This integration is most clearly seen in the development of social learning theory by the psychologist Albert Bandura (Bandura, 1977, 1986). Social learning theory gave rise to interventions that aimed to change 'internal' processes (i.e. cognitions) as well as overt behaviour, giving rise to the term 'cognitive-behavioural' and the associated methods of treatment.

Cognitive-behavioural interventions became increasingly popular for use with offenders (Hollin, 1990). For example, the social psychologist *Raymond Novaco* (Novaco, 1994) emphasized the central importance of anger in understanding some forms of violence. The use of anger-control treatments has become widespread with violent offenders.

The critical importance of appropriate cognitive development was emphasized by the American psychologist *Lawrence Kohlberg* (1927–1987), whose work was inspired by the ideas of the great developmental psychologist, *Jean Piaget* (1896–1980). Kohlberg argued that in order to achieve full moral maturity it was necessary for children to pass through six distinct stages of moral development: starting from a morality based on the threat of punishment, to moral reasoning based on an appreciation of the social value of order and reciprocity (Power, Higgins & Kohlberg, 1989). The link between the hypothesized stage individuals have reached and their actual behaviour has remained a source of controversy, but as a formal analysis of the development of moral judgment, Kohlberg's model remains influential in both understanding and working with offenders (Palmer, 2003).

A different line of development also took place in the UK in the form of crime prevention measures based on rational choice theory. Cornish and Clarke (1986) proposed that crime results from rational choice to offend by the criminal, with the prime motivation being personal gain, while avoiding detection, when the opportunities arose. This theory led to measures known as *situational crime prevention* in which the environment is changed, say by using electronic alarms to minimize the opportunities for crime; or increasing police patrols to maximize the chances of crime detection.

However, despite such developments in psychological theory and practice, the popular view was that *'nothing works'* in offender rehabilitation. This view led politicians and policy makers in some parts of the world, including the UK, to the pessimistic consensus that the only answer the criminal justice system could offer to rising crime was to build more prisons (Hollin, 2001). However, building on decades of research, this view was challenged by several groups of psychologists, principally from Canada and the UK, who rallied under the banner of *'what works'*. These psychologists argued that the meta-analyses of the results of treatment trials with offenders showed that interventions, principally employing cognitive-behavioural methods, *did* produce lower rates of recidivism compared to controls (Andrews *et al.*, 1990; McGuire 1995).

As we move into the twenty-first century, the emphasis placed by the 'what works' movement upon an evidence-based approach to penal policy within the criminal justice system has begun to find support among more pragmatic policy makers in Europe and North America. As the issue of crime and offending continues to grow in importance in society, it seems inevitable that policy makers will turn to psychology in general and forensic psychology in particular for answers to the questions of 'what makes a person offend?' and 'how can crime be curtailed?'

PROFESSIONAL ORGANIZATIONS FOR FORENSIC PSYCHOLOGISTS

The **European Association of Psychology and Law** (EAPL) was instituted in 1992 and is the principal European organization for psychologists and lawyers who work at the interface of the two disciplines. The Association aims to promote and develop research, and hosts regular conferences in different parts of Europe, the proceedings of which are regularly published. Membership of EAPL is not restricted to Europeans, and it currently has some 300 members in more than 20 countries. Membership is open to all professionals with a qualification in psychology, law, or a related discipline such as criminology or psychiatry. Full membership requires a university-level qualification or equivalent professional experience, but students and those without formal qualifications may join as affiliates. The official journal of the Association is *Psychology, Crime and Law.* The Association's website can be found at: http://www.law.kuleuven.be/eapl/

The **Division of Forensic Psychology** (DFP) of the British Psychological Society was founded in 1977 as the Division of Criminological and Legal Psychology, and renamed the Division of Forensic Psychology in 1999. The Division represents the interests of those psychologists who work in the criminal and civil justice systems. Division membership includes forensic psychologists working in academic settings, prison services, health, education and social services. Members must first qualify to join the BPS prior to applying for the DFP which has grades of membership. Full membership requires both postgraduate training and supervised practice in forensic psychology, but interested graduates in psychology may become general members. The official journal of the

Association is *Legal and Criminological Psychology*. The Division's website can be found at: www.bps.org.uk/dfp/dfp_home.cfm

The **American Psychology-Law Society (AP-LS)**, Division 41 of the American Psychological Association, is an interdisciplinary organization devoted to scholarship, practice, and public service in psychology and law. Members of AP-LS need not be members of APA, although many members belong to both organizations. Recent activities have included collecting course syllabi and teaching materials, surveying career opportunities in psychology and law and studying the special ethical problems of expert testimony. It sponsors a science policy forum and holds regular meetings often under the auspices of the APA. Membership is open to interested professionals and students in other disciplines beyond psychology. The official journal of the Division is *Law and Human Behavior*. Its website can be found at: http://www.ap-ls.org/.

A number of organizations for applied psychologists include a large membership of forensic psychologists. The **Society for Applied Research in Memory and Cognition (SARMAC)** was founded in 1994 and includes many researchers interested in psychology and law. It holds regular conferences, invariably with sessions devoted to legal themes and its membership is open to graduate and undergraduate students in psychology or related disciplines; other interested persons can join as affiliates. The official journal is *Applied Cognitive Psychology*. Its website can be found at: http://www.sarmac.org/society.html.

LEGAL PSYCHOLOGY

Legal psychology was one of the first areas of applied psychology to be explored by experimental psychologists. It then languished as a discipline until the 1970s when there was a great resurgence of interest in research at the interface of psychology and law, which continues today.

Legal psychology began in Europe around the turn of the twentieth century (see Sporer, 1982). Prominent among these pioneers was the Austrian *Hans Gross* (1847–1915) who in his career claimed to have performed over 45 000 pre-trial examinations on witnesses. As a result of his experiences, he became sceptical about the accuracy of witnesses and developed tests to try to discriminate those who might prove reliable. He described his experiences in probably the first textbook of legal psychology published in 1898.

One issue of concern to Gross was the suggestibility of witnesses under questioning. The French psychologist *Alfred Binet* (1857–1911) had conducted some of the earliest studies on suggestibility and conformity effects in children, described in his book *La Suggestibilité* (1900) and these ideas were taken up by the German psychologist *Louis William Stern* (1871–1938). It was Stern, who as part of his programme of research into what he termed the *Psychologie der Aussage* (the psychology of verbal reports), started the first journal devoted to witness psychology and introduced new methods such as the 'event test': a carefully rehearsed incident staged in front of onlookers who are subsequently asked to report the events in their own words and answer questions concerning details, a technique still in use today.

The *Aussage* movement continued to be active in Germany up until the First World War, but the man credited with publicizing the new science to the English-speaking world was Stern's friend, *Hugo Münsterberg* (1863–1916). Münsterberg moved from Germany to Harvard University in 1892 to accept an invitation from William James to set up their first experimental psychology laboratory. Münsterberg's interests in psychological aspects of the law went well beyond issues of testimony. In 1908 he published *On the Witness Stand*, a book aimed at publicizing and promoting the value of psychology to law enforcement in general and the courts in particular. The topics Münsterberg discussed include many issues researched by forensic psychologists today and indeed, most figure in this textbook. Among the topics discussed were:

- the accuracy of witness testimony
- the detection of deception
- false confessions
- suggestive questioning at court, and
- effective interviewing procedures.

Sadly, the emergence of Münsterberg's book did not usher in a new dawn for legal psychology. Its sometimes bombastic tone and casual generalizations alienated lawyers (he dismissed them as 'obdurate'), precisely the group to whom the implications of the book might most usefully have been directed. It drew from the distinguished American jurist, *John H. Wigmore* (1863–1943) a majestic rebuke in the form of a satirical account of an imaginary trial in which Münsterberg's more specious and expansive statements were held up to ridicule (Wigmore, 1909). Wigmore did concede that while psychology had little to offer to the law at present, there might come a time when psychology would have matured sufficiently to make a significant contribution. This rejection of Münsterberg's ideas was followed by his death in 1916, which effectively ended the study of legal psychology in the US until its revival in the 1970s.

One of the principal motives for the involvement of psychologists in legal matters was the concern around identification, which had led to miscarriages of justice. In Britain, Lord Justice Devlin published a report in 1976 on a series of cases involving mistaken identity. Devlin's enquiry into law and practice on identification was the first to take evidence from psychologists on perception and identification and one of his recommendations was that "Research should be directed as to establishing ways in which the insights of psychology can be brought to bear on the conduct of identification parades and the practice of the courts" (Devlin, 1976, p. 149). This led directly to Home Office funding of research into bodily and voice identification (Shepherd, Ellis & Davies, 1976; Bull & Clifford, 1984) and led in turn to a more positive approach generally toward the value of psychological research to the police and the law (Bull *et al.*, 1983).

In the US, the involvement of psychologists in identification issues took a rather different form. In the UK, psychologists with expertise in witness matters were not generally permitted to give evidence in criminal trials, with the exception of cases of alleged false confession (Gudjonsson, 2003). In the US, *Elizabeth Loftus* and *Robert*

Buckhout (1935–1990) were among the first psychologists permitted to testify as experts at trials regarding the reliability of eyewitness testimony in general and identification in particular. This testimony was routinely challenged at trial and this in turn led to a greater investment in research to better understand the processes that led to witness error. An important distinction emerged between *estimator* and *system* variables (Wells, 1978). Estimator variables concerned the haphazard circumstances surrounding an initial observation of a perpetrator, such as lighting and distance from the witness while system variables covered those factors in control of law enforcement officials, such as how many persons were present on an identification parade and their degree of similarity to the suspect. Much of this new research was summarized in Loftus's influential book *Eyewitness Testimony* (Loftus, 1979), which added to the growing interest among experimental psychologists in legal process.

Loftus's work had focused very much on the vagaries of witness testimony. It built on the findings of the *Aussage* movement by exploring the impact of so-called 'post-event information': information that witnesses to a crime read, saw or talked about after an incident and the adverse effect this might have on the reliability of their testimony at any subsequent trial. In the 1980s, universities in the US launched the first joint doctoral programmes involving the study of both psychology and law, which in turn led to research with a much wider focus on psychological aspects of legal procedure. Research in areas such as the wording and timing of legal pronouncements and in particular jury decision making (Hastie, Penrod & Pennington, 1987) laid the foundations for a psychology of jurisprudence.

One of the earliest concerns of forensic psychologists was the reliability of child witnesses and this issue also sprang back into prominence in the 1980s. In Britain and the US, children's evidence had traditionally been excluded or restricted by the courts because of concerns over suggestibility. However, there was increasing public concern that such restrictions effectively prevented most child complainants of abuse from seeking justice. New research, particularly by the US psychologist *Gail Goodman* (e.g. Rudy & Goodman, 1981) demonstrated that, under appropriate circumstances, children were capable of providing reliable testimony and this increased the pressure for reform of the law and the introduction of child-friendly measures at court, such as remote or video testimony (Davies, 1999). The dangers of the uncritical acceptance of particularly very young children's testimony are demonstrated by such miscarriages of justice as the Kelly Michaels trial in the US (Bruck, Ceci & Hembrooke, 1998) and the Shieldfield Nursery affair in the UK (Webster & Woffindon, 2002). Research particularly by the US developmental psychologist, *Stephen Ceci* has highlighted situations where children's testimony is likely to be more or less reliable. Official guidance written by psychologists for investigators charged with interviewing children is careful to take account of the vulnerabilities, as well as the strengths, of children's testimony.

Another concern dating from Münsterberg is the detection of deception. Psychologists have carefully researched the many assumptions surrounding so-called 'lie-signs' and have cast a critical eye over the various devices, from the polygraph to the fMRI brain imaging technique which have claimed infallibility in spotting lies (Vrij, 2008). In 2004, the British Psychological Society published a research review of all established methods to date and concluded that none had yet reached a point where their use in the courts for determining truth and falsity could be recommended.

The suggestibility and reliability of adult witnesses has been raised by the acrimonious debate over the status of *recovered memories*: memories of trauma often recovered during the course of therapy of which the person was previously unaware. This issue too came into prominence as a result of a trial: a murder trial in which there was a clash of expert testimony. In California, George Franklin stood trial for the murder of a young girl, Susan Nason, some 20 years previously. The principal evidence against him was the eyewitness account of his daughter who had recently recovered a vivid memory of her father carrying out the murder when she was a young child. The prosecution expert, psychiatrist *Lenore Terr* argued that the repression of memories was a commonplace among clinical patients and that Ms Franklin's memories fitted this pattern. For the defence, *Elizabeth Loftus* argued that Ms Franklin's testimony contained significant errors and that there was nothing in it that could not have been gleaned from local newspaper reports of the time: Ms Franklin was confusing real events with self-generated imagery, perhaps fuelled by suggestion in therapy. The jury found George Franklin guilty, but the sentence was reversed on appeal (Maclean, 1993). This reversal was due in part to the research evidence accumulated in the interim that recovered memories are often unreliable and *false memories* can be readily generated by established experimental techniques in the psychological laboratory. Cognitive and clinical psychologists continue to debate the circumstances in which recovered memories may be reliable or false, but there is no doubt that this and other contentious issues continue to generate significant research by psychologists, some of which is of direct relevance to the law and which is described in the ensuing chapters.

THE STRUCTURE OF THIS TEXT

This text attempts to introduce students to the core areas of forensic psychology. It is divided into four parts each devoted to a different facet of the discipline:

Part 1: The Anatomy of Crime

In Chapter 1 Joanna Jamel surveys our current understanding of criminals and crimes while in Chapter 2 Emma Palmer examines the principal psychological theories that have been proposed to explain this most perplexing and persistent aspect of human (mis)behaviour.

Part 2: Investigating Crime

In Chapter 3 Tim Valentine looks at the special problems that eyewitness identification presents for investigators. Ulf Holmberg and Ola Kronkvist (Chapter 4) consider how investigators can interview suspects in a way most likely to lead to a reliable confession of guilt while Robyn Holliday, Charles Brainerd and Valerie Reyna (Chapter 4) examine interviewing techniques to enable witnesses to provide the maximum amount of useful information with the minimum of error. Deception and lying can occur in any investigative interview and in Chapter 6, Pär Anders Granhag and Maria Hartwig review research on how to detect lies and deception in the police interview.

Part 3: The Trial Process

In Chapter 7 Jacqueline M. Wheatcroft describes how courts operate and reviews findings on how judges and juries reach decisions on the guilt or innocence of an accused. Chapter 8 by Helen Westcott is devoted to witnesses' concerns and fears of the legal process how witnesses can best be safeguarded, while in Chapter 9, Julie Blackwell-Young examines research on what factors influence the likely reliability and credibility of witnesses in general and vulnerable witnesses in particular. Finally, in Chapter 10 Brian R. Clifford considers the contentious role of the forensic psychologist as an expert witness, with particular reference to the possibility of mistaken identification, the testimony of children and recovered memories.

Part 4: After Sentencing

In Chapter 11 James McGuire asks the question 'What is the point of sentencing?' and answers it by reference to research on the impact of different regimes of punishment and rehabilitation on the likelihood of re-offending, while in Chapter 12, Ruth Hatcher looks at modern treatment regimes for offenders and research on their effectiveness relative to more traditional solutions which focus solely on incarceration.

BOOK COMPANION WEBSITE

This book is accompanied by a website at **www.wileyeurope.com/college/davies**. Lecturers will find PowerPoint slide presentations for each chapter as well as sample essay questions. Selected full-length journal articles and book chapters have also been provided to offer material for assignments and classroom discussions. Students will find an online version of the Glossary, Further Reading and Links to useful websites.

REFERENCES

Andrews, D.A., Zinger, I., Hoge, R.D. *et al.* (1990). Does correctional treatment work? A clinically relevant and informed meta-analysis. *Criminology, 28*, 369–404.

Bandura, A. (1977). *Social learning theory*. New York: Prentice-Hall.

Bandura, A. (1986). *Social foundations of thought and action: A social-cognitive theory*. Englewood Cliffs, NJ: Prentice-Hall.

Binet, A. (1900). *La suggestibilité* [On suggestibility]. Paris: Schleicher.

Bowlby, J. (1946). *Forty-Four juvenile thieves*. London: Bailliere Tindall & Cox.

British Psychological Society (2004). *A review of the current scientific status and Fields of application of the polygraphic deception detection*. Leicester: British Psychological Society.

Bruck, M., Ceci, S.J., & Hembrooke, H. (1998). Reliability and credibility of young children's reports: From research to policy and practice. *American Psychologist 53*, 136–151.

Bull, R., Bustin, R., Evans, P., & Gahagan, D. (1983). *Psychology for police officers*. Chichester: John Wiley & Sons. (Reprinted, 1985.)

Bull, R. & Clifford, B. (1984). Earwitness voice recognition accuracy. In G. Wells & E. Loftus (Eds), *Eyewitness testimony: Psychological perspectives*. New York: Cambridge University Press.

Cornish, D.B. & Clarke, R.V.G. (Eds) (1986). *The reasoning criminal: Rational choice perspectives on offending*. New York: Springer-Verlag.

Davies, G.M. (1999). The impact of television on the presentation and reception of children's evidence. *International Journal of Law and Psychiatry, 22*, 241–256.

Devlin, Lord P. (1976). *Departmental committee on evidence of identification in criminal cases*. London: HMSO.

Eysenck, H.J. (1977). *Crime and personality* (3rd edn). London: Routledge & Kegan Paul.

Goldstein, A.G., Chance, J.E., & Gilbert, B. (1984). Facial stereotypes of good guys and bad guys: A replication and extension. *Bulletin of the Psychonomic Society, 22*, 549–552.

Goring, C. (1913). *The English convict: A statistical study*. London: HMSO.

Gross, H. (1898) *Kriminalpsychologie*. [Criminal Psychology]. Leipzig: Vogel. (English translation downloadable at: http://manybooks.net/titles/grosshanetext98crmsy10.html.)

Gudjonsson, G.H. (2003). *The psychology of interrogations and confessions: A handbook*. Chichester: John Wiley & Sons.

Hastie, R., Penrod, S.D., & Pennington, N. (1986). *Inside the jury*. Cambridge, MA: Harvard University Press.

Hollin, C.R. (1990). *Cognitive-behavioral interventions with young offenders*. Elmsford, NY: Pergamon Press.

Hollin, C.R. (1999). Treatment programmes for offenders: Meta-analysis, 'what works', and beyond. *International Journal of Law and Psychiatry, 22*, 361–372.

Hollin, C.R. (Ed.) (2001). *Handbook of offender assessment and treatment*. Chichester: John Wiley & Sons.

Hollin, C.R. (2007). Criminological psychology. In M. Maguire, R. Morgan, & R. Reiner (Eds), *The Oxford handbook of criminology* (4th edn) (pp. 43–77). Oxford: Oxford University Press.

Jeffery, C.R. (1965). Criminal behavior and learning theory. *Journal of Criminal Law, Criminology, and Police Science, 56*, 294–300.

Johnson, M. (1998). Genetic technology and its impact on culpability for criminal actions. *Cleveland State Law Review, 46*, 443–470.

Loftus, E.F. (1979). *Eyewitness testimony*. Cambridge, MA: Harvard University Press.

Maclean, H.N. (1993). *Once upon a time*. New York: HarperCollins.

McGuire J. (Ed.) (1995). *What works: Reducing reoffending*. Chichester: John Wiley & Sons.

Milan, M.A. (2001). Behavioral approaches to correctional management and rehabilitation. In C.R. Hollin (Ed.), *Handbook of offender assessment and treatment* (pp.139–154). Chichester: John Wiley & Sons.

Münsterberg, H. (1908). *On the witness stand: Essays on psychology and crime*. New York: McClure.

Novaco, R.W. (1994). Anger as a risk factor for violence among the mentally disordered. In J. Monahan & H. Steadman (Eds), *Violence and mental disorder: Developments in risk assessment* (pp. 21–59). Chicago, IL: University of Chicago Press.

O'Connor, T.G & Zeenah, C.H. (Eds) (2003). Special Issue: Current perspectives on assessment and treatment of attachment disorders. *Attachment and Human Development, 5*, 219–326.

Palmer. E.J. (2003). *Offending behaviour: Moral reasoning, criminal conduct and the rehabilitation of offenders.* Cullompton: Willan.

Power, F.C., Higgins, A., & Kohlberg, L. (1989). *Lawrence Kohlberg's approach to moral education.* New York: Columbia University Press.

Rudy, L. & Goodman, G.S. (1991). Effects of participation on children's reports: Implications for children's testimony. *Developmental Psychology, 27,* 527–538.

Rutter, M. (1981). *Maternal deprivation reassessed* (2nd edn). Harmondsworth: Penguin.

Shepherd, J.W., Ellis, H.D., & Davies, G.M. (1982). *Identification evidence: A psychological evaluation.* Aberdeen: Aberdeen University Press.

Sporer, S.L. (1982). A brief history of the psychology of testimony. *Current Psychological Reviews, 2,* 323–340.

Taylor, I., Walton, P., & Young, J. (1973). *The new criminology: For a social theory of deviancy.* London: Routledge & Kegan Paul.

Vrij, A. (2008). *Detecting lies and deceit: Pitfalls and opportunities.* Chichester: John Wiley & Sons.

Webster, R. & Woffindon, B. (2002, 31 July). Cleared: The story of Shieldfield. *Guardian,* G2. Downloadable at: http://www.richardwebster.net/cleared.html

Wells, G.L. (1978). Applied eyewitness testimony research: System variables and estimator variables. *Journal of Personality and Social Psychology, 36,* 1546–1557.

Wigmore, J.J. (1909). Professor Münsterberg and the psychology of evidence. *Illinois Law Review, 3,* 399–445.

ANNOTATED READING LIST

Bartol, C.R. & Bartol, A.M. (2005). History of forensic psychology. In I.B. Weiner & A.K. Hess (Eds), *The handbook of forensic psychology* (2nd edn) (pp. 1–27). New York: John Wiley & Sons. *A very readable short introduction to the history of forensic psychology.*

Hollin, C.R. (2007). Criminological psychology. In M. Maguire, R. Morgan, & R. Reiner (Eds), *The Oxford handbook of criminology* (4th edn) (pp. 43–77). Oxford: Oxford University Press. *An in-depth look at the development of criminological aspects of psychology, setting contributions in the context of the often uneasy ideological relationship between psychology and criminology.*

Sporer, S.L. (1982). A brief history of the psychology of testimony. *Current Psychological Reviews, 2,* 323–340. *An expert assessment of the goals and achievements of the* Aussage *movement in Europe in the period leading up to the First World War.*

PART 1

THE ANATOMY OF CRIME

1

CRIME AND ITS CAUSES

Joanna Jamel
University of Leicester, United Kingdom

Everyone holds different views about what constitutes criminal behaviour and what to do about it. Historically, what behaviour has been defined as 'criminal' has been much influenced by moral conventions and political pressures. For example, in the UK, homosexual acts between consenting males were criminalized under the Criminal Law Amendment Act 1885 which decreed that "acts of gross indecency" between "men whether public or private" were punishable with up to two years of hard labour (Weeks, 1981, p. 117), an action which was only decriminalized in 1967 (Padfield, 2002). Likewise traditionally, physical assault or rape within a domestic setting were largely ignored by the law and only in 2004 was domestic violence the subject of new and stringent legislation under the Crime and Domestic Violence Victims Act (Office of Public Sector Information, 2007).

Definitions of crime can also vary according to who is describing them; for example, those who commit burglary may justify it as not 'really' a criminal act, because victims can recoup the costs through their insurance, or white-collar criminals may consider embezzlement to be an acceptable practice as the company can 'afford such losses'. Thus, definitions of criminal behaviour may be fluid depending on who is defining it (Walsh & Poole, 1983).

This chapter provides an introduction to the general topic of crime, and factors that contribute to offending behaviour. The key themes of this chapter are:

- how crime is classified
- how crime is measured
- explanations of why particular individuals engage in criminal behaviour and develop criminal careers, and
- the increasing importance of the victim's perspective and the victim's return to the political centre stage.

WHAT IS CRIME?

In order to address criminal behaviour, first it had to be defined. Cressey (1951) considered the classification of 'crime' as necessary for the following reasons: (i) democratic and legal agents needed to restrict the usage of this term to behaviours which contravene the law, and (ii) in accordance with the assumptions of proper scientific methodology, to facilitate the rigorous definition of "... *phenomena under investigation in criminology*" (p. 551). Padfield (2002) considered "... *crime* ... *[as] a legal wrong, which may result in* punishment" (p. 1). However, crime was thought by some criminologists to be (pre-) determined behaviour: individuals could not avoid committing crime as it was in their nature, a view illustrated in Lombroso's (1897) *L'Uomo Delinquente*. His theories will be discussed in more detail in the section below on biological explanations for criminal behaviour.

Criminal law is a corpus of laws that identify offences as crimes and their perpetrators as criminals; it also provides sentencing guidelines as to the appropriate punishment. The legislation in England and Wales has its origins in **common law** that dates from the time of the Norman Conquest. Laws may vary between countries and continents but there are certain types of behaviours which appear universally illegal, irrespective of the country of origin such as: robbery, theft, arson, burglary, murder and rape (Blackburn, 2001). Criminal behaviour may also be understood as the infringement of socially defined rules or 'norms', which dictate what types of behaviour are socially acceptable, but which, as has been illustrated, can vary across time and between countries. But, what are the fundamental underlying objectives of criminal law?

Firstly, legislation aims to maintain public moral standards. Secondly, to protect the weak and vulnerable in society. Thirdly, through linking punitive sanctions to law breaking, to deter criminal behaviour by other members of society. Finally, criminal legislation sometimes enables the rehabilitation of offenders through subjecting them to mandated interventions (such as drug relapse prevention programmes), targeting possible underlying causes (e.g. drug misuse) for their criminal behaviour while also facilitating legally sanctioned punishment such as incarceration (resulting in the removal of their personal freedom).

The definition of certain types of behaviour as 'criminal' may also be used to serve the political interests of the powerful in society and their definition of appropriate and publicly acceptable moral behaviour. Divided into its basic parts as defined under original common law, behaviour considered to be inherently evil was described in Latin as *mala in se*, whereas socially proscribed immoral behaviour was defined as *mala prohibita*. In addition to these concerns regarding moral behaviour, for certain acts to be defined as criminal two key factors must also be present. (i) *Mens rea*, which means that the person must intend to commit the act. To elaborate further, the person must plan or premeditate the perpetration of the particular behaviour, such as purposefully running over a person as opposed to accidentally hitting a pedestrian who walked out unexpectedly onto the road. Other factors may also impact upon the capacity of *mens rea* such as diminished responsibility, For example, in the *R. v. Ahluwalia* (1992) case, the victim endured years of domestic violence, and then one night after her husband threatened her with another beating, she set fire to him while he was asleep. She was originally convicted of murder, however at her appeal she pleaded guilty by reason of diminished responsibility, her defence being provocation: a sudden and temporary loss of control resulting in violent actions (Padfield, 2002). Other *mens rea* factors include insanity and automatism (e.g. where the offender committed the crime in their sleep). (ii) The other pivotal component in a criminal act is *actus reus* where the individual must perpetrate the act voluntarily and therefore was not coerced. For example, if in the case of rape the perpetrator states that the victim consented to sexual intercourse, then this refutes *actus reus*.

Criminal law also reinforces the paternalistic nature of society (sometimes described by the popular press as the 'nanny state') in the social control of the moral behaviour of individuals. This can result in paradigmatic shifts regarding the criminalizing of certain behaviours in accordance with the political concerns of the government of the time. For instance, as we have noted, homosexual acts between two consenting adult males in private was decriminalized in 1967, but it was not until the Criminal Offences Amendment Act (2000) that the age of consent for homosexual males was made the same as for heterosexual intercourse (16 years old). Media representation of particular behaviours can be used to increase support for passing certain legislation; for example, legislation aimed at reducing terrorism, but which infringes civil liberties (Burnett & Whyte, 2005). The media also socially construct issues regarding particular types of behaviour which they imply are a cause of concern for the general public and apply political pressure on the government to criminalize these behaviours, such as the introduction of anti-stalking legislation. Peelo and Soothill (2000) state that the media provide an outlet for facilitating a *"mass endorsement of morality"* (p. 136). These symbolic boundaries encourage social conformity to established rules, such as legislation.

The comprehension of criminal behaviour is pivotal in order to address the psychological factors that may contribute to criminal offending. Forensic psychology is utilized in many different contexts from assisting the initial stages of the investigative process, to developing risk assessment procedures, evaluating the effectiveness of offender treatment programmes, treating offenders, supporting victims, and generally assisting the criminal justice process through providing training and professional expertise. Psychology's individualistic interpretation of causes of criminal behaviour will be discussed later in this chapter. However, psychologists should not examine

CASE STUDY

R v Ahluwalia

The R v Ahluwalia case is an interesting one to consider further as there are a number of important factors which may have had a significant bearing on the outcome. Firstly, this case involved a well-educated Asian woman who murdered her husband in self-defence. She poured petrol over her husband and set fire to him as he slept. The initial defence used was provocation as it was stated that her actions were the result of 10 years of abuse perpetrated by the victim. She received a life sentence for her crime so the mitigating circumstances of the preceding years of abuse were not recognised. Thus, the judge's original directions to the jury were to consider whether a reasonable person with the accused's socio-demographic characteristics (e.g. her ethnicity, class and education) would have reacted in this manner. The basis of the appeal, however, was that the judge's directions should have included that Ahluwalia was suffering from Battered Woman's Syndrome (this medical condition is a form of Post-Traumatic Syndrome), a symptom of which is severe depression which was the result of years of domestic violence at the time of the incident. It was also highlighted that Ahluwalia had been unaware of the option to plead guilty to manslaughter on the grounds of diminished responsibility. The appeal was upheld in light of this additional information. Ahluwalia was subsequently released for time served. This Syndrome, while predominantly used in the defence of female offenders, can be described as "Battered Person's Syndrome" as it is not gender specific. This case highlights once more the categorization of female offenders as either "mad or bad". In order to launch a successful appeal Ahluwalia had to accept the label of "mad" and thus medicalization of the female body. However, the importance of this case lies in its fundamental impact on British legislation, in that, as a consequence of the Ahluwalia ruling, victims of partner violence could now use the mitigation of years of domestic violence. Thus, victims of domestic abuse who ultimately kill the perpetrators of their abuse are not treated as murderers who have coldly premeditated the attack. The distinction is the intent of the offender, in that Ahluwalia did not intend to kill her husband but to hurt him in order for him to experience what the abuse felt like. However, choosing the defence used by Ahluwalia has inherent implications regarding the agency of the defendant and the moulding of the accused's behaviour into such that is comprehended by society. Although this defence was successful in Ahluwalia's case, in the later case R v Thornton, Sara Thornton stabbed her husband to death while he slept and received a life sentence, which reflects the absence of recognition of the abuse which had been perpetrated against her over a number of years. The judicial reasons provided for the severity of sentence was that she should not have waited and then acted but responded to her partner's abuse on an immediate basis. Also, the fact that she suffered from a personality disorder and her eligibility for the Battered Women's Syndrome type of defence were not considered. The Thornton case provides an interesting contrast to the Ahluwalia case.

individual criminal behaviour in a social vacuum. Not only does the individual act on society but the reverse also occurs. Criminal behaviour therefore is an interactive process or as stated by Buckle (1861) "... *Society prepares the crime, and the guilty are only the instruments by which it is executed*" (p. 108).

Thus, the definition of criminal behaviour may be shaped by the power structures in society and societal moral concerns influenced by paradigmatic shifts in government policy or mass media sentiment. In the next section, the prevalence of criminal offending in society is considered.

MEASURING CRIME

England and Wales: Officially Recorded Crime Statistics and the British Crime Survey

Measuring the prevalence of crime is key to deciding the most effective methods for tackling and reducing crime. However, measures of crime are not without their shortcomings. For example, the dark figure of unreported and unrecorded crimes is a phenomenon that should always be borne in mind when considering officially recorded statistics. Self-report surveys such as the British Crime Survey ask individuals about their reasons for reporting or not reporting crime to the police, as well as highlighting general levels of fear of crime in society. A limitation of such self-report studies is that they are predominantly carried out on juveniles and focus on particular crimes. Thus, the findings may not be generalizable or representative of patterns of offending (which may vary with age, influencing the severity of crime committed) (Williams, 2004). There have been efforts to compensate for the limitations of officially recorded statistics and self-reported crime statistics. In the *Crime in England and Wales 2002–2003* report, both the British Crime Survey and officially recorded statistics were combined for the first time (Home Office, 2003). The aim was to provide a more holistic picture of the prevalence of criminal victimization in England and Wales. The introduction of the National Crime Recording Statistics in 2002 lead to a considerable augmentation in the recorded levels of crime in England and Wales (Home Office, 2006a).

Factors to Consider in Crime Reporting

Crime-reporting practices do not take place in a social and psychological void. There are a number of factors that determine the decision to report a crime to the police, such as the victim–offender relationship, the severity of the incident, the potential stigma or humiliation of the victim and implications for the honouring of insurance claims (Coleman & Moynihan, 2002). The type of crime also influences the likelihood of it being reported: missing persons, homicides, and burglaries are more readily reported than domestic violence, child abuse or rape, although recent improvements in the police response and treatment of survivors has had an impact on reporting (Williams, 2004). In addition, there is the likelihood of certain types of violence becoming normalized and thus not perceived as a crime by the victim.

It is not only officially recorded statistics and crime victimization surveys that provide insights into the level of crime in society. There are also self-report surveys that collate data regarding individuals' own criminal offending behaviour, which assists in illuminating the dark figure of crime. For example, child molesters whose only recorded crime was incest reported also being actively involved in assaults and property crimes (Weinrott & Saylor, 1991). However, these reports have inherent limitations. Firstly, there may be a tendency for some offenders to minimize their offending. Secondly, prior offences may be forgotten by the offenders. Thirdly, acts may be defined as criminal offences by respondents but may not in fact be illegal; for instance, in the UK prostitution is legal (it is the acts associated with it that are illegal such as soliciting).

There are also surveys that explore crime rates at a micro level such as local crime surveys. Examples of local surveys in the UK include Merseyside and Nottingham, both of which were conducted in 1985. Surveys were also carried out in Islington and Sheffield in 1986 and 1987 respectively. These examine the incidence of crime at a local level in order to inform crime reduction policies (Mawby & Walklate, 1995). For example, attention may be paid to contributing factors such as the social geography or level of socio-economic deprivation particular to that area (Williams, 2004). At a macro level, there is the International Crime Victims Survey (ICVS), which provides a contextualized representation of where England and Wales are situated relative to 31 other countries across a variety of crimes. However, comparisons can be problematic because of differential practices of law enforcement agencies, legislative variation and pervasive cultural differences (Williams, 2004).

Another factor that needs consideration regarding the accuracy of recorded statistics is gender. This is noteworthy due to the divergent responses provided by the criminal justice system when dealing with female offenders, which may impact on recording practices. Depending on the type of female offender, they may be responded to in a chivalrous manner or penalized harshly for their gender-deviant behaviour as in the case of juvenile offenders (Blackburn, 2001). The negative reaction to female offenders engaged in sex-role deviant offences involving revenge or confrontation are more likely to receive a custodial sentence, and also have higher conviction rates than their male counterparts for certain crimes such as prostitution-related acts (Armstrong, 1999). Regarding national sentencing trends, the gender differential in England and Wales remains marked: in 2004, 279 500 female offenders were sentenced versus 1 257 300 male offenders (Home Office, 2005) and the corresponding figures for 2005 were 282 700 females (a rise by 1% from the last year), against 1 192 500 males (a decline of 5%) (Home Office, 2006a).

How does the recording of crime in the UK compare to other countries? In the next section, the recording and reporting of criminal behaviour in the US will be considered, drawing on the FBI's Uniform Crime Reports, the National Incident-Based Reporting System, as well as self-report surveys such as the National Crime Victimization Survey.

The United States: FBI Uniform Crime Reports, National Crime Victimization Survey and National Incident-Based Reporting System

In the US, recorded crime has been measured since 1930 and is now published annually by the FBI in their Uniform Crime Reports. This is composed of two parts: Part I measures the prevalence nationally of serious offences such as homicide, robbery and forcible rape (these habitually occur across the country), which together compose the *crime index*. Part II covers sex offences such as incest, statutory rape and indecent exposure (it excludes prostitution and commercialized vice), weapon-related crimes (such as carrying, possessing etc.) and drug-abuse violations; however, only the *arrest data* are collected. The FBI crime rates are compiled by dividing the number of reported crimes by the number of people composing the national population size which are then stated as the number of crimes per 100 000 people (Conklin, 2004). The use of the terms *'prevalence'* and *'incidence'* in relation to the calculation of crime figures also requires consideration when interpreting crime statistics due to the significant difference in meaning. For example, *'prevalence'* refers to the quantity of offences over a number of years whereas *'incidence'* relates to the perpetration of offences over a specified period such as one year. In other words, 'prevalence' is composed of collective 'incidence'. There are similar limitations regarding FBI Uniform Crime Reports, as highlighted in relation to the international victimization surveys because of variations in police recording practices across states and between local police. This raises questions regarding the reliability and validity of such statistics. In an effort to overcome these limitations, in 2000, the FBI introduced a Quality Assurance Review to maintain consistent crime recording standards across states (Conklin, 2004). Rantala (as cited in Kilpatrick, 2004) discussed the differences in the recording of crimes between the FBI Uniform Crime Report and the National Incident-Based Reporting System (NIBRS) introduced in 2001.

According to the FBI, the NIBRS provides a better quantity, quality, and efficient collection of crime data by law enforcement and an improved methodology is used to compile, analyse and audit this material (FBI, n.d.). The NIBRS has several advantages in comparison to the summary reporting system (UCR): (i) it is more detailed as offence information on 46 major crimes is collected as compared to only eight in the UCR; (ii) the definition of rape in the NIBRS includes both male and female victims unlike the summary system where only female rape victims are reported; (iii) the NIBRS differentiates between attempted and completed offences whereas the summary system does not (FBI, n.d.).

Kilpatrick (2004) recommended standardizing the definition of rape used by the FBI Crime Reports so that it is more comprehensive (besides being gender neutral, the NIBRS definition recognizes non-consensual vaginal, anal, and oral penetration by penis, foreign objects and body parts) and consistent across states. In addition, *"incomplete coding rules increase the discretion of local agencies in completing various NIBRS data elements, a problem that potentially decrements reliability"* (Maxfield, 1999, p. 133).

The Bureau of Justice Statistics of the United States Department of Justice compiles a national crime victimization survey collating data across households asking residents aged 12 years and above to document their experiences of criminal victimization (including details regarding incidents, context and offenders where feasible) on an annual basis (Kilpatrick, 2004). There are flaws in the National Crime Victimization Survey (NCVS) similar to the British Crime Survey, which include victims forgetting, incorrectly defining crimes and omitting victimless crimes, and corporate and organized crime (Conklin, 2004). Furthermore, the measurement of particular types of crime, such as rape and domestic violence, may be unreliable due to the lack of sensitivity of the screening questions (those questions that are included to filter responses for the relevant information) and fail to capture the extent of the this type of criminal victimization due to the 'normalization' of these experiences. Researchers also suggest more sensitive screening questions should be used by the NCVS (Fisher, Cullen & Turner, 2000).

Conclusion

Thus, different measures of crime each have their limitations in assessing the prevalence and incidence of crime within society. However, official statistics, self-reported criminal victimization, and self-reported criminal offences taken together can assist in portraying the level of crime perpetrated and experienced. Hence, measures of crime are valuable as long as their limitations are taken into consideration and may be used by governments to inform their crime reduction policies, so that financial resources are allocated on a needs basis or used in a manner to support public policy. However, crime reports may also be manipulated by the media to invoke *moral panics* (Benedict, 1992) or to assert the media's claim to be the voice of the people in their concerns regarding the perceived level of crime (Peelo & Soothill, 2000).

This section examined the prevalence of crime within society, methodological concerns relating to officially recorded statistics, self-report measures, and how these may be used to support dominant political concerns. It is the criminal offender, and the psychological and criminological explanations for their offending behaviour, which will now be explored.

WHO BECOMES A CRIMINAL?

In this section, the definition of the criminal and offending behaviour patterns are examined, drawing on biological, social and environmental factors, longitudinal research and the influence of gender.

Biological Explanations of Criminal Behaviour

Historically, it has been hypothesized that offenders could be distinguished from non-deviant members of the public by their physical appearance. Lavater (as cited in Vold, Bernard & Snipes, 2002) was renowned for his claims regarding physiognomy (study of the face) and its relationship to deviant human behaviour. Phrenology, the study of the shape of the skull, was thought to mirror the internal contours of the brain. Thus, different undulations of the brain reflected differing potentials for criminal behaviour. Lombroso (1897) combined both physiognomy and phrenology and further developed these approaches to study the anatomical composition of the human body in its entirety. He claimed that criminals' brains differed in shape from law-abiding citizens, describing the criminal as " . . . *an atavistic being who reproduces in his person the ferocious instincts of primitive humanity and the inferior animals*" (p. 12). These individuals were considered to be sub-human or evolutionary throw-backs, and thus their criminal behaviour was determined in that they did not have the capacity to desist from such actions. These criminal individuals could be identified, for example, by their asymmetrical faces, thickset lips, receding chin, large jaws and cheekbones, long arms, extra digits or toes, and unusually large or small ears (or those that protruded from the head). Goring (1913) refuted Lombroso's assertions by carrying out an empirical study in England comparing physiological characteristics of convicts and officers of the Royal Engineers and found no significant differences. The only note-worthy finding was that criminal offenders tended to be of shorter stature than non-criminals.

It was not only the physical characteristics of criminals that were scrutinized by criminological theorists in their quest for an explanation of criminal behaviour but also body shape. Sheldon (1949) identified three physique types based on his study of juvenile offenders:

- endomorphs (soft, round body) would be calm, sensual, sensitive but extrovert
- mesomorphs (hard, muscular, athletic, lean) would be aggressive in verbal and behavioural manner
- ectomorphs (lean, fragile body) considered introverted, prone to allergies and skin conditions, sensitive to noise and crowds.

Sheldon found that delinquent boys were predominantly of a mesomorphic physique, with few cases of ectomorphic physique associated with criminal behaviour. His research was developed upon by Glueck and Glueck (1956) who supported his claims regarding a link between male delinquency and mesomorphic body type. In addition, they concluded that delinquent young males also possessed characteristics not usually associated with mesomorphs such as a proneness to contagious diseases, a sense of inadequacy, and being emotionally unbalanced. Moreover, there were cultural factors that were associated with delinquent behaviour, such as lack of access to recreational facilities and a disorganized home life. Subsequent studies have found only equivocal support for a causal link between body type and criminality; for example, Laub and Sampson (1988) and Feldman (1977) argue that the link may reflect stereotyping, such that persons of particular build are more likely to attract the attention of the police.

Another factor that may contribute to criminal behaviour is the elevated presence of certain hormones such as testosterone. There is evidence of a link between hormones and the likelihood of engaging in criminal behaviour. For example, some studies have found higher levels of testosterone in aggressive compared to non-aggressive prisoners (Ehrenkrantz, Bliss & Sheard, 1974). Researchers also suggest that there is a closer relationship between testosterone and dominance (Mazur, 1983). However, Raine (1993) has found conflicting evidence regarding this relationship: aggressive behaviour may increase levels of testosterone rather than the reverse. More recently, behavioural studies have found links between increased testosterone levels and both aggressive and violent behaviour (Archer, 1991; Dabbs, 1992; Harris, 1999; Mazur & Booth, 1999; Raine, 2002a).

Brain injuries and other neural abnormalities may also play a contributory role in the onset of criminal behaviour. Raine (2002b) suggests that there is a link between social and biological variables, in that, " . . . *head injuries leading to brain dysfunction are caused by the environment*" (p. 312). For example, damage may be caused to the brain at birth, through accident, disease or exposure to toxic chemicals. However, there is the frequently raised issue of the temporal sequence of the emergence of offending behaviour. For example, a person engaging in criminal behaviour may sustain brain injuries as a direct result of this, or the person may sustain damage to the frontal lobe through an accident, lowering their inhibitions resulting in criminal behaviour (Gorenstein, 1982).

In addition to biological factors, parents and siblings can also impact on the likelihood of criminal behaviour and this will be explored next, together with empirical studies on heredity and environment in shaping criminal behaviour.

Twin, Adoption, and Sibling Studies

As in other areas where the balance of heredity and environment is at issue, the significance of inheritance for criminal behaviour has been investigated by conducting research on sets of **monozygotic** and **dizygotic** twins. The results of studies conflict over the degree of **concordance** between monozygotic and dizygotic twins regarding their engagement in criminal activities. Overall, research studies suggest that the likelihood of monozygotic twins both engaging in criminal behaviour is higher than that regarding dizygotic twins (Christiansen, 1977; Lange, 1931). However, genetics alone are not responsible for the development of criminal behaviour. Sibling relationships also play a part (Rowe & Rodgers, 1989). Thus, a combination of genetics and familial relationships contributes to the development of criminal behaviour. Research on factors such as personality, intelligence and interest shows that monozygotic twins reared apart do not differ markedly from identical twins reared together (Bouchard *et al.*, 1990). Walters (1992) in his review of family, twin, and adoption studies found that there was a limited correlation between genetics and the onset of criminal behaviour. However, he emphasized the interplay between genetic, social, and environmental factors.

Research in this area has been criticized for its limited sample sizes, absence of control groups, and focus on institutionalized populations (Moffitt, 1988). In a review of studies regarding the impact of biological and social factors, Raine (2002b) found that *"to date the best replicated bio-social effect appears to consist of birth complications interacting with negative home environments in predisposing to adult violence, and there is also evidence that this effect particularly characterizes life-course persistent anti-social behaviour"* (p. 322).

Family Factors

Several studies, irrespective of their international origins and cultural differences, have found that parental criminal histories predict criminal behaviour in their offspring when they are older (Farrington *et al.*, 2001; Fergusson, Horwood & Nagin, 2000; Smith, 1991; West & Farrington, 1977). Murray, Gunnar-Janson and Farrington (2007) conducted a cross-national comparison of two longitudinal studies in Sweden and England. They found that parental incarceration resulting in a prolonged absence from the home may have a positive effect on the development of criminal behaviour in their children. Firstly, due to the absence of a role model to define socially and morally acceptable behaviour (Bandura & Walters, 1963). Secondly, negative effects as a result of poor parental attachment may contribute to offending behaviour due to an inability to trust and seek support from parents. Murray *et al.*'s (2007) study has limitations including differential penal policies, crime definitions and cultural disparities. However, they emphasized that their study made a valuable contribution to (the dearth of) available literature. It is not just criminal parents who can have a positive effect on the development of criminal behaviour but criminal siblings were found to be more influential than family size (Robins, West & Herjanic, 1975). Thus there are a number of familial factors such as parental and sibling criminality, and family size which contribute to the onset of criminal behaviour.

Developmental Criminology

A criminological perspective called **developmental criminology** examines the differing forms of deviant behaviour exhibited by offenders as their criminal career evolves. However, it recognizes that the underlying motivations for the commission of crimes remain constant. Le Blanc and Loeber (1998) define three developmental stages of offending behaviour, which are:

- activation (stability over time, increased frequency and variety of crimes committed)
- aggression (the augmentation in severity and seriousness of the criminal behaviour)
- desistance (the reduction in the seriousness of the crime but the evolution of more specialized offending).

Their approach may be used to clarify patterns that are identified in longitudinal studies, thus differentiating between the type and frequency of offending behaviours (see self-reports referred to above). There are a number of influences that contribute to the development of criminal behaviour in juveniles. It is suggested that the central tenet of the theories explaining criminal behaviour involves an interaction of three factors: *individual attributes* (e.g. age, and socialization) (Moffitt, 1993), *situational factors* (e.g. routine activities facilitating opportunities for commission of crime) (Felson, 2002) and *contextual influences* (such as protective factors like employment) (Sampson & Laub, 1993). Furthermore, criminal behaviour develops and varies with age, a pattern exemplifying the 'criminal career'.

Criminal Careers

The longevity of criminal careers can be age-limited and it is this aspect that will be considered here. The Cambridge study of juvenile criminal offending into middle adulthood found that brothers had similar criminal careers to the offenders studied but wives and sisters had shorter careers (Farrington, Lambert & West, 1998). Moffitt (2003) proposes a theoretical perspective based on a developmental taxonomic scale.

Type 1 offenders are "adolescence-limited". This type become involved in criminal offending through their adolescent peer group, which provides the social support network when attaining autonomy from parental control. However, once they reach an age when they are required to adopt adult roles with inherent responsibilities these conflict with their criminal behaviour and result in its gradual decline. This rejection of the criminal lifestyle may only occur if social skills (such as the ability to communicate well with others) and cognitive skills (e.g. reading) were successfully developed prior to the onset of criminal behaviour. Otherwise, they may not have the **psychosocial** capabilities to desist from criminal behaviour.

Type 2 offenders are described by Moffitt (2003) as "life-course-persistent" offenders whose varied criminality may involve the commission of violent offences; they are also not dependent on their peer group and act independently. They have a history of cognitive deficits (e.g. behavioural problems such as hyperactivity). Environmental factors such as socio-economic deprivation and poor attachment bonds with parents may also play a contributing role in life-course-persistent offending patterns. Their criminal behaviour advances into adulthood and the severity of their crimes may also increase. The reason suggested for this is that the adolescence-limited offender reaches adult maturity and develops legitimate resources to access material goods (and status) in accordance with socially ascribed goals. However, life-course-persistent offenders can only access these goals through illegal means. Ethnicity is also incorporated into this perspective. In the US, for instance, where social and political marginalization of African Americans results in poor healthcare and restricted employment opportunities, this can negatively affect access to legitimate resources and lead to a higher prevalence of persistent offending within this group.

Farrington (1986) suggested the increase in offending was one of differential prevalence not frequency. Moffitt's (1993) model of differential patterns of criminal offending considers their evolution to continue over the life-course of the offender. There has been much research carried out on the relationship between age and the onset of criminal behaviour. As the adolescent matures, their criminal behaviour increases till it peaks in the late teens and early twenties and then usually decreases as age increases (Adler, 2004). This is commonly referred to as the **age-crime curve**. However, critical consideration is required regarding the validity of claims made about the nature of individual criminal careers derived from such cumulative data, which focus solely on the relationship between age and criminal behaviour (Piquero, Farrington & Blumstein, 2003). The difficulty lies in interpreting the prevalence of criminal behaviour from the age-crime curve, as the peak may indicate a gradual increase in the committal of criminal offences by individual prolific offenders or alternatively, that more offenders are collectively committing offences during this period (Piquero & Moffitt, 2004). Studies evaluating Moffit's hypotheses regarding adolescence-limited offenders are scarcer with some exceptions (Aguilar *et al.*, 2000; Piquero & Brezina, 2001) than those assessing life-course-persistent offending. However, initial findings are supportive of the progression of less serious offending in late adolescence, which then declines during adulthood development.

A number of studies (Arseneault *et al.*, 2002; Gibson, Piquero & Tibbets, 2001; Kratzer & Hodgins, 1999; Piquero, 2001) have been conducted to assess the validity of developmental predictors (neuropsychological correlates and **bio-social** interaction factors) of life-course persistent offending. They confirmed that these predictors remained stable, despite cultural differences and diverse samples. Research findings are less clear regarding the influence of ethnicity within Moffitt's taxonomy. Donnellan, Ge & Wenk (2000) found that differential cognitive abilities discriminated between adolescent-limited and life-course-persistent criminal careers in Caucasian and Hispanic offenders. However, there was no such differentiation regarding cognitive abilities and the adolescent-limited and life-course-persistent criminal careers in African Americans. However, Donnellan *et al.* (2000) did not control for socio-economic status and thus the findings are limited because they only focused on one factor. Piquero, Moffitt & Lawton (2003) found that the developmental stages (such as low birth weight together with dysfunctional family backgrounds) which may act as precursors to serious criminal offending into adulthood did not differ according to ethnicity. However, risk factors did differentiate between ethnicities; Black participants showed higher levels of risk than White participants. Thus, the causality remained constant, irrespective of the ethnicity of offenders, unlike risk factors which differentiated between ethnicities, where level of risk was higher for other ethnic groups as opposed to Caucasians.

The influence of the criminal justice system on offending behaviour is not negligible. Johnson, Simons & Conger's (2004) study controversially found that involvement with the criminal justice system *increased* juveniles' criminal behaviour. Furthermore, Piquero, Brame & Lynam (2004) in their study of criminal careers found that incapacitation had a detrimental impact on criminal careers (long periods in prison and higher cognitive ability scores were associated with shorter criminal careers). Thus, Piquero *et al.* (2004) suggest that policy-making decisions should consider the criminal career literature more seriously, as incarcerating juvenile offenders for shorter periods would conserve resources and reduce offending in early adulthood. They also advocate programmes that provide assistance to offenders to improve their cognitive abilities. The importance of supporting offenders on release is also emphasized by Haapenen, Britton and Croisdale (2007) who found that offenders were 'arrested less' while on parole than those released without such assistance.

Gender may also influence the pattern of criminal careers. Research supports Moffit's (2003) gender-based hypothesis, in that females were likely to be involved in less serious offending than males and were rarely found to engage in life-course persistent offending (Fergusson & Horwood, 2002; Fergusson, Horwood & Nagin, 2000). However, Mazerolle *et al.* (2000) found the early onset of criminal behaviour in females produced a similar pattern of development to males regarding their life-course-persistent offending. Moffitt also suggests fewer females than males will become delinquent. The focus of the next section is the phenomenon that is the female offender.

Female Offenders

Similar to male offenders, the biological and psychological functioning of female offenders has also been subject to extensive scrutiny. However, females' agency and the likelihood of their engagement in acts of violence is often denied by these approaches (Morrissey, 2003). The subject of gender and crime cannot be understood without reference to social, class and racial influences (Kruttschnitt & Carbone-Lopez, 2006), but some of these factors lie outside the scope of this chapter.

CASE STUDY

'The Moors Murderers'

Myra Hindley and Ian Brady's crimes were nicknamed by the mass media "The Moors Murders". They abducted, tortured and killed several children but were only convicted of the murder of two children. They buried the children on the Saddleworth Moors in Yorkshire. A fact which was also highlighted was that they taped the physical abuse of their victims. Myra Hindley was jailed for life in 1966, and her infamy resulted in her being incarcerated for 36 years. She died in prison and is recorded as being the "longest serving" female offender in Britain. Ian Brady was deemed criminally insane and incarcerated in a secure psychiatric institution. In the first instance, there appears to be a gender differential relating to how these co-offenders were treated with regard to sentencing provisions. What is interesting about this case is again the dichotomous representation of Myra Hindley as intrinsically "bad"—a stark contrast with the implication that Ahluwalia was "mad" and thus not directly responsible for her actions. Therefore, the suggestion regarding Myra Hindley was that she was accountable for her actions. Also, there was much more media coverage focused on Myra Hindley than Ian Brady despite the fact that they committed the crimes jointly. White Hindley was demonized and portrayed as the personification of "evil", the same vilification was not directed at Brady. Thus, again one must query the disparity in the public reaction regarding the defendants based on their respective gender. It was implied that somehow because of Hindley's gender her actions were even more grievous than Brady's. This discriminatory portrayal of Hindley was reinforced by her initial stark black and white police photograph taken on arrest being constantly used when referring to her, even years later. This photograph appeared to embody her malevolent nature. What also needs to be remembered is that the media coverage, especially the tabloid press, chose to depict Hindley as this caricature devoid of humanity. One must consider why Brady did not receive the same level of negative press attention as Hindley. Might it be because the committal of such crimes against children by a female refutes the basic social stereotype of the female gender with her inherent characteristics of emotionality and maternal instincts? Again it is highlighted that the power of labelling, i.e. "mad" or "bad" can significantly affect the treatment of female offenders within the judicial system. Furthermore, what type of effect might these labels have on the psychology of the female offender? They may result in a self-fulfilling prophecy. The female offender may thus come to internalize this representation of self. A final point for consideration is that if blind justice is supposedly meted out then instead of being partial and reinforcing gender constructs should that justice also be gender neutral? Female offenders would then not be forced into the "choice" of the medicalization of their actions or the moralization of their behaviour.

The 'mad or bad' dichotomy is integral to the discussion of female offenders. Female offenders assigned 'bad' or even 'evil' status include demonized offender Myra Hindley who, with co-offender Ian Brady, tortured and murdered three children between 1963 and 1965. Both were convicted and imprisoned for life, and Myra Hindley's sentence was originally indeterminate. However, in accordance with sentencing practice, it was expected that she would receive a lesser sentence than her male co-offender. This was not the case, possibly due to her consistent iconic portrayal as a figure of evil. Murphy and Whitty (2006) provide a thought-provoking consideration of Myra Hindley and her 'evil' status, alongside two other recent female murderers: Beverley Allitt (a nurse who was convicted in 1993 of murdering four children in her care and attempted murder of three others), and Rose West (convicted in 1995 for allegedly murdering ten young females with her husband). Females are infrequently convicted of murder in the UK; as a consequence these three women were linked by the media and subsequently in the public consciousness. Murphy & Whitty (2006) criticize those feminists taking a legal perspective for overlooking such female offenders due to their incompatibility with an ideological stereotype of male violence. They argue that feminist critiques fail to recognize a woman's ability to commit violence in the absence of explanations in terms of self-defence or provocation which privilege the female victim.

The pathologizing and the medicalization of female offenders are challenging issues. Offenders who accept such labels ('mad' or 'bad') may receive a lesser sentence but may distort perceptions of female offenders. In order for women to benefit from a reduction in sentence, they must first accept the female gender stereotype, that they are the weaker sex and victims of their biology (menstruation, pregnancy, childbirth, menopause-related hormonal imbalances). According to this view, the normal woman's natural state is 'sickly' and medicalized as such (Carlen & Worrall, 1987). Furthermore, this permits women's criminal behaviour to be explained as being subject to uncontrollable impulses according to Tilt (as cited in Edwards, 1984). However, Loucks suggests offences committed by female offenders tend to be non-violent, such as shoplifting, soliciting and white-collar crimes such as fraud, forgery or embezzlement (as cited in Adler, 2004). Shoplifting may fit with the perception of women's uncontrollable impulses unlike the other offences, but they have one factor in common. These offences adhere to the gender stereotypes of what are considered to be female crimes.

Defence counsels frequently portray women as having an unstable psychology, which leaves them at the mercy of their emotions: they are 'mad', and thus not responsible for their crimes. The aim of this approach is to elicit a sympathetic and chivalrous response from the court and to reinforce social control (Armstrong, 1999). Alternatively, those female criminals whose behaviour is considered inherently bad or reminiscent of masculine criminal actions receive a more punitive response for their gender-deviant behaviour. Such severe sentences are consistent with the view that the crime is an affront to gender normative behaviour and a more serious infringement than the illegality of the action.

Armstrong (1999) discusses the ramifications of medicalizing women's criminal behaviour especially with regard to gender differential sentencing. Her study focused on 29 female and 29 male homicide offenders in Victoria, Australia. She found gender-discrepant sentencing was particularly evident in domestic homicide. For example, female offenders were pathologized more commonly than male offenders, and they received a more sympathetic response from the courts, increasing the probability of a lesser sentence than their male counterparts, with a custodial sentence a remote possibility. However, there was a marked contrast with those female offenders who committed non-domestic homicides. They did not receive a chivalrous, protective response from the courts, because their crimes appeared to be unprovoked and of a more masculine nature. However, the judicial response, while more punitive, was still less so compared with that received by male offenders. The majority received shorter sentences and more often the reduction of the charge from murder to manslaughter compared to their male counterparts.

In England and Wales, of the total offender population, 20% of those sentenced were females (Home Office, 2007). Hollin and Palmer (2006), in their critical review of the literature regarding **criminogenic need** in relation to female offenders, found some overlap between male and female offenders. However, there was also evidence of gender-specific needs, with females more likely to have experienced more adverse life events than male offenders.

Differential responses by the courts may also be due to the attractiveness and age of the victim, and the type of crime committed. For example, if the female is young and attractive, it is suggested by Heidensohn (1985) that the judge may behave chivalrously and hand down a more lenient sentence (for more on the possible role of attractiveness see Wheatcroft, Chapter 7). However, if the female is older and in an authoritative role or has engaged in a more masculine type of offence (motivated by revenge or the result of confrontation) then the response will be more punitive. According to Heidensohn, if the female is working class she is more likely to receive a custodial sentence, as social control of behaviour is required whereas a middle-class woman's control may be deflected to her 'husband'. It appears that in some countries, female offenders are treated paternalistically by the criminal justice system and subject to more pervasive social controls for their non-adherence to their assigned gender role.

The judicial response to female offenders may therefore be influenced by a number of factors including their attractiveness, age, type of offence committed and social position. Thus, the biological, social and environmental influences need to be considered cumulatively rather than independently when explaining the criminal behaviour of offenders. Next the impact of criminal victimization is considered in relation to financial, physiological, and psychological aspects.

WHAT HAPPENS TO VICTIMS?

Victims have been traditionally perceived by criminal justice systems as simply providing evidence to secure the prosecution and conviction of an offender. Thus, the psychological impact on victims may result in the perception that they are not valued as individuals but just another link in the chain of evidence. In contrast, the focus on offenders is considered of key importance having led to the development of criminology and forensic psychology. The neglect of the victim was the impetus for the 'victim movement': numerous groups lobbying for the government to redirect attention to victims. Feminists also played a role in placing the victim centre stage through highlighting male violence against women, such as domestic violence and rape (Barry, 1979; Brownmiller, 1971; Russell, 1984). Victim Support and the Criminal Injuries Compensation Board were products of this pressure.

The Criminal Injuries Compensation Board (CICB) in England and Wales evolved as a response to the lack of compensation for crime victims. The CICB was composed of a tariff-based system (originating in common law); for example, loss of a limb was allocated a nominal sum. It is the oldest compensation scheme in the world with 25 levels of compensation and awards ranging from £1000 to £250 000. The financial award recognizes the psychological, physiological and economic harm resultant from criminal victimization. This system has been replicated in other countries. The CICB has since been superseded by the Criminal Injuries Compensation Authority (CICA) (CICA, n.d.). Offenders who become crime victims, however, are not eligible for the Criminal Injuries Compensation Scheme. This suggests that once an individual engages in criminal behaviour, is charged and consequently labelled an '*offender*' they automatically lose the right to be recognized as a '*victim*' by the CICA, emphasizing the pervasiveness of labelling and its possible negative effects. Only 'innocent' victims may be considered for compensation. Thus eligibility is implicitly based on the culpability of the victim in their own criminal victimization. The psychological impact of this on victims could reinforce any self-blame already experienced and could delay their recovery.

The pioneering Bristol Victim Support Scheme was established by the National Association for the Care and Resettlement of Offenders (NACRO) in the UK (Mawby & Walklate, 1995). This scheme provided support to victims of burglary rather than victims of sexual violence (who required more specialist care, which was beyond the level of expertise offered by their volunteers). In 1977, the National Association of Victim Support Schemes (NAVSS) (now known as Victim Support) developed branches countrywide. By 1986, Victim Support extended their generic service to rape victims, implying that rape no longer required the specialized response provided by rape crisis and similar dedicated agencies. According to Mawby and Walklate (1995) this move could be construed as the "*normalization of rape*": the underlying message being that rape was no longer considered a serious offence but just another type of criminal victimization with a similar recovery period. One psychological implication of this move could be that rape victims might blame themselves for not being able to 'get on with their lives' in the aftermath of sexual violence. Expecting rape victims 'to get over it' without understanding the psychological and physiological complexities of this particular type of victimization will be considered later (see Westcott, Chapter 8, for information on how victims can be better supported by the criminal justice system).

Physiological And Psychological Impact of Crime on Victims

The impact of victimization can be all pervasive in that it can affect the person's self-assurance, self-confidence, self-perceptions and their world view. The rape victim in particular may also be subjected to secondary victimization experienced should their case progress through the criminal justice system as a result of the extremity of responses by agents such as the police or the courts, which can exacerbate the victim's social and psychological trauma (Campbell & Wasco, 2005). Intimate partners and family members may also experience indirect victimization. This may take several forms such as feelings of guilt by the victim's partner for not protecting them or alternatively anger, powerlessness or vulnerability may be felt (Schneider, 2001).

The physical, and psychological traumata that result from criminal victimization, include *post-traumatic stress disorder* (PTSD), defined as an anxious reaction to a situation which is outside of a person's normal range of trauma experienced, and characterized by anxiety, depression and the repeated experiencing of the traumatic incident (through flashbacks) according to the DSM IV (APA, 1994). Kilpatrick and Acierno (2003) suggest that ". . . proportionately rape was most strongly associated with PTSD in men and women" (p. 126). In addition, women develop PTSD symptoms irrespective of whether the crime is a physical or sexual assault, whereas males experience PTSD symptomology differentially: routinely in cases of rape but infrequently for physical assault (Kilpatrick & Acierno, 2003).

The coping strategies employed by victims of crime vary according to the severity of the violence experienced and the situational factors involved (e.g. location, victim-offender relationship). For example, the level of control victims felt they had over the incident will influence their coping strategy. If they felt they could have prevented the incident, such as a burglary, they may take a problem-focused approach and increase their security measures. However, if the incident was a physical or sexual assault (which they felt was beyond their control) then an emotional or avoidance coping strategy may be employed (Folkman *et al.*, 1986). Thus, victims of violent crime tend to use emotion-focused coping whereas victims of non-violent crimes tend to use problem-focused strategies. The underlying reason for these differential coping strategies was suggested as being the result of the loss of control experienced by victims of violent crimes. Therefore, they may be less able to employ a problem-solving coping style in these circumstances whereas in non-violent victimization incidents, there are sequential steps to be followed, for example, insurance claims to be filed (Green & Pomeroy, 2007).

Victims of sexual violence may suffer from *rape trauma syndrome* (RTS), this consists of two stages: *acute* and *long-term*. The *acute stage* is characterized as disorganized: an immediate reaction, which can be expressive screaming, crying or angry responses – or controlled – a more stoic response with little if any show of emotion. The *long-term* stage involves a reorganized approach and lifestyle changes, which can include avoidance of crowds, being home alone, change, of address or employment (Burgess, 1974; Burgess & Holmstrom, 1985). The situational context of criminal victimization can have psychological affects, for example, rape if perpetrated in the victim's house may lead to the victim no longer feeling safe in their home alone. The impact on burglary victims may also be considerable: they may have thought of their home as their 'castle' and find this invasion of their privacy and the sacredness of their possessions hard to bear.

If the crime took place outside, the person may fear being followed and even become agoraphobic (experiencing a fear of open spaces). Their entire lifestyle may be disrupted by their sense of vulnerability. The avoidance of situations similar to that in which the assault took place results in a reduction of fear, however, the person never 'learns' to address these fears (Kilpatrick & Acierno, 2003) thus perpetuating the RTS symptoms. Thus, a once outgoing person may become introverted and no longer able to go out after dark unaccompanied. There may also be a reverse effect on the victim's behaviour whereby they may engage in promiscuity as a coping mechanism to conquer their physical and psychological insecurities concerning physical boundaries and intimacy issues. If victims are repeatedly victimized, they may self-identify as a 'victim' and thus this becomes a defining part of their identity, which may reinforce this sense of *learned helplessness* in that 'traumatization appears as uncontrollable and inevitable' (Schneider, 2001, p. 543). This conceptualization may particularly apply to victims of domestic violence and child abuse (which may place them at a higher risk of victimization in adulthood) (Wiehe & Richards, 1995). It is therefore suggested that a crucial step in recovery for some rape victims is to address their cognitive distortions of themselves and their world view. This may be achieved by cognitive re-structuring so that they can recognize their distorted thought processes and how they may be inhibiting their recovery process. Psychological strategies need to be developed to address such factors as 'victim neutralizations' (Agnew, 1985), which increase victim proneness to anxiety and depression (Schneider, 2001).

Gender homogenization of the terms '*victim*' and '*offender*' persists whereby males are primarily perceived as 'offenders' and females as 'victims'. This can also affect the victim's psychological recovery from criminal victimization, despite official statistics reporting that young males are more likely to be subject to criminal victimization than females (Home Office, 2006b). This gender bias in the conceptualization of 'offender' and 'victim' is even more evident when it comes to sexual victimization and access to services. Male rape victims also suffer from symptoms of Rape Trauma Syndrome (Burgess & Holmstrom, 1979). The psychological impact of the attack may be further exacerbated by their lack of recognition as 'victims' and limited access to support services. They may also question their sexual orientation, irrespective of whether they previously self-identified as homosexual or heterosexual (Mezey & King, 1992; Scarce, 1997; Walker, Archer & Davies, 2005). Thus, the cumulative effects of these psychological and behavioural factors are highly influential in prolonging the victim's recovery period. The legacy of the victimological approach to criminal victimization regarding the inherent culpability of 'male victims' results in their ineligibility for needs-directed services because of the perception of their invulnerability and incompatibility with the notion of the '*blame-free*' and '*worthy*' victim (Goodey, 2005). Thus, they are often overlooked as '*victims*' by the judicial system and support organizations; considering the importance of social support in facilitating the recovery of the traumatized victim (Cobb, 1976), this further debilitates the victim. Thus, the traditional gender stereotyped approach of the agents of the criminal justice system continues to reinforce the gender homogenization of '*offenders*' and '*victims*' and impedes the recovery period for male victims of sexual violence.

SUMMARY

This chapter has provided an introduction to key areas pivotal to the understanding of crime including:

- the problems of definition and the inherent difficulties regarding crime measurement, using contrasting examples from England and Wales, and the US

- the possible explanations for the development of an offending, including whether it may be biologically determined or socially facilitated through agencies such as the family
- research on criminal careers and whether the concept of the offender is gender specific
- the consequences of criminal victimization and the psychological difficulties experienced by the victim and the problems of secondary victimization
- the power of labelling in relation to offenders and victims and resulting differential access to services, underlining the importance of understanding the development of criminal behaviour and its consequences.

ESSAY/DISCUSSION QUESTIONS

1. Discuss some of the problems of defining crime, using examples drawn from the UK and abroad.
2. Consider the relative contribution of heredity and environment to the creation of an offender.
3. Female offenders are fundamentally no different in their nature to male offenders. Discuss.
4. Discuss some of the psychological consequences of crime for victims.

WEB RESOURCES

Further information regarding the Criminal Injuries Compensation Authority can be accessed via the following link:

http://www.cica.gov.uk

Other useful resources to keep you updated regarding current research and prevalence statistics may be found here:

Centre for Crime and Justice Studies

http://www.kcl.ac.uk/depsta/rel/ccjs/home.htm

Home Office website is a crucial resource.

http://www.homeoffice.gov.uk

For Home Office research publications regarding offenders and victims as well as providing links to crime statistics.

http://www.homeoffice.gov.uk/rds/index.htm

National Crime Victimization Surveys entitled 'Criminal Victimization in the United States' can be accessed via:

http://www.ojp.usdoj.gov/bjs

American Society of Criminology

http://www.asc41.com

Sentencing Advisory Panel

http://www.sentencing-guidelines.gov.uk/about/sap/

American Psychological Society

http://www.apa.org

REFERENCES

Adler, J. (Ed.) (2004). *Forensic psychology: Concepts, debates and practice*. Cullompton, Devon: Willan.

Agnew, R.S. (1985). Neutralizing the impact of crime. *Criminal Justice and Behavior, 12*, 221–239.

Aguilar, B.L., Sroufe, A., Egeland, B., & Carlson, E. (2000). Distinguishing the early-onset/persistent and adolescence-onset antisocial behaviour types: From birth to 16 years. *Development and Psychopathology, 12*, 109–132.

American Psychiatric Association (APA) (1994). *Diagnostic and statistical manual of mental disorders* (4th edn). Washington, DC: APA.

Archer, J. (1991). The influence of testosterone on human aggression. *British Journal of Clinical Psychology, 82*, 1–28.

Armstrong, I. (1999). Women and their 'uncontrollable impulses': The medicalization of women's crime and differential gender sentencing. *Psychiatry, Psychology and Law, 6*, 67–77.

Arsenault, L., Tremblay, R.E., Boulerice, B., & Séguin, J.R. (2002). Obstetric complications and adolescent violent behaviours: Testing two developmental pathways. *Child Development, 73*, 496–508.

Bandura, A. & Walters, R.H. (1963). *Social learning and personality development*. New York: Holt, Rinehart & Winston.

Barry, K. (1979). *Female sexual slavery*. Englewood Cliffs, NJ: Prentice Hall.

Benedict, H. (1992). *Virgin or vamp: How the press covers sex crimes*. Oxford: Oxford University Press.

Blackburn, R. (2001). *The psychology of criminal conduct*. Chichester: John Wiley & Sons.

Bouchard, T.J., Lykken, D.T., McGue, M., & Segal, N.L. (1990). Sources of human psychological differences: The Minneapolis study of twins reared apart. *Science, 250*, 223–228.

Brownmiller, S. (1975). *Against our will: Men, women, and rape*. Harmondsworth: Penguin.

Buckle, H.T. (1861). *History of civilisation in England*. London: Parker.

Burgess, A.W. (1974). Rape trauma syndrome. *American Journal of Psychiatry, 131*, 981–986.

Burgess, A.W. & Holmstrom, L.L. (1979). *Male sexual victimization*. Bowie: Robert J. Brady.

Burgess, A.W. & Holmstrom, L.L. (1985). Rape trauma syndrome and post-traumatic stress response. In *Rape and Sexual Assault* (pp. 46–60). New York: Garland.

Burnett, J. & Whyte, D. (2005). Embedded expertise and the new terrorism. *Journal for Crime Conflict and the Media, 1*, 1–18.

Campbell, R. & Wasco, S.M. (2005). Understanding rape and sexual assault: 20 Years of progress and future directions. *Journal of Interpersonal Violence, 20*, 127–131.

Carlen, P. & Worrall, A. (Eds). (1987). *Gender, crime and justice*. Milton Keynes: Open University Press.

Christiansen, K.O. (1977). A review of studies of criminality among twins. In S.A. Mednick & K.O. Christiansen (Eds) (1977). *Biological Bases of Criminal Behaviour*. New York: Gardiner Press.

CICA (n.d.) *Criminal Injuries Compensation Authority*. Retrieved 16 March 2007, from http://www.cica.gov.uk

Cobb, S. (1976). Social support as a moderator to life stress. *Psychosomatic Medicine, 38*, 300–314.

Coleman, C. & Moynihan, J. (2002). The social construction of official statistics. In Y. Jewkes & G. Letherby (Eds), *Criminology: A reader* (pp. 96–104). London: Sage.

Conklin, J.E. (2004). *Criminology* (8th edn). Boston, MA: Pearson.

Cressey, D.R. (1951). Criminological research and the definition of crimes. *American Journal of Sociology, 56*, 546–551.

Dabbs, J.M. (1992). Testosterone measurements in social and clinical psychology. *Journal of Social and Clinical Psychology, 11*, 302–321.

Donnellan, M.B., Ge, X., & Wenk, E. (2000). Cognitive abilities in adolescence-limited and life-course-persistent criminal offenders. *Journal of Abnormal Psychology, 109*, 396–402.

Edwards, S. (1984). *Women on trial*. Manchester: Manchester University Press.

Ehrenkrantz, J., Bliss, E., & Sheard, M.H. (1974). Plasma testosterone: Correlation with aggressive behaviour and social domination in man. *Psychosomatic Medicine, 36*, 469–475.

Farrington, D.P. (1986). Age and crime. In M. Tonry & N. Morris (Eds), *Crime and Justice: An Annual Review of Research* (Vol. 7, pp. 189–250). Chicago: University of Chicago Press.

Farrington, D.P., Jolliffe, D., Loeber, R. *et al.* (2001). The concentration of offenders in families, and family criminality in the prediction of boys' delinquency. *Journal of Adolescence, 24*, 579–596.

Farrington, D.P., Lambert, S., & West, D.J. (1998). Criminal careers of two generations of family members in the Cambridge study in delinquent development. *Studies on Crime and Crime Prevention, 7*, 85–106.

FBI (n.d.). *National incident-based reporting system: General information (The Basics)*. FBI. Retrieved 8 July 2007, from http://www.fbi.gov/ucr/faqs.htm

FBI (n.d.). *Uniform crime reporting: National incident-based reporting system*. FBI. Retrieved 16 March 2007, from http://www.fbi.gov/hq/cjisd/ucr.htm

Feldman, M.P. (1977). *Criminal behaviour: A psychological analysis*. Chichester: John Wiley & Sons.

Felson, M. (2002). *Crime and everyday life* (3rd edn). Thousand Oaks, CA: Sage.

Fergusson, D.M. & Horwood, L.J. (2002). Male and female offending trajectories. *Development and Psychopathology, 14*, 159–177.

Fergusson, D.M., Horwood, L.J., & Nagin, D.S. (2000). Offending trajectories in a New Zealand birth cohort. *Criminology, 38*, 525–552.

Fisher, B.S., Cullen, F.T., & Turner, M.G. (2000). *The Sexual victimization of college women*. Washington DC: US Department of Justice.

Folkman, S., Lazarus, R.S., Dunkel-Schetter, C. *et al.* (1986). Dynamics of a stressful encounter: Cognitive appraisal, coping, and encounter outcomes. *Journal of Personality and Social Psychology, 50*, 992–1003.

Gibson, C., Piquero, A.R., & Tibbets, S.G. (2001). The contribution of family adversity and verbal IQ related to criminal behaviour. *International Journal of Offender Therapy and Comparative Criminology, 45*, 574–592.

Glueck, S. & Glueck, E. (1956). *Physique and delinquency*. New York: Harper.

Goodey, J. (2005). *Victims and victimology: Research, policy, and practice*. Harlow: Pearson.

Gorenstein, E.E. (1982). Frontal lobe function in psychopaths. *Journal of Abnormal Psychology, 91*, 368–379.

Goring, C.B. (1913). *The English convict: A statistical study*. London: HMSO.

Green, D.L. & Pomeroy, E. (2007). Crime victimization: Assessing differences between violent and non-violent experiences. *Victims and Offenders, 2*, 63–76.

Haapenen, R., Britton, L., & Croisdale, T. (2007). Persistent criminality and career length. *Crime and Delinquency, 53*, 133–155.

Harris, J.A. (1999). Review and methodological considerations in research on testosterone and aggression. *Aggression and Violent Behaviour, 4*, 273–291.

Heidensohn, F.M. (1985). *Women and crime: The life of the female offender*. New York: New York University Press.

Hollin, C. & Palmer, E. (2006). Criminogenic need and women offenders: A critique of the literature. *Legal and Criminological Psychology, 11*, 179–195.

Home Office (2003). Crime in England and Wales 2002/2003. *Home Office statistical bulletin 07/03*. London: Home Office.

Home Office (2005). Sentencing Statistics 2004. *Home Office statistical bulletin 15/05*. London: Research and Development Statistics and NOMS.

Home Office (2006a). Crime in England and Wales 2005/2006. *Home Office statistical bulletin 12/06*. London: Home Office.

Home Office (2006b). Criminal Statistics 2005: England and Wales. *Home Office statistical bulletin 19/06*. London: Research and Development Statistics Office and Criminal Justice Reform.

Home Office (2007). *Sentencing statistics 2005: England and Wales*. London: RDS NOMS.

Johnson, L.M., Simons, R.L., & Conger, R.D. (2004). Criminal justice system involvement and continuity of youth crime: A longitudinal analysis. *Youth and Society, 36*, 3–29.

Kilpatrick, D.G. (2004). What is violence against women? Defining and measuring the problem. *The Journal of Interpersonal Violence, 19*, 1209–1234.

Kilpatrick, D.G. & Acierno, R. (2003). Mental health needs of crime victims: Epidemiology and outcomes. *Journal of Traumatic Stress, 16*, 119–132.

Kratzer, L. & Hodgins, S. (1999). A typology of offenders: A test of Moffit's theory among males and females from childhood to age 30. *Criminal Behaviour and Mental Health, 9*, 57–73.

Kruttschnitt, C. & Carbone-Lopez, K. (2006). Moving beyond the stereotypes: Women's subjective accounts of their violent crime. *Criminology, 44*, 321–345.

Lange, J. (1931). *Verbrechen als Shicksal: Studien an kriminellen zwillingen*, trans. C. Haldane. New York: Charles Boni.

Laub, J.H. & Sampson, R.J. (1988) Unraveling families and delinquency: A reanalysis of the Gluecks' data. *Criminology 26*, 355–380.

Le Blanc, M. & Loeber, R. (1998). Developmental criminology updated. In M. Tonry (Ed.), *Crime and justice: A review of research* (Vol. 23, pp. 115–198). Chicago: University of Chicago Press.

Lombroso, C. (1897). *L'uomo delinquente* (5th edn). Torino: Bocca.

Mawby, R.I. & Walklate, S. (1995). *Critical victimology*. London: Sage.

Maxfield, M.G. (1999). The National Incident-Based Reporting System: Research and policy applications. *Journal of Quantitative Criminology, 15*, 119–149.

Mazerolle, P., Brame, R., Paternoster, R., Piquero, A., & Dean, C. (2000). Onset age, persistence, and offending versatility: Comparisons across gender. *Criminology, 38*, 1143–1172.

Mazur, A. (1983). Physiology, dominance, and aggression in humans. In A.P. Goldstein (Ed.), *Prevention and control of aggression*. New York: Pergamon Press.

Mazur, A. & Booth, A. (1999). The biosociology of testosterone in men. In D. Franks & S. Smith (Eds), *Mind, brain, and society: Toward a neurosociology of emotion* (Vol. 5, pp. 311–338). Stamford, CT: JAI Press.

Mezey, G.C. & King, M.B. (Eds) (1992). *Male victims of sexual assault*. Oxford: Oxford University Press.

Moffitt, T.E. (1988). Neuropsychology and self-reported early delinquency in an unselected birth cohort: A preliminary report from New Zealand. In T.E. Moffitt & S.A. Mednick (Eds), *Biological contributions to crime causation*. Dordrecht: Nijhoff.

Moffitt, T.E. (1993). Life-course-persistent and adolescence-limited anti-social behaviour: A developmental taxonomy. *Psychological Review, 100*, 674–701.

Moffitt, T.E. (2003). Life-course-persistent and adolescence-limited anti-social behaviour: A research review and a research agenda. In B. Lahey, T.E. Moffitt, & A. Caspi (Eds) *The Causes of conduct disorder and serious juvenile delinquency*. New York: Guilford Press.

Morrissey, B. (2003). *When women kill: Questions of agency and subjectivity*. New York: Routledge.

Murphy, T. & Whitty, N. (2006). The question of evil and feminist legal scholarship. *Feminist Legal Studies, 14*, 1–26.

Murray, J., Gunnar-Janson, C., & Farrington, D.P. (2007). Crime in adult offspring of prisoners: A cross-national comparison of two longitudinal samples. *Criminal Justice and Behavior, 34*, 133–149.

Office of Public Sector Information (2007). Domestic Violence, Crime and Victims Act 2004. Retrieved 16 March 2007 from http://www.opsi.gov.uk/acts/acts2004/20040028.htm

Padfield, N. (2002). *Criminal law* (3rd edn). London: Butterworths.

Peelo, M. & Soothill, K. (2000). The place of public narratives in reproducing social order. *Theoretical Criminology, 42*, 131–148.

Piquero, A.R. (2001). Testing Moffitt's neuropsychological variation hypothesis for the prediction of life-course-persistent offending. *Psychology, Crime and Law, 7*, 193–216.

Piquero, A.R., Brame, R., & Lynam, D. (2004). Studying criminal career length through early adulthood among serious offenders. *Crime and Delinquency, 50*, 412–435.

Piquero, A.R. & Brezina, T. (2001). Testing Moffitt's account of adolescence-limited delinquency. *Criminology, 39*, 353–370.

Piquero, A.R., Farrington, D.P., & Blumstein, A. (2003). The criminal career paradigm: Background and recent developments. In M. Tonry (Ed.), *Crime and justice: A review of research* (Vol. 30). Chicago: University of Chicago Press.

Piquero, A.R. & Moffitt, T.E. (2004). Life-course-persistent offending. In J.R. Adler (Ed.), *Forensic psychology: Concepts, debates and practice* (pp. 177–195). Cullompton, Devon: Willan.

Piquero, A., Moffitt, T.E., & Lawton, B. (2003). Race differences in life-course-persistent offending: Our children/their children: Race/ethnicity and crime. In D. Hawkins & K. Kempf-Leonard (Eds). *Race, crime and the juvenile justice system*. Chicago: University of Chicago Press.

R. v. Ahluwalia [1992] 4 All ER 889, CA 8.10, 8.16.

Raine, A. (1993). *The psychopathology of crime*. San Diego: Academic Press.

Raine, A. (2002a). The biological basis of crime. In J.Q. Wilson & J. Petersilia (Eds), *Crime: public places for crime control* (pp. 43–74). San Francisco: ICS Press.

Raine, A. (2002b). Biosocial studies of antisocial and violent behaviour in children and adults: A review. *Journal of Abnormal Child Psychology, 30*, 311–326.

Robins, L.N., West, P.A., & Herjanic, B.L. (1975). Arrests and delinquency in two generations: A study of black urban families and their children. *Journal of Child Psychology and Psychiatry, 16*, 125–140.

Rowe, D.C. & Rodgers, J.L. (1989). Behaviour genetic, adolescent deviance, and "d": Contributions and issues. In G.R. Adams, R. Montemayor, & T.P. Gullotta (Eds), *Advances in adolescent development* (pp. 38–67). Newbury Park: Sage Periodical Press.

Russell, D.E.H. (1984). *Sexual exploitation: Rape, child sexual abuse and workplace Harassment*. London: Sage.

Sampson, R. & Laub, J. (1993). *Crime in the making: Pathways and turning points through life*. Cambridge: Harvard University Press.

Sampson, R. & Laub, J. (2005). A general age-graded theory of crime. In D.P. Farrington (Ed.), *Integrated developmental and life-course theories of offending* (Vol. 14, pp. 165–182). New Brunswick, NJ: Transaction.

Scarce, M. (1997). *Male on male rape: The hidden toll of stigma and shame*. Cambridge: Perseus Publishing.

Sheldon, W.H. (with Hartl, E.M. & McDermott, E.) (1949). *Varieties of delinquent youth*. New York: Harper.

Schneider, H.J. (2001). Victimological developments in the world during the past three decades: A study of comparative victimology. *International Journal of Offender Therapy and Comparative Criminology, 45*, 539–555.

Smith, W.R. (1991). Social structure, family structure, child rearing, and delinquency: Another look. *Project Metropolitan Research Report No. 33*. Stockholm, Sweden: University of Stockholm.

Vold, G.B., Bernard, T.J., & Snipes, J.B. (2002). *Theoretical criminology* (5th edn). New York: Oxford University Press.

Walker, J., Archer, J., & Davies, M. (2005). Effects of rape on men: A descriptive analysis. *Archives of Sexual Behaviour, 34*, 69–80.

Walsh, D. & Poole, A. (Eds) (1983). *A dictionary of criminology*. London: Routledge & Kegan Paul.

Walters, G.D. (1992). A meta-analysis of the gene–crime relationship. *Criminology, 30*, 595–614.

Weeks, J. (1981). Inverts, perverts, and Mary-Annes: Male prostitution and the regulation of homosexuality in England in the nineteenth and twentieth centuries. *Journal of Homosexuality, 6*, 113–134.

Weinrott, M.R. & Saylor, M. (1991). Self-report of crimes committed by sex offenders. *Journal of Interpersonal Violence, 6*, 286–300.

West, D.J. & Farrington, D.P. (1977). *The delinquent way of life*. London: Heinemann.

Wiehe, V.R. & Richards, A.L. (1995). *Intimate betrayal: Understanding and responding to the trauma of acquaintance rape*. Thousand Oaks, CA: Sage.

Williams, K.S. (2004). *Textbook on criminology*. Oxford: Oxford University Press.

ANNOTATED READING LIST

Goodnow, J. J. (2006). Adding social contexts to developmental analyses of crime prevention. *Australian & New Zealand Journal of Criminology, 39,* Special issue: Pathways and Prevention, pp. 327–338. *A useful introduction to crime prevention.*

Hoyle, C. & Young, R. (2002). *New Visions of crime and victims.* Oxford: Hart Publishing.

Jones, S., Cauffman, E., & Piquero, A.R. (2007). The influence of parental support among incarcerated adolescent offenders: Moderating effects of self-control. *Criminal Justice and Behavior, 34,* 229–245. *Covers developmental approaches to criminal offending.*

Maguire, M., Morgan, R., & Reiner, R. (Eds) (2007). *The Oxford handbook of criminology* (4th edn). Oxford: Oxford University Press.

Mallicoat, S.L. (2007). Gendered justice: Attributional differences between male and females in juvenile courts. *Feminist Criminology, 2,* 4–30. *An excellent overview of issues around gender and crime.*

McGuire, J. (2004). *Understanding psychology and crime: Perspectives on theory and action.* Milton Keynes: Open University Press.

Wareham, J. & Dembo, R. (2007). A longitudinal study of psychological functioning among juvenile offenders: A latent growth model analysis. *Criminal Justice and Behavior, 34,* 259–273. *Covers developmental approaches to criminal offending.*

These texts provide a good introduction and overview of victimological, criminological and psychological conceptions of crime respectively.

2

CONTEMPORARY PSYCHOLOGICAL CONTRIBUTIONS TO UNDERSTANDING CRIME

Emma J. Palmer
University of Leicester, United Kingdom

As a discipline, psychology has contributed a number of theories that help our understanding of crime, and why people offend. At the same time, it is important to state that crime cannot only be explained by psychology. There are a number of other disciplines that can contribute to our understanding of crime, including sociology, philosophy, medicine and biological sciences, and law. However, the specific theories and methodologies of psychology do allow it to make a significant contribution to the important question of why people commit crime (see Jamel, Chapter 1).

This chapter will, therefore, cover three areas. First, it will outline three contemporary psychological theories of crime: (1) Eysenck's personality theory; (2) social learning theory; and (3) the social information-processing approach to explaining crime. Second, theories of three types of serious offending will be considered: interpersonal violence, sexual offending, and arson. Finally, the specific issue of mentally disordered offenders will be discussed. This section will cover the different types of mental disorder and their association to offending – mental illness, learning disability, and personality disorder, before considering in more depth issues relating to the psychopathic offender.

PSYCHOLOGICAL THEORIES

Eysenck's Personality Theory

Eysenck's personality theory proposes that personality affects behaviour through its effect on development of a conscience to control behaviour, and that this takes place through **classical conditioning** – with **punishment** being the consequence of antisocial behaviour (Eysenck, 1977). In this theory, conscience is seen as "a set of emotional responses conditioned to the adverse environmental events associated with the antisocial behaviour" (Hollin, 1989, pp. 55–56). Eysenck proposed that an individual's conditionability depends on their personality, which in turn is influenced via genetically inherited characteristics of their cortical and autonomic nervous systems.

Eysenck's theory of personality initially comprised two dimensions – Extraversion (E) and Neuroticism (N). A third dimension of Psychoticism (P) was later added to the theory (Eysenck & Eysenck, 1968). These dimensions are seen as continuous, with most people being in the middle and a few at the extremes. As E and N are proposed to be orthogonal, people's scores on these two dimensions can be plotted against each other.

According to Eysenck, E is linked to the arousal of the cortical nervous system (CNS), which in turn is genetically inherited. People with high E (i.e. extraverts) are proposed to be cortically *under-aroused*, and so seek environmental stimulation to heighten their arousal levels. Therefore, they are impulsive and seek excitement. In contrast, introverts (low E) are cortically *over-aroused*, and so avoid stimulation, and are quiet. As a result, extraverts (high E) condition less effectively than introverts (low E).

Neuroticism, or emotionality, is proposed to be linked to the autonomic nervous system (ANS). People with high N are argued to have a very labile ANS, which makes them have strong reactions to unpleasant environmental stimuli. As a result they show moody and anxious behaviour. Low N people have a stable ANS, making them calm and stable even under stressful circumstances. Therefore, high N individuals condition less effectively than those with low N.

The biological basis of psychoticism is less developed than for E and N. Although Eysenck claimed it had a genetic basis, this was never outlined in much detail. Its conceptualization has also changed over time. Initially it was seen as relating to personality characteristics associated with psychosis. Eysenck later suggested it was more closely related to psychopathy. As P relates to preference for solitude, sensation-seeking, callousness, aggression, and lack of empathy for other people (Eysenck, Eysenck & Barrett, 1985), these do appear similar to the characteristics associated with psychopathy, rather than psychoticism.

Therefore, it can be predicted that the combinations of low E/low N will condition most effectively, high E/high N will condition least effectively, with low E/high N and high E/low N falling in between. This suggests that those individuals who condition least effectively will be less likely to have learnt to control antisocial behaviour. It can be predicted, then, that the high E/high N combination will be over-represented in offender populations. In contrast, the low E/low N combination should be under-represented among offenders and be found most often among non-offenders, and the intermediate combinations being found among both offenders and non-offenders. Given the characteristics associated with high P, it is expected that this will be associated with criminal behaviour.

There has been much research evaluating Eysenck's theory of crime, with reviews of early research provided by Bartol (1999) and Eysenck and Gudjonsson (1989). This research concluded that there is support for offenders having high P and high N, although the evidence for E is more mixed.

However, these early studies did have a number of methodological limitations (cf. Hollin, 1989). Offenders were viewed as a homogenous group, the effect of imprisonment on offenders' scores was not considered, individual dimensions were compared rather than examining their combination, and the occurrence of undetected offending among control groups was not considered. The point about the combination of dimensions is important, as Eysenck emphasized the importance of the combination of dimensions.

Later research has attempted to address some of these issues. There have now been studies that have examined combinations of the personality dimensions and offending. McGurk and McDougall (1981) examined the clusters of E, N and P in 100 delinquents and 100 non-delinquents, finding four clusters within each group. The clusters predicted to occur only in one group were only found in that group, i.e. high E/high N and high E/high N/high P among offenders, and low E/low N among offenders. Furthermore, those clusters predicted to be found in both groups were found in both groups, i.e. low E/high N and high E/low N.

Eysenck, Rust & Eysenck (1977) took this methodology further, and examined the clusters of dimensions within five groups of offenders who had committed different types of crimes: property offences, major theft, violent offences, conmen, and general deviancy. The results showed that property and violence offenders scored lowest on N, and conmen had the lowest P scores. No differences were found between the groups for E.

Overall, research supports the link between combinations of personality dimensions and offending. As Hollin (1989) notes, criticisms remain of the theory. The focus on individuals at the extremes of the dimensions means that the theory is unlikely to apply to all offenders limiting its explanatory power. There is also a lack of empirical evidence for the proposed link between conditionability and socialization. Despite this, the strength of this theory lies in its attempt to integrate biological, psychological, and environmental factors.

Social Learning Theory

Social learning theory was developed by Albert Bandura (1977, 1986) as an extension of previous learning theories in which behaviour was seen as determined by **reinforcement** and **punishment** from the environment. As well as behaviour being learnt through the consequences of behaviour, social learning theory proposes that it is also learnt at a cognitive level by watching other people's behaviour (i.e. **modelling** of behaviour). Once behaviour is learnt in this way, it is reinforced or punished as a result of its consequences in the same way as **operant** behaviour.

Bandura (1977) also proposed two further principles of *motivation* in the learning of behaviours: **vicarious reinforcement** and **self-reinforcement**. **Vicarious reinforcement** occurs when behaviour is learnt through observing the reinforcing and punishing consequences of behaviour for other people. **Self-reinforcement** refers to motivations to behave in a certain way due to inner feelings of self-approval (e.g. feeling a sense of achievement or proud of oneself). Thus, social learning theory outlines how behaviour is learned at a cognitive level through observation, particularly if the model is perceived to have high status.

Social learning theory has been applied to offending behaviour by both psychologists (Bandura, 1973; Nietzel, 1979) and sociologists (Akers, 1990). These social learning approaches to offending suggest that criminal behaviour can be learnt through **reinforcement**, as in **operant** theory, or through **modelling** and imitation. Three sources of observational learning have been proposed in which criminal behaviour is learnt: the family, the individual's sub-culture (e.g. peers), and the wider culture (e.g. television, cinema, books, magazines). **Reinforcement** for crime is seen as coming from both internal and external sources, and can include material rewards (e.g. money, goods), social rewards (e.g. peer group status), or personal rewards such as avoiding detection or successfully committing a crime.

Hollin (1989) reviews some of the criticisms of learning theories in general, although he argues that a full understanding and appropriate use of these theories can answer many of these points. Instead, Hollin argues that learning theories' weakness is that they do not take full account of cognitive processes.

Social Information-Processing Theory

As social learning theory demonstrated, a complete model of cognitive functioning is needed to provide a fuller understanding of its role in offending. More recently, social information-processing theories have been applied to explaining crime. Although a number of such theories exist, an influential one in this area is that of Crick & Dodge (1994). This model is a six-step model of social information-processing that describes how individuals perceive their social world and process information about it, and the influence of previous experience on these processes. More recently some authors have begun to incorporate the role of affect into this model, such as emotions and motivations (Lemerise & Arsenio, 2000). Therefore, it is not just a model of criminal behaviour, but a general model of human functioning.

The six steps in the model are shown in Figure 2.1.

1. Encoding of social cues
2. Interpretation and mental representation of the situation
3. Clarification of goals/outcomes for the situation
4. Access or construction of responses for the situation
5. Choice of response
6. Performance of chosen response

Figure 2.1: Social information-processing model. Reproduced from Crick, N.R. & Dodge, K.A. (1994), A review and reformulation of social information-processing mechanisms in children's social adjustment, *Psychological Bulletin, 115*, 74–101, with permission of the American Psychological Association

Although these steps occur in sequence for a given situation stimulus, Crick & Dodge (1994) suggest that individuals can simultaneously perform the different steps, allowing for feedback between processes. Therefore, the model is conceptualized as circular, rather than a linear process. At all steps processing is influenced by social knowledge structures based on an individual's past experiences, such as social schema and scripts.

At the first stage social cues are perceived and encoded. These are used at the second stage along with social knowledge structures to interpret the situation and provide a mental representation of it. When interpreting the situation, attributions are made about the intent of other people and the causality of events. Throughout, these processes are influenced by previous experiences in the form of social schema and scripts, to provide cognitive short cuts to help process information quickly.

At the third stage individuals choose their preferred goals/outcomes for the situation. This is likely to be influenced by pre-existing goal orientations and the modification of these in line with the social cues associated with this situation.

The fourth stage requires individuals to generate a range of possible responses to the situation. This may be achieved with reference to past experience in similar situations or by creating new responses. These responses are evaluated at the fifth stage in order to choose one to perform. A range of criteria may be used when evaluating responses, including perceived efficacy of the behaviour with respect to the goals/outcomes identified at stage 3, perceived outcome of the behaviour, likelihood of success, appropriateness, what has worked in similar situations in the past, ease of execution, and the individual's belief systems (i.e. attitudes, moral values). Finally, at stage 6, the chosen response is enacted, requiring the individuals to have appropriate verbal and non-verbal social skills.

Social Information-Processing and Criminal Behaviour

There is now a large body of research showing that aggressive individuals show distinct patterns of social information-processing across the six steps (for a review, see Palmer, 2003a, 2003b).

At the first two steps, research suggests aggressive individuals experience a range of problems in encoding and interpreting social cues, leading to an inaccurate representation of the situation. Aggressive individuals appear to perceive fewer social cues (Dodge & Newman, 1981), take more notice of aggressive cues (Gouze, 1987), and pay more attention to cues at the end of interactions (Dodge & Tomlin, 1987). Aggressive people rely more on internal schema when interpreting situations (Dodge & Tomlin, 1987), with these schema tending to be aggressive in content (Strassberg & Dodge, 1987).

A number of studies have reported that aggressive individuals have a hostile attributional bias, and so often misinterpret situations as hostile (Slaby & Guerra, 1988). This tendency is exacerbated when individuals feel threatened (Dodge & Somberg, 1987) or react impulsively (Dodge & Newman, 1981). There is also a suggestion that aggressive people attribute greater blame to external factors (Fondacaro & Heller, 1990).

At the third step, research has found that aggressive individuals tend to have dominance and revenge-based goals, rather than prosocial goals (Lochman, Wayland & White, 1993).

When generating responses, aggressive individuals generate fewer responses than non-aggressive people, suggesting they have a limited repertoire from which to draw upon (Slaby & Guerra, 1988). The content of these responses is more aggressive as compared to the prosocial responses generated by non-aggressive people (Quiggle *et al.*, 1992).

Aggressive individuals also evaluate responses by different criteria, rating aggressive responses more positively than prosocial responses (Quiggle *et al.*, 1992), and having more positive outcome expectancies and perceptions of self-efficacy for aggression (Hart, Ladd & Burleson, 1990). Thus, aggression is viewed as being more effective to achieve their goals.

Finally, social skills are important at step 6, and there is some evidence that aggressive individuals have poor social skills (see Howells, 1986). If the chosen response is successful, it will be evaluated positively and reinforced, whereas if it is unsuccessful, it will be negatively evaluated and be less likely to be used in the future.

Taken together, the distinctive patterns of processing that are associated with aggressive and antisocial behaviour suggest that social information-processing is influential in the development of juvenile delinquency and adult offending. Furthermore, research showing these patterns among quite young children (for a review, see Palmer, 2003a, 2003b) really highlights the importance of early childhood experiences in the development of such behaviours. However, questions remain as to the exact role of emotion in this approach (cf. Lemerise & Arsenio, 2000), and this is an area that requires further research.

THEORIES, EVIDENCE AND CRIME

Interpersonal Violence

Media reports often give the impression that there are high levels of violent offending. However, in reality this is not the case. In the UK, recent statistics showed that in 2005–2006 violent crime comprised 22% of offences reported to the police and 23% of offences in the British Crime Survey (Walker, Kershaw & Nicholas, 2006). A range of crimes are included under the label of 'violence', including murder, manslaughter, and robbery. Domestic violence is gaining recognition as a serious problem and will also be considered here.

As noted by Polaschek (2006), research into violent offenders' criminal behaviour has revealed that they tend not to be specialists, but commit a wide range of offences. Indeed specialist violence offenders are quite rare. **Meta-analyses** also show violent offenders have an early onset of offending behaviour, and show considerable continuity of aggression and violence throughout their life (e.g. Zumkley, 1994).

There are a number of theories that attempt to provide explanations of violence and violent offending and these will be reviewed next.

Cognitive-Behavioural Theory and Violence

Cognitive-behavioural approaches to violence consider three stages: first, the situation in which the violence occurs; second, the individual's thoughts, feelings, and behaviour; and third, the consequences of the violence. Violence is viewed as a dynamic process, with consequences altering the situation, and the individual reacting accordingly.

Of greatest interest to psychological theories is the person stage, where cognitive appraisal and other internal processes are important. One way of examining these processes is through Crick and Dodge's (1994) six-step model of social information-processing. As outlined above, aggressive individuals show a range of distinctive processing patterns across these steps. The hostile attributional bias is one of the strongest findings, with a **meta-analysis** of 41 studies concluding it had a very strong relationship with aggressive behaviour (Orobio de Castro *et al.*, 2002). Empathy is another important factor, with a **meta-analysis** by Jolliffe & Farrington (2003) reporting a significant association between poor empathy and violent offending.

Emotional arousal can also impact on cognitive processes, with anger playing a significant role in understanding violence. Novaco's work showing that there are reciprocal relationships between angry emotional arousal and cognitive processes is important here. Novaco (1975; Novaco & Welsh, 1989) proposes that angry thoughts can be triggered by situational events; these angry thoughts then increase emotional arousal (including physiological and psychological components) and this arousal heightens the intensity of the angry thoughts. As this cycle continues, the level of cognition (angry thoughts) and affect increase in turn, with an increased risk of violence.

Various consequences can result from violence. These consequences can often be highly rewarding for the individual. For example, violent behaviour can allow goals to be achieved (acting as positive **reinforcement**), as well as providing a means to deal with difficult situations through using threats and displays of violence (acting as negative **reinforcement**).

Social Factors and Violence

A range of social factors have been shown to differ between violent and non-violent individuals and predict violent behaviour. These factors are similar to those associated with general offending. A **meta-analysis** conducted by Lipsey & Derzon (1998) found the best childhood predictors of later violence included being male, low socio-economic status, antisocial parents, poor relationship with parents, involvement in general delinquency and drug use from a young age, a history of aggression and violence, antisocial peers, poor attitudes towards school, and poor school performance. Similar factors were found in a narrative review of the literature conducted by Hawkins *et al.* (1998).

The role of harsh parenting has also been highlighted, with the Gulbenkian Foundation (1995) concluding research "emphatically confirms that harsh and humiliating discipline is implicated in the development of anti-social and violent behaviour" (p. 134). Socio-economic deprivation appears to increase the impact of adverse family and parenting factors on later violence (Dodge, Pettit & Bates, 1994). Research also shows a clear link between violence and severe abuse in childhood and witnessing family violence (Widom & Maxfield, 2001). This association appears to be mediated through the impact of abuse on children's psychological functioning, such as problem-solving and coping abilities.

Personality Theories of Violence

There is a body of research examining personality traits among violent offenders. Characteristics reported among violent offenders include a need for immediate gratification (Vachss & Backal, 1979), low self-esteem and strong feelings of rage (Strasberg, 1978), depression (Kulik, Stein & Sarbin, 1968), poor ego strength (Schoenfield, 1971), lack of impulse control and empathy, high fearfulness, and a failure to be fulfilled from consistent, long-term adaptive behaviour (Sorrels, 1977, 1980). However, instead of studying simple personality characteristics, modern personality approaches to violence seek to provide more complex explanations.

One such approach is **psychodynamic** explanations of violence. Rather than attempting to provide a general theory of violence, psychodynamic explanations are tailored to the specific individual. Violence is seen as the outward symptom of malfunctioning unconscious psychic problems of which the individual is mostly or wholly unaware. Therefore, violence is not necessarily seen as the main problem. Explanations of violence are derived from offenders' problems during their early development.

Neuropsychological Factors and Violence

There is some evidence that violence is associated with brain damage or dysfunction (Raine, 2002a). **Electroencephalogram** (EEG) studies with offenders have provided evidence that there is an increased level of brain abnormality among violent offenders (see Raine, 1993). Research suggests that damage and malfunctioning of the frontal and temporal lobes is most associated with violence. This is supported by what we know about the effect of lesions in these areas.

Frontal lobe lesions are associated with personality changes (Walsh, 1994), such as apathy, a lack of foresight or taking account of the consequences of behaviour, a tendency to continue with behaviours that are unsuccessful, irritability, and grandiose and unrealistic ideas. Together, these characteristics are often referred to as **disinhibition**. If individuals with frontal lobe lesions are both more irritable and likely to be disinhibited, they are more likely to be aggressive when irritated or provoked, which may include criminal violence. There is evidence to support this theory (Raine, 2002b).

Blair (2001) has suggested that there may be links between violence and structures in the temporal lobe – the amygdala and hippocampus. Some research has examined aggressive behaviour in temporal lobe epilepsy. However, there is mixed evidence for Blair's proposal.

Other research has examined **lateralization** patterns in the brain. Lateralization refers to the different functions performed in the brain's two hemispheres. However, this research has produced mixed results. A body of research shows that a proportion of violent offenders have suffered head injuries (see Diaz, 1995). It is likely that these injuries cause brain damage, which increases the likelihood of violence.

However, **neuropsychological** research suffers from various methodological problems. These include the need to establish cause and effect, the question of what constitutes an abnormality, inadequate control groups, and the representativeness of samples. Therefore, results should be interpreted cautiously.

Domestic Violence

Domestic violence refers to violence within the family, typically inter-partner violence. Many explanations of domestic violence are based on a feminist perspective. These hold that society is patriarchal, with an implicit assumption that men control the lives of women and children, both within the family and through social institutions (Stewart, Hall & Cripps, 2001). Men are proposed to maintain women's subordination through physical violence, as well as psychological and economic coercion. Social learning theory has also been applied to domestic violence. This approach views domestic violence as a behaviour that is learnt, through experiencing rewards from it and observing and **modelling** similar behaviour (**vicarious learning**). Other approaches view domestic violence as caused by psychopathology among abusers (Dutton, 1995), or resulting from dysfunctional relationships (Geffner, Barrett & Rossman, 1995).

CASE STUDY

Young People and Gangs in the UK

Barely a week seems to go past without mention of stabbings or worse carried out by youth gangs. Recent cases where youth gangs have been implicated in murders include those of Jessie James and Rhys Jones. Both are young people who were senselessly murdered by groups of other young people. This case study considers some factors that might be responsible for this type of violent crime.

A good place to start is by considering the social backgrounds from which young gang members are more likely to come. It is undoubtedly true that gangs proliferate in inner-city areas, with many of the media stories referring to cities such as London and Manchester. The areas within these cities that tend to be associated with gangs are usually those that are run-down and socially deprived.

(Continued)

The young people from these socially deprived areas often face other associated problems. For example, families living in these areas often live in poverty, with parents either being in low-paid jobs or unemployed, which can put pressure on family life. These problems can be increased for lone parents. For example, if a lone parent works, young children are looked after by older siblings and teenagers are left unsupervised for periods of time.

For some young people, this can leave them vulnerable to pressure from their friends and peers – either to take part in antisocial behaviour or commit offences. Where there is a gang culture, joining one of the groups can provide some protection from being victimized. This is illustrated by the fact that many young people admit they start carrying a knife (or other weapons) so they can defend themselves, rather than because they intend to use it. Being surrounded by a culture of violence often appears to lead to further violence through such incremental steps.

Schools in socially deprived areas are often also run-down and struggle with the behavioural and emotional problems of their pupils. Clearly, this can impact on the educational experience that students receive. Falling in with a bad group of friends can lead young people to stop valuing education – or rather, educational achievement is not seen as being 'cool' and respect is gained through other, more antisocial activities. For these young people, getting an ASBO (Anti Social Behaviour Order) is often valued more than passing their final school exams.

Unfortunately the problems of social deprivation, poor education, and family problems are difficult to address and require long-term solutions rather than a 'quick fix'.

Sexual Offending

The term 'sexual offences' covers a number of crimes, including rape, unlawful sexual intercourse, indecent assault, indecent exposure, and gross indecency with a child. Other non-sexual offences can also sometimes have a sexual element, such as sexually motivated murder. Due to problems of under-reporting of crimes, it is difficult to put a figure on the number of sexual offences committed. However, in the UK, figures for 2005/06 show there were 62 081 recorded sexual offences in this period (Walker *et al.*, 2006).

There are five major theories of sexual offending, three of which cover child sexual abuse, one relates to rape, and one that attempts to explain all types of sexual offending.

Finkelhor's (1984) 'Four Preconditions' model proposes that there are four preconditions that a child molester must pass through prior to an offence. First, there must be a motivation to sexually abuse, such as sexual arousal to a child, emotional congruence with a child, or blockage of sexual expression with an adult. Second, internal inhibitions against offending must be overcome. These inhibitions can be overcome through distorted beliefs about child abuse, becoming disinhibited through the use of alcohol or drugs, or experiencing severe stress. Third, external factors must be overcome to allow the abuse to occur, for example gaining the trust of the child and their family, or the child being left alone. Fourth, the child's resistance must be overcome, through using force or grooming techniques.

1. Motivation to sexually abuse children
2. Overcome internal inhibitions
3. Overcome external factors
4. Overcome child's resistance

Figure 2.2: Factors in Finkelhor's (1984) 'Four Preconditions' model of child sexual abuse

A second theory of child sexual abuse is Hall & Hirschmann's (1992) quadripartite model. Like Finkelhor's model this proposes there are four components necessary for an offence to take place: sexual arousal to children, attitudes and beliefs (cognitions) that justify child abuse, poor self-regulation, and personality problems. This theory suggests that vulnerability to committing child sexual abuse is caused by personality problems. Situational factors, including opportunity, determine when this vulnerability is triggered, leading to deviant arousal, emotional disturbance, and offence-permitting thinking. Subtypes of child molesters are also proposed, based on the relative level of each of these factors. Therefore, some child abusers have greater levels of deviant arousal, others have greater emotional disturbance, and others have more distorted cognitions. Research examining the risk factors for child molesters supports the four areas outlined in this theory.

The third theory is the 'Pathways Model' set out by Ward & Siegert (2002), which proposes four separate but interacting psychological mechanisms are involved in child sexual abuse. These are: intimacy/social deficits, distorted sexual scripts, cognitive distortions, and emotional dysregulation. The four components are involved in all sexual offences, but one component dominates each pathway into offending. Offenders with multiple dysfunctional mechanisms form a fifth pathway, hypothesized to be the 'pure paedophiles'. A recent update of this theory has attempted to incorporate biological, **neuropsychological**, and ecological factors (Ward & Beech, 2006).

Turning to theories of rape, an interaction model of sexual aggression was proposed by Malamuth, Heavey and Linz (1993). Specifically, this model proposes that sexual aggression is the result of the interaction of two 'paths': the hostile masculinity path and the sexual promiscuity path. The hostile masculinity path emphasizes the role of aggressive intimate relationships and sexual conquest in the concept of masculinity, along with valuing power, risk taking, dominance, and competitiveness. The sexual

1. Sexual arousal to children
2. Attitudes and beliefs that justify child sexual abuse
3. Poor self-regulation
4. Personality problems

Figure 2.3: Components in Hall and Hirschmann's (1992) quadripartite model of child sexual abuse

1. Intimacy/social deficits
2. Distorted sexual scripts
3. Cognitive distortions
4. Emotional dysregulation

Figure 2.4: Factors in Ward and Siegart's (2002) pathway models of child sexual abuse

promiscuity path focuses on the role of sexual behaviours in maintaining self-esteem and peer status, and the appeal of impersonal sex.

Malamuth *et al.* (1993) proposed that sexual promiscuity is more likely to lead to sexual aggression among men possessing a high level of the characteristics within the hostile masculinity pathway. This suggestion has been supported among non-offender samples using measures of self-reported sexual aggression. However, it remains to be validated on sexual offender samples.

The only theory to date that covers all types of sexual offending is Marshall & Barbaree's (1990) integrated theory. This approach takes account of biological, developmental, sociocultural, and situational variables that lead to psychological vulnerabilities. Negative childhood experiences (e.g. poor parenting, abuse) are proposed to lead children to experience problems in forming social, emotional, and sexual attachments with other people. During adolescence when hormonal changes occur, aggression and sex can become linked due to both drives originating from the same neural substrates. Poor social skills can lead to rejection of prosocial attempts to be sexually intimate, which results in anger and an increased likelihood of an aggressive response. If the individual experiences support for aggressive behaviour from sociocultural sources (e.g. peers, media), this will increase the likelihood of aggression. Other situational factors and emotional states, such as substance use, anger, or sexual frustration can also impact on the ability of the individual to inhibit antisocial behaviour. Taken together all these factors can result in a sexual offence being committed.

A weakness of Marshall and Barbaree's theory is its breadth, meaning that it does not provide explanations for why different types of sexual offending occur. Research has also found that some aspects emphasized by this theory, such as aggressive behaviour and disinhibition, are not shown by all sexual offenders.

There are certain factors common to all of these theories of sexual offending. They all suggest that sexual offending results from a mixture of distorted cognitions that allow sexual abuse of others, deviant sexual arousal, poor emotional and impulse management, and problems in relating to other people. Developmental adversity is a likely cause of these problems.

Research into the characteristics of sexual offenders has provided further understanding of their offences. Beech *et al.* (2005) provide a summary of such research among rapists. Characteristics commonly found among rapists include: sexual preoccupation, sexual interest in rape/violence against women, sexual entitlement, hostile masculinity and controlling sexual beliefs, distrust of women, lack of emotional intimacy with other adults, grievance schema, poor problem solving, poor emotional control, and lifestyle impulsiveness. Research with child sexual abusers have revealed some overlaps with these characteristics, including: sexual preoccupation, sexual interest or preference for children, sexual entitlement, beliefs supportive of child sexual abuse, lack of emotional intimacy with adults, emotional congruence with children, poor problem solving, and personal inadequacy, such as poor self-esteem, emotional loneliness, and personal distress (e.g. Bumby, 1999; Fisher, Beech & Browne, 1999; Hanson & Bussière, 1998; Hanson & Morton-Bourgon, 2005).

Arson

A large number of major fires within the UK are a result of arson, with Home Office figures showing 45 742 arson incidents were recorded by the police in 2005/2006 (Walker *et al.*, 2006). *Arson* refers to deliberate setting fire to property, whereas *firesetting* is a broader term often used when referring to young children, and does not necessarily imply intent. Geller (1992) proposed four categories of arson: arson associated with mental disorders, arson associated with medical or biological disorders, juvenile fire-play or firesetting and arson not associated with any psychobiological factors. Geller included within this last category arsons committed for profit, to conceal a crime, for revenge, vanity, or recognition, vandalism or political arson. The factors associated with arson and firesetting will be considered in more detail next.

Adult Arsonists

Among adults, the majority of research has focused on arson among psychiatric populations, even though they are responsible for a minority of arson incidents. This has raised questions as to the generalizability of findings to offenders within the criminal justice system. However, this literature suggests a number of factors that may be associated with arson.

Research with psychiatric populations suggests arson may be associated with a number of mental illnesses, including schizophrenia (Ritchie & Huff, 1999), personality disorders (Hurley & Monahan, 1969), depression (O'Sullivan & Kelleher, 1987), and bipolar affective disorders and mood disorders (Geller, 1992).

Although there is little research, there does not appear to be a relationship between arson and neurological disorders, such as epilepsy (Byrne & Walsh, 1989), other EEG abnormalities (Powers & Gunderman, 1978), or head trauma (Hurley & Monahan, 1969). While there is some evidence of a link with dementia, this is probably attributable to accidents and careless smoking (Cohen *et al.*, 1990).

More evidence exists for an association between arson and developmental disorders and learning disabilities (Murphy & Clare, 1996; Ritchie & Huff, 1999). It has been suggested that this relationship is due to a lack of awareness of the consequences of setting fires among these populations.

Functional analysis of arson behaviours has highlighted the importance of social and environmental stimuli in reinforcing arson (Swaffer, 1994), and the interaction of these stimuli with predispositions to committing antisocial behaviours (Fineman, 1995). Canter and his colleagues have attempted to understand the behavioural patterns of firesetting and arson. Canter & Fritzon (1998) used two facets to categorize arson: person-oriented v. object-oriented arsons, and expressive v. instrumental arsons. They argued that these two facets interact to give four types of arson: expressive person-oriented, expressive other-oriented, instrumental person-oriented, instrumental other-oriented. With a sample of adult and juvenile firesetters, Canter and Fritzon reported that individuals in their four categories differed on a number of characteristics. This research has since been replicated by Santilla *et al.*, (2003) and Almond *et al.* (2005).

Juvenile Firesetters

The research suggests that many of the characteristics of young firesetters overlap with those of general juvenile delinquent populations (for a review, see Kolko, 2001). Young firesetters are more likely to be male, with a **meta-analysis** of 22 studies revealing that 82% of young firesetters were male (Kolko, 1985). Firesetting in children is often associated with a range of other externalizing behaviours. These include aggression, extreme antisocial behaviour, and conduct disorder (Dadds & Fraser, 2006; Kolko, 1985; McCarty & McMahon, 2005). Other research has reported high levels of drug and alcohol abuse among firesetters (e.g. Repo & Virkkunen, 1997).

A range of psychological factors has been associated with firesetting in children and adolescents. These include poor interpersonal skills, such as impulsivity, poor assertion skills, and inability to resolve conflicts (Harris & Rice, 1984). There is also evidence that psychiatric problems are more prevalent among firesetting populations (Kolko & Kazdin, 1988; Räsänen *et al.*, 1995).

Parental and family functioning have also been implicated in firesetting. Factors include poor child-rearing practices, such as a lack of supervision and lax or inconsistent discipline (Kolko & Kazdin, 1990). Child abuse, maltreatment, and neglect are also prevalent among young firesetters. Firesetting has also been associated with parental relationship problems, conflict and violence, and parents who report experiencing personal difficulties and life stresses (Kolko & Kazdin, 1991; McCarty & McMahon, 2005). Young firesetters have also been found to be more likely to have experienced the loss of the mother as compared to non-firesetters, with 40% spending time in an orphanage, foster home, or psychiatric facility (Ritvo, Shanock & Lewis, 1982). There are also increased levels of academic underachievement, school disruption, and suspension/expulsions from school among young firesetters (Hollin, Epps & Swaffer, 2002).

One study comparing young firesetters with young delinquents who were not firesetters showed that firesetters have more problems than non-firesetters, with firesetting often used to obtain power over adults (Sakheim & Osborn, 1986). Kolko (2001) has also emphasized the role of children's exposure to fire materials and fire competence when examining motivations for firesetting behaviour.

MENTALLY DISORDERED OFFENDERS

'Mentally disordered offenders' is a legal term that refers to those individuals who have a mental disorder and who have also committed an offence. For many of these individuals, their mental disorder will have influenced their offending. The types of mental disorder include mental illness (schizophrenia and depression), learning disability, and personality disorder, along with the special case of psychopathic offenders. There is a body of research examining the relationship between mental disorder and offending. There certainly appears to be some relationship, with an increased prevalence of mental disorder among criminal populations (Fazel & Danesh, 2002; Shaw, 2001), particularly among women, older people, and ethnic minority groups. This is mirrored by higher levels of offending among psychiatric populations as compared to the general population (Taylor, 2001).

Why are Mentally Disordered Offenders a Special Case?

In the eyes of the law for a person to be found guilty of an offence they have to be criminally responsible. This relates to the distinction in law between *actus rea* (bad act) and *mens rea* (guilty state of mind). For an individual to be found guilty, both *actus rea* and *mens rea* must be proved, i.e. (1) that the act is an offence and the defendant did commit the offence; and (2) that *at the time of the offence*, the individual knew both (a) that what he was doing was bad, and (b) that what he was doing was wrong (i.e. against the law). In the UK, the McNaughton Rule states that an individual is not criminally responsible if:

At the time of committing the act, the party accused was labouring under such a defect of reason from a disease of the mind, as not to know the nature and quality of the act he was doing; or if he did know it, he did not know what he was doing was wrong.

If the defence can prove that such a 'defect' or mental disorder existed at the time of the offence, then individuals can be found 'not guilty' on the grounds that they are not criminally responsible.

Types of Mentally Disordered Offender

The different types of mental disorders and their association with offending will be considered next.

Mentally ill. The category of mental illness includes schizophrenia and depression, and these will be considered in turn. Schizophrenia refers to a group of disorders characterized by disturbances of perception, thought, affect, and actions. Individuals often experience hallucinations, delusions, paranoia (the psychotic symptoms of schizophrenia) and withdraw from others. The prevalence of schizophrenia in the general population is around 1%. The figure is far higher among offenders, with offenders referred for psychiatric treatment having often committed a violent offence. In a systematic review of 62 studies of prisoners from 12 countries, Fazel and Danesh (2002) reported 4% of male and female offenders had schizophrenia. These figures lead to the question of whether schizophrenia somehow causes the offending, or if there is simply an association caused by other factors.

When considering why schizophrenia may be associated with offending, it has been suggested that paranoid ideas, command hallucinations and other delusions associated with schizophrenia may influence behaviour, although research shows this is true in only a minority of cases (Smith & Taylor, 1999). Furthermore, the reliance on self-reports of the individual's state of mind at the time of the offence causes problems for researchers in this area.

The role of the individual's environment has also been considered. Research shows that similar factors are associated with both schizophrenia and violent behaviour, such as negative life experiences relating to families, relationship problems and loss of employment (McNeil, 1997). Therefore, it has been suggested that experiencing stressful life events can lead to both schizophrenia and offending/violence for individuals with a predisposing vulnerability. The role of co-morbid substance misuse has also been highlighted (Mueser, Drake & Wallace, 1998; Taylor, 2001). Use of alcohol and drugs is likely to exacerbate the psychotic symptoms of schizophrenia and may also lead to a reduced compliance with medication. Substance misuse is also associated with an elevated risk of offending in its own right (Home Office, 2002). Offenders with a diagnosis of schizophrenia may also have other mental health problems, further complicating the picture.

Depression can be split into two types: unipolar (major) depression and bipolar depression. Major depression is characterized by a pervasive sad mood, feeling of guilt and self-blame, disturbed appetite, tiredness, lethargy, and recurring thoughts of suicide. In bipolar depression individuals experience alternating periods of mania and depression. Of these, major depression is the most common and affects 8% of the general population, with bipolar experienced by about 1%. In contrast, research among offenders has found the prevalence of depression to be higher (Brinded *et al.*, 2001). For example in Fazel and Danesh's (2002) review, the prevalence of major depression was 10% among male prisoners and 12% among women prisoners.

There are a number of ways in which depression and offending may be linked: first, individuals may offend because they are depressed; second, depression may be triggered by guilt after an offence; and third, individuals may be depressed when they committed an offence, but the depression did not cause the offence. It is also possible that imprisonment for an offence may trigger depression.

It is also important to consider what factors may have triggered the depression. Social and environmental factors are often precursors to a depressive episode, such as losing a job or relationship problems (Kendler, Karkowski & Prescott, 1999; Kessler, 1997). As noted above these factors are themselves also associated with an increased risk of offending.

Overall, for both schizophrenia and depression, the mental illness may not be the only factor to consider when explaining the link with offending. Account should also be taken of the complex interactions between the individual, their mental state, predispositions, and social and environmental factors. The exacerbating influence of substance misuse should also not be ignored. Furthermore, the influence of each of these factors may vary for different people at different times.

CASE STUDY

Anatomy of a Gunman

In recent years there has been a spate of mass killings by gunmen in the US. A recent high-profile case occurred at Virginia Tech University in April 2007, in which a 23-year-old student (Seung-Hui Cho) shot 32 other students and staff before killing himself. In the days following the shootings, it emerged that the gunman had experienced mental health problems and had shown suicidal tendencies since he was 13 years. However, a closer look at his history reveals other issues that were implicated in what happened.

Cho's family had moved to the US when he was 8 years of age. Not knowing much English led to social isolation and even once his language skills improved Cho remained quiet and even withdrawn. At age 12, he was diagnosed with social anxiety disorder, specifically selective mutism. He was prescribed anti-depressants, which seemed to help, but was taken off these after about a year. Cho is reported as not having a good relationship with his father, and not speaking much to his parents. However, how much this was normal teenage behaviour rather than problematic is not clear.

At high school his teachers developed a programme to help him complete his school week and he continued to attend counselling. As a result, he graduated in 2003 with good grades. Although the school suggested he go to college close to home, he chose to apply to Virginia Tech. His counsellor gave Cho the name of someone there for him to call if he needed help, however he never used this.

The first few years at college appeared to go fine, with Cho achieving good grades and being in regular contact with his family. However, in autumn 2005 problems started to appear. He stopped writing home, argued with his teachers, and complaints were received from female students about receiving harassing emails, text messages and phone calls. As a result he was referred to counselling. A room-mate also reported that after one warning to stop contacting a woman Cho said "I might as well kill myself now". A psychiatric evaluation followed, along with a few brief phone calls with a counsellor.

Reviewing these facts, it would appear that Cho certainly had mental health problems. However, it is also clear that his social isolation and lack of social skills were also contributory factors to what happened. The strong support system that acted as a safety net at high school was simply not there at university, and he gradually became more isolated. These environmental factors were clearly important in the deterioration in Cho's mental health and the associated increase in his antisocial behaviour – and provide a good example of the complex nature of the mental illness/offending relationship.

Learning disabled. Learning disabled (LD) individuals are characterized by impairments of intelligence and social functioning. While there are no legal criteria of IQ score for LD, in clinical practice an IQ of 70 is normally seen as 'borderline'. When this is combined with below average social functioning, a diagnosis of LD is applied. An IQ of less than 50 represents a substantial amount of impairment. Learning disability can be present from birth or can result from hypoxia (lack of oxygen) at birth, serious illness, or brain damage.

Within the general population, 2–2.5% of people have an IQ of less than 70 (Holland, 2004). The corresponding figure among offender populations is less clear, although no UK studies have reported the figure to be greater than 2% in prisons

(Holland, 2004). However, this figure may be low due to learning disabled offenders receiving hospital orders under the Mental Health Act or being dealt with in the community, rather than being imprisoned. Other studies have examined the prevalence of offending among individuals known to services for learning disabled people. Again, these have shown low levels of offending, ranging from 2% (Lyall, *et al.*, 1995) to 5% (McNulty, Kissi-Deborah & Newsom-Davies, 1995).

Notwithstanding these figures, it is not at all clear how learning disabilities and offending are linked. The term 'learning disability' covers a wide range of individuals who can differ on a number of characteristics. As a result there is no clear definition of the term, particularly within the borderline area. Research suggests that there are two groups of learning disabled offenders (Holland, 2004). First, there are offenders with a mild learning disability who are not known to services, and often come from disadvantaged homes in which other family members are offenders and share many characteristics in common with general offenders. Second, are a more heterogeneous group of offenders who are known to learning disability services. These offenders are thought to commit fewer offences, but possibly to be more dangerous.

While learning disabled people commit a variety of offences, there appear to be a disproportionate number convicted for sexual offences (Law *et al.*, 2000). However, there seem to be distinct differences between the sexual offences committed by learning disabled offenders and the general sexual offender population. As compared to the general sexual offender population, the sexual offences committed by learning disabled offenders involve less planning and the victim often does not know the offender. This has led to suggestions that sexual offences by learning disabled people may represent inappropriate and impulsive behaviour towards other people, rather than being deliberate acts of sexual aggression. It may be that the learning disabled person is not aware of the social rules governing acceptable behaviours in such situations and lacks the social competence to express feelings and the social skills required to make acceptable sexual approaches to people (Hudson *et al.*, 1999).

Similar explanations have been suggested with regard to learning disabled offenders who have committed violent offences. Here, it may be that the violent behaviour is a result of impulsivity or frustration, or a lack of social skills in dealing with provocative situations. Research has also shown aggression in learning disabled samples to be associated with a poor self-concept (Jahoda *et al.*, 1998).

Personality disordered. A personality disorder is a persistent disorder that impacts on how the individual relates to themselves, others, and their environment, leading to major problems in their social functioning. There are 10 personality disorders, which are classified into three categories by DSM-IV (American Psychiatric Association, 1994).

Weismann (1993) suggests that about 10% of adults in the general population in North America suffer from some type of personality disorder, with this figure being considerably higher in forensic settings. Research has shown that 50–80% of adults in prison meet the diagnostic criteria for antisocial personality disorder (Hare, 1983; Robins, Tipp & Przybeck, 1991). There are often high levels of co-morbidity with other personality disorders and mental illness.

Research shows there to be some relationship between personality disorders and offending, especially violent offences. While the exact nature of this relationship is not fully understood, there are number of personality traits common to many personality

---

Cluster A: Odd-eccentric
- Paranoid
- Schizoid
- Schizotypal

Cluster B: Dramatic-erratic-emotional
- Antisocial
- Borderline
- Histrionic
- Narcissistic

Cluster C: Anxious-fearful
- Avoidant
- Dependant
- Obsessive-compulsive

Figure 2.5: Personality disorders as classified by DSM-IV

disorders that are related to offending (Hart, 2001). These traits include anxiety, emotional instability, insecure attachments, depressiveness, hostility, impulsivity and lack of empathy. Furthermore, being aggressive and a history of antisocial behaviour are diagnostic criteria for antisocial personality disorder (McMurran, 2001). However, care should be taken when attributing causality of offending to personality disorder, as there may be factors other than the personality disorder that increase the risk of offending.

In England and Wales, offenders suffering from personality disorders can be sentenced to prison or a probation order, or if they are considered 'treatable' they can be dealt with under the Mental Health Act 1983. Within legislation, personality disorder comes under the legal classification of 'psychopathic disorder' which is defined as "a persistent disorder or disability of the mind . . . which results in abnormally aggressive or seriously irresponsible conduct". However 'psychopathic disorder' is not a clinical diagnosis, and as is discussed below, although there are overlaps, psychopathy and personality disorder are not the same thing.

The Special Case of the Psychopathic Offender

The term 'psychopathic offender' refers to those offenders classified under the Mental Health Act 1983 as having a 'psychopathic disorder', defined as "a persistent disorder or disability of the mind (whether or not including significant impairment of intelligence) which results in abnormally aggressive or seriously irresponsible conduct". It is, therefore, a legal term, rather than a clinical diagnosis. Clinically, it appears that offenders detained under the term psychopathic disorder exhibit traits similar to a personality disorder, specifically antisocial personality disorder (ASPD). However, this diagnosis does not necessarily fit all offenders within this category.

There have been attempts to describe psychopathic offenders, and to develop diagnostic criteria for psychopathy. Some of the most important work in this area is that of Cleckley (1976) and Hare (1980). This work highlighted a number of characteristics as defining psychopaths. These include a lack of guilt and remorse, impulsiveness,

1.	Superficial charm
2.	Grandiose sense of self-worth
3.	Need for stimulation/easily bored
4.	Pathological lying
5.	Manipulative
6.	Lack of remorse or guilt
7.	No emotional depth
8.	Callous
9.	Parasitic lifestyle
10.	Poor behavioural control
11.	Promiscuous sexual behaviour
12.	Early behaviour problems
13.	Lack of long-term planning
14.	Impulsive
15.	Irresponsible
16.	Failure to accept responsibility for own actions
17.	Frequent marital failures
18.	Juvenile delinquency
19.	Poor record on probation or conditional release
20.	Criminal versatility

Figure 2.6: Hare, R.D. (2003). Hare Psychopathy Checklist-Revised (PCL-R) (2nd edn). North Tonawanda, NY: Multi-Health Systems

irresponsibility, pathological lying, manipulativeness, shallow affect, egocentricity, glibness, superficial charm, and a failure to learn from experience. Hare went on to develop a clinical assessment tool, the Psychopathy Checklist-Revised (Hare, 1991) comprising 20 items.

To be classified as a psychopath on the PCL-R, a cut-off score of 30 is used, although 25 has been suggested as more appropriate in some jurisdictions. Research suggests that these items assess three inter-related aspects of psychopathy: (1) an arrogant and manipulative interpersonal style; (2) affective deficits; and (3) an impulsive and irresponsible behavioural style (Cooke & Michie, 2001).

A large body of research exists showing that offenders with psychopathy (as assessed using the PCL-R) are persistent and serious offenders, with a particularly strong relationship between psychopathy and violence (for a review, see Hare, 2003). However, less is known about the mechanisms of this relationship. Three suggestions have been put forward by Hart (1998), relating to cognition, affect, and behaviour. First, psychopaths exhibit a cognitive pattern that includes a hostile attributional bias, attentional deficits, and beliefs that support the reinforcing nature of violence. Second, they show affective deficits in guilt, empathy and fear that can increase the likelihood of offending regardless of the consequences for the safety of themselves or other people. Third, psychopaths exhibit behavioural impulsiveness, often acting without thinking.

There are a number of problems with the legal term 'psychopathic disorder'. First, there is circularity in the diagnosis of 'psychopathic disorder' in that it is made on the basis of violent/very antisocial behaviour. Thus, no distinction is made between the psychiatric state of psychopathy and the behaviour which equals its symptoms. Therefore, it is perhaps no surprise that psychopathy is associated with violence. It is likely that there are people with psychopathic traits in the general population, who because they do not commit offences (or do not get caught) do not come to the attention of the criminal justice system. Second, research has shown that legally defined psychopaths and those identified using the PCL-R are not the same individuals. For example, Blackburn (1995) states that only a quarter of psychopaths in his research would be categorized as psychopaths by the PCL-R. Therefore, 'psychopathic disorder' and psychopathy do not represent the same construct. These issues have led to suggestions that psychopathy may actually be a severe personality disorder, or that it is not a mental disorder at all but an evolved lifestyle that is adaptive to certain situations (Rice, 1997). If the latter suggestion is the case, then psychopaths who commit violent acts may do so as a result of the same factors as other violent offenders.

CONCLUSIONS

Overall, it can be seen that psychology can make an important contribution to our understanding of why people offend. However, there remain a number of issues that we do not yet fully understand, and further research is required in these areas. Examples of these include the exact relationship of personality to offending, the developmental precursors to sexual offending, a coherent theory of arson and firesetting, and the true nature of the link between mental disorder and offending. The importance of this knowledge is in how it can be translated into practice with offenders, in terms of informing future developments in working with offenders to reduce their likelihood of reoffending.

SUMMARY

- This chapter has considered how psychological theory and research have contributed to our understanding of offending.
- Theories such as Eysenck's personality theory, social learning theory, and social information-processing approaches, have been applied with varying degrees of success to offending.
- Psychology has also been applied to the specific areas of violent offending, sexual offending and arson.
- Mentally disordered offenders cover a range of individuals with different problems. Examining these offenders by types of mental disorder has aided understanding of the associations between these disorders and offending.
- This research also provides some clarification of the question of whether mental disorder *causes* offending or if the association can be explained with reference to other factors. While it is true that an association does exist, it is often difficult to disentangle causality.
- Finally, the special case of the psychopathic offender was considered. This highlighted the problems with the legal definition of psychopathic disorder and its relationship to the concept of psychopathy as defined by Hare (1991).

ESSAY/DISCUSSION QUESTIONS

1. What factors lead to criminal behaviour?
2. What might lead to offenders having distinctive patterns of social information-processing?
3. Compare and contrast two different theories of violent offending.
4. Is crime caused by mental illness?

REFERENCES

Akers, R.L. (1990). Rational choice, deterrence, and social learning theory in criminology: The path not taken. *Journal of Criminal Law and Criminology, 81,* 653–676.

Almond, L., Duggan, L., Shine, J., & Canter, D. (2005). Test of the arson action system model in an incarcerated population. *Psychology, Crime and Law, 11,* 1–15.

American Psychiatric Association (1994). *Diagnostic and statistical Manual of mental disorders* (4th edn). Washington, DC: APA.

Bandura, A. (1973). *Aggression: A social learning analysis.* Englewood Cliffs, NJ: Prentice Hall.

Bandura, A. (1977). *Social learning theory.* Englewood Cliffs, NJ: Prentice Hall.

Bandura, A. (1986). *Social foundations of thought and action: A social cognitive theory.* Englewood Cliffs, NJ: Prentice Hall.

Bartol, C.R. (1999). *Criminal behavior: A psychosocial approach.* (5th edn). Upper Saddle River, NJ: Prentice Hall.

Beech, A., Oliver, C., Fisher, D., & Beckett, R. (2005). *STEP 4: The sex offender treatment programme in prison: Addressing the offending behaviour of rapists and sexual murders.* University of Birmingham: Centre for Forensic and Family Psychology. Also available from www.hmprisonservice.gov.uk/assets/documents/100013DBStep_4_report_2005.pdf

Blackburn, R. (1995). Psychopaths: Are they bad or mad? In N.K. Clark & G.M. Stephenson (Eds), *Criminal behaviour: Perceptions, attributions, and rationality. Issues in Criminological and Legal Psychology, No. 22.* Leicester: The British Psychological Society.

Blair, R.J.R. (2001). Neuro-cognitive models of aggression, the antisocial personality disorders and psychopathy. *Journal of Neurology, Neurosurgery and Psychiatry, 71,* 1–4.

Brinded, P.M.J., Simpson, A.I.F., Laidlaw, T.M. *et al.* (2001). Prevalence of psychiatric disorders in New Zealand prisons: A national study. *Australian and New Zealand Journal of Psychiatry, 35,* 166–173.

Bumby, K. (1995). Assessing the cognitive distortions of child molesters and rapists: Development and validation of the RAPE and MOLEST scales. *Sexual Abuse: A Journal of Research and Treatment, 8,* 37–54.

Byrne, A. & Walsh, J.B. (1989). The epileptic arsonist. *British Journal of Psychiatry, 155,* 268–271.

Canter, D.V. & Fritzon, K. (1998). Differentiating arsonists: A model of firesetting actions and characteristics. *Legal and Criminological Psychology, 3,* 73–96.

Cleckley, H. (1976). *The mask of sanity* (5th edn). St. Louis, MO: Mosby.

Cohen, M.A.A., Aladjem, A.D., Bremin, D., & Ghazi, M. (1990). Firesetting by patients with the Acquired Immunodeficiency Syndrome (AIDS). *Annals of International Medicine, 122,* 386–387.

Cooke, D.J. & Michie, C. (1998). Predicting recidivism in a Scottish prison sample. *Psychology, Crime and Law*, *4*, 169–211.

Cooke, D.J. & Michie, C. (2001). Refining the construct of psychopathy: Towards a hierarchical model. *Psychological Assessment*, *13*, 171–188.

Crick, N.R. & Dodge, K.A. (1994). A review and reformulation of social information-processing mechanisms in children's social adjustment. *Psychological Bulletin*, *115*, 74–101.

Dadds, M.R. & Fraser, J.A. (2006). Fire interest, firesetting and psychopathology in Australian children: A normative study. *Australian and New Zealand Journal of Psychiatry*, *40*, 581–586.

Diaz, F.G. (1995). Traumatic brain injury and criminal behaviour. *Medicine and Law*, *14*, 131–140.

Dodge, K.A. & Newman, J.P. (1981). Biased decision-making processes in aggressive boys. *Journal of Abnormal Psychology*, *90*, 375–379.

Dodge, K.A., Pettit, G.S., & Bates, J.E. (1994). Socialisation mediators of the relation between socio-economic status and child conduct problems. *Child Development*, *65*, 649–665.

Dodge, K.A. & Somberg, D.R. (1987). Hostile attributional biases among aggressive boys are exacerbated under conditions of threat to the self. *Child Development*, *58*, 213–224.

Dodge, K.A. & Tomlin, A.M. (1987). Utilization of self-schemas as a mechanism of interpersonal bias in aggressive children. *Social Cognition*, *5*, 280–300.

Dutton, D.G. (1995). *The domestic assault of women: Psychological and criminal justice Perspectives*. Vancouver, Canada: UBC Press.

Eysenck, H.J. (1977). *Crime and personality*. (3rd edn). London: Routledge & Kegan Paul.

Eysenck, H.J. & Eysenck, S.B.G. (1968). A factorial study of psychoticism as a dimension of personality. *Multivariate Behavioural Research* (special issue), 15–31.

Eysenck, H.J. & Gudjonsson, G.H. (1989). *The causes and cures of criminality*. New York: Plenum Press.

Eysenck, S.B.G., Eysenck, H.J., & Barrett, P. (1985). A revised version of the psychoticism scale. *Personality and Individual Differences*, *6*, 21–29.

Eysenck, S.B.G., Rust, J., & Eysenck, H.J. (1977). Personality and the classification of adult offenders. *British Journal of Criminology*, *17*, 169–179.

Fazel, S. & Danesh, J. (2002). Serious mental disorder in 23,000 prisoners: A systematic review of 62 surveys. *Lancet*, *359*, 545–550.

Fineman, K.R. (1995). A model for the qualitative analysis of child and adult fire deviant behaviour. *American Journal of Forensic Psychology*, *13*, 31–60.

Finkelhor, D. (1984). *Child sexual abuse: New theory and research*. New York: Free Press.

Fisher, D., Beech, A.R., & Browne, K. (1999). Comparison of sex offenders to non-sex offenders on selected psychological measures. *International Journal of Offender Therapy and Comparative Criminology*, *43*, 473–491.

Fondacaro, M.R. & Heller, K. (1990). Attributional style in aggressive adolescent boys. *Journal of Abnormal Child Psychology*, *18*, 75–89.

Geffner, R., Barrett, J.J., & Rossman, B.B.R. (1995). Domestic violence and sexual abuse: Multiple systems perspectives. In R.H. Mikesell, D.-D. Lusterman, & S.H. McDaniel (Eds), *Integrating family therapy: Handbook of family psychology and systems theory* (pp. 501–517). Washington, DC: APA.

Geller, J.L. (1992). Arson in review. *Clinical Forensic Psychiatry*, *15*, 623–645.

Gouze, K.R. (1987). Attention and social problem solving as correlates of aggression in pre-school males. *Journal of Abnormal Psychology, 15*, 181–197.

Gulbenkian Foundation (1995). *Children and violence.* London: Calouste Gulbenkian Foundation.

Hall, G.C.N. & Hirschmann, R. (1992). Sexual aggression against children: A conceptual perspective of etiology. *Criminal Justice and Behavior, 19*, 8–23.

Hanson, R.K. & Bussière, M.T. (1998). Predicting relapse: A meta-analysis of sexual offender recidivism studies. *Journal of Consulting and Clinical Psychology, 66*, 348–362.

Hanson, R.K. & Morton-Bourgon, K.E. (2005). The characteristics of persistent sexual offenders: A meta-analysis of recidivism studies. *Journal of Consulting and Clinical Psychology, 73*, 1154–1163.

Hare, R.D. (1980). A research scale for the assessment of psychopathy in criminal populations. *Personality and Individual Differences, 1*, 111–119.

Hare, R.D. (1983). Diagnosis of antisocial personality disorder in two prison populations. *American Journal of Psychiatry, 140*, 887–890.

Hare, R.D. (1991). *The Hare psychopathy checklist-revised.* Toronto, Ontario: Multi-Health Systems.

Hare, R.D. (2003). *Hare psychopathy checklist-revised (PCL-R)* (2nd edn). North Tonawanda, NY: Multi-Health Systems.

Harris, G.T. & Rice, M.E. (1984). Mentally disordered firesetters: Psychodynamics versus empirical approaches. *International Journal of Law and Psychiatry, 7*, 19–34.

Hart, C.H., Ladd, G.W., & Burleson, B.R. (1990). Children's expectations of the outcomes of social strategies: Relations with sociometric status and maternal disciplinary styles. *Child Development, 61*, 127–137.

Hart, S.D. (1998). Psychopathy and risk for violence. In D.J. Cooke, A.E. Forth, J. Newman, & R.D. Hare (Eds), *Psychopathy: Theory research and implications for society* (pp. 355–373). Netherlands: Kluwer Academic Publishers.

Hart, S.D. (2001). Forensic issues. In W.J. Livesley (Ed.), *Handbook of personality disorders: Theory, research, and treatment* (pp. 555–569). New York: The Guilford Press.

Hawkins, J.D., Herrenkohl, T., Farrington, D.P. *et al.* (1998). A review of predictors of youth violence. In R. Loeber & D.P. Farrington (Eds), *Serious and violent juvenile offenders*, (pp. 106–146). Thousand Oaks, CA: Sage Publications.

Holland, A.J. (2004). Criminal behaviour and developmental disability: An epidemiological perspective. In W.R. Lindsay, J.L. Taylor, & P. Sturmey (Eds), *Offenders with developmental disabilities* (pp. 23–34). Chichester: John Wiley & Sons.

Hollin, C.R. (1989). *Psychology and crime: An introduction to criminological psychology.* London: Routledge.

Hollin, C.R., Epps, K.J., & Swaffer, T.J. (2002). Adolescent firesetters: Findings from an analysis of 47 cases. *Pakistan Journal of Psychological Research, 17*, 1–16.

Home Office (2002). *Offender assessment system OASys: User manual, V2.* London: Home Office.

Howells, K. (1986). Social skills training and criminal and antisocial behaviour in adults. In C.R. Hollin & P. Trower (Eds), *Handbook of social skills training, Volume 1: Applications across the life span.* Oxford: Pergamon.

Hudson, A., Nankervis, K., Smith, D., & Phillips, A. (1999). *Identifying the risks: Prevention of sexual offending amongst adolescents with an intellectual disability.* Melbourne: Research Unit, DisAbility Services Division, Victorian Department of Human Services.

Hurley, W. & Monahan, T.M. (1969). Arson: The criminal and the crime. *British Journal of Criminology, 9,* 145–155.

Jahoda, A., Pert, C., Squire, J., & Trower, P. (1998). Facing stress and conflict: A comparison of the predicted responses and self-concepts of aggressive and non-aggressive people with intellectual disability. *Journal of Intellectual Disability Research, 42,* 360–369.

Jolliffe, D. & Farrington, D.P. (2003). Empathy and offending: A systematic review and meta-analysis. *Aggression and Violent Behavior, 9,* 441–476.

Kendler, K.S., Karkowski, L.M., & Prescott, C.A. (1999). Causal relationship between stressful life events and the onset of major depression. *American Journal of Psychiatry, 156,* 837–841.

Kessler, R.C. (1997). The effects of stressful life events on depression. *Annual Review of Psychology, 48,* 191–214.

Kolko, D.J. (1985). Juvenile firesetting: A review and methodological critique. *Clinical Psychology Review, 5,* 345–376.

Kolko, D.J. (2001). Firesetters. In C.R. Hollin (Ed.), *Handbook of offender assessment and treatment* (pp. 391–414). Chichester: John Wiley & Sons.

Kolko, D.J. & Kazdin, A.E. (1988). Prevalence of firesetting and related behaviours among child psychiatric patients. *Journal of Consulting and Clinical Psychology, 56,* 628–630.

Kolko, D.J. & Kazdin, A.E. (1990). Matchplay and firesetting in children: Relationship to parent, marital and family dysfunction. *Journal of Clinical Child Psychology, 19,* 229–238.

Kolko, D.J. & Kazdin, A.E. (1991). Motives of childhood firesetters: Firesetting characteristics and psychological correlates. *Journal of Child Psychology and Psychiatry, 32,* 535–550.

Kulik, J.A., Stein, K.B., & Sarbin, T.R. (1968). Dimensions and patterns of adolescent antisocial behaviour. *Journal of Consulting and Clinical Psychology, 32,* 375–382.

Law, J., Lindsay, W.R., Quinn, K., & Smith, A.H.W. (2000). Outcome evaluation of 161 people with mild intellectual disabilities who have offending or challenging behaviour. *Journal of Intellectual Disability Research, 45,* 130–138.

Lemerise, E.A. & Arsenio, W.E. (2000). An integrated model of emotion processes and cognition in social information processing. *Child Development, 71,* 107–118.

Lipsey, M.W. & Derzon, J.H. (1998). Predictors of violent or serious delinquency in adolescence and early adulthood: A synthesis of longitudinal research. In R. Loeber & D.P. Farrington (Eds), *Serious and violent juvenile offenders: Risk factors and successful interventions,* (pp. 86–105). Thousand Oaks, CA: Sage Publications.

Lochman, J.E., Wayland, K.K., & White, K.J. (1993). Social goals: Relationship to adolescent adjustment and to social problem solving. *Journal of Abnormal Child Psychology, 21,* 135–151.

Lyall, I., Holland, A.J., Collins, S., & Styles, P. (1995). Incidence of persons with learning disability detained in police custody: A needs assessment for service development. *Medicine, Sciences and the Law, 35,* 61–71.

Malamuth, N.M., Heavey, C.L., & Linz, D. (1993). Predicting men's antisocial behavior against women: The interaction model of sexual aggression. In G.C.N. Hall, R. Hirschman, J.R. Graham, & M.S. Zaragoza (Eds), *Sexual aggression: Issues in etiology, assessment and treatment* (pp. 63–97). Washington DC: Taylor & Francis.

Marshall, W.L. & Barbaree, H.E. (1990). An integrated theory of sexual offending. In W.L. Marshall, D.R. Laws, & H.E. Barbaree (Eds), *Handbook of sexual assault: Issues, theories and treatment of the offender* (pp. 257–275). New York: Plenum.

McCarty, C.A. & McMahon, R. (2005). Domains of risk in the developmental continuity of fire-setting. *Behavior Therapy*, *36*, 185–195.

McGurk, B.J. & McDougall, C. (1981). A new approach to Eysenck's theory of criminality. *Personality and Individual Differences*, *2*, 338–340.

McMurran, M. (2001). Offenders with personality disorders. In C.R. Hollin (Ed.), *Handbook of assessment and treatment* (pp. 467–479). Chichester: John Wiley & Sons.

McNeil, D.E. (1997). Correlates of violence in psychotic patients. *Psychiatric Annals*, *27*, 683–690.

McNulty, C., Kissi-Deborah, R., & Newsom-Davies, I. (1995). Police involvement with clients having intellectual disabilities: A pilot study in South London. *Mental Handicap Research*, *8*, 129–136.

Mueser, K.T., Drake, R.E., & Wallach, M.A. (1998). Dual diagnosis: A review of the etiological theories. *Addictive Behaviours*, *23(6)*, 717–734.

Murphy, G.H. & Clare, I.C.H. (1996). Analysis of motivation in people with mild learning disabilities (mental handicap) who set fires. *Psychology, Crime and Law*, *2*, 153–166.

Nietzel, M.T. (1979). *Crime and its modification: A social learning perspective*. Oxford: Pergamon.

Novaco, R.W. (1975). *Anger control: Development and evaluation of an experimental treatment*. Lexington, KT: D.C. Heath.

Novaco, R.W. & Welsh, W.N. (1989). Anger disturbances: Cognitive mediation and clinical prescriptions. In K. Howells & C.R. Hollin (Eds), *Clinical approaches to violence*, (pp. 39–60). Chichester: John Wiley & Sons.

Orobio de Castro, B., Veerman, J.W. *et al.* (2002). Hostile attribution of intent and aggressive behavior: A meta-analysis. *Child Development*, *73*, 916–934.

O'Sullivan, G.H. & Kelleher, M.J. (1987). A study of firesetters in the south-west of Ireland. *British Journal of Psychiatry*, *151*, 818–823.

Palmer, E.J. (2003a). An overview of the relationship between moral reasoning and offending. *Australian Psychologist, 38*, 165–174.

Palmer, E.J. (2003b). *Offending behaviour: Moral reasoning, criminal conduct and the rehabilitation of offenders*. Cullompton: Willan Publishing.

Polaschek, D.L.L. (2006). Violent offenders: Concept, theory, and practice. In C.R. Hollin & E.J. Palmer (Eds), *Offending behaviour programmes: Development, application, and controversies* (pp. 113–154). Chichester: John Wiley & Sons.

Powers, P.S. & Gunderman, R. (1978). Kleine-Levin syndrome associated with firesetting. *Pediatrics and Adolescent Medicine*, *132*, 786–792.

Quiggle, N.L., Garber, J., Panak, W.F., & Dodge, K.A. (1992). Social information processing in aggressive and depressed children. *Child Development*, *63*, 1305–1320.

Raine, A. (1993). *The psychopathology of crime*. San Diego, CA: Academic Press.

Raine, A. (2002a). Biosocial studies of antisocial and violent behavior in children and adults: A review. *Journal of Abnormal Child Psychology*, *30*, 311–326.

Raine, A. (2002b). Annotation: The role of prefrontal deficits, low autonomic arousal, and early health factors in the development of antisocial and aggressive behavior in children. *Journal of Child Psychology and Psychiatry*, *43*, 417–434.

Räsänen, P., Hirvenoja, R., Hakko, H., & Vaeisaenen, E. (1995). A portrait of the juvenile arsonist. *Forensic Science International*, *73*, 41–47.

Repo, E. & Virkkunen, M. (1997). Young arsonists: History of conduct disorder, psychiatric diagnosis and criminal recidivism. *Journal of Forensic Psychiatry, 8*, 311–320.

Rice, M.E. (1997). Violent offender research and implications for the criminal justice system. *American Psychologist, 52*, 414–423.

Ritchie, E.C. & Huff, T.G. (1999). Psychiatric aspects of arsonists. *Journal of Forensic Science, 44*, 733–740.

Ritvo, E., Shanock, S., & Lewis, D. (1982). Firesetting and nonfiresetting delinquents: A comparison of neuropsychiatric, psychoeducational, experiential and behavioural characteristics. *Child Psychiatry and Human Development, 13*, 259–267.

Robins, L.N., Tripp, J., & Przybeck, T. (1991). Antisocial personality. In L.N. Robins & D. Regier (Eds), *Psychiatric disorders in American: The epidemiological catchment area study* (pp. 258–290). New York: Free Press.

Sakheim, G.A. & Osborn, E. (1986). A psychological profile of juvenile firesetting in residential treatment: A replication study. *Child Welfare, 45*, 495–503.

Santilla, P., Häkkänen, H., Alison, L., & Whyte, C. (2003). Juvenile firesetters: Crime scene actions and offender characteristics. *Legal and Criminological Psychology, 8*, 1–20.

Schoenfeld, C.G. (1971). A psychoanalytic theory of juvenile delinquency. *Crime and Delinquency, 17*, 469–480.

Shaw, J. (2001). *Prison healthcare*. NHS National Programme on Forensic Mental Health Research and Development. Department of Health.

Slaby, R.G. & Guerra, N.G. (1988). Cognitive mediators of aggression in adolescent offenders. 1 Assessment. *Developmental Psychology, 24*, 580–588.

Smith, A.D. & Taylor, P.J. (1999). Serious sex offending against women by men with schizophrenia. *British Journal of Psychiatry, 174*, 233–237.

Sorrels, M. (1977). Kids who kill. *Crime and Delinquency, 23*, 312–320.

Sorrels, M. (1980). What can be done about juvenile homicide? *Crime and Delinquency, 26*, 132–161.

Stewart, L., Hill, J., & Cripps, J. (2001). Treatment of family violence in correctional settings. In L.L. Motiuk & R.C. Serin (Eds), *Compendium 2000 on effective correctional programming*. Ottawa, Ontario: Ministry of Supply and Services.

Strasberg, P.A. (1978). *Violent delinquents: A report to Ford Foundation from the Vera Institute of Justice*. New York: Monarch/Simon & Schuster.

Strassberg, Z. & Dodge, K.A. (1987). *Focus of social attention among children varying in peer status*. Paper presented at the annual meeting of the Association for the Advancement of Behavior Therapy, Boston, MA.

Swaffer, T.J. (1994). Predicting the risk of reoffending in adolescent firesetters II: The key to success. In N.K. Clark & G.M. Stephenson (Eds), *Rights and risks: The application of forensic psychology* (pp. 64–67). Leicester: The British Psychological Society.

Taylor, P.J. (2001). *Mental illness and serious harm to others*. NHS National Programme on Forensic Mental Health Research and Development. Department of Health.

Vachss, A.H. & Backal, Y. (1979). *Life-style violent juvenile: The secure treatment approach*. Lexington, MA: Heath Lexington Books.

Walker, A., Kershaw, C., & Nicholas, S. (2006). *Crime in England and Wales 2005/06*. Home Office Statistical Bulletin, 12/06. London: Home Office.

Walsh, K.W. (1994). *Neuropsychology: A clinical approach*. Edinburgh: Churchill Livingstone.

Ward, T. & Beech, A.R. (2006). An integrated theory of sexual offending. *Aggression and Violent Behavior, 11*, 44–63.

Ward, T. & Siegert, R.J. (2002). Toward a comprehensive theory of child sexual abuse: A theory knitting perspective. *Psychology, Crime & Law, 8*, 319–351.

Weismann, M.M. (1993). The epidemiology of personality disorders: A 1990 update. *Journal of Personality Disorders, 7*, 44–62.

Widom, C.S. & Maxfield, M.G. (2001). *An update of the cycle of violence.* Washington, DC: National Institute of Violence. (Available online at: http://www.ojp.usdoj.gov/nij.)

Zumkley, H. (1994). The stability of aggressive behavior: A meta-analysis. *German Journal of Psychology, 18*, 273–281.

ANNOTATED READING LIST

Eysenck, H.J. (1996). Personality and crime: Where do we stand? *Psychology, Crime and Law, 2*, 143–152. *Eysenck provides an up-to-date review of his personality theory of crime and the associated research.*

Hollin, C.R. (2007). Criminological psychology. In M. Maguire, R. Morgan, & R. Reiner (Eds), *The Oxford handbook of criminology* (4th edn), (pp. 43–77). Oxford: Oxford University Press. *Reviews psychological theories of criminal behaviour.*

Kolko, D.J. (2004). Firesetters. In C.R. Hollin (Ed.), *The essential handbook of offender assessment and treatment* (pp. 177–199). Chichester: John Wiley & Sons. *Provides a review of research on young firesetters, including their characteristics, assessment and treatment.*

Lipsey, M.W. & Derzon, J.H. (1998). Predictors of violent or serious delinquency in adolescence and early adulthood: A synthesis of longitudinal research. In R. Loeber & D.P. Farrington (Eds), *Serious and violent juvenile offenders: Risk factors and successful interventions*, (pp. 86–105). Thousand Oaks, CA: Sage Publications. *Reviews the predictors of violent offending among young people.*

Prins, H. (2005). *Offenders, deviants or patients?* (3rd edn). Hove: Routledge. *Highlights the complexity of the issues relating to mentally disordered offenders.*

Ward, T., Polaschek, D.L.L., & Beech, A.R. (Eds) (2006). *Theories of sexual offending.* Chichester: John Wiley & Sons. *A good source on the theories of sexual offending.*

PART 2

INVESTIGATING CRIME

3

IDENTIFYING PERPETRATORS

Tim Valentine

Goldsmiths, University of London, United Kingdom

This chapter examines the psychological processes involved when an eyewitness identifies a perpetrator, and explores reasons for the fallibility of eyewitness identification. Throughout the chapter evidence is drawn both from laboratory experiments and from analysis of actual identifications made by real witnesses or victims of crime. The processes involved in human memory are discussed, and the demands of the task facing an eyewitness are explored. This analysis helps us to understand the nature of the errors that often arise. The design of procedures commonly used to obtain identification evidence is critically evaluated. Legal guidance relating to factors that affect the reliability of eyewitness identification is introduced, and their basis in the scientific literature is reviewed. Other factors discussed include the effects of stress, the age of the witness and the confidence with which an identification is made. Ways in which procedures used for identification can affect reliability are discussed. The factors considered include the instructions given to witnesses, the selection method for people to include in a line-up with a suspect, and the effect of previous identification attempts. Procedures that may change the confidence that eyewitnesses express after the identification are discussed. For example, telling witnesses that they identified the police suspect will bolster confidence. An understanding of how subtle influences can lead to erroneous identification can inform development of procedural safeguards. Official guidance on identification procedures is critically evaluated in the light of the research literature. Widespread availability of CCTV increasingly provides an appealing opportunity to avoid the frailty of witness memory and to use video imagery to identify a perpetrator. However, psychological science shows that identifying unfamiliar people from CCTV-type images can itself be error-prone.

THE PROBLEM OF MISTAKEN IDENTIFICATION

Identification of a perpetrator is often disputed in criminal cases. In the absence of forensic evidence, for example a DNA profile or fingerprints, the central issue for a court is to evaluate the accuracy of eyewitness identification. Recent evidence from the US has shown that mistaken identification is a factor in three-quarters of wrongful convictions, overturned by DNA evidence that was not available at the original trial (Innocence Project, 2007). More than 200 people wrongly convicted have now been exonerated by new DNA evidence. Case histories show that mistaken eyewitnesses may be confident in their identification and more than one eyewitness may make the same mistaken identification.

The evidence, provided by DNA exonerations in the US, that mistaken identification has played a major role in wrongful conviction, has again focused attention on the methods used to collect eyewitness identification. Previously the British government commissioned an enquiry into eyewitness identification following a number of wrongful convictions which occurred as a result of mistaken eyewitness identification in the 1970s (Devlin, 1976). The considerable challenge in developing policy for eyewitness identification procedures is to minimize the possibility of mistaken identification, whilst making it as easy as possible for a reliable witness to identify a guilty suspect, thereby enhancing the **probative** value of eyewitness identification evidence. A further challenge for the criminal justice system is to ensure that eyewitness identification evidence is appropriately interpreted and the limitations of eyewitness identification evidence are properly recognized in the courts.

EYEWITNESS IDENTIFICATION AND HUMAN MEMORY

To be remembered, information must first be **encoded** by the eyewitness at the crime scene. Eyewitnesses may be unable to remember some aspect of an event because they did not attend to relevant detail and therefore it was not encoded in memory. The information must be **stored** for the intervening period without being lost or corrupted. Finally it must be **retrieved** at the appropriate time, either by **recall** or **recognition**.

Human memory is an active process of reconstructing an account of an event or object from incomplete information encoded in memory. It is a mistake to think of memory as being like a video recording, which allows the viewer to freeze a frame and examine in close detail some aspect not previously noticed. When remembering, available information is used to reconstruct the event actively. This information may include the witness' own prior knowledge, expectations and assumptions. We tend to fill in gaps in our memory with expectations of what 'must have happened'. The person remembering is usually unaware of this process, and so is unable to distinguish genuinely remembered information from new information included in the memory. Expectations are derived from memory of typical everyday events (**scripts**), such as buying goods in a shop or going out for a drink (Schank & Abelson, 1977) or **stereotypes** (e.g. that the driver of a van was a man). For example, a witness recalling a man getting into a car and driving away may assume that he got into the driver's seat. When remembering, we may also use information acquired since the event (**post-event information**), which may be derived from an investigator's questions, or another witness' account. For example, a witness may be asked: "Another witness mentioned that the man had a knife. Did you see a knife?" In summary, human memory is an active process that involves a creative component. This is why it is vulnerable to **suggestion** (from post-event information) and **bias** (from prior knowledge or assumptions).

Eyewitnesses are asked to perform a feat of **episodic** memory. They are required to remember what they saw at a specified place and time (i.e. an episode). When recalling an event a witness may misattribute a detail from a different event to the one being recalled. For example, a car seen earlier in the day may erroneously be remembered as being at the crime scene. This is known as a **source attribution error**.

Encoding may be affected by the extent to which attention is paid to the relevant item and the extent of cognitive processing of the item, or its **level of processing**. For example, consider two witnesses who notice that a car was parked near a crime scene at the relevant time. One witness may have noticed that it was a maroon car. This witness has engaged in a relatively shallow level of processing, which may make the item relatively vulnerable to retrieval failure when the witness is subsequently questioned about the event. The other witness may notice that it is a maroon Jaguar Mk II, similar to one driven by the television detective Inspector Morse. This witness has processed the item to a greater depth, relating its characteristics to their existing knowledge. The details of the car may be more resistant to retrieval failure for this witness.

The extent to which one can recall an event may be strongly dependent on the cues available when retrieval is attempted. The success of retrieval is related to the overlap of cues available at the time of retrieval and the cues stored in memory (the **encoding specificity principle**). For example, consider these two questions. "Can you remember what were you doing on 31 August 1997?" Providing the date is a poor cue to elicit a memory. 'Can you remember what you were doing when you first heard that Princess Diana had died?' The death of Princess Diana was a shocking event that is likely to be relatively distinctive in your memory. The point to note is that Diana died on 31 August 1997, so these two questions may provide different retrieval cues for the same information. One is much more effective than the other.

Every time one attempts to remember, a new memory of the retrieval attempt may be created. When repeatedly questioned about an event, for example, subsequent questions may be answered by recalling the answer given previously rather than recalling the original memory. Ultimately the memories of previous recall attempts can interfere with recall of the original event. Aspects recalled previously are more likely to be recalled subsequently, but aspects excluded from previous recall, perhaps because the details were not relevant to the question or because the witness was interrupted, are less likely to be recalled subsequently (e.g. Bauml, Zellner & Vilimek, 2005).

Psychologists distinguish **explicit** memory, such as giving a free recall of an event, from **implicit** memory. When memory has an effect of which one is not aware, it is said to be implicit memory. An example of implicit memory may be the influence of a script in memory used to fill in details of an everyday event.

The principles of memory described up to this point apply to eyewitness testimony in general. When asked to identify the face of a perpetrator, visual memory is involved. The general principles of memory described apply equally to visual memory. However, when giving testimony a witness is giving a free recall or recall in response to questions. Recall of visual memory, especially memory for faces, is very difficult partly because we do not have sufficient language to describe each face uniquely. Therefore when attempting to identify the face of a perpetrator we rely on recognition. Recognition yields superior memory performance to recall. The purpose of organizing an identification procedure (such as a line-up) is to test whether a witness recognizes the face of the suspect. A witness may recognize a face because she or he can **recollect** seeing that person on a specific occasion (episodic memory). However, she or he may recognize the face merely because it is seems familiar. The influence of implicit memory may make a face seem familiar, in absence of any recollection of when the face was seen previously. Recognition memory for a face exceeds the ability to recall the context of encounter. Familiarity may then be misattributed to presence at the crime scene and potentially may lead to a mistaken identification.

DESIGN REQUIREMENTS OF IDENTIFICATION PROCEDURES

Equipped with some understanding of human memory in general and recognition memory in particular, the design of appropriate procedures used to obtain eyewitness identification can be evaluated. It is useful to consider an identification procedure as a scientific experiment (Wells, 1993). The police have an hypothesis that the suspect is the perpetrator. The purpose of an identification procedure is to test the hypothesis, by establishing whether the witness can identify the suspect as the perpetrator. Such an experiment should enable a compliant but unreliable witness to be distinguished from a witness who makes a reliable identification of the perpetrator.

The simplest identification procedure is to allow the witness to see the suspect or their photograph and ask if this person is the perpetrator. This procedure is known as a **show-up** in the US and as a **confrontation** in the UK. It is most commonly used at or near the scene shortly after a crime has been reported when there is insufficient justification for arrest of a suspect. In these circumstances the procedure would be referred to as a **street identification** in the UK. Essentially the same procedure is also used (much later) as a **dock identification** during a trial under Scots law, when a witness is asked whether they see the perpetrator present in the courtroom. The problem with this procedure is that there is no means of establishing whether a witness who makes an identification is mistaken. There are only two possible outcomes: a witness may decline to identify the person or they identify the suspect. The procedure leads the witness to believe that the person concerned is the police suspect, or in the case of dock identification, is the person who has been charged with the offence. The procedure is highly suggestive. The information implied by seeking the identification may bias the witness' response.

A much better procedure is to ask the witness whether the perpetrator is present amongst a line-up of people, which includes one police suspect. The **foils** in the line-up are not suspects. This procedure has three possible outcomes: the witness may identify the suspect, providing evidence that the suspect is the perpetrator; the witness may make no identification; or the witness may identify a foil, making a known mistaken identification. Line-ups are widely used, especially in the UK and US. In the US line-ups may consist of a live line-up of people standing in a line or an array of photographs (**a photo-spread**). In the UK, official guidance states that photographs should not used to obtain formal identification evidence of an arrested suspect. Historically, identification has been made by use of live line-ups, known as **identity parades** in the UK. Recently, virtually all live line-ups in the UK have been replaced by **video identification** procedures (which are described in more detail below).

There is an extensive research literature on the factors which affect the ability of eyewitnesses to identify a perpetrator from a line-up. It is useful to distinguish between factors that are under the control of the criminal justice system (known as 'system variables') from those which are not (known as 'estimator variables': see Wells, 1993; see Box). The influence of estimator variables is important to evaluate

---

ESTIMATOR AND SYSTEM VARIABLES

Estimator variables, which concern the circumstances of the opportunity to view the culprit and are not under the control of the criminal justice system, include:

- the time to view the perpetrator, the distance of the witness, the lighting and other circumstances of the incident
- the distinctiveness of the appearance of the perpetrator
- whether the perpetrator is known to the witness
- the presence of a weapon
- the number of perpetrators
- the stress induced in the witness
- differences in ethnicity between the witness and perpetrator
- the age of the witness.

(Continued)

System variables, which are generally under the control of the criminal justice system, include:

- the selection of identification method (e.g. street identification, line-up procedure, dock identification)
- the mode of presentation (e.g. photographs, live, video)
- instructions given to the witness
- 'blind' vs. 'non-blind' administration of a line-up
- use of prior identification procedures (e.g. showing photographs prior to a line-up procedure)
- method used to select foils for a line-up
- method of line-up administration (e.g. simultaneous v. sequential presentation of line-up members)
- feedback given to witnesses.

the likely performance of eyewitnesses under various conditions. However, system variables are especially interesting to psychologists who aim to develop the most reliable methods of obtaining eyewitness identification. Psychological scientists can make recommendations about the best practice by studying the effect of system variables in experiments.

CASE STUDY

The Murder of Justin McAlroy

Justin McAlroy was suspected of involvement in drug dealing and was said to owe £50 000 in connection with a drugs deal. After visiting serious criminals in Perth Prison on 7 March 2002 he returned to his home shortly before 10 p.m. where a gunman was waiting for him. His wife was in the house with her sister. She heard three or four loud bangs and ran to the front door. She looked out of the windows at the top of the door and saw a man at the top of her driveway. She described him as wearing a blue-green hooded bomber jacket with the hood up and a similar coloured scarf or snood, covering his nose and mouth. In her first statement, made about 40 minutes after the shooting, she said she would not be able to identify him.

Other witnesses provided similar descriptions of a padded jacket. One witness, Mr Madden, reported seeing a man in similar clothing get into a white car and remove a ski mask. At about 10.30 p.m. a white Saab car was found abandoned some miles from the murder scene. An attempt had been made to set it on fire. Inside were a set of clothing including a hooded jacket and a drinks bottle. William Gage's DNA was found on the bottle and on the jacket. His DNA was also found on gloves and a snood, with traces of the DNA of at least two other individuals. Firearms discharge of the same type as that at the crime scene was found on the jacket and the snood.

William Gage was arrested and charged with murder. The prosecution case depended on establishing that the white Saab was the getaway car used by the killer and on identification evidence. The defence contended that the police had not traced the getaway car, that the white Saab was not connected to the offence and that William Gage had an alibi. He had spent the evening with a girlfriend and was with her when the offence was committed.

In the course of the investigation, the police had shown Mrs McAlroy a tailor's mannequin dressed in the clothing recovered from the abandoned car and she identified the clothing as similar to that worn by the gunman, although it differed in a number of respects from her earlier description. For example, the jacket was a thin waterproof cagoule rather than the padded jacket described previously by Mrs McAlroy and other witnesses. An identification parade had been arranged, but had to be abandoned when Gage objected to the selection of foils. Neither Mrs McAlroy nor Mr Madden were asked to attend the parade, but instead, the prosecution sought to rely on dock identifications.

At trial, Mrs McAlroy identified Gage by his eyes: she said that the man running away had "scary eyes" which she would never forget, but she had never mentioned his eyes in her earlier statements to the police. Mr Madden did not identify Gage at trial. The jury convicted Gage of murder and he was sentenced to life imprisonment.

The case went to appeal, but this was dismissed. The court noted that, in a case involving circumstantial evidence, it is necessary to look at the evidence as a whole. Each piece of evidence might not be incriminating in itself, but the concurrence of testimony was critical. It was for the jury to decide how to interpret this evidence, and whether to draw the inference that the accused was guilty, beyond reasonable doubt. In reaching their conclusion, they were entitled to reject inconsistent evidence if they so chose.

REFERENCE

Gage v. Her Majesty's Advocate [2006] Scot HCJ AC 7. Downloaded 20 February 2007 from: http://www.bailii.org/scot/cases/ScotHC/2006/HCJAC_7.html

ESTIMATOR VARIABLES

Is it possible to judge whether an eyewitness is likely to be accurate in their identification from the circumstances of their view of the culprit? In this section the effects of the estimator variables that have received most attention from researchers in laboratory studies will be briefly reviewed. To begin, estimator variables that have a special status in English law will be considered from a psychological rather than a legal perspective.

The section will conclude by examining the effect of estimator variables in archival studies of real criminal cases.

The Turnbull Guidelines

English case law is based on the premise that a distinction between good and poor eyewitness identification evidence is possible. Following a landmark ruling in the Appeal Court in London (*R v. Turnbull*, 1976), when identity is disputed a trial judge must advise the jury to consider carefully the circumstances of an identification (see Box).

The judgment in Turnbull arose from an enquiry into eyewitness identification evidence that the British government has set up in response to public concern amount a number of well publicized wrongful convictions which had occurred as a result of mistaken identification (Devlin, 1976). Subsequent laboratory research has confirmed that most of the factors mentioned in the Turnbull guidelines are likely to affect the accuracy of eyewitness identification. For example, witnesses who had 45 seconds to view a culprit were more likely to identify him from a line-up than witness who had

---

THE TURNBULL GUIDELINES

(*R v. Turnbull and Others*, 1976)

In a case that relies substantially on disputed eyewitness identification evidence, the trial judge must warn the jury about the special need for caution before relying on the accuracy of eyewitness identification evidence to convict the defendant. The judge should make some reference to the possibility that a convincing witness may be mistaken and that a number of witnesses who make the same identification may all be mistaken. The judge should direct the jury to consider carefully the circumstances of each witness, identification. The relevant factors are often summarized by the acronym ADVOKATE.

1. **A**mount of time for which the perpetrator was in view.
2. **D**istance of the witness from the perpetrator.
3. **V**isibility of the perpetrator. How good was the lighting?
4. **O**bstruction to the witness's view?
5. **K**nown to the witness? Has the witness seen the suspect before? How often?
6. **A**ny reason to remember? If only seen occasionally before, did the witness have any reason to remember the suspect?
7. **T**ime delay between the incident and the formal identification procedure.
8. **E**rror. Is there any material discrepancy between the description given to the police at the time of the incident and the appearance of the suspect?

only 12 seconds to view (Memon, Hope & Bull, 2003). The ability to identify faces viewed under different levels of lighting and at a range of distances has been investigated (Wagenaar & Van der Schrier, 1996). Faces of people known to the viewer are remembered in an episodic memory task with much greater accuracy than are unfamiliar faces, when a different view of the face is presented in the study and test phase of the experiment (Bruce, 1982). Laboratory studies have found that fewer correct identifications are made after a long delay. For example, Shepherd (1983) reported that 65% of faces were recognized after one week, 55% after a month, 50% after three months and 10% after eleven months. In contrast there was no effect of delay on mistaken identifications. Shapiro & Penrod (1986) found an effect of delay in a **meta-analysis** of 18 face recognition and eyewitness identification studies on both correct identifications (**effect size** = 0.43) and mistaken identifications (effect size = 0.33). The delay in the studies analysed had a mean of 4.5 days with a standard deviation of 21 days. The only factor mentioned in the Turnbull warning that seems difficult to justify from laboratory research is the issue of any material error of description. The research suggests that the quality of a verbal description is not strongly associated with the accuracy of a subsequent identification (e.g. Pozzulo & Warren, 2003).

Laboratory Studies of Estimator Variables

In this section the effect of several factors on the accuracy of eyewitness identification will be reviewed. The intention is not to provide an exhaustive review of eyewitness identification but to highlight issues that have attracted research attention in recent years.

Weapon focus: When confronted by a perpetrator wielding a knife or a gun, the weapon captures the attention of a witness. Under these circumstances there is believed to be a narrowing of attention, meaning that less attention is paid to other aspects of the scene. Therefore eyewitnesses are very capable of describing the detail of the knife or gun, but may be less able to recognize the face of the perpetrator. Steblay (1992) conducted a systematic analysis of 19 tests of the hypothesis and found a reliable but small effect (effect size = 0.13) on identification. Witnesses were less accurate in identifying a perpetrator when a weapon was present.

Stress: The presence of a weapon may exert its influence through inducing fear or stress in a witness, rather than directly by the capture of attention *per se*. Are witnesses who experience a very frightening or stressful event less reliable than witnesses who experience less stress? Morgan *et al.* (2004) examined the ability of soldiers to recall a person present at an interrogation. The soldiers had been detained for 12 hours in a mock prisoner of war camp. Each soldier then underwent a high-stress interrogation involving physical confrontation and a low-stress interrogation. Twenty four hours later the soldiers took part in an identification procedure. Identification was more accurate for the target person seen during a low-stress interrogation (67%) than for the person seen during a high-stress interrogation (29%).

Deffenbacher *et al.* (2004) reported a meta-analytic review of studies that successfully manipulated stress, demonstrated by measures taken as soon as possible after encoding the target person. They found that heightened stress had a moderate negative effect on identification and on recall of a target person. The effect of stress on identification was restricted to the number of correct identifications made when the target person was included in the line-up; there was no effect of stress on the rate of correctly rejecting the line-up when the target person was not present.

'Cross-race' identification: Witnesses tend to be less accurate in recognizing a perpetrator of an ethnic origin different from their own. The effect is moderate and may depend upon the experience of the witness. Chiroro & Valentine (1995) found that experience of people of a different ethnic origin in daily life may reduce or eliminate any effect of ethnicity, but does not necessarily do so. The quality of the social contact may be an important mediating factor. The effect of ethnicity on face recognition can be interpreted within a framework in which individual faces are recognized by their distinctive qualities in relation to the population of faces experienced in one's lifetime (Valentine, 1991; Valentine & Endo, 1992). For a review of what has typically been referred to as 'cross-race' recognition see Meissner & Brigham (2001).

Witness age: Laboratory studies have found that older people make fewer correct responses in tests of face recognition (e.g. Bartlett & Fulton, 1991; O'Rourke, Penrod & Cutler, 1989). O'Rourke et al. (1989) found that identification accuracy declined sharply at around age 50. The effect of witness age has been found in terms of older witnesses making both fewer correct identifications and more mistaken identifications. (Searcy, Bartlett & Memon, 1999, 2000; Searcy et al., 2001).

Confidence: A confident eyewitness may provide compelling evidence in court and can be highly influential on a jury (or on judges in countries that do not have juries). It has been appreciated for a long time that a confident witness may be mistaken. Indeed a caution to this effect is included in the Turnbull judgment on eyewitness evidence. Many studies on eyewitness identification have suggested that the relationship between confidence and accuracy is low or negligible, leading psychologists to point out that witness confidence is a poor way to assess accuracy. In recent years our understanding of the confidence–accuracy relationship has become more sophisticated. The confidence–accuracy relationship is stronger when a wide range of viewing conditions is considered (Lindsay, Read & Sharma, 1998). One factor that may have restricted the relationship in experimental studies is that witness participants usually view a live or video mock crime under identical viewing conditions. Furthermore, the correlation coefficient is moderate to strong (typically in the region of $r = 0.5$) if we only consider witnesses who identify somebody at a line-up; it is close to zero amongst witness who reject the line-up (Sporer et al., 1995). However, a correlation of this order will still mean that confident but mistaken eyewitnesses will be encountered fairly frequently. Recently psychologists have begun to plot 'calibration' of the confidence–accuracy relationship, which allows one to see when witnesses tend to be over-confident or under-confident of their accuracy. (See Brewer (2006) for a review.)

Decision speed: In a series of studies Sporer (1992, 1993, 1994) found that fast identification decisions are associated with accurate choices. It has been suggested that identification decisions latencies in the range of 10 to 12 seconds are most likely to be accurate (Dunning & Perretta, 2002). However, the range of the latency associated with most accurate decisions is affected by the context of the procedure used (Weber et al., 2004). Nevertheless, the finding that fast decisions tend to be more likely to be accurate has proved reliable in laboratory studies.

Archival Studies of Estimator Variables

Studies of live line-ups conducted in England and Wales as part of real criminal cases show remarkable consistency (Slater, 1994; Valentine, Pickering & Darling, 2003; Wright & McDaid, 1996). Note that in archival studies it is not known how many line-ups contained the actual perpetrator. Approximately 40% of witnesses identified the suspect, approximately 40% of witnesses did not make any identification, and 20% of witnesses made a mistaken identification of an innocent foil. The known mistaken identifications were made despite the witness having been cautioned that the person they saw may or may not be present in the line-up. Archival data collected by the police from 1776 identity parades showed that the suspect was identified in 48% of cases, but did not distinguish non-identifications from identification of a foil (Pike, Brace & Kyman, 2002). An archival analysis of 58 live line-ups conducted in US criminal cases found that the suspect was identified in 50% of cases, a foil was identified in 24% of cases and the witness was unable to make an identification or rejected the line-up in 26% of cases (Behrman & Davey, 2001).

Valentine *et al.* (2003) examined the effect of a range of estimator variables on the outcome of identification attempts made by approximately 600 witnesses who viewed over 300 live line-ups organized by the London Metropolitan Police during the investigation of criminal cases. The suspect was more likely to be identified if the witness was younger than 30, the suspect was a white European (rather than African-Caribbean), the witness gave a detailed description, viewed the culprit at the scene for over a minute and made a fast decision at the line-up. There were no independent, statistically reliable effects of the use of a weapon during the incident, 'cross-race' identification or of the delay before the identification attempt. However, the data did suggest that the proportion of witnesses who identified the suspect was higher for identifications made after a very short delay of less than one week after the offence. Sixty-five per cent of witnesses identified the suspect from line-ups held up to seven days later, while only 38% of witnesses identified the suspect in line-ups held eight days or more after the incident. Pike, Brace & Kyman (2002) also reported an effect of witness age, no effect of the use of a weapon during a crime, and no effect of 'cross-race' identification on the outcome of live line-ups conducted by British police.

Most research on eyewitness identification has focused on the use of photographs to obtain formal identification evidence, because this procedure is widely used in the US and Canada. The typical format is to present the witness with six photographs simultaneously arranged in two rows of three images in a single array. Behrman and Davey's (2001) archival analysis of eyewitness identification in American criminal cases included an analysis of the outcome of 289 photographic line-ups. They found that 48% of witnesses identified the suspect. In common with the British studies cited above, there was no effect of the presence of a weapon in the crime on the likelihood of the suspect being identified. There was an effect of delay prior to the identification. Line-ups held within seven days of the incident produced a higher rate of identifications of the suspect (64%) than line-ups held after eight days or more (33%). However, in contrast to the British data, Behrman and Davey did find an effect of 'cross-race' identification in their sample of US photograph line-ups. Sixty per cent of witnesses of the same ethnicity as the suspect identified the suspect, compared to 45% of witnesses of different ethnicity.

SYSTEM VARIABLES

The criminal justice system can exert influence over some aspects of identification procedures (system variables). For example a line-up may be presented in photographs, video or live. What is the best way to select the 'foils', and instruct the witness?

The Presentation Mode

The effect of presenting line-ups in different media (photographs, video, live) and manipulating the richness of cues available (e.g. stills, moving images, people walking) is surprisingly small. A possible reason is that the face is the most reliable way to recognize somebody and the face can be sufficiently well perceived from a good quality still photograph. Therefore, relying on cues such as gait, build or colour images would add little extra benefit. Reviewing the literature, Cutler *et al.* (1994) concluded: "With respect to current practices, the conservative conclusion is that, based on available research, there is no reason to believe that live line-ups, video-taped line-ups or photo arrays produce substantial differences in identification performance" (p. 181).

Fairness of Video Identification

Traditionally in England and Wales formal identification evidence has been obtained by use of live line-ups. However, since 2003 video technology has been used to replace virtually all live identity parades. The video line-ups consist of 15-second clips of a head and shoulders shot of each line-up member. First they are looking at the camera and then rotate their head to show both profiles before looking back at the camera. The images are captured under standardized conditions. Each line-up member is shown sequentially one at a time, with a digit in the top left corner of the screen that can be used to identify each individual. The benefits of video identification as compared to live line-ups are listed in Box.

Research has shown that video line-ups from real criminal cases were fairer to the suspects than conventional 'live' line-ups (Valentine & Heaton, 1999) and that video line-ups were equally fair to white European and African-Caribbean suspects (Valentine *et al.*, 2003). In these studies, participants (known as '**mock witnesses**') were given the first description of the offender provided by the original witness and were required to guess which line-up member was the suspect. As a 'mock witness' has not seen the perpetrator, the suspect should be chosen no more often than predicted by chance if the line-up is perfectly fair (i.e. 11% (one in nine) of choices from line-ups contained a suspect and eight foils). Valentine & Heaton (1999) found that the mock witnesses identified the suspect in live line-ups more frequently (25%) than by chance but were not able to select the suspect from video line-ups (15%) significantly more often than chance. Valentine *et al.* (2003) found video line-ups of African-Caribbeans and of white Europeans were equally fair, using equal numbers of mock witness witnesses from both ethnic backgrounds.

Instructions Given to Witnesses

Witnesses may assume that they would not have been invited to attempt an identification if the police did not have good reason to believe that their suspect was guilty, and

THE BENEFITS OF VIDEO IDENTIFICATION PROCEDURES

- Video can dramatically reduce the delay before an identification can be organized. Live line-ups have been subject to long delays to enable a selection of appropriate foils to be available to stand on a line-up (typically of one to three months, see Valentine *et al.*, 2003). In contrast a video line-up can be produced and transmitted via a secure network within two hours of request.

- Approximately 50% of live line-ups were cancelled, for example, because a bailed suspect failed to attend. With video identification the cancellation rate has fallen to around 5% (Pike *et al.*, 2000).

- A large database of video clips (approximately 14 000) is available providing more foils for selection. This helps to make line-ups fairer (see text for further details).

- Video is less threatening to victims, who no longer have to attend an identification suite where, for example, their attacker may be physically present. Intimidation can result in a witness feeling too threatened to make a positive identification of a police suspect at a line-up. Use of video does not prevent witness intimidation but any means of reducing the perceived level of threat at an identification procedure is beneficial.

- Video equipment can be taken to a witness who is unable to attend the police station. In a recent case, Abigail Witchalls, a victim of an attack who was left paralysed, was able to view a video line-up from her hospital bed. As a result a suspect was eliminated from the enquiry.

it will help the police if the witness identifies the suspect. It is important that the instructions to the witness should emphasize the possibility that making no identification may be the right thing to do because the suspect may not be guilty. Most commonly this point is made by including an instruction that the person who the witness saw 'may or may not be present'. Instructions that do not point out that the culprit may not be in the line-up are regarded as 'biased' instructions (e.g. "Look at these photographs. Can you identify the man who assaulted you?").

A meta-analysis of 18 studies shows that when biased instructions are given, witnesses are more likely to make an identification whether it is correct or incorrect. Biased instructions increase the likelihood of an innocent suspect being identified from culprit-absent line-ups (Steblay, 1997).

Blind Administration of Line-Ups

'Blind' is used in the sense of meaning that the person who administers the line-up procedure to the witness does not know (i.e. is blind to) the identity of the suspect in a line-up. The procedure is often referred to as 'double-blind' meaning that both the witness and the line-up administrator are blind to the identity of the suspect.

The expectations of the experimenter can influence the outcome of behavioural research (Harris & Rosenthal, 1985). The line-up administrator should be blind to the identity of the suspect in order to prevent any inadvertent influence on the witness. Such influence can be very subtle and entirely unconscious. For example, the administrator may look at the witness when the suspect's image is being viewed, or be more likely to accept a tentative identification if it is of the suspect. Phillips *et al.* (1999) found that double-blind line-up administration led to a reduced rate of mistaken identification under some circumstances. Double-blind administration of identification procedures removes all possibility of leading the witness. Therefore, the integrity of identification evidence is enhanced and any potential claim of bias can be rebutted. Widespread use of photographs for identification in the US and of video in the UK greatly facilitates use of a double-blind identification procedure.

Prior Exposure To Photographs

If the police have not identified a suspect they may show photographs (**mugshots**) to the witness of people previously convicted of a similar offence, in the expectation that the witness may be able to identify the perpetrator. In this procedure all of the people are suspects. Therefore any identification will lead to that person being investigated. Later in the investigation the police may want to collect formal identification evidence from a line-up. Would a subsequent line-up be biased against suspects if witnesses has previously seen their photograph in a mugshot album?

Deffenbacher, Bornstein & Penrod (2006) provide a systematic review of the effects of mugshot exposure. They found that prior viewing of a photograph of somebody who subsequently appears in a line-up increases the probability of a mistaken identification from the line-up. The effect is due to transference of familiarity from the photograph which is mistakenly attributed to having being seen at the crime scene. The effect is stronger when few mugshots were viewed (eight to 15 or less) than when more mugshots have been viewed. The effect is particularly strong if the person was mistakenly identified as the perpetrator from the mugshot photographs. This is known as an effect of **commitment** to the earlier identification. There was no ill-effect of showing photographs if none of the people seen appeared in the subsequent line-up.

Deffenbacher *et al.* (2006) point out that transference of familiarity can occur for a bystander in the original mock crime who is included in the line-up. Experiments using this bystander design showed a significant effect of increased mistaken identification but the effect was stronger when the face had been seen in a mugshot rather than as a bystander. The increased risk of a mistaken identification when a bystander but not the perpetrator is included in a line-up is very relevant to cases in which the suspect admits presence at the scene but denies involvement in the offence (e.g. a bystander at a fight).

Selection Of Foils

The code of practice in England and Wales specifies that the foils for line-ups must be selected to 'resemble the suspect'. This is known as a **suspect-resemblance** strategy. Luus and Wells (1991) argued that a better strategy is to select foils who match the witness' description of the culprit. It is reasonable to assume that the witness can remember the description that he or she gave to the police, and may expect to identify somebody who matches their description. Therefore, the witness may be inclined to disregard any foils that do not match their description, or conversely pay special attention to anybody who is a better match to their description than the rest. To be fair, all line-up members should match the witness's description of the culprit.

Luus & Wells (1991) suggested it does not introduce a bias against the suspect if line-up members differ on some feature that was not mentioned in the original description. Heterogeneity of features not mentioned in the description will help a witness with a reliable memory to distinguish the culprit from the foils. If the suspect is not the culprit, he or she is no more likely to be mistakenly identified by some feature not mentioned in the description, because the witness has not seen the suspect before. A line-up that consists of a number of people chosen because they closely resemble the suspect in all aspects of their appearance will make it difficult even for a reliable witness to identify the culprit, if present.

When constructing a **culprit-description** line-up it may be necessary to take account of **default values** in descriptions. Sometimes people may not describe the sex or race of the person, or may neglect to say that somebody did not have a beard or was not wearing glasses. This may occur because the witness assumes a default value (Lindsay, Martin & Webber, 1994).

Wells, Rydell & Seelau (1993) conducted an experiment in which students witnessed a live staged theft and were asked to identify the perpetrator from an array of photographs in an immediate test. There were more correct identifications from culprit-description line-ups (67%) than from suspect-resemblance line-ups (22%). When the culprit was not present in the line-up, there were fewer mistaken identifications of foils from culprit-description line-ups (32%) than from suspect-resemblance line-ups (47%), but this difference was not statistically significant. Juslin, Olsson & Winman (1996) found a similar result. Forty-four percent of participants correctly identified the perpetrator from a suspect-resemblance line-up and 52% identified the culprit in a culprit-description line-up. When the perpetrator was not in the line-up, 9% of participants identified the innocent suspect from both line-ups. Lindsay *et al*. (1994), Tunnicliffe & Clark (2000) and Valentine, Darling & Memon (in press) did not find a statistically significant difference in the rate of correct or mistaken identification between culprit-description and suspect-resemblance line-ups. At present there is little empirical evidence on which to base a recommendation that a match-to-description strategy is a superior method than a suspect-resemblance strategy to construct a line-up.

Relative and Absolute Judgments: Sequential and Simultaneous Presentation

A persistent problem in understanding eyewitness identification is to explain why a sizeable minority of witnesses (about one in five) make mistaken identifications, despite appropriate warnings that the perpetrator may not be present in the line-up. Wells (1993) demonstrated that at least part of the problem may be attributable to witnesses who make a **relative** judgment rather than an **absolute** judgment. When confronted with

	Line-up member						
	1	2	3(p)	4	5	6	No choice
Perpetrator present	3%	13%	54%	3%	3%	3%	21%
Perpetrator removed	6%	38%	-	12%	7%	5%	32%

Table 3.1: The distribution of identifications across members of a photograph line-up with the perpetrator present and with the perpetrator removed. Data from Wells, G.L. (1993). What do we know about eyewitness identification? *American Psychologist, 48*, 553–571. Reproduced by permission of the American Psychological Association

a line-up a witness may only identify a person if their resemblance to the culprit exceeds some criterion of recollection (an absolute judgment). Alternatively a witness may examine all the members of a line-up and identify the person who most closely resembles the perpetrator (a relative judgment). The influence of relative judgments was demonstrated using a method of removal without replacement (Table 3.1).

The top line of Table 3.1 shows the distribution of selections made by 100 witnesses to a mock crime who saw a six-person line-up in which the perpetrator was present. Fifty-four percent identified the perpetrator and twenty-one percent rejected the line-up. Other participants were presented with a five-person line-up from which the perpetrator was removed. One might expect that the witnesses who would correctly identify the perpetrator if he had been present, would reject the line-up. Instead the number of mistaken identifications increases dramatically. In the absence of the culprit many witnesses appear to identify the foil who most closely resembles their memory of the perpetrator. Clark & Davey (2005) replicated this shift of choices from the perpetrator to the foils. These data suggest that relative identification decisions may be a cause of mistaken identifications.

The method of sequential line-up presentation was developed to prevent witnesses from making a relative judgment. In a sequential presentation, photographs of faces are presented one at a time (Lindsay & Wells, 1985). The line-up administrator should be blind to the identity of the suspect. The witness is not told how many faces will be presented, but must decide when each face is presented whether it is or is not the culprit before the next face is presented (Lindsay, Lea & Fulford, 1991). Furthermore, witnesses must not be allowed a second choice or to see again a face previously presented.

Steblay *et al.* (2001) carried out a meta-analytic comparison of the accuracy rates in sequential and simultaneous line-up presentations based on data from nine published and 14 unpublished papers. When present in the line-up more witnesses identified the culprit from simultaneous line-ups than from sequential line-ups (50% v. 35% respectively). When the culprit was not in the line-up there were substantially fewer correct rejections from simultaneous line-ups than from sequential line-ups (49% v. 72%), and fewer incorrect identifications of a foil from sequential line-ups (28% v. 51%). In summary, sequential presentation reduces the rate of choosing from both culprit-present and culprit-absent line-ups. Meissner *et al.* (2005) found that sequential line-ups induce a more conservative response criterion but do not affect discrimination accuracy. The effect is to provide some protection against mistaken identification from culprit-absent line-ups, but at a cost to the sensitivity of the identification procedure when the culprit is in the line-up.

Malleability of Witness Confidence

A very important research finding is that witness confidence is changeable and is influenced by information that the witness acquires after attending an identification procedure. Receiving feedback that it was the suspect whom they identified, or that somebody else made the same identification, will increase witnesses' confidence in their identification. Not only does confirming feedback tend to make witnesses subsequently more confident in their identification, but it also tends to inflate estimates of a range of subsequent testimony including how long the culprit was seen for, how close they were, how much attention the witness paid (Wells & Bradfield, 1998). Furthermore, confirming post-identification feedback tends to make eyewitnesses over-confident. That is, they now express more confidence in their identification than is warranted (Semmler, Brewer & Wells, 2004). By the time witnesses give evidence in court they will have received confirming feedback, if only by virtue of the fact that they have been called upon to give evidence. Witnesses are less likely to be asked to attend court if they had identified the 'wrong' person.

CASE STUDY

The Murder of Jill Dando

Jill Dando was a well-known British TV presenter. In April 1999 she returned to her home at about 11.30 a.m. She was killed on her doorstep by a single shot from a handgun. Nobody saw the murder, but two neighbours heard a muffled cry, looked out of their window and saw a man walking away from the house but neither realized at the time that there was anything wrong. It was accepted that the man seen by these two witnesses was undoubtedly the murderer. Initially, the police suggested that the murder had been carried out by an assassin, but a year later the police arrested Barry George, a local unemployed man, and charged him with the murder.

Identification evidence was central to the case. Sixteen people who saw a man in Gowan Avenue either on the morning of the murder or the previous day attended an identification procedure. The first five witnesses saw a live parade and the remainder a video parade after George was advised by his solicitor not to attend any further live parades. Barry George had been clean shaven at the time of the murder but now had a beard. Therefore, all of the men in the line-up had beards. Neither of Jill Dando's neighbours identified George. He was positively identified

(*Continued*)

by only one witness. This witness had seen the face of a man for five to six seconds some hours before the murder and made her identification after 17 months.

After making her identification, the identifying witness was given a lift home in a police car with two other witnesses. During the journey the two other witnesses discovered the positive identification she had made and, apparently influenced by this knowledge, both subsequently made statements that they too would have identified George but were hindered by not being able to see his build and height in the video.

The case set a legal precedent because identification evidence was admitted from four witnesses who did not make a positive identification at the line-up. In addition to the two retrospective identifications, a postman stated that the man he saw was not in the line-up, but he recognized a man he had had a conversation with about the Dando case in the days after the murder, a fact confirmed by Barry George. The prosecution argued that there is an underlying unity of the description of the man these witnesses saw which pointed to George as the murderer.

Barry George was convicted of murder in July 2001 by a majority verdict and was sentenced to life imprisonment. In July 2002 the Court of Appeal upheld the principle that a witness who did not identify the suspect can still give evidence in court (*R v. George*, 2002). However, in June 2007 the Criminal Cases Review Commission referred Barry George's conviction back to the Court of Appeal.

REFERENCE

R v. George [2002] EWCA Crim 1923. Downloaded 20 February 2007 from: http://www.bailii.org/ew/cases/EWCA/Crim/2002/1923.html

OFFICIAL GUIDANCE

The conduct of identification procedures in England and Wales is governed by Code D of the Police and Criminal Evidence Act (1984) Codes of Practice. The current code, which came into force in 2008, can be downloaded from the Home Office website (included in the list of references). The code is a lengthy document that covers a wide range of circumstances but the major provisions are as follows. If identification is disputed, a video identification procedure containing moving images must be offered unless it is not practicable or 'live' identity parade is more suitable. All line-ups should consist of a minimum of eight foils and one suspect. The foils should "resemble the suspect in age, general appearance and position in life". Witnesses must be advised that the person they saw may not be present and must view the entire line-up at least twice. The person who runs the procedure should not be involved in the investigation of the case. The suspect has the right for his or her legal representative to be present. The suspect and the legal representative may object to the procedure (e.g. the selection of foils) and their reason for objection must be recorded. If the witness has previously been shown photographs, details of the photographs shown should be recorded. Anything the witness says should be written down before he or she leaves the identification room.

The situation in the US is more complicated. In general identification procedures are much less regulated. Practice is governed at state level or below, so there is no one federal code of practice. Identification from photographs is commonplace. Procedures are often conducted by an investigating police officer. A few years ago, the US Department of Justice issued a guide on identification procedures, but it does not have the force of law (Technical Working Group for Eyewitness Evidence, 1999). The guide makes recommendations for sequential and simultaneous line-ups of photographs or 'live' volunteers, but does not endorse one method over another. A minimum of five foils are required. Advice is provided on selecting foils so that the suspect does not unfairly stand out, giving unbiased instructions and carefully recording all identifications or non-identifications.

IDENTIFICATION FROM CCTV

In view of the fallibility of eyewitnesses it may be a comforting thought that in many cases we can rely on CCTV images to identify perpetrators, thus cutting out the human error involved in eyewitness testimony. In the UK, in particular, this idea has proved highly attractive to politicians and the public alike. Growth of CCTV has been rapid. There are estimated to be more than four million CCTV cameras in the UK, which is believed to be the highest density of CCTV surveillance in the world. (See Norris, McCahill & Wood, 2004 for a review.) CCTV may have benefits including use in the investigation of crime. However, *identification of perpetrators* from CCTV has proved to be surprisingly susceptible to human error.

People are extremely good at recognizing highly familiar individuals (e.g. work colleagues, friends and family) even from low-quality images. Familiar people can be recognized from poor-quality CCTV images with over 90% accuracy (Bruce *et al.*, 2001; Burton *et al.*, 1999). However, we are surprisingly poor at matching images, taken by different cameras, of an otherwise unfamiliar person. For example, Bruce *et al.* (1999) asked participants to choose the face from an array of ten high-quality photographs that they thought matched a target face. The photograph of the target was taken from a studio video recording made on the same day as the still photographs in the array were taken. The set of faces consisted of 120 young, male, clean-shaven Caucasian police trainees supplied by the Home Office. The arrays consisted of faces judged to resemble each other so that selections could not be based on substantial differences in hairstyle, weight or age. When the viewpoint and facial expression of the target and the correct image in the array matched (i.e. a comparison is made under ideal conditions), participants only made the correct selection in 79% of the arrays. Bruce *et al.* conclude: "The implication of these findings is that courts must be aware that caution should be used when the impressions of resemblance are used to establish the identity of unfamiliar people, *even when the quality of videotape is high*" (emphasis as in the original).

The forensic implications of a separate study of recognition of faces from a poor-quality video, typical of that recorded by a commercial security CCTV system, was summarized as follows: " . . . identification of these types of video sequences is very unreliable, unless the viewer happens to know the target person" (Burton *et al.*, 1999).

FORENSIC IMPLICATIONS OF USING CCTV IMAGES FOR IDENTIFICATION

- Photographs of different people can look remarkably similar to each other.
- Two images of the same person can look very different, when taken with different cameras.
- Faces of familiar people (e.g. colleagues, friends or family) can be recognized accurately even from low-quality images, such as those obtained from CCTV.
- Matching the identity of unfamiliar people in images taken by different cameras is error-prone, even if the images are high quality.
- Both inclusion errors (judging two different people to be the same person) and exclusion errors (judging images of the same person to be different people) are common.
- Matching facial identity is error-prone even when there is no requirement to remember a face.
- CCTV is a powerful investigative tool, which can help identify potential suspects worthy of further investigation. Evidential use of CCTV as a means of establishing disputed identification in court should be treated with great caution.

Furthermore, Burton *et al.*'s study showed that police officers, with experience in forensic identification and an average of over 13 years' service, perform as poorly as other participants unfamiliar with the targets. A police officer is no more likely to correctly identify somebody from video than anybody else who has a similar level of familiarity with the target.

Davis (2007) examined people's ability to match a person filmed in a 40-second high-quality video to somebody physically present in the room. This comparison was intended to simulate the task facing a member of the jury who watches a video sequence in a court in the presence of the defendant. The video displayed views of each actor's face and body from a number of different angles and was played up to three times. In half of the trials the defendant was not the person in the video. The overall error rate was approximately 20% (22% target present; 17% target absent). That is, one in five 'witnesses' was mistaken under ideal conditions when there was no requirement to remember the culprit's face, and there was no time pressure. In the case of one particular actor, 44% of participants incorrectly judged an 'innocent defendant' to be the actor in the video sequence.

Studies by Henderson, Bruce & Burton (2001) and by Davies & Thasen (2000) have found similarly high error rates in identifying previously unfamiliar persons from CCTV. Davies & Thasen report identification accuracy between 15–30% with false alarm rates between 60–65%, showing that people are particularly prone to making a mistaken identification when the person they expect to identify is not present.

Why is recognition of familiar faces so robust but recognition of previously unfamiliar faces so vulnerable? It is known that familiar faces are relatively better recognized from their internal features (eyes, nose, mouth) than are unfamiliar faces (Ellis, Shepherd & Davies, 1979). When looking at unfamiliar faces more reliance is placed on the external features (hair, face shape). The configuration of the internal features is a more reliable cue to identity across different views and lighting conditions. When recognizing unfamiliar faces we are more likely to rely on superficial similarities that are changeable (e.g. hairstyles, hairline).

Stills from CCTV are often circulated to police officers in an attempt to obtain an identification from an officer who may have previously arrested or interviewed the offender. Recognition by police officers from CCTV is often used as identification evidence in court. The experimental evidence discussed above suggests that the degree of familiarity of the perpetrator to the police officer is a critical variable in assessing the reliability of the identification. This type of identification evidence raises the question: How familiar does one have to be with a face to recognize it reliably from video?

At present the scientific evidence on this point is rather sparse. Bruce *et al.* (2001) looked at matching performance for faces that had been familiarized by 30 seconds' or one minute's exposure of a wide range of different views of the face immediately before performing the matching task. The task required matching of a target photograph to an array of 8–10 photographs. In half of the trials the target was not present in the array. There was little benefit of prior familiarization, except when two participants viewed the faces together and were encouraged to discuss the faces during familiarization. In these circumstances when matching *good quality images in the same view*, participants who had received the prior 'social' familiarization identified 98% of targets and correctly rejected 68% of 'target absent' arrays. This compares to 81% and 39% respectively for participants who received no prior familiarization. In conclusion, prior brief social familiarization can enhance matching under ideal conditions with no memory load. However, even under these ideal conditions (good-quality video images in the same view) there is a substantial false alarm rate when the 'target' is not present in the array (32% of responses).

CONCLUSIONS

Our ability to judge that a face has been seen before can exceed our ability to recall the circumstances in which it was encountered. Reliance on a feeling of familiarity at a formal identification procedure can be especially prone to mistaken identification. There is ample evidence that mistakes by eyewitnesses occur frequently, and are a leading cause of wrongful convictions. Therefore, the procedures to obtain formal identification evidence should be designed and used with care.

Procedures that do not require selection amongst alternatives (e.g. dock identification, a show-up, street identification in some circumstances) are particularly prone to mistaken identification. A witness should not participate in repeated identification procedures. In selection methods careful consideration must given to the design of the procedure, including the choice of plausible foils and the instructions given to the witness. Two methods have been advocated to improve the probative value of line-up procedures: selection of foils who match the witness' description of the culprit (rather than on the basis of their similarity to the suspect) and sequential rather than simultaneous presentation of images. However, recent evidence, especially in an operational context, shows at best mixed results. Recommendations to change existing practice in these respects would be inappropriate.

Increasing surveillance by CCTV has had a marked impact on criminal investigations. Identification of unfamiliar faces from CCTV images can be surprisingly error-prone. Images of different people can look very similar, whilst images of the same person, especially when taken with different cameras, can look very different. Although CCTV may appear to give an opportunity to overcome the frailties of human eyewitness memory, CCTV itself poses significant issues of human misidentification.

We are familiar with the image of crime scene investigators dressing in paper suits and latex gloves taking care not to contaminate the crime scene by introducing rogue samples or destroying evidence, whilst endeavouring to detect extend every last-minute trace that might link the offender to the scene. It is useful to extend this approach, by thinking of the memory of an eyewitness as part of a crime scene. The investigators need to use sensitive, unbiased procedures to obtain reliable eyewitness identification. Equally the investigators must take great care to avoid contaminating the witness' memory by using multiple identification procedures, biased line-ups, or providing feedback to witnesses.

SUMMARY

- Mistaken identification by eyewitnesses is the leading cause of wrongful convictions.
- Reliance on a feeling of familiarity can be especially error-prone.
- Factors that affect the accuracy of eyewitness identification include the length of time the witness was able to view the culprit, high stress experienced by a witness, and the age of the witness.
- A witness should not participate in repeated identification procedures to avoid a potential misattribution of familiarity.
- Witnesses who make an accurate identification generally express higher confidence than witnesses who make a mistaken identification, however it is not uncommon for confident witnesses to be mistaken.
- The confidence of an eyewitness is affected by information acquired afterwards. For example, being told whether the person identified is the police suspect.
- Identification of unfamiliar faces from CCTV images can be surprisingly error-prone. Images of different people can look very similar, whilst images of the same person can look very different.
- The memory of an eyewitness should be regarded as part of a crime scene. Therefore, procedures must be designed to avoid distorting the witness' memory.

ESSAY/DISCUSSION QUESTIONS

1. What insights does psychological science provide to our understanding of mistaken eyewitness identification?

2. Compare the strengths and weaknesses of laboratory studies of eyewitness identification with those of archival studies.

3. What practical advice, based on psychological research, would you offer to the police authorities regarding the fair and effective conduct of identification parades?

4. Discuss the strengths and limitations of CCTV evidence as an aid to identifying offenders.

REFERENCES

Bartlett, J.C. & Fulton, A. (1991). Familiarity and recognition of faces in old age. *Memory and Cognition, 19*, 229–238.

Bauml, K-H., Zellner, M., & Vilimek, R. (2005). When remembering causes forgetting: Retrieval-induced forgetting as recovery failure. *Journal of Experimental Psychology: Learning, Memory and Cognition, 31*, 1221–1234.

Behrman, B.W. & Davey, S.L. (2001). Eyewitness identification in actual criminal cases: An archival analysis. *Law and Human Behavior, 25*, 475–491.

Brewer (2006). Uses and abuses of eyewitness identification confidence. *Legal and Criminological Psychology, 11*, 3–23.

Bruce, V. (1982). Changing faces: Visual and non-visual coding processes in face recognition. *British Journal of Psychology, 73*, 105–116.

Bruce, V., Henderson, Z., Greenwood, K. *et al.* (1999). Verification of face identities from images captured on video. *Journal of Experimental Psychology: Applied, 5*, 339–360.

Bruce, V., Henderson, Z., Newman, C., & Burton, A.M. (2001). Matching identities of familiar and unfamiliar faces caught on CCTV images. *Journal of Experimental Psychology: Applied, 7*, 207–218.

Burton, A.M., Wilson, S., Cowan, M., & Bruce, V. (1999). Face recognition in poor quality video: evidence from security surveillance. *Psychological Science, 10*, 243–248.

Chiroro, P. & Valentine, T. (1995). An investigation of the contact hypothesis of the own-race bias in face recognition. *Quarterly Journal of Experimental Psychology, 48A*, 879–894.

Clark, S.E. & Davey, S.L. (2005). The targets-to-foils shift in simultaneous and sequential line-ups. *Law and Human Behavior, 29*, 151–172.

Cutler, B.L., Berman, G.L., Penrod, S., & Fisher, R.P. (1994). Conceptual, practical and empirical issues associated with eyewitness identification test media. In D.F. Ross, J.D. Read, & M.P. Toglia, *Adult eyewitness testimony: Current trends and developments*. Cambridge: Cambridge University Press (pp. 163–181).

Davies, G. & Thasen, S. (2000). Closed-circuit television: How effective an identification aid? *British Journal of Psychology, 91*, 411–426.

Davis, J.P. (2007). *The forensic identification of CCTV images of unfamiliar faces*. Unpublished PhD Thesis. Goldsmiths, University of London.

Deffenbacher, K.A., Bornstein, B.H., & Penrod, S.D (2006). Mugshot exposure effects: retroactive interference, mugshot commitment, source confusion and unconscious transference. *Law and Human Behavior, 30,* 287–307.

Deffenbacher, K.A., Bornstein, B.H., Penrod, S.D., & McGorty, K. (2004). A meta-analytic review of the effects of high stress on eyewitness memory. *Law and Human Behavior, 28,* 687–706.

Devlin, Lord P. (1976). *Report to the secretary of state for the Home Department of the departmental committee on evidence of identification in criminal cases.* London: HMSO.

Dunning, D. & Perretta, S. (2002). Automaticity and eyewitness accuracy: A 10–12 second rule for distinguishing accurate from inaccurate positive identifications. *Journal of Applied Psychology, 87,* 951–962.

Ellis, H.D., Shepherd, J.W., & Davies, G.M. (1979). Identification of familiar and unfamiliar faces from internal and external features: Some implications for theories of face recognition. *Perception, 8,* 431–439.

Harris, M.J. & Rosenthal, R. (1985). Mediation of interpersonal expectancy effects: 31 meta-analyses. *Psychological Bulletin, 97,* 363–386.

Henderson, Z., Bruce, V., & Burton, A.M. (2001). Matching the faces of robbers captured on video. *Applied Cognitive Psychology, 15,* 445–464.

Innocence Project (2007). Downloaded 8 January 2007 from: http://www.innocenceproject. org/understand/Eyewitness-Misidentification.php.

Juslin, P., Olsson, N., & Winman, A. (1996). Calibration and diagnosticity of confidence in eyewitness identification: comments on what can be inferred from the low confidence–accuracy correlation. *Journal of Experimental Psychology: Learning, Memory and Cognition, 22,* 1304–1316.

Lindsay, D.S., Read, J.D., & Sharma, K., (1998). Accuracy and confidence in person identification: The relationship is strong when witnessing conditions vary widely. *Psychological Science, 9,* 215–218.

Lindsay, R.C.L., Lea, J.A., & Fulford, J.A. (1991). Sequential line-up presentation: Technique matters. *Journal of Applied Psychology, 76,* 741–745.

Lindsay, R.C.L., Martin, R., & Webber, L. (1994). Default values in eyewitness descriptions: A problem for the match-to-description line-up foil selection strategy. *Law and Human Behavior, 18,* 527–541.

Lindsay, R.C.L. & Wells, G.L. (1985). Improving eyewitness identification from line-ups: Simultaneous versus sequential presentation. *Journal of Applied Psychology, 66,* 343–350.

Luus, C.A.E. & Wells, G.L. (1991). Eyewitness identification and the selection of distracters for line-ups. *Law and Human Behavior, 15,* 43–57.

Meissner, C.A. & Brigham, J.C. (2001). Thirty years of investigating the own-race bias in memory for faces. *Psychology, Public Policy and Law, 7,* 3–35.

Meissner, C.A., Tredoux, C.G., Parker, J.F., & MacLin, O. (2005). Eyewitness decisions in simultaneous and sequential line-ups: A dual-process signal detection theory analysis. *Memory and Cognition, 33,* 783–792.

Memon, A., Hope, L., & Bull, R. (2003). Exposure duration: Effects on eyewitness accuracy and confidence. *British Journal of Psychology, 94,* 339–354.

Morgan, C.A., Hazlett, G., Doran, A. *et al.* (2004). Accuracy of eyewitness memory for persons encountered during exposure to highly intense stress. *International Journal of Law and Psychiatry, 27,* 265–279.

Norris, C., McCahill, M., & Woods, D. (2004). The growth of CCTV: A global perspective on the international diffusion of video surveillance in publicly accessible space. *Surveillance and Society, 2*, 110–135. Downloaded 14 May 2007 from: http://www.surveillance-and-society. org/cctv.htm.

O'Rourke, T.E., Penrod, S.D., & Cutler, B.L. (1989). The external validity of eyewitness identification research: Generalizing across subject populations. *Law and Human Behavior, 13*, 385–397.

Phillips, M.R., McAuliff, B.D., Kovera, M.B., & Cutler, B.L. (1999). Double-blind photoarray administration as a safeguard against investigator bias. *Journal of Applied Psychology, 84*, 940–951.

Pike, G., Brace, N., & Kyman, S. (2002). *The visual identification of suspects: procedures and practice*. Briefing note 2/02, Policing and Reducing Crime Unit, Home Office Research Development and Statistics Directorate. Downloaded 14 May 2007 from: www.homeoffice. gov.uk/rds/prgbriefpubs1.html.

Pike, G., Kemp, R., Brace, N., Allen, J., & Rowlands, G. (2000). The effectiveness of video identification parades. *Proceedings of the British Psychological Society, 8*, 44.

Police and Criminal Evidence Act 1984 (s.60(1)(a), s.60(1) and s.66(1)) Codes of Practice (2005). Downloaded 16 February 2007 from: http://police.homeoffice.gov.uk/operational-policing/powers-pace-codes/pace-code-intro/.

Pozzulo, J. & Warren, K.L. (2003). Descriptions and identifications of strangers by youth and adult eyewitnesses. *Journal of Applied Psychology, 88*, 2, 315–23.

R. v. Turnbull [1976] 3 All ER 549.

Schank, R.C. & Abelson, R.P. (1977). *Scripts, plans, goals and understanding*. Hillsdale NJ: Lawrence Erlbaum Associates Inc.

Searcy, J.H., Bartlett, J.C., & Memon, A. (1999). Age differences in accuracy and choosing in eyewitness identification and face recognition. *Memory & Cognition, 27*, 538–552.

Searcy, J.H., Bartlett, J.C., & Memon, A. (2000). Relationships of availability, line-up conditions, and individual differences to false identification by young and older eyewitnesses. *Legal and Criminological Psychology, 5*, 219–236.

Searcy, J.H., Bartlett, J.C., Memon, A., & Swanson, K. (2001). Ageing and line-up performance at long retention intervals. Effects of metamemory and context reinstatement. *Journal of Applied Psychology, 86*, 207–14.

Semmler, C., Brewer, N., & Wells, G.L. (2004). Effects of post-identification feedback on eyewitness identification and non-identification confidence. *Journal of Applied Psychology, 89*, 334–346.

Shapiro, P.N. & Penrod, S.D. (1986). Meta-analysis of facial identification. studies. *Psychological Bulletin, 100*, 139–156.

Shepherd, J.W. (1983). Identification after long delays. In S.M.A. Lloyd-Bostock & B.R. Clifford (Eds), *Evaluating Eyewitness Evidence*. Chichester: John Wiley & Sons (pp. 173–187).

Slater, A. (1994). *Identification parades: A scientific evaluation*. London: Police Research Group (Police Research Award Scheme), Home Office.

Sporer, S. (1992). Post-dicting accuracy: Confidence, decision times and person descriptions of choosers and non-choosers. *European Journal of Social Psychology, 22*, 157–180.

Sporer, S. (1993). Eyewitness identification accuracy, confidence and decision times in simultaneous and sequential line-ups. *Journal of Applied Psychology, 78*, 22–33.

Sporer, S. (1994). Decision times and eyewitness identification accuracy in simultaneous and sequential line-ups. In D.F. Ross, J.D. Read, & M.P. Toglia (Eds), *Adult eyewitness testimony: Current trends and developments*. Cambridge: Cambridge University Press (pp. 300–327).

Sporer, S., Penrod, S., Read, D., & Cutler, B.L. (1995). Choosing, confidence and accuracy: A meta-analysis of the confidence-accuracy relations in eyewitness identification studies, *Psychological Bulletin, 118*, 315–327.

Steblay, N.M. (1992). A meta-analytic review of the weapon focus effect. *Law and Human Behavior, 16*, 413–423.

Steblay, N.M. (1997). Social influence in eyewitness recall: A meta-analytic review of line-up instruction effects. *Law and Human Behavior, 21*, 283–297.

Steblay, N., Dysart, J., Fulero, S., & Lindsay, R.C.L. (2001). Eyewitness accuracy rates in sequential and simultaneous line-up presentations: A meta-analytic comparison. *Law and Human Behavior, 25*, 459–473.

Technical Working Group for Eyewitness Evidence (1999). *Eyewitness evidence: A guide for law enforcement*. Washington: US Department of Justice Downloaded 14 May 2007 from: http://www.ncjrs.org/nij/eyewitness/tech_working_group.html.

Tunnicliff, J.L. & Clark, S.E. (2000). Selecting foils for identification line-ups: Matching suspects or descriptions? *Law and Human Behavior, 24*, 231–258.

Valentine, T. (1991). A unified account of the effects of distinctiveness, inversion and race in face recognition. *Quarterly Journal of Experimental Psychology, 43A*, 161–204.

Valentine, T., Darling, S., & Memon, A. (in press). Do strict rules and moving images increase the reliability of sequential identification procedures? *Applied Cognitive Psychology*.

Valentine, T. & Endo, M. (1992). Towards an exemplar model of face processing: The effects of race and distinctiveness. *Quarterly Journal of Experimental Psychology, 44A*, 671–703.

Valentine, T. Harris, N., Colom Piera, A., & Darling, S. (2003). Are police video identifications fair to African-Caribbean suspects? *Applied Cognitive Psychology, 17*, 459–476.

Valentine, T. & Heaton, P. (1999). An evaluation of the fairness of police line-ups and video identifications. *Applied Cognitive Psychology, 13*, S59–S72.

Valentine, T., Pickering, A., & Darling, S. (2003). Characteristics of eyewitness identification that predict the outcome of real line-ups. *Applied Cognitive Psychology, 17*, 969–993.

Wagenaar, W.A. & Van der Schrier, J. (1996). Face recognition as a function of distance and illumination: A practical tool for use in the courtroom. *Psychology, Crime and Law, 2*, 321–332.

Weber, N. Brewer, N., Wells, G.L., Semmuler, C., & Keast, A. (2004) Eyewitness identification accuracy and response latency: The unruly 10–12 second rule. *Journal of Experimental Psychology: Applied, 10*, 139–147.

Wells, G.L. (1993). What do we know about eyewitness identification? *American Psychologist, 48*, 553–571.

Wells G.L. & Bradfield, A.L. (1998). "Good you identified the suspect": Feedback to eyewitnesses distort their reports of the witnessing experience. *Journal of Applied Psychology, 66*, 688–696.

Wells, G.L., Rydell, S.M., & Seelau, E. (1993). The selection of distractors for eyewitness line-ups. *Journal of Applied Psychology, 78*, 835–844.

Wright, D.B. & McDaid, A.T. (1996). Comparing system and estimator variables using data from real line-ups. *Applied Cognitive Psychology, 10*, 75–84.

ANNOTATED READING LIST

Schachter, D.L. (1999). The seven sins of memory. Insights from psychology and cognitive neuroscience. *American Psychologist, 54*, 183–203. *An authoritative review of the evidence of the fallibility of human memory including memory distortions such as misattribution, suggestibility and bias. It is argued that these flaws of human memory are the by-product of otherwise adaptive features of memory.*

Thompson, J. (2000). I was certain but I was wrong. *New York Times*, 18 June 2000. Downloaded 27 September 2007 from: http://truthinjustice.org/positive_id.htm. *A compelling statement by Jennifer Thompson, who confidently identified Ronald Cotton as the man who raped her. Ronald Cotton was subsequently exonerated by DNA evidence after serving 11 years of a life sentence.*

Valentine, T. (2006). Forensic facial identification. In A. Heaton-Armstrong, E. Shepherd, G. Gudjonsson, & D. Wolchover (Eds), *Witness testimony; Psychological, investigative and evidential perspectives*. Oxford: Oxford University Press (pp. 281–309). *A literature review of eyewitness identification and identification from CCTV, which integrates the psychological literature with the procedures and cases in English Law.*

Wells, G.L., Memon, A., & Penrod. S. (2006). Eyewitness evidence. Improving its probative value. *Psychological Science in the Public Interest, 7*, 45–75. *An up-to-date and extensive review of eyewitness identification evidence, principally from an American perspective. Features a substantial review of interviewing witnesses and the cognitive interview.*

4

INTERVIEWING VULNERABLE WITNESSES

Robyn E. Holliday
University of Kent at Canterbury, United Kingdom

Charles J. Brainerd & Valerie F. Reyna
Cornell University, USA

The number of vulnerable witnesses testifying in the courts has increased significantly in most Western countries in recent years. The most publicized are probably children, frequently testifying in cases of alleged sexual abuse, but other vulnerable witness groups are also increasingly seen and heard in court, notably the elderly and witnesses with learning disabilities. The appearance of such witnesses reflects the need to ensure that all groups in society have the opportunity to have their 'day in court', to have their testimony heard and tested and to ensure offenders are successfully prosecuted (see Westcott, Chapter 8). "Eyewitness testimony is the most damning of all evidence that can be used in a court of law" (Loftus, 1996: v). Reliable eyewitness testimony depends on accurate memory for the witnessed or experienced event. Psychological science and the legal system have become closely intertwined. The courts have taken notice of groundbreaking research on eyewitness testimony of vulnerable witnesses, and this research is now routinely applied to actual cases. The contribution of psychological science has not been peripheral. Rather, research has changed the outcomes of important cases involving long prison terms and lifetime labelling of individuals as sex offenders, sometimes absolving and sometimes implicating the accused (see Ceci & Bruck, 1995, for actual cases).

This chapter begins by examining how memory operates and the strategies that must be employed in order to encode, store and later retrieve material accurately from memory. This leads onto a discussion of what causes failures of memory, particularly the role of suggestibility and misinformation in producing memories which are false, but nonetheless confidently held. Such *false memories* are particular areas of difficulty for some vulnerable witnesses. It then goes on to consider the special interviewing techniques that have been developed to enable such witnesses to provide the police and the courts with the maximum amount of accurate information with the minimum of error.

HOW DO EXPERIENCES GET TURNED INTO INFORMATION IN THE BRAIN?

Information-processing theories are based on a view of the brain as a complex symbol-manipulating system through which information flows – a computer metaphor. There is not a single information-processing theory but rather an account of the processes by which information passes in and out of the brain. It is widely accepted that what we remember is a combination of verbatim memory (exact details, which rapidly become inaccessible) along with reconstruction, two processes that are largely independent. *Fuzzy-trace theory* (e.g. Brainerd & Reyna, 1998) proposes that *verbatim memories* (i.e. exact details – *red car*) and *gist memories* (i.e. semantic and relational information – *car* in this instance is vaguely specified – it could be any colour) are encoded, stored, and retrieved in parallel. When asked to remember information, for instance during a police interview or in identifying a perpetrator from a line-up, remembering a verbatim memory is made on the basis of an *exact* match between the target details (e.g. a line-up face) and the details held in memory. In contrast, remembering a gist memory is made on the basis of the *similarity* between the target details (e.g. a line-up face) and the details held in memory (Brainerd, Reyna & Mojardin, 1999). Fuzzy-trace theory proposes that the bulk of false memories are spontaneous products of understanding the gist of experience and that this tendency is increased when repeated, connected events have occurred, as in repeated abuse (Reyna *et al.*, 2007). However, this biasing tendency to spontaneously connect related events is lower in children than adults (Brainerd & Reyna, 2007).

Memory Strategies for Encoding, Storing and Retrieving Information

Memory strategies are deliberate mental activities used to hold details in working memory, to store information, and to transfer information to long-term memory and existing knowledge. In other words, memory strategies are cognitive or behavioural activities that are under the deliberate control of an individual, which are typically employed so as to enhance memory performance.

Information from the environment must be encoded; for example, details of a suspect such as clothing, hair and eye colour, age, height, and build. Once information is encoded, it must be stored within our brains. Encoded details are transferred from short-term memory to long-term memory. A number of memory storage strategies such as rehearsal, elaboration and organization are employed to store details. This newly stored information is integrated into our existing knowledge base. For example, we might use a rehearsal memory strategy of repeating information when trying to learn a phone number, remember a list of items to buy at the supermarket, or the license plate of a car. We might make meaning connections between to-be-remembered details by the elaboration strategy. For example, in order to remember the words *elephant, pin, trunk*, we could put the words into a memorable sentence: *the elephant had a pin in his trunk*, or memorize the first letter of each word, *e, p, t*.

HOW DO THE CONTENTS OF MEMORY GET OUT OF OUR BRAIN?

Just as there are strategies for storing information in our brain, there are memory strategies for retrieving information. Retrieval strategies are deliberate operations designed to access information from long-term memory and move information to short-term memory ready for use. Using the example above, the encoded information about a suspect must be recollected when required, such as in a police interview. Recognition is the simplest and easiest method for such recollections. Asking a witness to identify the individual from a series of mug shots or from a police line-up is easier for them than asking them to recall details because the mug shot or line-up serve as retrieval cues. Recall is the hardest memory task because it requires generating memory information about an absent stimulus in order to recall it. Importantly, the accuracy of witness testimony can be affected at encoding, storage and retrieval.

Children and Memory Strategies

Memory strategy use develops: there are age differences in the type, number and efficiency of strategy use (Bjorklund, 2005). Employment of strategies starts to emerge during preschool years but is not very successful at first. During mid-childhood, usage of memory strategies increases dramatically.

Storage Strategies

Rehearsal: Seminal research on this topic was reported by Flavell, Beach & Chinsky (1966). These researchers presented 5-, 7- and 10-year-old children with pictures of objects to remember. Results showed a clear increase with age in the spontaneous use of verbal rehearsal as a memory encoding strategy and a resultant increase in levels of recall.

Organization: Grouping information into meaningful chunks, for example, when you learn a phone number you may typically chunk the digits into groups of three digits. In a classic piece of research, Miller (1956) reported that adults can hold in memory an average of seven random numbers or letters (+ or −2). Moely, Olson, Halwes & Flavell (1969) investigated children's use of the organization strategy. Children aged 5–6, 8 and 10–11 years were allowed two minutes in which they were free to move around and touch pictures of objects from different categories (e.g. animals) which they recalled later. Moely *et al.* were interested in the number of times children sorted the pictures (e.g. lion, dog) into categories (e.g. animals). The oldest group spontaneously sorted the pictures into categories whilst the youngest children rarely did so, and this, in turn, was linked to improved recall.

Elaboration: Creating a relationship between two items, for example, in order to remember the words *pig* and *mud*, the words could be included in a sentence: *the mud swallowed the pig.* Beuhring & Kee (1987) investigated the use and efficacy of such a strategy in 5th and 12th grade participants. These researchers found that performance on a paired-associate learning task was improved to a greater extent by instructions in elaboration techniques in the older participants. So, efficient use of elaboration strategies appears late in development (late adolescence). Indeed, often university students need to be taught to use effortful elaboration because adults typically use this strategy inconsistently (for a review, see Bjorklund, 2005).

Retrieval Strategies

As with storage strategies, use of retrieval strategies varies developmentally. The contents of memory are retrieved more accurately if the context in which the material was learned is reinstated. Using our earlier example, returning a witness to the location in which the suspect was seen committing the crime has positive benefits on recollection. Context is particularly important for young children (Bjorklund, 2005). On memory tests, young children perform better on recognition tests due in part to the representation of the original retrieval cues (e.g. a word or picture). Kobasigawa (1974) reported evidence of an age-related increase in the efficient employment of available retrieval cues (i.e. cue cards) from 5–6 to 10–11 years. The younger children encoded as much information as the older children but did not spontaneously use the available retrieval cues to assist with recall.

The Misinformation Paradigm

The contents of our memories are subject to interference from a number of sources (e.g. parents, friends, the media, and photographs). Arguably, the most important factor influencing accurate eyewitness testimony, however, is suggestibility.

The notion of memory reconstruction (i.e. gap filling – cf. Bartlett, 1932) is at the heart of research on the reliability of eyewitness testimony. Elizabeth Loftus is a recognized pioneer in the investigation of eyewitness testimony in the laboratory. Loftus and her colleagues (Loftus, Miller & Burns, 1978) introduced the misinformation paradigm in which participants witness an event, are then misled about some aspects of the original event, and then try to recollect the original event. In Loftus

(1977), for example, college students were shown a series of coloured slides of a road traffic accident. A red Datsun car knocked down a pedestrian, which was witnessed by the driver of a *green* car who did not stop. Subjects were misinformed that this latter car was *blue*. Misled participants were more likely than controls to select a blue or a bluish-green colour (from an array of colours) for the car that did not stop. In other words, witnesses showed evidence of blended memories for this car; a blend of green (the colour in the witnessed event) and blue (the colour suggested).

When asked to choose between the original event and the post-event misleading details, research with adults (Loftus *et al.*, 1989; Loftus, Miller & Burns, 1978) and children (Ceci, Ross & Toglia, 1987; Holliday, Douglas & Hayes, 1999; Lampinen & Smith, 1995) has consistently found that misled participants are significantly more likely than controls (who have not been misled) to mistakenly select the misleading suggestions. This paradigm has come to be termed the 'standard test' of recognition memory in both the adult and child misinformation literature.

McCloskey & Zaragoza (1985) developed a 'modified test' that resembles the standard test except that at test the misled item is replaced by a new item (see Table 4.1). In the final phase of the standard test, participants choose between the original and the misled item (e.g. *red* ball v. *green* ball). In the modified test condition, the misled alternative is replaced by a previously unseen novel item (e.g. *blue* ball). McCloskey and Zaragoza argued that if misinformation impairs original memories, participants in a misled condition would choose the original event detail (e.g. *red* ball) less often than those in a control condition. In a series of experiments using modified recognition tests with adults, McCloskey and Zaragoza found no significant differences in recognition accuracy between misled and control groups, providing evidence against the memory impairment view. They concluded that misinformation effects detected in the 'standard' testing paradigm were, in all likelihood, due to demand factors and/or response biases, and did not reflect true memory alteration.

Experimental condition	Phase 1 Original detail	Phase 2 Post-event misinformation	Standard test	Modified test
Control	(e.g. red ball)	(e.g. ball)	(e.g. red ball v. green ball)	(e.g. red ball v. blue ball)
Misled	(e.g. red ball)	(e.g. green ball)	(e.g. red ball v. green ball)	(e.g. red ball v. blue ball)

Table 4.1: The Standard and Modified Testing Paradigms

A number of researchers have replicated McCloskey & Zaragoza's (1985) finding that the modified test eliminates the misinformation effect (e.g. Belli *et al.*, 1994; Bowman & Zaragoza, 1989). Others, however, have found a reduced but reliable misinformation effect on modified tests (e.g. Belli *et al.*, 1992; Holliday, Douglas & Hayes, 1999; Schreiber & Sergent, 1998) (see Holliday, Reyna & Hayes, 2002; Reyna, Holliday & Marche, 2002, for reviews of this literature).

CHILD WITNESSES AND VICTIMS

Historically, in many countries children have been regarded by legal practitioners and other concerned professionals as unreliable eyewitnesses. Indeed, prior to the 1980s, children were believed to be poor witnesses, prone to making things up, highly suggestible and not able to distinguish fantasy from reality – in essence, second-class witnesses (see Westcott, Chapter 8). At the turn of the twentieth century one of the most influential pioneers in memory and intelligence testing, the French developmental psychologist, Alfred Binet (1857–1911) published his classic book *La Suggestibilité;* (1900). Binet proposed that auto-suggestion (the influence of a prominent thought) which originates inside an individual was the primary factor underlying suggestibility (Ceci & Bruck, 1995). Binet presented children aged 7 to 14 years with a number of lines that steadily increased in length followed by a series of target lines, which were equal in length to the last line in the study phase. Each child then drew each target line one at a time. Binet reported that children drew progressively longer lines (as they had seen in the study phase) even though each target line was the same length.

In 1910, the German psychologist, William Stern (1871–1938) asked children, adolescents and young adults (7- to 18-year-olds) to recall the details of a picture they had studied a few minutes earlier. Next the participants responded to questions some of which were about the picture and some of which were misleading questions. In a prelude to modern research on false memories and suggestibility, Stern reported that the misleading questions produced the most errors, free recall produced the least amount of errors and the youngest children were more suggestible than the adolescents and young adults (Ceci & Bruck, 1995). In 1911, another German psychologist, Otto Lipmann (1880–1933) proposed that children encode details of a witnessed event differently from adults. He also noted that children were more compliant than adults in response to questions posed by an adult authority figure. Lipmann's views on child testimony and suggestibility, that is the role of both cognitive (internal) and social (external) factors remain the focus of contemporary research (e.g. Bruck & Ceci, 1999).

The last two decades have seen an explosion in eyewitness research, including many studies involving child witnesses (Brainerd & Reyna, 2005; Ceci & Bruck, 1995). Such research is timely because: (1) Expert witnesses began providing the courts with opinions about the reliability of eyewitness testimony (e.g. see Loftus & Ketcham, 1991); (2) the societal beliefs of the 1960s and 1970s were rapidly changing with increasing numbers of instances of child abuse being reported; (3) few cases of child abuse were successfully prosecuted; and (4) in a growing number of countries the admissibility of child testimony and the abolition of legal constraints on children's evidence known as the corroboration rule (i.e. the statements given to juries regarding the risk of convictions solely on the basis of a child's evidence) (see Westcott, Chapter 8).

Factors Affecting Children's Testimony

How reliable is a 6-year-old child's memory for an experienced or witnessed event? The answer is it very much depends on a number of factors. Young children tend to forget information faster than older children (Brainerd *et al.*, 1990; Howe, 1991), so the time delay between the witnessed event and testifying is critical. Young children report fewer details than older children and adults. However, the information that they do recollect is typically quite accurate (Holliday, 2003a). In 1981, Nelson and Gruendel published a study that evaluated preschoolers' verbal reports about routine and familiar events such as going to MacDonald's. They found that children as young as three years accurately remembered details of events if such events were experienced a number of times. However, young children tend to provide adult questioners with the details that they think the adult wants to hear (Holliday, Douglas & Hayes, 1999) and sometimes confuse the source of their memories – a child who has experienced an event and has received false information about that event may subsequently confuse memories of the event with memories of the false information.

We will now consider a range of factors that impact on children's testimony.

Cognitive Factors

Memory

Young children's free recall accounts tend to be accurate but less complete than older children. Hence, an interviewer must probe for detail with specific questions. Questioning increases the amount of information recollected but such information is often less accurate than that obtained with a free recall request, especially in young children (Brainerd, Reyna & Forrest, 2002; Holliday, 2003a). Open-ended questions (e.g. *Tell me what happened?*) are generally answered more accurately than specific questions (e.g. *What colour was the man's hat?*) but this ability improves with age (Holliday, 2003a; Poole & White, 1995).

Event-Based Knowledge

An important source of variability in children's true and false memory is prior knowledge (Bruck, Ceci & Melnyk, 1997; Reyna, Holliday & Marche, 2002). Studies examining children's event-relevant knowledge focus on the beneficial effects on accurate memory of prior knowledge that is consistent with experience (e.g. Chi, 1978; Goodman & Quas, 1997; Schneider, Korkel & Weinert, 1989) and on memory errors when children are asked to remember information that is inconsistent with prior knowledge (e.g. Ceci, Caves & Howe, 1981; Pillemer, Picariello & Pruett, 1994; Welch-Ross & Schmidt, 1996). Ornstein *et al.* (1998) examined the influence of prior knowledge on children's immediate and delayed recall of their memory for a physical examination and found that their knowledge of such an event had both positive and negative effects on recall, indicating that children confuse experience and expectation.

Language

Children's comprehension and production skills affect their susceptibility to misinformation acceptance. Children may fail to understand the questions (Waterman, Blades & Spencer, 2002). Interviewers may misinterpret children's answers and jump to conclusions about the meaning of a child's statement. Of particular relevance for eyewitness testimony are the concepts of time, date, and height, all of which are gradually acquired throughout childhood. Indeed, estimation of the height of an alleged perpetrator is quite difficult for children to make (and for some adults, too). Accurate estimations of when and for how long an abusive incident took place are not likely to be accomplished until around 10 years of age (Saywitz & Camparo, 1998).

Social Factors

Compliance

Children's compliance to adult authority figures who question them (e.g. police officers, judges, and social workers) also affects their vulnerability to misinformation acceptance. Young children are very aware of the high status of these people and are likely to report the suggested information because they view adult authority figures as credible sources of information (Ceci, Ross & Toglia, 1987; Lampinen & Smith, 1995; Toglia et al., 1992). For example, in Ceci et al.'s (1987) study, suggestibility effects were reduced but not eliminated in the youngest children (4 year olds) when another child (a 7 year old) provided the misinformation. Hence, for these very young children, suggestibility effects were in part influenced by a stronger belief in information provided by adult authority figures.

Interviewer Bias

Allegations that an interviewer had shaped the course of the interview to maximize disclosures that were consistent with what he/she believed a child witnessed or experienced were a common feature of several prominent trials during the 1980s and 1990s (e.g. Ceci & Bruck, 1995; Garven et al., 1998; Guilliatt, 1996; Pendergrast, 1996). It appeared that interviewers only sought details that confirmed what they believed happened. In their discussions of a series of the US day-care cases of the 1980s and 1990s (e.g. Little Rascals, Kelly Michaels, and Country Walk), Ceci & Bruck (1995) highlight evidence of blatant interviewer biases: "blind pursuit of a single hypothesis, and failure to test alternate, equally believable explanations of the children's behaviour" (p. 99).

Repeated Interviews and Questions

In many countries, children are typically interviewed several times by different professionals and family members before a case comes to court. However, in other countries video recording the first professional interview has replaced multiple interviewing (see Westcott, Chapter 8). Laboratory research suggests that repeated requests for information *within* an interview may signal to a child that their earlier answer was incorrect. Young children especially are prone to change their answers when questioned repeatedly and are often reluctant to say *I don't know* (although repeated questioning can sometimes improve recall; Reyna & Titcomb, 1997). This reluctance is particularly pertinent when yes/no questions are asked (Poole & White, 1991; see also Bruck et al., 1995).

CASE STUDY

Old Cutler Presbyterian Nursery School

In *State v. Fijnje* (1991), Robert Fijnje was accused of sexually abusing a large number of preschool children who attended a church-sponsored day-care centre in Miami, Florida over a two-year period. At the time of the alleged abuse, Fijnje, a teacher's assistant in the Old Cutler Presbyterian day care, was between 11 and 13 years old.

"The initial disclosure came from a 3-year-old child who was in therapy for regressive toileting practices, nightmares, and refusal to attend the church day care. When questioned by her therapist during the initial session as to why she did not want to attend the day care, the young child said that there was a boy who played too roughly, tossing her into the air and catching her. (It was subsequently confirmed by the staff that the defendant did indeed do this, ignoring protests by the children that he was tossing them too high.) Despite an absence of any disclosures of sexual abuse by the child during that session or any physical or corroborative evidence, the therapist appears to have held the hypothesis from the very first session that sexual abuse was at the root of the child's difficulties, because she made her beliefs known after the initial therapy session and soon after she made her first report to the state's Hotline for Abuse" (Ceci & Bruck, 1995: 13–14).

"After approximately three more months of therapy, with the assistance of anatomical dolls, the child disclosed the first details of her alleged sexual molestation. Over the course of the following seven months, she named a number of other children and adults who she claimed were present during the abuse" (Ceci & Bruck, 1995: 14).

Fijnje was arrested soon after his 14th birthday. He was acquitted on all charges after spending two years in a youth offender facility.

Further study: This case involved therapy-induced false memory reports in very young children, many of whom did not disclose sexual abuse until several months into therapy. Moreover, the first child who disclosed was recalling an incident that occurred at least six months before disclosure. How reliable would this child's account at age three be for abuse that allegedly occurred when she was two-and-a-half years? None of the children testified in court. Instead, each child's therapist gave evidence on the child's behalf (hearsay).

In your further study, find a case or cases of alleged sexual and/or ritual abuse and look for any examples of interviewer or confirmatory bias, compliance to authority, peer pressure, and leading and suggestive questioning.

The Misinformation Effect

Researchers continue to identify the conditions under which children are adversely affected by the implantation of misinformation after a witnessed event. Initial research interest in this area was precipitated by increased participation of young children in the legal system. In the UK, several legislative changes were introduced to promote inclusion of child witnesses, including abolition of the corroboration requirement, court evidence given via CCTV (closed-circuit television), video-recorded interviews as evidence, and relaxation of the competency request (see Westcott, Chapter 8). If the sole witness is a child, the credibility of that child's testimony is crucial in determining the outcome of the case (Reyna, Holliday & Marche, 2002). One of the key issues affecting the reliability of children's reports in such cases is suggestive questioning. Such questioning can be seen in high profile cases involving claims of sexual assault made by young children in the 1980s–1990s in a number of countries including the UK (see Ceci & Bruck, 1995; Guilliatt, 1996; Pendergrast, 1998). In this chapter we have adopted a broad definition of the *suggestibility* or *misinformation effect* that incorporates social (acquiescence) and psychological (memory) factors which affect "children's encoding, storage, retrieval, and reporting of events" (Ceci & Bruck, 1993: 404). Children are vulnerable to misinformation effects yet the nature of the underlying mechanisms responsible for these effects continues to be debated (Brainerd & Reyna, 2005; Holliday, Reyna & Hayes, 2002).

In a widely cited series of studies, Ceci, Ross & Toglia (1987) found evidence of misinformation effects in children aged 3 to 12 years, with the magnitude of these effects largest in the 3- and 4-year-olds. Zaragoza (1987, 1991) found evidence of suggestibility effects only when children aged 3 to 6 years were tested with the standard (Loftus) memory test. Zaragoza concluded that social demand factors and response biases inherent in the standard test were responsible for suggestibility effects in children rather than changes in their memory of the target event. Holliday, Douglas & Hayes (1999) investigated the relationship between memory trace strength of the original event and post-event misinformation, when 5- and 9-year-old children responded on either a standard or a modified test. Suggestibility effects were found on both types of tests implying that both memory and social factors are responsible for suggestibility effects in children (see also Holliday & Hayes, 2001; for reviews see Bruck & Ceci, 1999; Holliday, Reyna & Hayes, 2002; Reyna, Holliday & Marche, 2002).

Dual Memory Processes and Suggestibility in Children

Is suggestibility a process of which we are consciously aware? Or is it an unconscious process? Or is it both? These are important questions because if suggestibility is for the most part a conscious process it might be possible to devise methods to minimize its negative effects on memory. Such questions have been addressed in a series of studies conducted in Holliday's laboratory over the last decade (e.g. Holliday, 2003b; Holliday & Albon, 2004; Holliday & Hayes, 2000, 2001, 2002).

Holliday & Hayes (2000) showed that misinformation effects in children were due to two memory processes – recollection (intentional acceptance of suggestions) and familiarity (automatic acceptance of suggestions) (for a related approach, see Brainerd, Stein & Reyna, 1998). Five- and eight-year-old children were read a story, followed by misleading post-event details and a final recognition memory test.

Holliday and Hayes established that both recollection and familiarity were impli-cated in children's reporting of misinformation but the relative roles of these processes were affected by the method of encoding of misinformation. A larger recollection component was found for self-generated misinformation than for misinfor-mation that was simply read aloud. Such findings accord with the view that misinformation effects in children can be influenced by social demand factors such as compliance (Zaragoza, 1991). In general, however, misinformation effects were more often due to familiarity than recollection. A large familiarity component to suggestibility is predicted by trace alteration (post-event suggestions automatically overwriting initial memory details) (Loftus, Miller & Burns, 1978), retrieval inter-ference (post-event suggestions blocking retrieval of initial memory details) (Morton, 1991) and source-monitoring theories (individuals adopt a response crite-rion of familiarity, reporting the misinformation because it was the most recently presented without considering the source of their memories which implies that, for the most part, source-monitoring errors reflect automatic memory processes) (Johnson, Hashtroudi & Lindsay, 1993). However, theories that propose *both* recollection and familiarity such as fuzzy-trace theory (Brainerd & Reyna, 1998) provide the closest fit to these data. The results reported in Holliday & Hayes' (2000) findings were replicated in subsequent studies with children aged 4 to 10 years (Holliday, 2003b; Holliday & Albon, 2004; Holliday & Hayes, 2001, 2002) and in a real-life event (Memon, Holliday & Hill, 2006). Importantly, familiarity-based suggestibility *decreased* from 4 to 5 years to 10 years.

Familiarity and recollection memory processes and models of the misinformation effect		(Holiday & Hayes, 2000)
Misinformation model	Automatic processing of suggestions?	Intentional processing of suggestions?
Trace-alteration (strong) (Loftus *et al.*, 1978)	Yes	No
Trace strength (Brainerd & Reyna, 1998)	Yes	Yes
Trace competition (Chandler & Gargano, 1998; Morton, 1991)	Yes	No
Social demands/response bias (McCloskey & Zaragoza, 1985; Zaragoza, 1991)	No	Yes
Source-monitoring (Johnson *et al.*, 1993)	Yes	No

Table 4.2: The assumptions of current models of the misinformation effect in children: Evidence for dual memory processes, familiarity and recollection

CASE STUDY

Can The Children Be Believed?

"On 2nd August 1988 Margaret Kelly Michaels, a 26-year-old nursery school teacher, was convicted of sexually abusing children in the Wee Care Nursery School in Maplewood, New Jersey (*State v. Michaels*, 1988). Kelly was said to have licked peanut butter off children's genitals, played the piano while nude, made children drink her urine and eat her faeces, raped and assaulted children with knives, forks, spoons, and Lego blocks. She was accused of performing these acts during regular school hours over a period of seven months. None of the alleged acts were noticed by staff or reported by children to their parents, nor did any of the parents notice any signs of strange behaviour or genital soreness in their children, or smell urine or faeces on them when they collected them from school at the end of the day" (Ceci & Bruck, 1995: 11–12).

The major premise behind the explosion of allegations of sexual abuse made by very young children in the 1980s and early 1990s at their day care centres was that children never fabricate such details – on the contrary, children are often reluctant to disclose such things (Dr Roland Summit, 1983 – *Child Sexual Abuse Accommodation Syndrome*).

Professors Maggie Bruck and Steve Ceci and colleagues published research in 1995 which had far-reaching implications for all these cases. Bruck *et al.* found quite the opposite – 3-year-old children do make up tales of being touched on their genitals.

- Bruck *et al.* (with permission) installed hidden cameras in a doctor's office and filmed individual 3-year-old children's routine medical examinations. Some were touched on their genitals as part of the exam.

- Immediately after this examination each child was taken to the room next door and asked whether the doctor had touched them (experimenter pointed to genitals of an **anatomically-detailed doll**).

- More than half the children gave inaccurate descriptions of their examinations.

- Many showed on the doll genital and anal touching that did not occur.

- Nearly 60% of the children used the dolls in a sexualized or aggressive manner.

Further study: What are the strengths and weaknesses surrounding the use of other methods, for example props (toys, models) and drawing, in forensic interviews of children? Are these other methods more reliable than the anatomically-detailed dolls?

Implications for Children's Eyewitness Testimony

Holliday and colleagues' research suggests that questioning techniques that inadvertently encourage children to themselves generate an incorrect detail may be even more detrimental to the accuracy of subsequent testimony than the overt provision of a (wrong) suggestion by the questioner (Reyna, Holliday & Marche, 2002). Similarly, researchers have found that generating a mental image of events that did *not* occur in their childhood (e.g. breaking a window) increased the subjective likelihood that such events actually occurred (Garry *et al.*, 1996).

In the day care cases discussed earlier, children were frequently subjected to therapeutic interventions (e.g. imagery induction) and investigative techniques that directed them to speculate or 'think hard' about events that *might* have happened to them (Ceci & Bruck, 1995). In the McMartin Preschool case, for example, these techniques were most often employed when alternative means failed to result in allegations of abuse. Researchers have reported that young children who are repeatedly encouraged to imagine or visualize false events come to believe that such events actually occurred and provide elaborate descriptions of the contextual and emotional details surrounding these events (e.g. Ceci *et al.*, 1994a; Ceci *et al.*, 1994b).

Stereotype Induction and Suggestibility

Leichtman & Ceci (1995) evaluated the effect of stereotypes on 3- to 6-year-old children's memories of a subsequent visit by an adult male, Sam Stone. At weekly intervals before Sam's visit, children were read stories that portrayed Sam as a good-hearted but awkward person. Ten weeks after Sam's visit, children were given an interview that included two leading questions about actions that Sam did not perform (destroying a book, dirtying a teddy bear). Significantly, 30% of the children falsely reported that Sam performed at least one of these actions. Children's false reports were thus likely to have been based on their negative stereotypes of Sam induced before he visited the school (see also Blackwell-Young, Chapter 9).

In the forensic context, the impact of negative stereotypes on children's recollections can be seen in the Little Rascals Day Care and the McMartin Preschool cases, and in the 1987 death row case of Frederico Macias in Texas (Ceci & Bruck, 1995). In the Macias case, it was possible that the child's false testimony could have been influenced by negative information about Macias supplied to the child by her parents *prior* to the episode which the child was alleged to have witnessed. Recent research by Memon, Holliday & Hill (2006) showed that young children were less able to reject misinformation presented prior to a classroom visit by an adult male when that misinformation was positive. An applied analogy can be made to the murders of two British schoolgirls in the summer of 2003 (known as the Soham murders). Both the murderer Ian Huntley and his girlfriend Maxine Carr (guilty of conspiracy to pervert the course of justice) were known to the girls through their connections with the local schools. Indeed, Huntley pretended to assist in early searches for the girls and even appeared on television during the days after the girls' disappearance. It is possible that witnesses did not come forward at first with information about Huntley and Carr's movements and behaviours because they held positive images of them.

VULNERABLE ADULTS

Elderly Eyewitnesses

Older adults represent a special group of witnesses. The fact that in some countries growing numbers of older adults remain active in the community makes it likely that some will witness or be the victim of a crime. Elder abuse (physical, psychological, financial, sexual and neglect) is being reported with increasing frequency. Adults over 75 years are particularly vulnerable and men and women are equally affected (Action on Elder Abuse, 2004). Obtaining eyewitness testimony from young-old and oldest-old individuals, which is forensically relevant, is now becoming a major concern to policy makers and professionals (see Westcott, Chapter 8).

Only a handful of laboratory studies have evaluated older adults' recall accuracy in an eyewitness context. In general, recall is less complete and less accurate (in comparison to young adults) whether the event is a slide show (Yarmey & Kent, 1980), a video clip (List, 1986) or a live staged event (Yarmey, 1993). Similar age-related differences are evident when memory is tested immediately, minutes or days after the to-be-remembered event (Brimacombe *et al.*, 1997; List, 1986; Yarmey, 1993; see also Blackwell-Young, Chapter 9).

Learning-Disabled Witnesses

Individuals with learning disabilities (LDs) are another group of eyewitnesses who are regarded in the criminal justice system as vulnerable witnesses. Such adults are typically reported as slower than normal developing adults to encode, store and retrieve details of an event (Milne & Bull, 2001). This not to say that what they recollect is inaccurate. On the contrary, the number of details recollected is fewer, but just as accurate as for other adult witnesses.

As regards the learning disabled, studies have shown that they are particularly susceptible to the negative effects of social demand factors. Indeed, Kebbell & Hatton (1999) reviewed the research literature and reported that LD adults are more likely to respond 'yes' to questions irrespective of the content of such questions. LD adults are also more likely than other adults to make up answers in response to questioning. Given these characteristics it is not surprising that LD adults (and children) can be highly suggestible depending on how well they are questioned/interviewed. Caution must be taken when interviewing these most vulnerable witnesses.

Learning-disabled adults may have particular problems with retrieving information from memory. Indeed, given that these witnesses have been found to be highly suggestible (e.g. Cardone & Dent, 1996; Milne, Clare & Bull, 1999), it is of major importance that LD adults, like other groups of vulnerable witnesses, be questioned appropriately and non-suggestively. Some of the special protocols which have been developed for interviewing vulnerable witnesses are described in the next section.

FORENSIC INTERVIEW PROTOCOLS

The Cognitive Interview

The *Original Cognitive Interview* protocol was devised by Geiselman, Fisher, Firstenberg *et al.* (1984) for use with adult witnesses. Memory trace retrieval is usually enhanced when there is an overlap between the encoding and retrieval environments (i.e. encoding specificity) (Tulving & Thomson, 1973). This overlap is achieved by context reinstatement: mental reconstruction of the physical and personal contexts surrounding the event to be recalled. A second instruction is to report all: relate all details regardless of their perceived relevance. Individual memory traces may also be accessed via several different retrieval paths minimizing reliance on prior knowledge and expectations. Varied retrieval (Tulving, 1974) is facilitated by a change perspective instruction: recall the event from several relevant perspectives; and a change order instruction: recall the event in a different temporal order (e.g. backwards).

The *Revised Cognitive Interview* (Fisher & Geiselman, 1992) retains the four cognitive mnemonics. However, it also stresses the importance of social and communication factors (e.g. rapport, transfer of control of the interview to the interviewee). Social factors also play a role in determining the extent to which memory performance is influenced by advancing age. For example, older adults' accuracy on memory tests was reduced if they were first read a statement that portrayed a negative stereotype about memory in old age (e.g. ageing is detrimental for memory) (Hess & Hinson, 2006). Such stereotypes probably make older adults overly cautious about reporting information. A Cognitive Interview may ameliorate this in part because it stresses the importance of reporting any detail, regardless of its perceived relevance (Report All instruction) and it emphasizes that the witness is the expert about the to-be-remembered event (Transfer of Control instruction). For practitioners, shortened modified interview protocols that facilitate accurate recollections are important given the potential problems surrounding interviewing vulnerable witnesses (limited attention span, faster forgetting) and pressures on police and other professionals to obtain maximum information as soon as possible after a crime.

Misinformation Effects and the Cognitive Interview

A few studies have examined whether Cognitive Interview memory-jogging methods minimize the impact of misleading questions on school-aged child witnesses. In Memon, Holley, Wark *et al.*'s (1996) study, for example, 8- and 9-year-olds watched a short film, then 12 days later were given misleading and neutral questions before and after a Cognitive Interview employing only two of the Cognitive Interview mnemonics, *context reinstatement* and *report all*. Memon *et al.* (1996) found no differences in responding to pre-interview questions. When children were questioned post-interview, however, those given a prior Cognitive Interview gave more correct responses to misleading questions than those given a structured (control) interview (for similar findings see Milne & Bull, 2003). Hayes & Delamothe (1997) reported that the *context reinstatement* and *report all* mnemonics failed to reduce 6- and 10-year-old children's acceptance of misleading information if presented *before* the interview. It is clear that the timings of the misinformation and the forensic interview are the keys to these disparate findings. Indeed, Holliday (2003b) evaluated this proposition and reported that 5- and 8-year-old children's reporting of misinformation during interviews and on subsequent recognition memory tests was significantly reduced if they had been interviewed with a developmentally modified Cognitive Interview before they were asked for a free recall narrative and before they were given a memory test. Importantly, these findings only held for misinformation that was self-generated in response to cues given by the experimenter in the post-event misinformation phase.

Which Cognitive Interview Mnemonics are Responsible for the Improvements in Children's Recollection?

Given the findings outlined above, the next step in Holliday's programme of research was to see whether a shorter version of the Modified Cognitive Interview could be as effective at reducing suggestibility. Given the brief attention span of very young children, a short version of Holliday's (2003b) Modified Cognitive Interview would be advantageous.

Hence, Holliday and Albon (2004) examined the effects of several variations of a Cognitive Interview on 4- and 5-year-old children's correct recall and subsequent reporting of misinformation. Children viewed an event followed by misinformation that was read or self-generated before completing a Cognitive Interview. Developmentally modified Cognitive Interviews elicited significantly more correct details than control interviews. As Holliday (2003b) found, a Cognitive Interview presented after misleading information reduced children's reporting of misinformation during the interview and reduced reporting of self-generated misinformation on memory tests. Crucially, however, just two Cognitive Interview mnemonics, report all and context reinstatement in combination offered some protection against the negative effects of misinformation on memory. The implication of this research is that a developmentally appropriate interview comprising these two Cognitive Interview mnemonics would take approximately 70% of the time of a full Cognitive Interview.

The Cognitive Interview with Learning-Disabled Adults

A small handful of researchers have tested Cognitive Interview protocols with LD adults. For example, Brown and Geiselman (1990) reported a one-third increase in correct details in a Cognitive Interview in comparison to a control interview. (LD adults recalled fewer correct details than other adults, which did not vary by interview condition.)

In Milne, Clare & Bull's (1999) study, adults with mild LD adults and typically developed adults watched a short film of an accident and were interviewed the next day with either a Cognitive Interview or a structured (control) interview (Structured: Köhnken, 1993). An increase in correct details was found for those given a Cognitive Interview. Unfortunately, however, LD adults in the Cognitive Interview condition reported more confabulated details about the witnessed persons in the video than LD adults in a structured interview (Milne & Bull, 2001). Clearly, there is a great need for more research attention to be given to these vulnerable witnesses and victims.

Interview Protocols: Enhanced Rapport Cognitive, Modified Cognitive, Full Cognitive, Report All & Change Order, Report All & Context Reinstatement and Structured interviews	
Cognitive Interviews	*Structured Interview*
1. *Rapport building phase*	1. *Rapport building phase*
a. Describe favourite game[1]	
b. Explain aims/rules of interview[a]	1a. Explain aims/rules of interview
2. *Free recall phase*	2. *Free recall phase*
a. Context Reinstatement[1-3,5]	Free recall report request
b. Report all[1-5]	
c. Change Order[1-4]	
d. Change perspective[3]	
e. Free recall report request[a]	
3. *Questioning phase*	3. *Questioning phase*
Information provided by child only is used as a basis of open-ended & specific questions[a]	Information provided by child only is used as a basis of open- ended & specific questions
4. *Closure*[a]	4. *Closure*

Notes: [a]All interviews; [1]Enhanced rapport Cognitive interview; [2]Modified Cognitive interview; [3]Full Cognitive interview; [4]Report all + Change Order interview; [5]Report all + Context Reinstatement interview.

Table 4.3: Minimizing Misinformation Effects in Young Children with Cognitive Interview Mnemonics. From Holliday, R.E. & Albon, A.J. (2004). Minimizing Misinformation Effects in Young Children with Cognitive Interview Mnemonics, *Applied Cognitive Psychology, 18,* 263–281. Reproduced by permission of John Wiley & Sons, Ltd.

The 'Memorandum' and 'Achieving Best Evidence'

In 1989, following the recommendations of an official committee headed by Justice Pigot, video-recorded interviews have been used as a substitute for live examination-in-chief at trial in cases of child witnesses. The Criminal Justice Act 1991 incorporated the admissibility of video-recorded interviews as evidence-in-chief and courts have followed this law, leading to a significant increase in the number of cases in which children give evidence at court (see Chapter 8).

    Given the evidential status of the recommended interviews, the Pigot Committee recommended that specific guidance should be prepared to ensure that interviews were conducted in a manner acceptable to the courts with the minimum of suggestion or mis-information. The Criminal Justice Act 1991 also established that police officers and social workers should have joint responsibility for conducting such interviews with children involved in cases of alleged abuse. Interviewers must follow the guidance first outlined in the *Memorandum of Good Practice on video-recorded interviews with child witnesses for criminal proceedings* (MOGP) (Home Office & Department of Health, 1992) and then incorporated in *Achieving Best Evidence in Criminal Proceedings:*

The MOGP (1992) and the ABE (2001) make the following recommendations:

Initial phase:
- Develop rapport with the child.
- Interview the child as soon as possible after the crime/abuse.
- Conduct interviews in an informal setting with trained interviewers.
- Explain the purpose and process of the interview.
- Establish the ground rules for responding to questions; tell the child that not every question must be answered, nor has every question a right or wrong answer. This minimizes social demand suggestibility; tell the child to answer *don't know* when necessary.

Free narrative phase:
Encourage free narrative.

Employ a phased-approach in questioning:
Begin with open-ended questions (e.g. *Please tell me in your own words what happened?*), followed by specific questions (e.g. *What colour was his shirt?*) and non-leading questions (e.g. *Where was your sister when this was happening?*), then closed questions (*Do you remember anything about his clothing?*) and leading questions only when necessary (*What happened after he took you into the bathroom?* – when the child has not mentioned being taken into the bathroom.)

Avoid repeated questions.

Minimize or avoid forced-choice questions (*Was the shirt red or blue?*).

Minimize or avoid multi-part questions (*Did he ask you to go upstairs with him and did you then go into the bedroom?*).

At the end of the interview summarize what the child has said (in the child's own words) and invite questions.

Guidance for vulnerable or intimidated witnesses, including children (ABE) (Home Office & Department of Health, 2001). While the Memorandum was specifically designed for child witnesses, ABE was written for all vulnerable witnesses, including the elderly and the learning disabled. Both protocols were developed with substantial input from psychologists with expertise in interviewing and eyewitness testimony.

How Effective Has the Memorandum of Good Practice Been in the Field?

Davies, Westcott & Horan (2000) evaluated a number of MOGP interviews conducted by police officers with children aged 4 to 14 years in the context of alleged sexual abuse. Davies *et al.* found that the length of the interviews varied considerably from 20 to 90 minutes (the MOGP recommended no longer than 60 minutes). Little time was spent developing rapport (on average less than 10 minutes). Specific questions produced more information in the young children; open-ended questions were more effective in the oldest children.

Likewise, Sternberg *et al.* (2001) evaluated the quality of 119 videoed MOGP interviews in which children aged 4 to 13 years appeared to allege abuse. The police interviewers employed forced-choice questions much more often than open-ended questions. Indeed, Sternberg *et al.* found that more than a third of the details reported by the children were in response to forced-choice and leading questions.

Guidance on Interviewing Child Witnesses in Scotland (Scottish Executive, 2003)

In 2003, the Scottish Executive published a set of investigative interview protocols for use with children and other vulnerable witnesses such as learning-disabled and elderly adults. The Steering Committee was headed by Professor Amina Memon and her colleague Lynn Hulse from the University of Aberdeen. This comprehensive document is very similar to ABE and can be downloaded at: http://www.scotland.gov.uk/Publications/2003/09/18265/27045.

Which Works Best with Children – A Cognitive or A Memorandum-Type Interview?

Researchers have reported mixed results concerning the effectiveness of the Cognitive Interview with children. An important finding is that, in general, a Cognitive Interview elicits more correct information than standard or structured interviews without compromising accuracy in children aged 7 to 12 years (Geiselman & Padilla, 1988; Granhag & Spjut, 2001; Holliday, 2003a, b; McCauley & Fisher, 1996; Saywitz, Geiselman & Bornstein, 1992). Nonetheless, some researchers (e.g. Hayes & Delamothe, 1997; McCauley & Fisher, 1995; Memon *et al.*, 1997) have found a concomitant increase in reporting of incorrect and/or confabulated details.

Researchers now examine the types of details that are enhanced by a Cognitive Interview. Milne and Bull (2003), for example, reported that 8- to 9-year-old children recalled more correct person and action details in a Cognitive Interview than in a structured interview. Granhag & Spjut (2001) and Memon *et al.* (1997), on the other hand, found no such differences in reporting of person details in school-aged children. More correct information was reported in a Cognitive Interview with 5- to 12-year-olds than a control interview based on the MOGP and ABE (Granhag & Spjut, 2001; McCauley & Fisher, 1996; Saywitz *et al.*, 1992).

Holliday (2003b) compared two interview techniques, a modified Cognitive Interview based on the revised protocols developed by Fisher & Geiselman (1992) and an interview modelled on the MOGP (Home Office & Department of Health, 1992). The study found that children's reports were more complete and they recalled 27% more correct information during a modified Cognitive Interview than in a MOGP interview. Importantly, a Cognitive Interview enhanced reporting of correct details in children as young as four and five years. Of forensic relevance were the findings that a modified Cognitive Interview produced more pieces of person, action and object information relative to a MOGP interview.

A recent study conducted by Wright & Holliday (2007a) evaluated older witnesses' recall of a short film using either the *Memorandum of Good Practice* or a revised Cognitive Interview. Recall was less complete and less accurate for older than for young adults. There was a trend for correct recall of person, action and object details to be improved using a revised (i.e. shortened) Cognitive Interview irrespective of age (see also Wright & Holliday, 2007b).

SUMMARY

- Vulnerable witnesses and victims of crime include children, the elderly and learning-disabled.
- Such witnesses present special difficulties in ensuring that they give their best evidence.
- Interview procedures need to be based on knowledge of how memory operates.
- The stages of memory-encoding, storage and retrieval – and strategies employed to ensure material is accurately retained and retrieved from memory.
- Factors that could produce unreliable evidence in vulnerable witnesses especially young children (interviewer bias, knowledge, compliance to adult authority figures, memory).
- Children's suggestibility and the theoretical explanations of this factor.
- Interview protocols have been especially developed for children and other vulnerable witnesses.
- These include the Cognitive Interview and the various guidance documents produced by the Home Office and Department of Health (MOGP in 1992; ABE in 2001).
- Research which has evaluated the effectiveness of these procedures with different groups of vulnerable witnesses.

ESSAY/DISCUSSION QUESTIONS

1. Compare and contrast the trace-alteration and trace-blocking theories of the misinformation effect.
2. How does fuzzy-trace theory explain age differences in suggestibility in children?
3. Is a cognitive interview viable with young children?
4. Discuss the impact of compliance on children's memories for events in which they have been witnesses or participants?

REFERENCES

Action on Elder Abuse. (2004). *Hidden voices: Older people's experience of abuse*. London: Help the Aged.

Bartlett, F. (1932). *Remembering: A study in experimental and social psychology*. Cambridge: Cambridge University Press.

Belli, R.F., Lindsay, D.S., Gales, M.S., & McCarthy, T.T. (1994). Memory impairment and source misattribution in post-event misinformation experiments with short retention intervals. *Memory and Cognition, 22*, 40–54.

Belli, R.F., Windschitl, P.D., McCarthy, T.T., & Winfrey, S.E. (1992). Detecting memory impairment with a modified test procedure – manipulating retention interval with centrally presented event items. *Journal of Experimental Psychology: Learning, Memory and Cognition, 18*, 356–367.

Beuhring, T. & Kee, D.W. (1987). Developmental relationships among metamemory, elaborative strategy use, and associative memory. *Journal of Experimental Child Psychology, 44*, 377–400.

Bjorklund, D.F. (2005). *Children's thinking*, 4th edn. Belmont, CA: Wadsworth/Thomson.

Bowman, L.L. & Zaragoza, M.S. (1989). Similarity of encoding context does not influence resistance to memory impairment following misinformation. *The American Journal of Psychology, 102*, 249–264.

Brainerd, C.J. & Reyna, V.F. (1998). Fuzzy-trace theory and children's false memories. *Journal of Experimental Child Psychology, 71*, 81–129.

Brainerd, C.J. & Reyna, V.F. (2005). *The science of false memory*. New York: Oxford University Press.

Brainerd, C.J. & Reyna, V.F. (2007). Explaining developmental reversals in false memory. *Psychological Science. 18*, 442–448.

Brainerd, C.J., Reyna, V.F., & Forrest, T.J. (2002). Are young children susceptible to the false-memory illusion? *Child Development, 73*, 1363–1377.

Brainerd, C.J., Reyna, V.F., & Mojardin, A.H. (1999). Conjoint recognition. *Psychological Review, 106*, 160–179.

Brainerd, C.J., Reyna, V.F., Howe, M.L., & Kingma, J. (1990). The development of forgetting and reminiscence. *Monographs of the Society for Research in Child Development, 55*.

Brainerd, C.J., Stein, L., & Reyna, V.F. (1998). On the development of conscious and unconscious memory. *Developmental Psychology, 34*, 342–357.

Brimacombe, C.A., Quinton, N., Nance, N., & Garrioch, L. (1997). Is age irrelevant? Perceptions of young and old adult eyewitnesses. *Law and Human Behaviour, 21*, 619–634.

Brown, C.L. & Geiselman, R.E. (1990). Eyewitness testimony of mentally retarded: Effect of the Cognitive Interview. *Journal of Police and Criminal Psychology, 6*, 14–22.

Bruck, M. & Ceci, S.J. (1999). The suggestibility of children's memory. *Annual Review of Psychology, 50*, 419–439.

Bruck, M., Ceci, S.J., Francoeur, E., & Renick, A. (1995) Anatomically detailed dolls do not facilitate preschoolers' reports of a pediatric examination involving genital touching. *Journal of Experimental Psychology: Applied, 1*, 95–109.

Bruck, M., Ceci, S.J., & Melnyk, L. (1997). External and internal sources of variation in the creation of false reports in children. *Learning and Individual Differences, 9*, 289–316.

Cardone, D. & Dent, H. (1996). Memory and interrogative suggestibility: The effects of modality of information presentation and retrieval conditions upon the suggestibility scores of people with learning disabilities. *Legal and Criminological Psychology, 1*, 165–177.

Ceci, S.J. & Bruck, M. (1993). Suggestibility of the child witness: An historical review and synthesis. *Psychological Bulletin, 113*, 403–439.

Ceci, S.J. & Bruck, M. (1995). *Jeopardy in the courtroom: A scientific analysis of children's testimony*. Washington, DC: American Psychological Association.

Ceci, S.J., Caves, R.D., & Howe, M.J.A. (1981). Children's long-term memory for information that is incongruous with their prior knowledge. *British Journal of Psychology, 72*, 443–450.

Ceci, S. J., Huffman, M. L. C., Smith, E., & Loftus, E. F. (1994a). Repeatedly thinking about a non-event: Source misattributions among preschoolers. *Consciousness and Cognition, 3*, 388–407.

Ceci, S.J., Loftus, E.F., Leichtman, M.D., & Bruck, M. (1994b). The possible role of source mis-attributions in the creation of false beliefs among preschoolers. *International Journal of Clinical and Experimental Hypnosis, 42*, 304–320.

Ceci, S.J., Ross, D.F., & Toglia, M.P. (1987). Suggestibility of children's memory: Psycho-legal implications. *Journal of Experimental Psychology: General, 116*, 38–49.

Chi, M.T. (1978). Knowledge structures and memory development. In R.S. Siegler (Ed.), *Children's thinking: What develops?* (pp. 73–96). Hillsdale, NJ: Erlbaum.

Davies, G.M., Westcott, H.L., & Horan, N. (2000). The impact of questioning style on the content of investigative interviews with suspected child sexual abuse victims. *Psychology, Crime and Law, 6*, 81–97.

Fisher, R.P. & Geiselman, R.E. (1992). *Memory-enhancing techniques for investigative interviewing: The Cognitive Interview*. Springfield, IL: Charles C. Thomas.

Flavell, J., Beach, D.R., & Chinsky, J.M. (1966). Spontaneous verbal rehearsal in a memory task as a function of age. *Child Development, 37*, 283–299.

Garry, M., Manning, C.G., Loftus, E.F., & Sherman, S.J. (1996). Imagination inflation: imagining a childhood event inflates confidence that it occurred. *Psychonomic Bulletin and Review, 3*, 208–214

Garven, S., Wood, J.M., Malpass, R.S., & Shaw, J.S. (1998). More than suggestion: The effect of interviewing techniques from the McMartin Preschool case. *Journal of Applied Psychology, 83*, 347–359.

Geiselman, R.E., Fisher, R.P., Firstenberg, I., *et al.* (1984). Enhancement of eyewitness memory: An empirical evaluation of the cognitive interview. *Journal of Police Science and Administration, 12*, 74–80.

Geiselman, R.E. & Padilla, J. (1988). Interviewing child witnesses with the cognitive interview. *Journal of Police Science and Administration, 16*, 236–242.

Goodman, G.S. & Quas, J.A. (1997). Trauma and memory: Individual differences in children's recounting of a stressful experience. In N.L. Stein, P.A. Ornstein, B. Tversky, & C. Brainerd (Eds), *Memory for Everyday and Emotional Events* (pp. 267–294). Mahwah, NJ: Erlbaum.

Granhag, P.A. & Spjut, E. (2001). Children's recall of the unfortunate fakir: A further test of the enhanced cognitive interview. In R. Roesch, R.R. Corrado, & R. Dempster (Eds). *Psychology in the courts,* (pp. 209–222). London: Routledge.

Guilliatt, R. (1996). *Talk of the devil: Repressed memory and the ritual abuse witch-hunt*. Melbourne: Text Publishing.

Hayes, B.K. & Delamothe, K. (1997). Cognitive interviewing procedures and suggestibility in children's recall. *Journal of Applied Psychology, 82*, 562–577.

Hess, T.M. & Hinson, J.T. (2006). Age-related variation in the influences of aging stereotypes. *Psychology and Aging*, 621–625.

Holliday, R.E. (2003a). The effect of a prior cognitive interview on children's acceptance of misinformation. *Applied Cognitive Psychology, 17*, 443–457.

Holliday, R.E. (2003b). Reducing misinformation effects in children with Cognitive interviews: Dissociating recollection and familiarity. *Child Development, 74*, 728–751.

Holliday, R.E. & Albon, A.J. (2004).Minimising misinformation effects in young children with cognitive interview mnemonics. *Applied Cognitive Psychology*, 18, 263–281.

Holliday, R.E., Douglas, K., & Hayes, B.K. (1999). Children's eyewitness suggestibility: Memory trace strength revisited. *Cognitive Development, 14*, 443–462.

Holliday, R.E. & Hayes, B.K. (2000). Dissociating automatic and intentional processes in children's eyewitness memory. *Journal of Experimental Child Psychology, 75*, 1–42.

Holliday, R.E. & Hayes, B.K. (2001) Automatic and intentional processes in children's eyewitness suggestibility. *Cognitive Development 16*, 617–636.

Holliday, R.E. & Hayes, B.K. (2002). Automatic and intentional processes in children's recognition memory: the reversed misinformation effect. *Applied Cognitive Psychology, 16*, 1–16.

Holliday, R.E., Reyna, V.F., & Hayes, B.K. (2002). Memory processes underlying misinformation effects in child witnesses. *Developmental Review, 22*, 37–77.

Home Office and Department of Health (1992). *Memorandum of good practice on video recorded interviews with child witnesses for criminal proceedings*. London: HMSO.

Home Office and Department of Health (2001). *Achieving best evidence in criminal proceedings: Guidance for vulnerable or intimidated witnesses, Including Children*. London: HMSO.

Howe, M.L. (1991). Misleading children's story recall: Forgetting and reminiscence of the facts. *Developmental Psychology, 27*, 746–762.

Johnson, M.K., Hashtroudi, S., & Lindsay, D.S. (1993). Source monitoring. *Psychological Bulletin, 114*, 3–28.

Kebbell, M. & Hatton, C. (1999). People with mental retardation as witnesses in court: a review. *Mental Retardation, 37*, 179–187.

Kobasigawa, A. (1974). Utilization of retrieval cues by children in recall. *Child Development, 45*, 127–134.

Köhnken, G. (1993). *The structured interview: A step-by-step introduction*. Lampinen, J.M. & Smith, V.L. (1995). The incredible (and sometimes incredulous) child witness: Child eyewitnesses' sensitivity to source credibility cues. *Journal of Applied Psychology, 80*, 621–627.

Leichtman, M.D. & Ceci, S.J. (1995). The effects of stereotypes and suggestions on children's suggestibility. *Developmental Psychology, 31*, 568–578.

List, J.A. (1986). Age and schematic differences in the reliability of eyewitness testimony. *Developmental Psychology, 22*, 50–57.

Loftus, E.F. (1977). Shifting human color memory. *Memory and Cognition, 5*, 696–699.

Loftus, E.F. (1996). *Eyewitness testimony*. Cambridge, MA: Harvard University Press.

Loftus, E.F., Donders, K., Hoffman, H.G., & Schooler, J.W. (1989). Creating new memories that are quickly accessed and confidently held. *Memory and Cognition, 17*, 607–616.

Loftus, E.F. & Ketcham, K. (1991). *Witness for the defense: The accused, the eyewitness and the expert who puts memory on trial*. New York: St Martin's Press.

Loftus, E.F., Miller, D.G., & Burns, H.J. (1978). Semantic integration of verbal information into visual memory. *Journal of Experimental Psychology: Human Learning and Memory, 4*, 19–31.

McCauley, M.R. & Fisher, R.P. (1995). Facilitating children's eyewitness recall with the revised cognitive interview. *Journal of Applied Psychology, 80*, 510–516.

McCauley, M.R. & Fisher, R.P. (1996). Enhancing children's eyewitness testimony with the cognitive interview. In G. Davies, S. Lloyd-Bostock, M. McMurran, & C. Wilson (Eds). *Psychology, Law, and Criminal Justice* (pp. 127–133). Berlin: De Gruyter.

McCloskey, M. & Zaragoza, M. (1985). Misleading post-event information and memory for events: Arguments and evidence against memory impairment hypotheses. *Journal of Experimental Psychology: General, 114*, 1–16.

Melissa, K., Welch-Ross, M.K., & Schmidt, C.R. (1996). Schema development and children's constructive story memory: evidence for a developmental model. *Child Development, 67*, 820–835.

Memon, A., Holliday, R.E., & Hill, C. (2006). Pre-event stereotypes and misinformation effects in young children. *Memory, 14*, 104–114.

Memon, A., Holley, A., Wark, L., *et al.* (1996). Reducing suggestibility in child witness interviews. *Applied Cognitive Psychology, 10*, 503–518.

Memon, A., Wark, L., Bull, R., & Köhnken, G. (1997). Isolating the effects of the cognitive interview techniques. *British Journal of Psychology, 88*, 179–197.

Miller, G.A. (1956). The magical number seven, plus or minus two: Some limits on our capacity for processing information. *Psychological Review, 63*, 81–97.

Milne, R. & Bull, R. (2001). Interviewing witnesses with learning disabilities for legal purposes. *British Journal of Learning Disabilities, 29*, 93–97.

Milne, R. & Bull, R. (2003). Does the cognitive interview help children to resist the effects of suggestive questioning? *Legal and Criminological Psychology, 8*, 21–38.

Milne R., Clare I.C.H., & Bull R. (1999). Using the cognitive interview with adults with mild learning disabilities. *Psychology, Crime Law, 5*, 81–101.

Moely, B.E., Olson F.A., Halwes, T.H., & Flavell, J.H. (1969). Production deficiency in young children's clustered recall. *Developmental Psychology, 1*, 26–34.

Morton, J. (1991). Cognitive pathologies of memory: A headed records analysis. In W. Kessen, A. Ortonly, & F. Craik (Eds), *Memories, thoughts, and emotions: Essays in honor of George Mandler* (pp. 199–210). Hillsdale, NJ: Erlbaum.

Nelson, K. & Gruendel, J. (1981). Generalised event representations: Basic building blocks of cognitive development. In M.E. Lamb & A.L. Brown (Eds), *Advances in developmental psychology* (Vol. 1), pp 131–158. Hillsdale, NJ: Lawrence Erlbaum.

Ornstein, P.A., Merritt, K.A., Baker-Ward, L., *et al.* (1998). Children's knowledge, expectation, and long-term retention. *Applied Cognitive Psychology, 12*, 387–405.

Pendergrast, M. (1996). *Victims of memory.* London: HarperCollins.

Pillemer, D.B., Picariello, M.L., & Pruett, J.C. (1994). Very long-term memories of a salient pre-school event. *Applied Cognitive Psychology, 8*, 95–106.

Poole, D.A. & White, L.T. (1991). Effects of question repetition on the eyewitness testimony of children and adults. *Developmental Psychology, 27*, 975–986.

Poole, D.A. & White, L.T. (1995). Tell me again and again: Stability and change in the repeated testimonies of children and adults. In M. Zaragoza, J.R. Graham, G.N.N. Hall, R. Hirschman, & Y.S. Ben-Porath (Eds), *Memory, suggestibility, and eyewitness testimony in children and adults.* Thousand Oaks, CA: Sage.

Reyna, V.F., Holliday, R.E. & Marche, T. (2002). Explaining the development of false memories. *Developmental Review, 22*, 436–489. Special issue on developmental forensics.

Reyna, V.F., Mills B., Estrada, S., & Brainerd, C.J. (2007). False memory in children: Data, theory, and legal implications. In M. Toglia & D. Read (Eds), *The handbook of eyewitness psychology* (Vol. 1): *Memory for Events*. Mahwah, NJ: Erlbaum.

Reyna, V.F. & Titcomb, A.L. (1997). Constraints on the suggestibility of eyewitness testimony: A fuzzy-trace analysis. In D.G. Payne & F.G. Conrad (Eds), *A synthesis of basic and applied approaches to human memory* (pp. 157–174). Hillsdale, NJ: Erlbaum.

Saywitz, K. & Camparo, L. (1998). Interviewing child witnesses. A developmental perspective. *Child Abuse and Neglect, 22*, 825–843.

Saywitz, K.J., Geiselman, R.E., & Bornstein, G.K. (1992). Effects of cognitive interviewing and practice on children's recall performance. *Journal of Applied Psychology, 77*, 744–756.

Schneider, W., Korkel, J., & Weinert, F.E. (1989). Domain-specific knowledge and memory performance: A comparison of high- and low-aptitude children. *Journal of Educational Psychology, 81*, 306–312.

Schreiber, T. & Sergent, S. (1998). The role of commitment in producing misinformation effects in eyewitness memory. *Psychonomic Bulletin and Review, 5*, 443–448.

Sternberg, K.J., Lamb, M.E., Davies, G.M., & Westcott, H.L. (2001). The Memorandum of Good Practice: theory versus application. *Child Abuse Neglect, 26*, 669–681.

Summit, R.C. (1983). The child sexual abuse accommodation syndrome, *Child Abuse and Neglect, 7*, 177–193.

Toglia, M.P., Ross, D.F., Ceci, S.J., & Hembrooke, H. (1992). The suggestibility of children's memory: A social-psychological and cognitive interpretation. In M.L. Howe, C.J. Brainerd, & V.F. Reyna (Eds), *Development of long-term retention* (pp. 217–241). New York: Springer-Verlag.

Tulving, E. (1974). Cue-dependent forgetting. *American Scientist, 62*, 74–2.

Tulving, E. & Thomson, D.M. (1973). Encoding specificity and the retrieval processes in episodic memory. *Psychological Review, 80*, 352–373.

Waterman, A., Blades, M., & Spencer, C. (2002). How and why do children respond to nonsensical questions? In H.L. Westcott, G.M. Davies, & R.H.C. Bull (Eds). *Children's testimony*. Chichester: John Wiley & Sons.

Wright, A.M. & Holliday, R.E. (2007a). Enhancing the recall of young, young-old and old-old adults with the cognitive interview and a modified version of the cognitive interview. *Applied Cognitive Psychology, 21*, 19–43.

Wright, A.M. & Holliday, R.E. (2007b). Interviewing cognitively impaired older adults: How useful is a cognitive interview? *Memory, 15*, 17–33.

Yarmey, A.D. (1993). Adult age and gender differences in eyewitness recall in field settings. *Journal of Applied Social Psychology, 23*, 1921–1932.

Yarmey, A.D. & Kent, J. (1980). Eyewitness identification by elderly and young adults. *Law and Human Behavior, 4*, 359–371.

Zaragoza, M.S. (1987). Memory, suggestibility, and eyewitness testimony in children and adults. In S.J. Ceci, M. Toglia, & D. Ross (Eds), *Children's eyewitness memory*. (pp. 53–78). NY: Springer-Verlag.

Zaragoza, M.S. (1991). Preschool children's susceptibility to memory impairment. In J. Doris (Ed.), *The suggestibility of children's recollections: Implications for eyewitness testimony* (pp. 27–39). Washington, DC: American Psychological Association.

ANNOTATED READING LIST

Ceci, S.J. & Bruck, M. (1995). *Jeopardy in the courtroom: A scientific analysis of children's testimony*. Washington, DC: American Psychological Association. *Essential reading – detailed accounts of day care cases in the United States. Also very good for misinformation theories.*

Bjorklund, D.F. (2005). *Children's thinking*, 4th edn. Belmont, CA: Wadsworth/Thomson. *Very good coverage of issues such as memory strategies, memory theories.*

Garven, S., Wood, J.M., Malpass, R.S., & Shaw, J.S. (1998). More than suggestion: The effect of interviewing techniques from the McMartin preschool case. *Journal of Applied Psychology, 83*, 347–359. *Interviewing methods used in this important case.*

Holliday, R.E. (2003). Reducing misinformation effects in children with cognitive interviews: Dissociating recollection and familiarity. *Child Development, 74*, 728–751. *Latest research on evaluating the usefulness of Cognitive Interview protocols with children.*

Holliday, R.E., Douglas, K., & Hayes, B.K. (1999). Children's eyewitness suggestibility: memory trace strength revisited. *Cognitive Development, 14*, 443–62. *Evaluation of memory trace strength theory of suggestibility.*

Reyna, V.F., Holliday, R.E., & Marche, T. (2002). Explaining the development of false memories. *Developmental Review, 22*, 436–489. *A review article covering suggestibility, misinformation, and memory illusions in children.*

5

INTERVIEWING SUSPECTS

Ulf Holmberg
Kristianstad University, Sweden

Ola Kronkvist
Växjö University, Sweden

 Imagine the situation where a crime has occurred, for example an assault outside a restaurant or a burglary at your home. Many questions will arise about what exactly has happened and, if the suspect has been caught in the act, why did he or she commit the crime? If the suspect was not caught in the act and an investigation has identified a certain person as a possible suspect, the police will ask questions about the suspect's alibi. During the crime investigation and the trial, many questions need to be answered about when, where, what, who and why a certain crime has been committed. According to the United Nations Convention on Human Rights, the suspect must be given an opportunity to express and explain his or her perspective regarding an accusation. Thus, it is necessary for the police to interview the suspect.

The following three convicted criminals' experiences of police interviews will give the reader a glimpse of what really happens during police interviews with suspects. In the first interview, with a suspect accused of murder, the police officer repeatedly asked the same questions about what the suspect had been doing during the previous 24 hours. This confession-seeking police interview resulted in conflict. As the police officer continually asked the same kind of questions, it forced the suspect to conclude that the officer was just trying to 'grill' him and so the suspect remained silent (Holmberg, Christianson & Wexler, 2007, p. 357). Such a confrontational approach can create external pressures that lead to suspects displaying 'avoidance' during the interview (Gudjonsson & Petursson, 1991; Gudjonsson & Sigurdsson, 1994).

In the second interview, a man convicted of rape described his encounter with a police officer who recognized his needs and emotions. In his own words he said,

then I got some questions and I started to talk, she [the police officer] was quite, quite broad-minded. She showed respect for me, I felt that it was something more than just a job for her, like 'now interrogation – bang boom' and nothing more – but she might possibly talk about it. (Holmberg, Christianson & Wexler, 2007, p. 361)

In the third case, a convicted rapist's description of his police interview indicates that the police interview may 'open doors' as well as 'shut doors' (Holmberg, 1996):

It was easier for me to talk to people who acted properly because people who interview people, they should not punish you, but they can do so just that by their way of talking, showing their hate for me as a human being, and at that moment you turn around and return their hate.

Obviously, one of the most important parts of a crime investigation, the interview with the suspect, may be conducted and experienced in different ways and in this chapter we will discuss different kinds of police interview. As an introduction, we start by examining the recommendations found in interrogation manuals. This throws light on the confession culture, the assumption that most suspects are liars and the emphasis upon psychologically coercive tactics. The next section describes the effects on a police officer's behaviour while interrogating and questioning a suspect according to the guidance embodied in such manuals. One possible consequence of a confession-seeking interrogation is a false confession and the impact of this, as well as other explanations as to why some people falsely confess to a crime, will be discussed in the third part. Finally, we take a step from interrogation to investigative interviewing and give an account of what research has found regarding interviewing suspects. In other words, what could work from a human rights perspective that could also increase a suspect's readiness to talk (with the added hope that this might be a first step toward rehabilitation and a life without crime).

INTERROGATION MANUALS: WHAT ARE POLICE OFFICERS TOLD TO DO?

In almost any profession, there are manuals available providing normative guidelines as to how people should go about their work. Policing, and the interrogation of suspects, is no exception. A close look at 20 interrogation manuals and handbooks published in

> **The nine steps of the Reid Technique**
> Direct positive confrontation
> Theme development
> Handling denials
> Overcoming objections
> Procurement and retention of suspect's attention
> Handling suspect's passive mood
> Presenting an alternative question
> Having suspect orally relate various details of offence
> Converting an oral confession into a written confession

Figure 5.1: The nine steps of the Reid Technique

English reveals some concerns regarding strategy and an apparent neglect of human rights issues. A review of these manuals raises several issues and a crucial question about whether police interviews with suspects are about eliciting information or obtaining confessions.

One of the more obvious differences between the manuals is how they portray the very purpose of interrogation. Manuals from the US totally dominate the market (18 out of 20 in this review) and lay great emphasis on how to obtain a confession from a suspect. Several of them appear to have been strongly influenced by the 'Reid Technique' (Inbau *et al.*, 2001). This involves a nine-step interrogation process, during which the suspect's resistance to confess is gradually broken down.

Several manuals (e.g. Inbau *et al.*, 2001; Palmiotto, 2004; Royal & Schutt, 1976) promote the idea that an interrogation is to be preceded by an interview. Thus, the spokespersons for this approach make a distinction between the interview and the inter-rogation, and argue that the purpose of the interview is to obtain information and facts in order to establish whether the suspect is guilty or not. According to Buckley (2006), the interview step/phase should be non-accusatory during which the suspect may vol-unteer useful information and reveal behaviour that the interviewer should evaluate in depth to make assessments of the suspect's credibility (Kassin, 2006). The founders of the 'Reid Technique' claim that interviewers can be trained to detect lies at an 85% level of accuracy (which exceeds the success rate found in any lie-detection experiment in published research). Thousands of people, all over the world, have been tested in lie-detection studies and these psychological studies have found that individuals cannot detect lies at levels much above chance (Kassin, 2006; Vrij, 2000; see Granhag, Chapter 6). According to Buckley (2006), when the interviewer believes that the sus-pect has not revealed the truth, the suspect is ready to be interrogated. This second step/phase urges the interrogator to provide at least 95% of the conversation and not to ask any questions. Weinberg (2002) argues that if the interrogator asks questions, this reveals insecurity regarding the guilt of the suspect, which is not regarded as a good strategy. The sole purpose of the interrogation appears to be to obtain a confes-sion, and for some suspects it means to be persuaded to tell the truth (Buckley, 2006). You must ask, whose truth? Here the advocates of the 'Reid Technique' have the inves-tigators, the police officers, in mind. However, some innocent people may be being interrogated without evidence of their involvement, but solely on the basis of a police hunch (Kassin, 2006). This means that the interrogation is a guilt-presumptive process where biases affect police officers' behaviour, instead of it being an objective information-gathering process. (Later in this chapter we discuss how guilt-presumptions may affect an interviewer's behaviour.)

A confession is, of course, very valuable for the police, provided it is not a false one. It makes it easier to recover goods, leads to compensation and satisfaction for the victims, enables other culprits to be pursued and probably results in a conviction at trial. However, an interrogation technique with the sole purpose of obtaining confessions breaks one of the cardinal principles of investigative policing, the presumption of innocence (UN General Assembly, 1966, Art. 14:2). If the investigation and the initial interview conclude that the suspect is guilty, then the suspect who denies their guilt during the interrogation will naturally be considered a liar. Under these circumstances the interrogator will see no need to consider the suspect's credibility any further.

One of the techniques for obtaining a confession is so-called *theme-building*. It is one of the nine steps in the Reid Technique and the idea is to give the suspect a morally justifiable way out, given that the way out also includes an admission of guilt. The idea is that the suspect is unwilling to admit to the crime because her/his deeds are morally objectionable, an admission that would disturb the self-image. The interrogator then constructs a theme, a fake story, which is consistent with the known details of the crime. The story relieves the suspect of guilt, but if he or she agrees to the story, the individual simultaneously admits to the crime. It could be something like "Okay, the money was taken; you might have borrowed it, just in order to pay for food for your family. You wanted to pay it back, didn't you?" Other methods are the use of fake evidence or the introduction of evidence that does not exist, all to persuade the suspect that he/she is caught and might as well admit to the crime. One of the problems with this is that innocent but suggestible suspects might confess to a crime they did not commit, especially if they are influenced into believing that an admission might result in leniency from the justice system. Thus, in some cultures, police interrogation methods can be problem makers rather than problem solvers for the criminal justice system.

One confusing circumstance is how the different manuals use the words 'interrogation' and 'interview'. Commonly, the interview phase is understood as being an information-seeking conversation. Several manuals (e.g. Benson, 2000; Butterfield, 2002; Rutledge, 2001) do not describe methods for conducting the interview phase but those which do normally emphasize the importance of good communication. They generally advise establishing rapport with the suspect and actively seeking information with an open mind. Unfortunately, some manuals advise the police not to reveal any suspicions to the suspect at this point (e.g. Bristow, 1964; Inbau *et al.*, 2001; Yeschke, 2003). This is highly questionable according to the UN Covenant on Civil and Political Rights (UN General Assembly, 1966, Art. 9), which states that suspects have the right to be immediately informed about the reasons for an arrest and the accusations made against them.

The interrogation phase is normally described as a confrontational process, the sole purpose of which is to obtain a confession. Twelve of 20 manuals contain methods that are highly questionable or actually illegal under international law (e.g.

Benson, 2000; Inbau *et al.*, 2001; Starrett, 1998). These are mainly methods involving trickery and/or deceit, but in some manuals (e.g. Butterfield, 2002) advocate methods very close to actual torture, as defined by the UN Universal Declaration of Human Rights Art. 5 (UN General Assembly, 1948). When coercive interrogation techniques, trickery and deceit are applied by the interrogator, other legal conflicts will arise with the principles of voluntariness and the presumption of innocence in the UN Covenant on Civil and Political Rights (UN General Assembly, 1966, Art. 14). A majority of the manuals seem to contain implicit contradictions that can confuse their readers. The contradictions mainly concern whether one is supposed to act with a humane attitude and establish rapport with the suspect, or if it is more effective to be rough and coercive. Some manuals (e.g. Inbau *et al.*, 2001) discuss the influence of interview stress and its impact on correct assessments of credibility. A stressed suspect is supposed to give away more clues to deception; hence the creation of stress within a suspect is argued to be good. Now, stress does not promote rapport, so in context of conversation management, stress is often discouraged. Here it should be noted with regard to the interview phase that use of the stereotypical clues to deception is very ineffective and sometimes directly counterproductive when it comes to detecting deception accurately (for overviews see Vrij, 2000; DePaulo *et al.*, 2003; see Granhag, Chapter 6).

Several manuals are also inconsistent in their advice concerning the use of evidence known to the police (e.g. Inbau *et al.*, 2001; Starrett, 1998). They may have a well-reasoned strategy about the late disclosure of evidence, but usually contradict themselves in another chapter. This comes from the persistent promotion of the so-called factual approach. This method encourages a direct disclosure of all available evidence to the suspect, sometimes even false information. This is promoted as likely to lead to a quick confession, as the suspect immediately sees that he or she is caught and that further resistance is useless. There is research supporting the notion that strong (and valid) evidence encourages a guilty suspect to confess (e.g. Gudjonsson & Bownes, 1992; Gudjonsson & Petursson, 1991). Thus, it is not very surprising that it is a preferred technique among interrogators to use all the evidence available in the beginning of the interrogation. Unfortunately, many intelligent suspects then choose to make up a deceptive story, now including all the disclosed evidence. It doesn't have to be entirely credible, provided it raises sufficient doubt in the mind of the investigator.

In conclusion, there are many manuals available and they are of varying quality concerning their evidence base, utility, effectiveness of the guidelines given, adherence to the law and consistency. A majority of the manuals have serious shortcomings concerning conflict with research findings, risk of false confessions, voluntariness and presumption of innocence, and some of them are in direct conflict with basic human rights issues such as the principle of protection against torture.

EFFECTS ON INTERVIEWER BEHAVIOUR

Returning to the first example cited in this chapter, where the suspect was exposed to a coercive and confession-seeking interrogation that came to nothing more than conflict, the suspect felt himself coerced under external pressure, and thus, perceived the situation as the police officer attempting to 'grill' him, which in turn led to the suspect's conclusion that he would say no more and stay silent. The third example provides an explanation about the possible effects of police officers' behaviour while interviewing suspects. The man argued that it was easier to talk about the crime he had committed when the interviewer acted 'properly', compared to when the interviewer adopted an aggressive and punitive approach. The suspect noted that when a police officer shows hate toward a suspect it is likely that the suspect returns the hate towards the police officer. From the investigative perspective, such suspect is seen as resistant and not co-operative. However, this attitude may actually reflect the behaviour of the police officer.

Having analysed 400 video recordings and 200 audio recordings of British police interviews, Baldwin (1992, 1993) emphasized the need for professionalism. Some officers adopted a confession-seeking approach and tried to persuade suspects to accept a predetermined description of their alleged crimes. These interviewers did not listen to what the suspects said, but instead continually interrupted them. Such interviewers occasionally became unduly flustered, aggressive and provocative. Some used a 'macho' style and were incapable of recognizing how counter-productive **this** was. Baldwin was critical of such confession-seeking approaches.

Moston & Engelberg (1993) analysed 118 taped police interviews that involved a wide range of offences and a wide variety of suspects. A common interviewing style was found that was confrontational and confession-seeking, which in turn created a major problem. When such interviewers directly accused suspects of having committed crimes and simply asked them to confirm the allegations, many suspects denied involvement, showed resistance, or exercised their right to remain silent. Interviewees can show resistance through verbal or non-verbal blocking behaviours that obstruct interviewers' efforts to establish rapport and create appropriate communication. Unwillingness often depends on interviewee psychological blocks such as anxiety, fear, depression, anger and antipathy (Shepherd, 1993). Such unwillingness may appear when the interviewer fails to orientate suspects sufficiently toward the purpose of the interview: suspects need to know the 'route map' if they are to deal in realities. Resistance may also depend on an interviewer's disruptive talk, inappropriate listening, and inappropriate pacing when he or she immediately asks another question or makes a comment after an interviewee's response, filling pauses and allowing no time for reflection.

In their study of confession-seeking approaches, Stephenson & Moston (1993) studied 1067 interviews and found that in 73% of these cases the police interviewers seemed sure of the guilt of the suspect. In a widely cited article, Kassin & Gudjonsson (2004) have reviewed in detail the literature on confessions. They describe interrogation as a guilt-presumptive process where the police officer, affected by a strong prior belief concerning the guilt of the suspect, behaves accordingly. The officer's success is measured by whether the suspect confesses or denies. Beliefs about guilt may influence a police officer's interaction with a suspect, explaining why police officers adopt a confession-seeking interrogating approach (Mortimer & Shepherd, 1999). Psychological research has found that when people have formed a belief they become selective when seeking and interpreting new information (see e.g. Kassin, Goldstein & Savitsky, 2003). In this distorted, selective process, people strive for information to verify their belief. This process of cognitive confirmation bias may make a police officer's beliefs resistant to change, even in the presence of contradictory facts (Nickerson,

1998). Innes (2002) argued that during crime investigations police officers may be overwhelmed by the amount of evidence in a case, leading the officer not to search for new facts which might reveal the whole truth. The officer may search for an amount of evidence that is sufficient to construct a satisfying internal representation of the criminal event, and in such construction, gaps (without evidence) may be filled by imagination and conjecture to fashion a coherent story. Such a construction may feed into a presumption of the suspect's guilt, which in turn may shape the police officer's interviewing behaviour. Kassin, Goldstein & Savitsky (2003) conducted an experiment that used students as interrogators to test the hypothesis that guilt presumption affects interviewers' behaviour. This study showed that when interviewers adopted a presumption of guilt rather than innocence, they asked more guilt-oriented questions and used more techniques and pressure in order to elicit a confession. This prior belief sets into motion a confession-seeking process of behavioural confirmation that affects the behaviour of the interviewer as well as the suspect, as in the introductory example, where the suspect perceived that the police officer as just trying to 'grill' him. In their study of confession-seeking procedures, Stephenson & Moston (1993, 1994) distinguish between accusatorial strategies and information-gathering strategies. When the evidence was judged as strong, the interviewer used an accusatorial approach, accusing the suspect early on in the interview. Thus, police officers' perceptions that the evidence is strong may promote a presumption of guilt, where the officer acts in a coercive and dominant manner, which in turn can elicit resistance and denials from the suspect. Such an analysis is supported by Holmberg & Christianson's (2002) study of 83 convicted murderers and sexual offenders' experiences of their police interviews. They found that these men perceived the interview as either *dominant* or *humanitarian*. In the dominant experience, these offenders perceived their interviewers as impatient, rushing, aggressive, brusque, nonchalant, unfriendly, deprecating and condemning. The dominant experience was also associated with the offenders' feelings of anxiety and tendency to deny the alleged crime. Thus, a police officer who shows a dominant, coercive and confession-seeking approach may be seen as an anti-therapeutic agent because such behaviour may be counterproductive not only for the crime investigation but also for offenders' rehabilitation. This approach is clearly an example of the external pressure that convicted criminals experience when police officers use a confession-seeking approach (Gudjonsson & Petursson, 1991; Gudjonsson & Sigurdsson, 1999).

A serious problem with a question-based approach to seeking information is that asking too many questions can be counterproductive. First, human beings have limited mental resources to process information (Baddeley, 1998). Imagine yourself in a rapid-fire interview concerning what you have eaten for lunch the previous week, where and with whom. Think about three, four and six days ago and imagine someone asking several hard-hitting questions about where you were sitting, with whom, as well as exactly what you had on your plate. The questions shift between different days and aspects of the events. It is likely that when you try to recall you will need some time to remember. In a situation where an interviewer asks many questions, perhaps jumping between different phases in the course of events, the interviewee needs time to recover detail. In such a situation, the interviewee's mental resources will be overloaded by the rain of questions to which he or she can only provide superficial answers. Without the knowledge that psychologists have regarding the effects of limited mental resources, a police officer might wrongfully interpret the interviewee's pauses and hesitations as a reluctance to tell the truth, rather than a situation created by the police officer's rapid-fired questions. Interviewees need time to think and time to remember. Second, the information contained in questions may affect a suspect's memory, because all remembering is constructive, meaning that an interviewee may incorporate information provided in the questions subsequently to construct an incorrect, fabricated account (see Holliday, Chapter 4 for the same process operating with witness testimony). Thus, an interviewer who asks lots of questions may distort a suspect's memories of his or her criminal conduct (for a more detailed description of offenders' memories, see Christianson, 2007).

Thus, following the advice of the manuals described above and using a confession-seeking procedure will not only generate suspect resistance, but may also lead to confessions, some of which are false.

CASE STUDY

False Confession, A Precursor of A Miscarriage of Justice

On Monday 30 March 1998, the journalist Jan Hoffman published an article on the front page of *The New York Times* entitled *Police Refine Methods So Potent, Even The Innocent Have Confessed*. In his article, Hoffman argued that American interrogators use tricks, deceptions and lies to extract confessions from suspects and that these techniques were so powerful that even innocent people confessed to the crime. Describing a case involving a false confession, Hoffman reported that the innocent man had said what they (the interrogators) wanted to hear. This was a man, suspected of the murder of a local shop owner, who falsely confessed after insisting on his innocence for nearly nine hours. During these nine hours, seven police officers had handled the questioning. The officers lied and told the suspect that they had found his fingerprints and hair on the crime scene, as well as that he did not pass the lie detector test. After these many hours of interrogation, the innocent man had given up the hope that telling the truth would give him his freedom back. With the hope of being released to go home, he told the police officers what they wanted to hear.

Is it possible for an innocent person to confess to a crime that he or she has not committed? Yes, and it is not a new phenomenon. Munsterberg wrote about false confessions as early as 1908, and described it as a normal reaction to the emotional shock of being arrested and interrogated. Historically, there are many examples of voluntary false confessions, for example, about 200 people confessed to the kidnapping of Charles Lindbergh's son in 1932. One of the most well-known confessors in the 1980s was Henry Lee Lucas, who confessed to hundreds of unsolved murders. In Sweden, more than a hundred persons have been investigated after having falsely confessed the murder of former Prime Minister Olof Palme in 1986 (Detective Superintendent

Per-Olof Palmgren, personal communication). Gudjonsson & Sigurdsson (1994) describe a self-report study of 229 Icelandic prison inmates of whom 27 (12%) revealed that they had sometimes made false confessions to the police. In a similar study on 509 Icelandic prison inmates, Sigurdsson & Gudjonsson (1996) found that the same number of inmates (12%) reported that they had made one or more false confessions to the police at some time in their past lives. The most frequent motives for false confessions were **to** protect somebody else (50%), to escape from police coercion (48%) or to avoid detention (42%) (respondents could choose more than one category, which explains the overlaps between the motives reported).

There are several other documented cases of false confessions and the numbers grow, showing that false confessions are a reality that may well lead to miscarriages of justice, and for that reason, it is important to understand the mechanisms underlying them. Research suggests that false confessions can be provoked by a number of different causes (Kassin & Gudjonsson, 2004). Gudjonsson (2003) distinguishes between a voluntary false confession, a coerced-compliant false confession and coerced-internalized false confession. Sometimes it happens that a person, without any external pressure, voluntarily makes a self-incriminating statement and falsely confesses a crime he or she has not committed. This situation can occur when the person knows the culprit and tries to protect him or her from being sentenced for the offence. Obviously, the reasons why innocent people make a *voluntary self-confession* are full of nuances; it may be a pathological desire for notoriety, which may be stimulated by media reports about high-profile cases. Other explanations might be a person's inability to separate his or her fantasy from reality and facts or the need to satisfy a person's desire for self-punishment based on feelings of guilt over previous offences or sins or the result of mental illness. Voluntary false confessions originate entirely from the confessor without any influence from the police, which is not the situation regarding the next type of false confession.

When a police officer interrogates a suspect and exposes this person to pressure or coercion, a *coerced-compliant false confession* can arise. In such a situation, the suspect gives in to explicit coercion in the expectation of receiving some kind of immediate instrumental gain or favour (Gudjonsson, 2003; Kassin & Gudjonsson, 2004). The confessor is completely aware of his or her innocence and the confession is an act of compliance. The motive of a coerced-compliant false confession may be to avoid a threatening situation from which the confessor is desperate to escape. Another reason for a confession of this type may be based on a sound promise, an expectation or a hope of a reward.

The third type is the *coerced-internalized false confession* that may occur when a suspect, often a vulnerable person, temporarily or more persistently, comes to believe that he or she must have committed the crime in question (Gudjonsson, 2003; Kassin & Gudjonsson, 2004). Importantly, in such cases the suspect may have no memories of the alleged event through, for example, drink or drugs and this lack of memory may sometimes make him or her more likely to confabulate a false memory. In major investigations, the suspect may be exposed to several long interviews and he or she may start to doubt his or her own denials. Such a situation may occur without any tricks, deceit or pressure from the police officer. The person is co-operative, tries to remember and without memories may come to believe that he or she must have committed the crime. For the police interviewer, it is extremely important not to continue with

CASE STUDY

Coerced-Compliant False Confession

In 1989, a female jogger was found brutally beaten, raped, and left for dead in Central Park in New York City, but she survived (Kassin & Gudjonsson, 2004). Within two days, the police had arrested five African-American and Hispanic-American boys aged between 14 and 16 as suspects for the attack. The brutal crime became a high-profile case for the national news media. The police aggressively interrogated the boys and they confessed to the crime. Four of these resultant confessions were then video recorded and presented during the trial so that a successful conviction was almost inevitable. The videotapes showed the four boys describing in detail how they attacked the female jogger and carried out the crime, and during the trial, one of the boys even expressed remorse and assured the court that he would not commit such a crime again. While there was no forensic evidence or physical traces linking the boys to the crime, they were all found guilty and sentenced to long terms of imprisonment. However, in many ways the boys' descriptions of the brutal crime were erroneous. Thirteen years later, a man sentenced for a murder and three rapes committed at the time of the jogger attack, revealed on his own initiative that he was the one, and only one, who had attacked and raped the female jogger. The subsequent investigation showed that the new suspect had unique and corroborated knowledge of the crime and the crime scene. In this investigation, a DNA test also showed that the semen samples found on the victim excluded the boys as perpetrators, but incriminated the new suspect. In December 2002 and after 13 years in prison, the five boys' convictions based on their false confessions were withdrawn. The boys explained that when they confessed, they believed and expected that they would be released and allowed to go home once they had confessed. These confessions show specific motives for this kind of compliance, for example, being allowed to go home, sleep and make a phone call. Police officers' desire to end an interview and solve a crime may be extremely coercive for young people, especially those who are desperate, or phobic of being locked up in custody.

questions that might introduce false memories. Instead, the interviewer must close the interview because the interviewee (likely innocent in the scenario described) is highly vulnerable, and particularly vulnerable to suggestion. Otherwise, there is a high risk for a coerced-internalized false confession as a result of memory distrust syndrome (MDS) (Gudjonsson, 2003). A person with MDS is especially vulnerable to suggestive cues, especially those implicit in questions, and the presence of an authority figure like a police officer might add to the likelihood of a person creating false memories. The creation of false memories occurs because the individual doubts his or her own autobiographical memory and is in a heightened state of suggestibility. He or she is cooperative, may be socially isolated and puts trust in the police officer who, deliberately or unintentionally, offers hints and cues that lead to false memories. The source of the memory becomes confused, the reality distorted and a fertile base for internalized false confession is created.

To prevent false confessions, Davis & Leo (2006) suggest that the police should interrogate a person as a suspect only where there is sufficient ground to support a presumption of guilt. The authors also suggest that the police should organize education for their officers about the risk and causes of false confessions, which would include education about how confirmatory bias may affect the work of a criminal investigator. Police officers should be aware of and avoid practices that may promote false confessions (e.g. not use confession-seeking tactics). That means that police officers need to acquire knowledge of, and be sensitive to, the psychological vulnerabilities that make some suspects particularly susceptible to such influences, and to adjust their interviewing techniques accordingly. In many countries, the concept of *interrogation* is seen as synonymous with single-minded confession-seeking, whereas the concept of *interviewing* is seen as a much wider notion involving both the giving and receiving of information. The latter will be the focus in the final section of this chapter.

THE CHANGE FROM INTERROGATION TO INVESTIGATIVE INTERVIEWING

The term *interrogation* has given way in Britain to investigative interviewing (Milne & Bull, 2003), which has emphasized and promoted the importance of changing attitudes towards the police interview. In order to understand the historical connections between police information-gathering techniques, the public and research, a brief review of the evolution of interrogation into investigative interviewing will be provided.

From antiquity to the first half of the twentieth century, some interrogators have used acts of cruelty to discover criminal facts. Suspects have tried to hide their knowledge by silence or lies, and historically, the method chosen to obtain confessions has been the use of physical and mental force. Münsterberg (1908/1923) argued that threats and torture have been used all over the world for thousands of years to force suspects to confess. The term 'third degree' was introduced in 1900 to describe interrogating a prisoner by means of mental or physical torture to extract a confession (Merriam-Webster, 2004). Münsterberg (1908/1923) described the 'third degree' as including the use of dazzling light, the cold-water hose and secret blows that left few marks and he maintained that it was still in regular use by the police in some countries in the early decades of the twentieth century. Public opinion was firmly against such methods, the public not being convinced that the 'third degree' was effective in bringing out the real truth from suspects. Up to the early 1930s and perhaps longer, police interview tactics in some countries were generally characterized by coercion (Leo, 1992).

In Sweden, Hassler (1930) argued that the police interview should be inquisitorial, marked by coercive questioning. The suspect should, in the absence of inflicted pain, threat or deceit, be induced to provide a voluntary confession. Peixoto (1934), from a

Brazilian standpoint, argued that the 'third degree' was coercive and of doubtful value. In the 1930s and 1940s, the use of coercive interviewing methods began to decline (Leo, 1992). Swedish police officers were recommended to try to win the interviewee's trust and then let the interviewee provide a free account before the police officer began to ask open-ended questions (Leche & Hagelberg, 1945). Leche and Hagelberg also emphasized the necessity for police officers to understand people's emotions and reactions, to have knowledge about how human memory functions, and to understand how a statement could be affected by different tactics adopted by the interviewer.

In order to secure the truth and to judge a witness' veracity, Gerbert (1954) stressed the need for understanding an interviewee's personality. Gerbert stated that some tense interviewees, who appeared to be guilty, were actually reacting to the interview, and became relaxed only when they were assured that the interview would be conducted in a fair and impartial way. However, in the 1960s, police deceptive techniques, tactics and stratagems became commonplace in interviews with suspects. These methods were, as discussed above, based on an uncritical and subjective use of psychological knowledge.

The psychologist Dr Eric Shepherd trained police officers of the City of London Police in the early 1980s. Shepherd developed a script for managing conversations with anybody a police officer would be likely to meet. In the context of this training, Shepherd coined the term Conversation Management (CM) for this technique, which means that the police officer must be aware of and manage the communicative interaction, both verbally and non-verbally (Milne & Bull, 1999). Conversation Management comprises three phases: *pre-, within- and post-interview behaviour.*

In the pre-interview phase the officer has to work objectively and without any biases. He or she analyses the case in detail and develops questions to be answered, that is, to prepare and plan the interview. A method known as SE3R (Shepherd, 1988) aims to help the investigator rapidly to record, analyse, collate, process, collate and register all the information from interviews and written statements. The five steps are *Skim, Extract, Read, Review* and *Recall.* In the *within-interview* phase, the interviewer is encouraged to pay attention to four sub-phases: *Greeting, Explanation, Mutual Activity* and *Closure,* abbreviated as GEMAC. The *greeting* phase concerns an appropriate introduction of the interviewer, which means establishing rapport. In the *explanation* phase, the interviewer must set out the aims and objectives, and develop the interview further. *Mutual activity* concerns the elicitation of narrative from the interviewee and clarifying questions from the interviewer. *Closure* is the important phase in which the interviewer attempts to create a positive end to the interview, aiming at mutual satisfaction with the content and performance of the session. CM was consistent with the Police and Criminal Evidence Act (known as PACE) introduced in England and Wales in 1984. PACE can be seen as a reaction, from the public, researchers and to some extent, the police, to criticism of the existing methods used to interrogate suspects (Bull, 1999). The advent of PACE encouraged further research into police interviewing techniques in England and Wales.

To facilitate the communicative interaction between a police interviewer and a suspect, Shepherd (1991) emphasized the importance of the interviewer showing human feeling towards suspects, and advocated ethical interviewing (EI). Shepherd argued that the EI approach lends itself to professional investigations. It also improves investigative

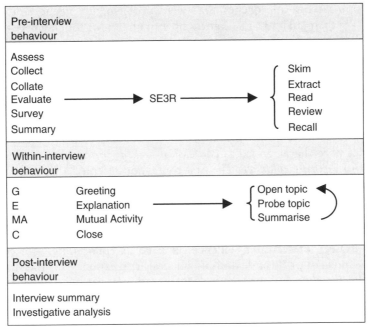

Figure 5.2: Conversation Management. Reproduced from Milne & Boone (1999), *Investigative Interviewing: Psychology and Practice,* 0471987298, p. 57, Fig. 4.1, by permission of John Wiley & Sons, Ltd

quality leading to a greater degree of success in crime prevention, detection, and conviction of the guilty. This approach rests on ethical principles, signifying that individuals show mutual respect and treat each other as equal human beings with the same rights to dignity, self-determination and free choice. It also emphasizes empathy, which means treating each other with a degree of mutual understanding. However, specialist investigative interviewers have been found to rate showing empathy and compassion amongst the least important interviewing skills (Cherryman & Bull, 2001).

As stated above, Baldwin's (1992, 1993) observation of video and audio recordings of police interviews emphasized the need for professionalism and he called for the use of the basic rules of sound interviewing practice. Such professionalism provides for a fair and calm interview in which suspects may express their own point of view. Additionally, professional police interviewers must also pay attention to the suspects' responses, avoid harrying tactics and coercion. Thus, an open-minded interviewer gives suspects time for reflection and the opportunity to express their own position. Professional interviewers establish rapport and listen actively to the suspects' responses. However, many officers showed difficulties in creating rapport with suspects, adopted a confession-seeking approach, and tried to persuade suspects to accept a predetermined description of the event. Baldwin concluded in the early 90s that the competence of the police interviewers was unacceptably low. Moston and Engelberg's (1993) analysis of taped police interviews showed that the police used *confrontational* and *confession-seeking* approaches that were problematic. Stephenson & Moston (1993, 1994) in their analysis of a large number of interviews found where the evidence against the accused was perceived as strong, police interviewers invariably assumed their guilt and adopted a confession-seeking approach. However, when the evidence was perceived as weak, they employed an information-gathering strategy. The latter approach increased the probability of obtaining a suspect's own account of the event.

Consistent with Stephenson and Moston's results, Williamson (1993) identified four interviewing styles that different police officers sought to adopt with suspects. Williamson's study used a questionnaire which was completed by 80 detectives. Two of these styles were characterized as *confession-seeking procedures* and the other two by *searches for securing evidence*. The first confession-oriented approach was conceptualized as *collusive*, implying that the interviewer acts in a cooperative, paternalistic, helpful, and problem-solving way. The second confession-oriented style was the dominant one, in which the investigators adopted a *confrontational* approach and displayed impatience and showed their emotions towards the suspects. The third involved a strategy of securing evidence, labelled as *counselling*, and comprised a cooperative, unemotional and non-judgmental demeanour. In the fourth style, labelled as *businesslike* and marked by confrontational, brusque, factual and formal demeanour, the interviewer tried to secure evidence. Williamson's research revealed that interviewers who obtained many true confessions showed a positive attitude towards suspects. They also manifested sympathetic and cooperative behaviour. Dominant interrogators, on the other hand, kept up pressure on suspects through quick questioning. These police officers were regarded as unsympathetic and confrontational towards the suspects, who in turn often responded with resistance and denials. Considering his findings, Williamson found the results congruent with the concept of *investigative interviewing*.

Investigative interviewing was developed in the early 1990s under the aegis of the British Home Office and Association of Chief Police Officers and incorporated into the PEACE model of interviewing (Milne & Bull, 2003). It arose partly as a response to the shortcomings researchers had revealed with existing approaches and followed outcry from the public and the media over such methods. The mnemonic PEACE denotes *Planning and preparation, Engage and explain, Account, clarification and challenge, Closure* and *Evaluation,* which are seen as important phases in a good interview (Bull, 1999; Bull & Milne, 2004; Milne & Bull, 1999, 2003).

First, interviewers are obliged to carefully plan and prepare themselves before the interview. Both experienced police officers and researchers have repeatedly shown the benefits of being well prepared prior to an interview. They underline the importance of the planning and preparation phase as cost effective, and one of the most fundamental and crucial skills upon which the interview outcome is dependent. *Planning and preparation* not only includes reading the case file and being familiar with the facts. It also encourages police officers to seek out knowledge about the individual to be interviewed, in particular, aspects that might complicate or facilitate the interview (e.g. vulnerabilities, religious and cultural aspects, addiction, physical and environmental circumstances). Armed with knowledge about the specific case and the individual concerned, police officers are now in a position to plan how to conduct the interview with the suspect in question. *Engage and explain* is the first phase in the real

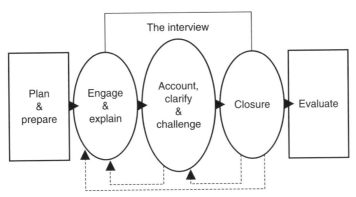

Figure 5.3: The five phases of the PEACE model. In the interview phases, it may be necessary to go back to a previous phase to develop something more and then continue the interview

interview, where interviewers inform the suspect about the allegation, their rights and the procedure to be followed in the interview. Here, it is also most important for interviewers to build rapport, engage suspects and try to motivate them to provide their perspective on the key events. The aim of this introduction to the interview is to provide suspects with a 'route map' for a fair and just interview of which they are going to be a part. In the phase of *account, clarification and challenge*, suspects are invited to give their account of what happened during the event in question. Interviewers then ask questions about aspects of the suspect's account that need to be clarified and challenge any inconsistencies. The *closure* phase involves interviewers summing up what has been said and checking with suspects that everything has been correctly understood. It is also important to inform suspects, as far as is possible, about the next steps in the investigation, and bring the interview to an end on a positive note. The positive closure may prepare the way for a further interview. The final phase of the PEACE model, *evaluation*, requires officers to evaluate the facts revealed in the interview and relate these to pre-existing information and to the aims of the interview. Additionally, is it important for interviewers to evaluate how they have conducted the interview and reflect on how the interview could have been improved. The aim of the PEACE model is to obtain correct and reliable evidence and to discover the truth in a crime investigation. This model emphasizes ethical principles, which differentiate this method from other coercive and persuasive approaches to interviewing suspects described earlier.

As regards the humanitarian experience, Holmberg & Christianson's (2002) study of convicted murderers and sexual offenders' experiences of police interviews revealed that some offenders perceived their interviewers as cooperative, accommodating, positive, empathic, helpful and engaging. Experience of a humanitarian interview related significantly to the offenders' own perception of being respected by the interviewers. This study also found a significant positive relation between the humanitarian interviewing style and the offenders' admissions of crime. Kebbell, Hurren & Mazerolle (2006) reported similar findings. In their first study, they interviewed 19 sexual offenders about their feelings during their most recent police interview and their reasons for confessing or denying the crime in question. In the second study 44 convicted sexual offenders completed a questionnaire regarding their perceptions of police interviews and what they perceived as effective police interview practices. From the outcomes of these two studies, Kebbell *et al.* suggested that in order to maximize the likelihood of genuine confessions, police officers should be open-minded, act according to ethical principles and show humanity.

Therapeutic jurisprudence is a growing movement within the philosophy of law and within the legal and judicial practice areas. Its roots can be found in the American legal realism movement which developed in the first half of the twentieth century. Therapeutic jurisprudence focuses on human problems and conflicts and encourages police officers, prosecutors and other legal parties to understand that conflicts produce social and psychological effects on the individuals involved. It sees the law and its procedures as therapeutic agents because the law and its execution can have both therapeutic and anti-therapeutic consequences (Petrucci, Winick & Wexler, 2003). The purpose of therapeutic jurisprudence is to develop legal procedures that promote the social and psychological well-being of the individual involved in a juridical action. The idea is that legal actors can use theories and empirical knowledge from the behavioural sciences to influence the practice of the law. In this way, jurisprudence can be seen as a therapeutic tool to promote psychological well-being in legal practice. The suspects who had felt themselves highly respected in Holmberg & Christianson's (2002) study showed significant higher psychological well-being compared to those who felt themselves less respected (Holmberg, Christianson & Wexler, 2007). Even those offenders who admitted their crimes showed a significantly higher psychological well-being than those who did not. Admissions of guilt should not only be seen from an investigative and legal perspective. It is likely that admissions in the context of therapeutic jurisprudence may also enable the offender to work through the crime committed. Such admissions may enhance the suspect's memory for the crime as well as promoting their psychological well-being **which** in turn may prevent offending in the future.

CONCLUSION

- Most manuals on police information-gathering techniques embody a concept of interrogation that is characterized by confession-seeking, often violating basic human rights legislation.

- These manuals, implicitly or explicitly, encourage a presumption of the suspect's guilt that in turn may prevent a fair investigation and may lead to a miscarriage of justice.

- Police officers' presumption of guilt and coercive questioning of suspects often leads to resistance from the suspect and can lead to a false confession and miscarriage of justice.

- Gudjonsson (2003) distinguishes between voluntary false confessions; coerced-compliant false confessions, and coerced-internalized false confessions.

- Recent innovations, such as the PEACE interview encourage establishing proper rapport with the suspect, free responding and emphasize establishing facts rather than assuming guilt.
- Such an approach is characterized by a regard for justice and human rights and may minimize the risk of a miscarriage of justice.

ESSAY/DISCUSSION QUESTIONS

1. What tactics do interrogation manuals recommend for interviewing suspects and how do these accord with human rights legislation?
2. In what ways may a police interviewer be biased and how might such biases influence an interviewer's behaviour?
3. Describe three types of false confession and consider their causes.
4. Apart from investigative advantages, discuss at least two other advantages possibly promoted by a suspect freely making admissions.

REFERENCES

Baddeley, A. (1998). *Human memory: Theory and practice*. Boston, MA: Allyn & Bacon.

Baldwin, J. (1992). Video taping police interviews with suspects – an evaluation. *Police Research Series: Paper No. 1*. London: Home Office Police Department.

Baldwin, J. (1993). Police interview techniques; Establishing truth or proof? *The British Journal of Criminology, 33*, 325–352.

Benson, R. (2000). *Ragnar's guide to interviews, investigations, and interrogations*. Boulder CO: Paladin Press.

Bristow, A.P. (1964). *Field interrogation* (2nd edn). Springfield, IL: Charles C Thomas Publisher Ltd.

Buckley, J.P. (2006). The Reid Technique of interviewing and interrogation. In T. Williamson (Ed.), *Investigative interviewing: Rights, research, regulation*. Cullompton: Willan Publishing.

Bull, R. (1999). Police investigative interviewing. In A. Memon & R. Bull (Eds), *Handbook of the psychology of interviewing*. Chichester: John Wiley & Sons.

Bull, R. & Milne, R. (2004). Attempts to improve police interviewing of suspects. In G.D. Lassiter (Ed.) *Interrogations, confessions and entrapment* (pp. 181–196). New York: Kluwer.

Butterfield, R. (2002). *The official Guide to interrogation*. Philadelphia: Xlibris Corporation.

Cherryman, J. & Bull, R. (2001). Police officers' perceptions of specialist investigative skills. *International Journal of Police Science and Management, 3*, 199–212.

Christianson, S.Å. (2007). *Offenders' memories of violent crimes*. Chichester: John Wiley & Sons.

Davis, D. & Leo, R. (2006). Strategies for preventing false confessions and their consequences. In M.R. Kebbell & G.M. Davies (Eds) *Practical psychology for forensic investigations and prosecutions*, (pp. 121–149). Chichester: John Wiley & Sons.

DePaulo, B.M., Lindsay, J.J., Malone, B.E., *et al.* (2003). Cues to deception. *Psychological Bulletin, 129*, 74–118.

Gerbert, K. (1954). The psychology of expression and the technique of criminal interrogation. *Jahrbuch fuer Psychologie und Psychotherapie, 2*, 85–98.

Gudjonsson, G.H. (2003). *Psychology of Interrogations and Confessions: A Handbook.* Chichester: John Wiley & Sons.

Gudjonsson, G.H. & Bownes, I. (1992). The reasons why suspects confess during custodial interrogation: Data from Northern Ireland. *Medicine, Science and the Law, 32*, 204–212.

Gudjonsson, G.H. & Petursson, H. (1991). Custodial interrogation: Why do suspects confess and how does it relate to their crime, attitude and personality? *Personality and Individual Differences, 12*, 295–306.

Gudjonsson, G.H., & Sigurdsson, J.F. (1994). How frequently do false confessions occur? An empirical study among prison inmates. *Psychology, Crime and Law, 1*, 21–26.

Gudjonsson, G.H. & Sigurdsson, J.F. (1999). The Gudjonsson Questionnaire-Revised (GCQR): factor structure and its relationship with personality. *Personality and Individual Differences, 27*, 953–968.

Hassler, Å. (1930). *Föreläsningar över den Svenska kriminalprocessen, I.* Stockholm: A.B. Nordiska Bokhandeln i Distribution.

Holmberg, U. (1996). Sexualbrottsförövares upplevelser av polisförhör. Report series 1996:7. Kristianstad: Kristianstad University.

Holmberg, U. & Christianson, S.Å. (2002) Murderers' and sexual offenders' experiences of police interviews and their inclination to admit or deny crimes. *Behavioural Sciences and the Law, 20*, 31–45.

Holmberg, U., Christianson, S.Å., & Wexler, D. (2007). Interviewing offenders: A therapeutic jurisprudential approach. In S.Å. Christianson (Ed.), *Offenders' memories of violent crimes* (pp. 355–371). Chichester: John Wiley & Sons.

Inbau, F.E., Reid, J.E., Buckley, J.P., & Jayne, B.C. (2001). *Criminal interrogation and confessions* (4th edn). Sudbury: Jones & Bartlett.

Innes, M. (2002). The 'process structure' of police homicide investigations. *British Journal of Crimonology, 42*, 669–688.

Kassin, S.M. (2006). A critical appraisal of modern police interrogations. In T. Williamson (Ed.), *Investigative interviewing: Rights, research, regulation.* Cullompton: Willan Publishing.

Kassin, S.M., Goldstein, C.J., & Savitsky, K. (2003). Behavioral confirmation in the interrogation room: On the dangers of presuming guilt. *Law and Human Behavior, 27*, 187–203.

Kassin, S.M. & Gudjonsson, G.H. (2004). The psychology of confessions: A review of the literature and issues. *Psychological Science in the Public Interest, 5*, 33–67.

Kebbell, M., Hurren, E., & Mazerolle, P. (2006). An investigation into the effective and ethical interviewing of suspected sex offenders. *Trends and Issues in Crime and Criminal Justice*, No. 327. Canberra: Australian Institute of Criminology.

Leche, E. & Hagelberg, V. (1945). *Förhör i brottmål.* Stockholm: P.A. Nordstedt & Söners Förlag.

Leo, R.A. (1992). From coercion to deception: The changing nature of police interrogation in America. *Crime, Law and Social Change, 18*, 35–59.

Merriam-Webster (2004). *Merriam-Webster online dictionary.* Available online at: http://www.m-w.com.

Milne, R. & Bull, R. (1999). *Investigative interviewing; Psychology and practice.* Chichester: John Wiley & Sons.

Milne, R. & Bull, R. (2003). Interviewing by the police. In D. Carson & R. Bull (Eds), *Handbook of Psychology in Legal Contexts* (pp. 111–125). Chichester: John Wiley & Sons.

Mortimer, A., & Shepherd, E. (1999). Frames of mind: Schemata guiding cognition and conduct in the interviewing of suspected offenders. In A. Memon & R. Bull (Eds), *Handbook of the psychology of interviewing* (pp. 293–315). Chichester: John Wiley & Sons.

Moston, S. & Engelberg, T. (1993). Police questioning techniques in tape-recorded interviews with criminal suspects. *Policing and Society, 3*, 223–237.

Munsterberg, H. (1908). *On the witness stand.* Garden City, NY: Doubleday. Available online at http://psychclassics .yorku.ca/Munster/Witness.

Nickerson, R.S. (1998). Confirmation bias: A ubiquitous phenomenon in many guises. *Review of General Psychology, 2*, 175–220.

Palmiotto, M.J. (2004). *Criminal Investigation* (3rd edn). Lanham: Rowman & Littlefield.

Peixoto, A. (1934). The interrogation and confessions in the judiciary process. *Revista de Criminologia Buenos Aires, 21*, 383–395.

Petrucci, C.J., Winick, B.J., & Wexler, D.B. (2003). Therapeutic jurisprudence: An invitation to social scientists. In D. Carson & R. Bull (Eds), *Handbook of psychology in legal contexts* (pp. 579–601). Chichester: John Wiley & Sons.

Royal, R.F. & Schutt, S.R. (1976). *The gentle art of interviewing and interrogation – A professional manual and guide.* Upper Saddle River: Pearson Prentice Hall.

Rutledge, D. (2001). *Criminal interrogation, law and tactics* (4th edn). Boston: Wadsworth Publishing.

Shepherd, E (1988). Developing Interview Skills. In P. Southgate (Ed.), *New directions in police training.* London: HMSO.

Shepherd, E. (1991). Ethical interviewing. *Policing, 7*, 42–60.

Shepherd, E. (1993). Resistance in interviews: The contribution of police perception and behaviour. *Issues in Criminal and Legal Psychology, 18*, 5–12.

Sigurdsson, J.F. & Gudjonsson, G.H. (1996). Psychological characteristics of 'false confessors': A study among Icelandic prison inmates and juvenile offenders. *Personality and Individual Differences, 20*, 321–329.

Starrett, P. (1998). *Interview and interrogation for investigations in the public or private sector.* San Clementine CA: LawTec Publishing Co. Ltd.

Stephenson, G.M. & Moston, S.J. (1993). Attitudes and assumptions of police officers when questioning criminal suspects. *Issues in Criminological and Legal Psychology, No. 18*, pp. 30–36.

Stephenson, G.M. & Moston, S.J. (1994). Police interrogation. *Psychology, Crime and Law, 1*, 151–157.

UN General Assembly (1948). UN Universal Declaration of Human Rights, Art. 5.

UN General Assembly (1966). UN Covenant on Civil and Political Rights, Art. 9, 14:2 (presumption of innocence)

Vrij, A. (2000). *Detecting lies and deceit.* Chichester: John Wiley & Sons.

Weinberg, C.D. (2002). *Effective interviewing & interrogation techniques.* San Diego: Academic Press.

Williamson, T.M. (1993). From interrogation to investigative interviewing: Strategic trends in police questioning. *Journal of Community and Applied Psychology, 3*, 89–99.

Yeschke, C. L. (2003). *The Art of investigative interviewing* (2nd edn). Burlington: Butterworth-Heinemann.

ANNOTATED READING LIST

Bartol, C.R. & Bartol, A.M. (2007) *Criminal behavior: A psychosocial approach.* Upper Saddle River, NJ: Prentice Hall. *This book offers a detailed insight about suspects and considers the behavioural, emotional and cognitive aspects of criminals.*

Christianson, S.Å. (2007) *Offenders' memories of violent crimes.* Chichester: John Wiley & Sons. *To conduct investigative interviewing, interviewers need knowledge of how memory and memory distortion function, which this textbook provides.*

Gudjonsson, G. H. (2003). *The Psychology of interrogation and confessions.* Chichester: John Wiley & Sons. *In this text, Gudjonsson offer a comprehensive description about false confessions and the suggestibility of suspects.*

Kebbell, M.R. & Davies, G.M. (2006). *Practical psychology for forensic investigations and prosecutions.* Chichester: John Wiley & Sons. *This book is a comprehensive practicable guide to investigative interviewing, making decisions to prosecute, and enhancing the quality of evidence presented at court.*

Memon, A. & Bull. R. (2000). *Handbook of the psychology of interviewing.* Chichester: John Wiley & Sons. *This Handbook provides a genuine text on the psychology of interviewing, reviewing diagnosis and assessment in several contexts, e.g. forensic and social.*

Williamson, T. (2006). *Investigative interviewing: Rights, research, regulation.* Cullompton, Devon: Willan. *In this book, Williamson, together with researchers and practitioners, reviews the position of investigative interviewing in a variety of different countries, with different types of criminal justice systems.*

CHAPTER 6

DETECTING DECEPTION

Pär Anders Granhag
University of Gothenburg, Sweden

Maria Hartwig
John Jay College of Criminal Justice, City University of New York

 To define the topic under investigation is often a good point of departure. However, to define 'deception' is a far from easy task, and the conceptualizations offered in the literature are many. For the present context we think that it will suffice to say that in order to label a statement 'deceptive', an intentional act is required (to unintentionally misremember is not to lie). Furthermore, it is possible to make distinctions between falsification (everything being told is contrary to the truth), distortion (the truth is altered to fit the liar's goal), and concealment (the liar holds back the truth).

In the field of deception detection, the most frequently studied situation is that in which a person, frequently referred to as a target, provides a statement that is either truthful or deceptive. The target is often video-taped while providing his or her statement and this videotape is shown to observers, sometimes referred to as lie catchers. The task of these lie catchers is to make a judgment of whether the target is lying or not, on the basis of the verbal content of the statement as well the target's non-verbal demeanour. For some four decades now, researchers have expended considerable effort studying human deception and its detection.

In this chapter, we will provide an overview of the findings from this extensive body of work. First, we will discuss the characteristics of deceptive and truthful behaviour. Our discussion will be guided by the different theoretical approaches and perspectives offered within the field. In relation to this, we will report what strategies people commonly apply when attempting to assess veracity, and to what extent these strategies have been shown to be successful.

Second, we will turn to methods focusing on verbal content, that is, methods designed to trace differences between liars' and truth tellers' statements. In this section we describe several different methods – all focusing on analyses of the verbal content – and make clear which methods have scientific support, and which do not.

Third, we will provide an overview of findings generated from studies on psychophysiological detection of deception, simply put, the research surrounding the polygraph. The section describes the most frequently used test methods and research on their respective validity, as well as some of the applications of polygraph testing.

Finally, we will focus on some of the new directions within the field of deception detection. Specifically, we will discuss to what extent deception detection can be improved by (i) brain scanning (such as fMRI), (ii) a more eclectic approach with regard to the lie-detection methods used, and (iii) by different training programmes. We will also address the issue of authentic and simulated amnesia.

What cognitive and emotional processes can we expect to be at play during deception? And how might these processes cause liars' overt behaviour to differ from truth tellers'? Answers to these questions can be sought by way of four different approaches: the emotional approach, the content complexity approach, the attempted control approach and the self-presentational perspective (DePaulo & Morris, 2004).

THE EMOTIONAL APPROACH

The emotional approach states that lying causes emotions that differ from those experienced while telling the truth (Ekman, 2001). For example, a liar may experience fear of being judged as not being truthful. The consequences of being judged as a liar, and hence the fear of apprehension, may differ depending on the context. For example, being judged as deceptive when suspected of having committed a serious crime could have serious consequences, which can create a great deal of fear. According to the emotional approach, experiencing emotions when lying can have behavioural consequences. It is predicted that fear of apprehension will cause liars to experience stress and arousal, causing the pitch of voice to rise and increasing blushing, sweating and the amount of speech errors, while feelings of guilt will cause liars to avert their gaze. According to the approach, the stronger the emotions experienced by the liars, the more likely that these emotions will leak, leaving visible traces in demeanour (Ekman, 2001).

The emotional approach	Lying causes emotions that differ from those experienced while telling the truth. These can have behavioural consequences such as stress and arousal, visible signs include raised voice pitch and increased sweating.
The content complexity approach	Lying is more cognitively demanding than telling the truth and the concentration required can result in gaze aversion, fewer body movements and long pauses.
The attempted control approach	Attempting to control behaviour in order to prevent detection through visible signs may in itself result in cues such as an unnaturally stiff presentation.
The self-presentational perspective	Liars and truth tellers are seen as having a mutual goal: to appear honest. But as liars don't have the same grounds for their claims there will be cognitive and behavioural differences in the way they present themselves and the information they give.

Table 6.1: Approaches to detecting deception

THE CONTENT COMPLEXITY APPROACH

In the content complexity approach, outlined by Zuckerman and colleagues (1981), emphasis is put on the cognitive demand accompanying lying. Lying can be a more difficult task than telling the truth, in that a liar must provide a story consistent with the facts known by the interviewer, detailed enough to appear based on something self-experienced, but simple enough to be remembered if one is asked to repeat the story later on (Burgoon, Buller & Guerrero, 1995). Research has shown that cognitively demanding tasks can result in gaze aversion (Ekman, 2001), since it can be distracting to look at the conversation partner. Moreover, this approach predicts that engaging in a cognitively demanding task will result in fewer body movements (Ekman & Friesen, 1972) and long pauses within a statement as well as between the interviewer's question and the reply.

THE ATTEMPTED CONTROL APPROACH

The attempted control approach suggests that liars may be aware that internal processes (such as emotions) could result in cues to deception; consequently, they may try to minimize such cues in order to avoid detection (Vrij, 2004). Paradoxically, attempting to control one's behaviour in order to prevent leakage of deceptive cues may in itself result in cues to deception (DePaulo & Kirkendol, 1989). For example, trying to inhibit movements caused by nervousness and arousal is predicted to result in overcontrol, creating an unnaturally stiff impression.

THE SELF-PRESENTATIONAL PERSPECTIVE

The above approaches describe lying as an activity that differs qualitatively from telling the truth. In contrast to these approaches stands the self-presentational perspective (DePaulo, 1992; DePaulo *et al.*, 2003), in which some similarities between liars and truth tellers have been emphasized. Self-presentation has been defined as regulating one's own behaviour to create a particular impression on others (DePaulo, 1992). Liars and truth tellers are seen as having a mutual goal: to appear honest. The major difference between liars' and truth tellers' claims of honesty is that truth tellers have grounds for their claims, and that they stay within the boundaries of the truth. As a consequence of this, liars and truth tellers are predicted to differ cognitively and behaviourally in two important ways. First, deceptive statements could be less embraced by the communicator than truthful ones. Liars are aware that their claims of honesty are illegitimate, which may result in more negative feelings, making them appear less pleasant and more tense (DePaulo *et al.*, 2003). Moreover, since liars may be less familiar with the events or domains which their stories concern, they will provide less information.

Liars and truth tellers are predicted to differ in a second way. Liars provide stories that they know depart from the truth, which may result in a deliberate attempt to seem credible. In contrast to providing an account based on a self-experience, liars are likely to experience acting in a more effortful way (DePaulo, LeMay & Epstein, 1991). Liars' attempts to control their behaviours, as well as their feelings of deliberateness, may cause their actions to appear less convincing, less involved and more tense, and may make them seem to hold back.

OBJECTIVE CUES TO DECEPTION

The above predictions were assessed in a very extensive **meta-analysis**, which focused on objective cues to deception, that is, behavioural differences between liars and truth tellers (DePaulo *et al.*, 2003; see also DePaulo & Morris, 2004). The majority of the studies covered in the analysis included college students as participants, and were carried out in laboratory settings. The studies included people lying or telling the truth about personal opinions, about an event they had witnessed, and about mock transgressions (i.e. a **mock crime**).

The most important results emanating from this meta-analysis were that (a) reliable cues to deception are scarce, and (b) behaviours that actually are related to deception lack strong predictive value. Liars seem to be somewhat more tense than truth tellers. This is shown in that their pupils are more dilated, and the pitch of their voice is higher. People who are asked to rate the appearance of liars and truth tellers (without knowing that some of them are lying while others are telling the truth) tend to perceive liars as being more tense and nervous. Liars are also perceived as markedly less cooperative than truth tellers (however, for a contrasting finding, see Vrij, 2005b) and their faces are perceived as less pleasant.

There are a few indications that liars' stories differ from those of truth tellers. Liars talk for a shorter time and include fewer details compared to truth tellers. Also, liars' stories make less sense in that they are less plausible, less logically structured and more ambivalent. Liars also sound more uncertain and appear less vocally and verbally immediate, meaning that observers perceive liars to be less direct, relevant and personal in their communication. There are some differences in terms of specific details between deceptive and truthful accounts: liars spontaneously correct themselves and admit not remembering to a lesser extent than truth tellers, indicating that liars' stories may lack some of the so-called ordinary imperfections of truthful accounts (this is in line with some predictions and findings from research on **Statement Validity Analysis**, which will be described later in this chapter). Taken together, both the self-presentational perspective and the attempted control approach received some support in the results of the meta-analysis.

LIE CATCHERS' PERFORMANCE

There is a huge body of research investigating human deception detection accuracy. With few exceptions, accuracy levels fall between 45% and 60% (Vrij, 2000). In a recent extensive **meta-analysis**, an average accuracy level of 54% was found (Bond & DePaulo, 2006). Keeping in mind that the level of chance is 50%, this is hardly an impressive performance. However, considering the scarcity and weakness of valid cues to deception, this result is not surprising.

Not only lay people, but also presumed lie experts – such as police officers, judges and customs officers – have participated in studies on deception detection. It could be assumed that these groups are more skilled at assessing veracity since they face this task in their working life (Mann, Vrij & Bull, 2004). Also, police officers themselves sometimes believe that they are better lie detectors than the average person (Inbau *et al.*, 2001; Vrij, 2004). The studies conducted so far on police officers' ability to detect deception indicate that this notion is incorrect (for an overview, see Vrij, 2005a). In these studies, accuracy rates tend to fall between 45–60%, in other words very similar to rates observed for lay people (for an exception, see Mann *et al.*, 2004). As will be discussed further below, it might be problematic, on the basis of these studies, to draw conclusions about police officers' ability to detect deception in real-life settings.

Misconceptions about Deceptive Behaviour

It has been argued that people's poor lie detection ability is partly dependent upon wrongful beliefs about the characteristics of deceptive behaviour (Strömwall, Granhag & Hartwig, 2004). Research has supported this by showing a lack of overlap between objective (i.e. actual) and subjective cues to deception (behaviours that people associate with deception). For example, the most frequent subjective cue to deception is gaze aversion (a decrease in eye contact). People also tend to associate lying with an increase in speech disturbances such as hesitations and speech errors, a slower speech rate, longer and more frequent pauses, and an increase in smiling and movements such as **self-manipulation**, hand/finger and leg/foot movements (Vrij, 2000). Generally, these subjective deception cues are identical to indicators of nervousness, implying that people make the assumption that liars are more nervous than truth tellers. However, liars are not necessarily more nervous than truth tellers (Köhnken, 1989; in Vrij & Semin, 1996). It should be noted that studies on beliefs about cues to deception have been carried out both on lay people and presumed lie experts. Similar to research on deception detection accuracy, these studies have shown that presumed lie experts do not outperform lay people. In fact, these two groups report similar stereotypical and incorrect beliefs about cues to deception (Strömwall *et al.*, 2004). Interestingly, Mann *et al.* (2004) found that those police officers who held the weakest stereotypical beliefs were the better lie/truth detectors.

CASE STUDY

When Training to Detect Deception Fails

As will be discussed later in this chapter, there have been several attempts to improve people's deception detection accuracy by providing various types of training. A training study of a slightly different nature was carried out by Kassin & Fong (1999). Instead of providing a training programme predicted to increase accuracy levels, the training consisted of recommendations on how to detect deception taken from a highly influential police interrogation manual.

In the study, 16 participants either committed one of four mock crimes such as vandalism or shoplifting, or a non-criminal act. They were all asked to deny involvement in the crime, creating a sample of both false denials (statements from guilty participants) and true denials (statements from innocent participants). Subsequent interrogations with the participants were video-taped, and used as stimulus materials. A sample of 40 lay people acted as lie catchers, who were randomly allocated to either a training condition or a naïve condition. The training was based on parts of the interrogation manual *Criminal Interrogation and Confessions* by Inbau, Reid and colleagues (most recently Inbau, Reid, Buckley & Jayne, 2001). The manual, and the techniques described in it (referred to as the Reid technique) have received fierce criticism for the heavy emphasis on manipulative and psychologically coercive elements (Gudjonsson, 2003), and lately also for the provision of cues to deception that completely lack diagnostic value (Vrij, 2003). In the study, lie catchers in the training condition watched two videotape segments taken from a training seminar produced by Reid and colleagues. The first segment concerned cues to deception to be found in the verbal content, and described truthful statements as direct, spontaneous, unqualified, and truth tellers' denials as unequivocal (Inbau *et al.*, 2001). In contrast, deceptive statements were said to be hesitant, general, evasive and unspecific. The second segment concerned non-verbal cues to deception, which were said to include gaze aversion, slouching in their seat, covering of the eyes and mouth, and self-manipulations such as grooming gestures. It should be noted that the authors of the manual have much faith in the value of these cues: they state that using them can result in deception detection accuracy rates exceeding 80%.

The results from the study by Kassin and Fong contradict the bold statements from the interrogation manual. Not only did the training group fail to outperform the naïve group (who achieved an accuracy level of nearly 56%), they actually performed *worse* (nearly 46% accurate judgments). However, the group who received training were more confident than the naïve group that they had made an accurate judgment of veracity. The trained group of lie catchers also reported more reasons for their judgment, and a large proportion of these reasons were related to cues recommended in the training material. Taken together, the study shows that exposure to and use of the cues recommended in the Reid manual is not only inefficient, but directly counterproductive in improving accuracy in detecting deception and truth. Unfortunately, according to the authors themselves more than 150 000 people working in various parts of law enforcement have already been trained in using the technique (John E. Reid and Associates, 2007) and it is likely that many more legal professionals have access to the manual in their everyday work life. The results directly point to the problems associated with relying on empirically unsupported methods when making judgments of veracity, and indirectly to the need for scientifically sound and empirically validated approaches to the detection of deception and truth.

Realism in Deception Detection Studies

The external validity of the typical deception detection study has been questioned. The most important and persistent criticism has concerned two aspects: first, the realism in the target material (the statement to be assessed by the lie catchers), and second, the realism of the situation in which the lie catchers are put. The targets in the paradigmatic deception detection experiment provide either a true or a false statement regarding their opinions, feelings or about their involvement in some event (sometimes a mock crime). This could be characterized as a **low-stake situation**, in that failing to give a credible impression has little or no consequences. This does not mirror a situation in the legal system, for example, in which a suspect is assessed in order to determine the likelihood of guilt. Failing to act in a credible way in such a situation can have severe and far-reaching consequences for the suspect. It could be argued that the deceptive patterns are different in low- and **high-stake situations** and that it thus would be premature to draw conclusions about, for example, police officers' ability to detect high-stake lies (Miller & Stiff, 1993). Aldert Vrij and his colleagues have taken an important step in investigating real high-stake lies and truths in a police interrogation (e.g. Mann *et al.*, 2004). Although the pattern is not entirely clear, these studies indicate that realistic target materials slightly improve police officers' ability to detect lies.

The second part of the criticism of the realism in deception detection studies concerns the context in which the assessment occurs. In the typical study, participants watch a video-clip of the target. Hence, they are restricted to passively watching the suspects, without any background information and without the possibility to plan and ask questions as they find necessary in order to form the basis for a veracity assessment (Hartwig *et al.*, 2004). This is very different from the situation in which police officers normally make judgments of veracity. Instead, they often make judgments on the basis of their background information, and on their own interaction with the suspect. It could be argued that one reason for the modest accuracy rates often found in studies on police officers' deception detection ability is that they are unfamiliar with catching lies from passive observation. Research has disproven this notion. For example, it has been shown that experienced criminal investigators fail to accurately assess veracity even when getting the chance to plan and conduct an interrogation in the manner of their own choice (Hartwig *et al.*, 2004).

DETECTING DECEPTION FROM VERBAL CONTENT

Is it possible to detect deception on the basis of what is being said? If so, what should one listen for and is it better to use human coders or computer programs? Or are you better off totally ignoring the verbal content, and instead using special equipment in order to analyse the speaker's voice? Below we will address these questions by describing the basic features of a number of deception detection methods, and (where possible) report on each method's discriminative power.

Statement Validity Assessment

Statement Validity Assessment (SVA) is the most widely used technique for assessing veracity on the basis of verbal content. Originally, it was developed in Germany and Sweden for assessing children's accounts of alleged sexual abuse (Trankell, 1963; Undeutsch, 1967). Underlying the technique is the Undeutsch hypothesis, stating that if a child's statement is based on the memory of an actual experience, it will differ in content and quality from a statement based on fabrication (Steller & Köhnken, 1989). A full **SVA** is a four-stage procedure (Köhnken, 2004). The first stage consists of a thorough analysis of the case-file, which – in turn – forms the basis for the generation of hypotheses about the source of the statement. Second, a semi-structured interview is conducted, where the child tells his or her own story. The interview is audio-taped and transcribed. Third, the statement is assessed in terms of credibility, using a so-called **Criteria-Based Content Analysis (CBCA)**. The CBCA is based on a list of 19 different criteria, which are listed in Table 6.2. For an in-depth discussion of each criterion, see Köhnken (2004). Finally, by using a so-called **Validity Checklist**, alternative explanations to the CBCA outcome are considered (Steller & Köhnken, 1989).

The CBCA is the core of the SVA, therefore a few aspects of this particular stage will be highlighted. The 19 criteria derive from 5 different categories: (i) General characteristics, (ii) Specific contents, (iii) Peculiarities of content, (iv) Motivation-related contents, and (v) Offence-specific elements. Furthermore, each of the 19 criteria is scored in terms of absence or presence (for example, using a 3-point scale, where '0' = absent, '1' = present, and '2' = strongly present). In essence, the more criteria present and the stronger the presence of each criterion, the stronger the hypothesis that the memory is based on a genuine personal experience.

Content criteria for statement analysis
General characteristics
1. Logical structure
2. Unstructured production
3. Quantity of details
Specific contents
4. Contextual embedding
5. Descriptions of interactions
6. Reproduction of conversation
7. Unexpected complications during the incident
8. Unusual details
9. Superfluous details
10. Accurately reported details misunderstood
11. Related external associations
12. Accounts of subjective mental state
13. Attribution of perpetrator's mental state
Motivation-related contents
14. Spontaneous corrections
15. Admitting lack of memory
16. Raising doubts about one's own testimony
17. Self-deprecation
18. Pardoning the perpetrator Offence-specific elements
19. Details characteristic of the offence

Table 6.2: Adapted from Steller, M. & Köhnken, G. (1989). Criteria-Based Content Analysis. In D.C. Raskin (Ed.), *Psychological Methods in Criminal Investigation and Evidence* (pp. 217–245). New York: Springer-Verlag

Critically, to what extent can CBCA discriminate between genuine and fabricated accounts? Before attempting to answer this question, one needs to consider that although the CBCA is widely used in court in some countries (Vrij, 2000), it is very problematic to use real-life cases in order to assess the diagnostic value of the technique. In most cases where the technique is used, there is no other evidence than the statement itself. In such cases, we simply do not know whether the accounts are based on genuine or fabricated experiences (i.e. the 'ground truth' is unknown).

In order to get information on the technique's diagnostic value, laboratory studies are needed. Vrij (2005a) reviewed the first 37 studies from laboratory settings. The majority of these studies focused on adults' statements, which is not considered problematic as the **Undeutsch hypothesis** is not limited to children's statements (Köhnken, 2004). Vrij's review showed an overall accuracy rate of 73%, and the technique proved to be equally good for detecting truthful accounts as for detecting fabricated accounts.

Reality Monitoring

The term 'reality monitoring' (RM) has been used in basic memory research for many years, and refers to people's ability to discriminate between self-experienced and imagined events (Johnson & Raye, 1981). Research on RM supports the notion that real experiences are products of perceptual processes, whereas imagined events are products of reflective processes. As a consequence memories of real events tend to differ from memories of imagined events. Specifically, memories of real events tend to contain more perceptual information (e.g. details concerning taste, touch, smell) and contextual information (i.e. spatial and temporal details), than memories of imagined events. Memories of imagined events tend to contain more cognitive operations (e.g. "*I must have been tired, because it was late*") than do memories of real events.

The Spanish psychologist Maria Alonso-Quecuty (1992) was first to suggest that RM could be used as a tool not only to distinguish between *one's own* real and imagined events, but also between *other people's* real and imagined events, thus framing RM as a tool for distinguishing between truthful and deceptive accounts. Many researchers have later picked up on her idea (Sporer, 2004), and the list of RM criteria is now slowly finding its final form.

Recently, Masip and his colleagues (2005) presented the first systematic overview of RM studies conducted within the deception detection framework. Overall accuracy was 75%, and the technique proved to be about equally accurate in detecting truths and lies. Interestingly, the technique seemed to work equally well for children's and adults' statements. In sum, considering that the technique rests upon a well-established theoretical framework, and that the criteria are relatively easy to learn, the RM technique is a rather interesting complement (or alternative) to the CBCA. However, one should note that although the scientific studies on the CBCA and the RM technique constitute a 'critical mass' – showing an overall positive result – the evaluation of these techniques is still at a rather early stage (Davies, 2001).

Scientific Content Analysis

The **Scientific Content Analysis (SCAN)** technique was developed by Sapir, a former Israeli polygraph examiner. Similar to SVA and RM, the underlying assumption of SCAN is that a statement based on memory of an actual experience differs in content from a statement based on invention. SCAN uses written statements, preferably statements that are handwritten by the examinee (to ensure that the examinee's own words are produced). The list of SCAN criteria is extensive, and includes 'Denial of allegations', 'Emotions' and 'Change in language'. For a list of the 12 most commonly used criteria, see Vrij (2008) and Smith (2001). Compared to the CBCA and RM, a SCAN is much less standardized in terms of coding.

To date, there has been very little research on the diagnostic value of SCAN. Vrij (2008) could only find three published studies on the SCAN, one laboratory study and two field studies. The laboratory study showed that truthful and deceptive statements did not differ with regard to the SCAN criteria tested (Porter & Yuille, 1996), and for both field studies the '**ground truth**' is unknown (Driscoll, 1994; Smith, 2001, both cited in Vrij, 2008). The name of the method implies scientific status, but one should be aware that the scientific evidence supporting the technique is meagre (Shearer, 1999).

Computer-Based Linguistic Analysis

Yet another approach to the detection of deception is to examine the language that people use when lying. Scientific studies within this approach started to appear already in the late 1960s, and the basic idea is easy to grasp: it is assumed that a person's choice of words reveals more about their underlying mental state than the actual message (Pennebaker & King, 1999). Simply stated, liars are expected to use different words from truth tellers. There are several methods for conducting a linguistic analysis (basically, decomposing text, based on natural language, to word level), but we will restrict our discussion to a recent method: **Linguistic Inquiry and Word Count (LIWC)**. The LIWC is a computer-based technique which creates linguistic profiles by means of categorizing words into different classes, such as (a) standard language dimensions (e.g. pronouns and articles), (b) psychological processes (e.g. emotional and sensory processes), and (c) relativity (e.g. space and time).

By using LIWC it has been found that some words are less frequent in deceptive statements (e.g. first-person pronouns), whereas other words are more frequent in deceptive statements (e.g. negative emotions words). An examination of the hit rates for the linguistic methods reveals plenty of room for improvement, even if the LIWC has proven to discriminate between deceptive and truthful statements at a rate better than chance level. For example, Newman and colleagues (2003) found an average hit rate (over three studies) of 67%. Interestingly, recent research shows that an automatic coding of RM criteria of liars' and truth tellers' statements utilizing the LIWC software programme resulted in less verbal cues to deception than a manual coding of the very same criteria (Vrij *et al.*, 2007). Finally, and importantly, by decomposing text to word level one loses context. Since the context of a statement is very important in forensic settings (e.g. the statement's development over time), it may render linguistic analysis limited in legal contexts.

Computer Analysis of Voice Stress

Another approach to deception detection is to analyse the voice as such, and neglect the verbal content. We will discuss two such approaches: **Voice Stress Analysis** and **Layered Voice Analysis**. The basic assumption behind the *Voice Stress Analysis* (**VSA**), sometimes called **Psychological Stress Evaluator** (**PSE**), is quite straightforward: by measuring the activity in the muscles responsible for producing speech, it may be possible to infer the speaker's mental state (e.g. experiences of stress). The main phenomena of interest are so-called 'micro tremors', weak involuntary muscle activities that it is possible to register with electrodes. It is well established that such tremors occur in larger groups of muscles, for example, the biceps. Unfortunately, there is very little scientific evidence for the existence of tremors in the muscles that produce speech (Shipp & Izdebski, 1981). In brief, if there is no tremor in the muscles that produce speech, there is no tremor to measure in the voice. Also, even if it was possible to show tremor in the voice, a major challenge remains: to find scientific support for an association between

(a) a certain type of tremor and lying, and (b) another type of tremor and telling the truth. Taken together, the VSA seems to suffer from problems related to both reliability and validity. For a similarly sceptical view of this technique, see the evaluation conducted by the National Research Council (2003).

The **Layered Voice Analysis (LVA)** is a more recent method, and its advocates claim that the method rests upon highly sophisticated technology. The LVA uses a computer program for analysing errors occurring when a raw signal (sound) is digitized. These errors are very difficult for the human ear to pick up, but it is argued that these can be measured by more refined methods. Such errors are not exclusive for the human voice, and can be found for any type of sound (e.g. a clock ticking or a washing machine). The LVA offers statistical output on two such errors, and uses these for calculating a so-called 'truth value'. Experts on forensic phonetics have equated the diagnostic value of the LVA to flipping a coin (Eriksson, forthcoming).

PSYCHOPHYSIOLOGICAL DETECTION OF DECEPTION

Previously in this chapter, we have discussed cues to deception in demeanour and in the verbal content of a statement. The third major branch of research on deception detection focuses on differences in physiological patterns, and is referred to either simply as research on the polygraph, or as psychophysiological detection of deception (PDD).

Development of Psychophysiological Detection of Deception

Throughout history, humans have attempted to detect deception using a variety of techniques. In China, suspected transgressors were forced to chew rice powder and spit it out. If the rice powder was still dry, the suspect was deemed to be guilty (Sullivan, 2001). Underlying such a technique is the assumption that liars and truth tellers differ in terms of physiological responses. In the case of the rice powder technique, a decrease in saliva production was interpreted as a result of fear of being caught lying. The same assumption was the foundation for late nineteenth-century attempts by Lombroso and others to measure changes in blood volume during an interrogation with a suspect (Grubin & Madsen, 2005).

The polygraph, in its present form, is an instrument built to measure the same physiological processes as both the Chinese and Lombroso attempted to tap. Although the modern polygraph is more technically sophisticated, the basic function of the polygraph is the same today as almost 100 years ago (Grubin & Madsen, 2005). The polygraph of today measures at least three physiological systems, all governed by the autonomic nervous system (Fiedler, Schmid & Stahl, 2002), typically galvanic skin response (sweating from the palm), cardiovascular activity such as systolic and diastolic blood pressure (measured by a cuff on one of the upper arms) and breathing patterns (measured by sensors attached around the chest).

Although it is difficult to give exact information about how and where the polygraph is used, it is safe to say that it is used in a vast number of contexts in all parts of the world. In the US, polygraph testing occurs in many parts of law enforcement (Honts, 2004), and polygraph tests play a role in the legal systems of among others Belgium, Canada, Israel, Japan, Korea, Mexico, Thailand and Turkey (Honts, 2004;

Pollina *et al.*, 2004; Vrij, 2000). Its use in these countries varies: in Japan, polygraph evidence is generally admissible (Hira & Furumitsu, 2002), while most countries impose restrictions on the use of polygraph tests in court (Vrij, 2000). Traditionally, the use of the polygraph in the UK has been limited. However, in the 1980s, the Geoffrey Prime spy scandal sparked the British government's interest in the polygraph (Segrave, 2004). A working group was appointed to evaluate the reliability, validity and ethical aspects of the polygraph, and its use both in criminal investigations and for employment evaluations (Grubin & Madsen, 2005). The working group came to the conclusion that the empirical support for the use of the polygraph was limited and that some aspects might be inconsistent with the British Psychological Society's codes of conduct (BPS, 1986). The report of a more recent working group concurred with the earlier report, and concluded that the body of ecologically valid research on the polygraph is limited, and that there are a number of problems related to its use as a lie detector (BPS, 2004). Nevertheless, British researchers have recently explored the possibilities of using the polygraph for sex offender monitoring and treatment. So far, such attempts have shown promising results (Grubin & Madsen, 2006).

The polygraph serves a number of purposes. In the US, the outcomes of polygraph tests are used as evidence in trials only occasionally (Faigman *et al.*, 2002), but they are ubiquitous in other parts of the legal system, such as in criminal investigations (Vrij, 2000). Moreover, in the US the polygraph is used in a number of states as a condition for probation orders and parole licenses (Grubin & Madsen, 2005). Similar to recent British practice, the polygraph is also used in post-conviction testing of sexual offenders (Honts, 2004).

The Control Question Test

There are two main types of test in which the polygraph is used to assess veracity. The most frequently used is the Control Question Test (CQT, sometimes referred to as the Comparison Question Test; Honts, 2004), which is widely applied in law enforcement in the US, Canada and Israel (Ben-Shakhar, Bar-Hillel & Kremnitzer, 2002).

The CQT is administered in several stages (Lykken, 1998). In the introductory phase, rapport is established, basic information is obtained and the subject is invited to provide free recall. Questions are then formulated, and the subject and the polygraph examiner discuss these questions. The first reason for this is that the examiner wants to establish that the subject has understood all the questions. The second reason is that the examiner wants to be sure that the subject will respond to the questions with 'yes' or 'no' (Vrij, 2000). After this, the question phase commences. This phase is run several times, and the responses are averaged across the different test occasions. Subjects are asked a number of questions belonging to one of three categories. In the first category are *irrelevant questions* or *neutral questions* ('Is your last name Morris?', 'Do you live in the United States?'); these questions are not included in the analysis of the results. The second category of questions are the *relevant questions*, which directly concern the crime being investigated ('Did you break into the house on Stanley Street?' 'Did you shoot Mr Philip?'). The third category are the *control questions*, which concern transgressions in the past, unrelated to the event under scrutiny ('Before the age of 25, did you ever take something that did not belong to you?'). These questions are designed to

N1:	Do you live in the USA? 'Yes'
C1:	During the first 20 years of your life, did you ever take something that did not belong to you? 'No'
R1:	Did you take that camera? 'No'
N2:	Is your name Rick? 'Yes'
C2:	Prior to 1987, did you ever do something dishonest or illegal? 'No'
R2:	Did you take that camera from the desk? 'No'
N3:	Were you born in the month of November? 'Yes'
C3:	Before the age of 21 did you ever lie to get out of trouble or to cause a problem for someone else? 'No'
R3:	Did you participate in any way in the theft of that camera? 'No'

Table 6.3: An Example of a Control Question Sequence. Table 7.1 from Vrij, A. (2000), Detecting Lies and Deceit: The Psychology of Lying and Implications for Professional Practice, 047185316X, p. 176. Reproduced by permission of John Wiley & Sons, Ltd.

force everyone to give a deceptive response, both because they are vague enough to cover the most frequent transgressions (such as lies for social purposes) and because the subject has been steered into denying such transgression during the introductory phase of the test. The purpose of the control questions is to establish a deception baseline, to which responses to the relevant questions are compared. Simply put, it is the difference in physiological responses between the relevant questions and the control questions that determine the outcome of the test. The idea is that a guilty subject will react more strongly to the relevant questions than to the control questions, while the opposite pattern is expected for innocent people (Fiedler *et al.*, 2002).

Validity of the CQT

There are two types of studies evaluating the accuracy of polygraph-assisted judgments of guilt. The first one is the *field study*, which focuses on the accuracy of the polygraph in real-life situations. These studies show that the CQT is rather good at classifying guilty suspects. In an overview by Vrij (2000), it was concluded that 87% of the guilty suspects failed the test. However, more than 21% of the innocent suspects were incorrectly classified as guilty. This indicates that the test has a tendency towards false positive errors which poses a problem in the legal system, where false positives are considered more severe mistakes than false negatives (classifying guilty suspects as innocent). The results of field studies must however be interpreted with caution. The main problem associated with these studies is being able to establish ground truth – to know whether the subject really is guilty or not. In some of the studies, a main source of information leading to classifications is confession evidence. It is a well-known fact within the scientific community that innocent people sometimes confess to crimes they have not committed (Kassin, 2004).

In laboratory studies, the ground truth is not problematic. Rather, the challenge is to create externally valid situations, taking into account among other things the high-stake nature of polygraph tests in the investigative context. One problem with giving an overall accuracy figure for laboratory-based studies on the polygraph is variability in the criteria for deciding whether a study is externally valid. Honts (2004) lists three criteria for categorizing studies as high quality. However, these criteria are not absolute: for example, one of the criteria is that the instrumentation and testing should be as similar as possible to those applied in the field setting. There could be different opinions about whether the testing is identical to that of the field setting. For example, there might be disagreement about what physical setting is the most common in real-life polygraph examinations. A second problem with estimating overall accuracy is that some reviews exclude the inconclusive results (arguing that they are not decisions, e.g. Honts, 2004), while others include these outcomes. Hence, estimates of accuracy might vary. In one estimate of accuracy (Vrij, 2000) it was concluded that the CQT was 73% accurate when it comes to classifying guilty suspects, but slightly worse (66%) when it comes to innocent suspects. In an overview by Honts (2004), average accuracy for classifying suspects was 91%, with no prominent tendency towards either false negatives or false positives. A third summary of studies produced an overall accuracy of 86% (NRC, 2003). In conclusion, although it is difficult to provide an exact figure, field and laboratory studies indicate that the CQT has some discriminative value.

Problems with the CQT

For decades, the CQT has been the target of harsh criticism (Ben-Shakhar & Furedy, 1990; Lykken, 1998). There is no room in this chapter to provide a detailed presentation of this criticism; however, we will briefly present some core arguments against the use of the CQT. First, and perhaps most importantly, a central assumption of the CQT is that innocent suspects will give more aroused responses to control questions than to relevant questions. Ekman (2001) argues that such an assumption is far from safe to make, and cites a number of reasons for such scepticism. For example, it is conceivable that innocent suspects would react more strongly to the details of the crime they are being falsely accused of (the relevant questions), than to a control question about a rather mild transgression in the past.

Some have attacked the CQT on problems related to scoring the polygraph chart, such as its subjective nature (Elaad, Ginton & Shakhar, 1994, but see Olsen *et al.*, 1997 for a possible remedy). Others have thoroughly investigated psychometric aspects of the test, such as a study based on a German review. In this study, the validity of the CQT was deemed to be clearly insufficient, and the authors concluded that the use of the test was unethical (Fiedler *et al.*, 2002). The results from this particular review led a German Supreme Court to abandon the test.

The Guilty Knowledge Test

The second type of test is the Guilty Knowledge Test (Lykken, 1959; Lykken, 1960). The test has been suggested as an alternative to the CQT (Furedy & Heslegrave, 1991). The basic idea behind the GKT is straightforward: it aims to detect concealed knowledge that only the guilty suspect has. This is done by presenting a question together with a number of answer alternatives, one of which is correct (e.g. 'What weapon was used to kill Mr Sylvester? Was it a knife? A dagger? A pair of scissors?' and so on). The assumption is that a guilty suspect, who will recognize the correct answer, will experience more physiological arousal when the correct alternative is presented, compared to the incorrect alternatives. In contrast, an innocent suspect will react on average similarly to all alternatives, since they lack the so-called guilty knowledge (MacLaren, 2001).

Validity of the GKT

The same methodological problems with field and laboratory studies as with the CQT also apply to studies evaluating the validity of the GKT, and will not be repeated. In contrast to the CQT, the GKT seems to be slightly more accurate in classifying innocent than guilty. In an overview by Vrij (2000), 96% of innocent suspects and 82% of guilty suspects were correctly classified in laboratory studies. A review of 20 such studies showed somewhat lower figures, with 83% of innocent suspects and 76% of the guilty ones were correctly classified (MacLaren, 2001). Results from real-life studies (cf. Elaad, 1990; Elaad, Ginton & Jungman, 1992) support the asymmetric pattern, and in a summary of field studies (Vrij, 2000), 96% of innocent suspects were found to be cleared by the test, while only 59% of the guilty suspects failed it.

Problems with the GKT

A survey showed that 75% of a sample of both general psychologists and psychophysiologists considered the GKT to be based on scientifically sound principles, while only 33% considered this to be true for the CQT (Iacono & Lykken, 1997). Despite this, there are problems with the GKT, of which we will address two. First, the validity of the test can be seriously challenged if the correct alternative stands out in any way. Such transparency could make the reaction pattern of innocent suspects look like that of guilty ones. One could partly solve that problem by presenting the answer alternatives to a group of naïve subjects, but Honts (2004) notes that this does not protect against idiosyncratic biases in individuals.

The second type of criticism concerns the applicability of the GKT. If the test is to be used, innocent suspects *must not* know the correct alternatives, otherwise an innocent suspect might give 'guilty' responses because of having been exposed to the critical information, for example, via the media. Moreover, the guilty suspect *must* know the answer. If a guilty person failed to perceive a certain detail at the crime scene, the guilty person might give 'innocent' responses to questions about the detail because of lack of knowledge. These conditions drastically affect the applicability of the technique, which has been estimated to be lower than 10% of FBI cases (Podlesny, 2003; cited in Honts, 2004).

Countermeasures

There has been some debate in the research field concerning the extent to which it is possible for subjects to influence the outcome of polygraph tests. Any attempts with such a purpose are called countermeasures. The aim would be (during a CQT) to purposely enhance reactions to control questions or (during a GKT) to purposely provide similar responses to all answer alternatives. It has consistently been shown that people's spontaneous countermeasures are not effective in producing false negative outcomes (Honts & Amato, 2002). However, coaching subjects in countermeasures before the test occasion is a more serious threat to the polygraph. In experimental research, subjects who received training in countermeasures managed to impair the accuracy of the CQT. The countermeasures were both physical, such as biting the tongue or pressing the toes to the floor (Honts, Hodes & Raskin, 1985), and cognitive, such as counting backwards (Honts, Raskin & Kircher, 1994). For a classification and discussion on different types of countermeasures, see Honts & Amato (2002).

DETECTING DECEPTION USING OTHER PROCEDURES

Brain Scanning

There are many methods for scanning the human brain, and one of the more common is called functional magnetic resonance imaging (fMRI). This method enables monitoring of neural activity during, for example, cognitive operations. In recent years fMRI has been used for many different purposes; among these being to study the brain activity taking place during deception. The findings from this research indicate that neural activity during lying may be different compared to activity during telling the truth (Spence *et al.*, 2004). Specifically, fMRI studies show an increased activity in the prefrontal cortex during deception (i.e. the 'executive' part of the brain, supporting complex human behaviour such as speech and problem solving). These studies can be taken to indicate that lying is more cognitively demanding than telling the truth (Vrij *et al.*, 2006).

The use of fMRI as a deception-detection tool has received extensive media coverage. Indeed, the studies on neural correlates of deception are intriguing, and the findings reported are (so far) promising. Importantly though, this does not mean that the deception enigma is solved once and for all. Besides the fact that fMRI equipment is extremely expensive, immobile and demands a target to remain still, the studies conducted so far are very few. It still remains to be shown whether fMRI is diagnostic for deception in situations of high forensic relevance. It is probably safe to assume that studies using fMRI will shed some light on the cognitive processes taking place during deception, but we will refrain from speculating on potential future applications of these techniques in forensic settings.

Combining Methods to Detect Deception

Research on deception detection is, as reflected in the structure of the current chapter, very much divided into camps. Some researchers focus on the diagnostic value of verbal content techniques, others examine people's ability to detect deception from non-verbal behaviour, and yet others examine the accuracy of psychophysiological methods. The combination of methods is an understudied topic (Granhag & Strömwall, 2004), which to some extent can be explained by the fact that some methods are very difficult to combine, for example, verbal content techniques and the polygraph. Recent research does however suggest that some combinations might be worth exploring. It has, for example, been demonstrated that lie catchers who use verbal and non-verbal cues simultaneously, outperform those using only verbal cues, or only non-verbal cues (e.g. Vrij & Mann, 2004; Vrij *et al.*, 2004). It is also reasonable to assume that future work on deception will profit from combining different methods. For example, fRMI research can offer relatively detailed information on liars' and truth tellers' cognitive processes; such knowledge could be used both in theoretical work and for developing interview techniques focused on suspects' cognitive load (Vrij *et al.*, 2006).

The Effects of Training to Detect Deception

Workshops on 'deception detection' are very popular and exist in a number of countries. Some of these workshops offer to train participants in becoming better lie catchers. The effectiveness of these training programmes is rarely evaluated, therefore we know little thereof. Turning to scientific studies on the effect of training, that is, controlled attempts to train people to become better at distinguishing between liars and truth tellers, a few things should be noted. First, such studies have been conducted for quite some time (for summaries of this line of research, see Bull, 1989; 2004). Second, the methodologies used in order to train the participants vary extensively over the different studies. Some programmes have included information about cues to deception (e.g. Fiedler & Walka, 1993), whereas others include both information on cues to deception and outcome feedback about one's own deception detection performance (e.g. Porter, Woodworth & Birth, 2000). Third, the effects of training are generally small. A meta-analysis by Frank and Feeley (2003), based on 20 training v. no training comparisons (extracted from 11 published studies), showed a very small overall effect in terms of deception detection accuracy (the positive effect was significant, but added only to a 4% gain for trained participants).

CASE STUDY

When Training to Detect Deception Works

A study by Hartwig and colleagues (2006) showed that it is possible to train police trainees to become better at detecting deception. Their study set out to investigate the effects of the so-called *Strategic Use of Evidence technique* (the SUE technique). This technique draws on the assumption that guilty and innocent suspects use different strategies when being interviewed about a crime (Hartwig, Granhag & Strömwall, 2007). In brief, guilty suspects tend to use self-regulative methods aiming at controlling what to admit, avoid and deny (i.e. the goal is to withhold, at least, some self-incriminating information from the interviewer). In contrast, innocent suspects' self-regulative methods are often driven by the belief that 'their innocence will shine through' (Kassin, 2005). Hence, their strategies are much less sophisticated (i.e. the goal is that the interviewer will come to know what they know, at least with respect to their own actions). Drawing on these differences the SUE technique suggests that the interviewer should use the information that he or she holds about the crime (the evidence), strategically during the interview. That is, not to disclose this information early in the interview and to make sure that the suspect addresses this information (by asking questions that do not reveal how much he or she knows).

The study was carried out at a Police Academy in Sweden, and a total of 82 police trainees participated. In the first phase of the study (day 1), half of the trainees received a three-hour training session in the SUE technique, while the other half received no such training. In the second phase of the study (day 2), a group of 82 university students acted as mock suspects, and half of these committed a mock theft by stealing a wallet from a briefcase in a bookstore (guilty suspects). The other half visited the same bookstore, searched for a particular item, but committed no mock theft (innocent suspects). Later on the same day, each suspect (either guilty or innocent) was interviewed by one police trainee (either trained or untrained). The trained and untrained police trainees were given exactly the same case file, containing pieces of evidence pointing to the suspect's guilt (e.g. information that the suspect's fingerprints had been found on the briefcase). This evidence was 'true' for all suspects, in that all guilty suspects had to touch the briefcase in order to steal the wallet, and all innocent suspects had to touch the briefcase in order to properly search a particular box for a paper punch. The trained ones were asked to interview in line with the SUE technique, and the untrained ones were free to interview as they wished. By providing the police trainees with background information, and allowing them to interview the suspect (instead of passively watching a video taped interview), the design of this study is very different from all previous training studies.

The results showed that the trained interviewers did indeed use the SUE technique, whereas the untrained interviewers did not. Furthermore, the analysis showed that (a) guilty suspects avoided mentioning incriminating information during the free recall phase of the interview (whereas innocent suspects showed a much less avoidant strategy), and (b) guilty suspects denied holding incriminating information when asked specific questions addressing this information (whereas innocent suspects showed much less denial). This boiled down to the fact that guilty suspects interviewed by trained interviewers produced statements that were much more inconsistent with the existing evidence than did guilty suspects interviewed by untrained interviewers. Specifically, the more statement-evidence inconsistency, the more likely were the trained interviewers to assess the suspect as guilty (the same association did not prove significant for untrained interviewers). In brief, by using the SUE technique, the trained interviewers created and used a diagnostic cue to deception: statement-evidence inconsistency. The overall deception accuracy was 85.4% for trained interviewers and 56.1% for untrained interviewers. The accuracy score for the trained interviewers is one of the highest in the scientific literature, whereas the accuracy score for the untrained is in line with most other groups tested (Bond & DePaulo, 2006).

Detecting Simulated Amnesia

To falsely claim not to remember is to lie; it is to conceal the truth. It has been estimated that between 20% to 30% of violent crime offenders claim amnesia and that a large portion of these offenders feign their amnesia (Christianson & Merkelbach, 2004). To distinguish between simulated and real amnesia is a far-from-easy task. Therefore, researchers have started to systematically compare crime-related amnesia to non-crime amnesia (authentic amnesia). Such work shows a number of interesting mismatches: (i) crime-related amnesia is typically described as a total memory loss, whereas non-crime amnesic victims tend to report fragments of memories from the event; (ii) crime-related amnesia is typically described as having a sharp beginning and end, whereas these are fuzzy for non-crime amnesic victims, and (iii) those claiming crime-related amnesia tend to be more dogmatic ("I will never ever remember"), whereas non-crime amnesic victims are more willing to try different memory-enhancing techniques. In sum, when offenders claim amnesia, the characteristics of this amnesia deviate from the characteristics of amnesia of non-criminals' events. Well-established theories and findings on human memory suggest that authentic amnesia for an entire crime event is unlikely (Christianson & Merkelbach, 2004).

CONCLUSIONS

Research on deception detection has exploded over the past years, and the current zeitgeist tells us that this particular sub-area of forensic psychology will continue to grow. In an era of threat, violence and terrorism a premium is placed on research dealing with security and control. We believe that research on deception detection has an important role to play in the struggle for justice and a safer society. However, in order for research to make a significant contribution, and to have a fair chance to reach the desks of policy makers, several tough challenges must be faced and dealt with. In short, it is not enough to debunk the 'foolproof-way-to-detect deception' claims flourishing in the media and in pseudo-science; researchers also need to pay close attention to their own activities. It is true that the field offers many new and intriguing problems (e.g. deception over the Internet), as well as a number of old problems still awaiting solutions (e.g. how to train people to become better lie catchers). In order to properly address these problems, the ecological validity of the overall research agenda must be increased. For example, researchers must come up with creative designs that better mirror the interactive processes at play in most real-life interview situations. On a positive note, it is possible to discern a paradigmatic shift in research focus from studies mapping people's judgement errors and wrongful beliefs, toward studies with an aim of enhancing people's deception detection performance (Granhag & Vrij, 2005). This is indeed promising, but our conclusion is that much significant work on deception has yet to be conducted.

SUMMARY

- In order to predict liars' and truth tellers' behaviour, four different approaches have been suggested: the emotional approach, the content complexity approach, the attempted control approach, and the self-presentational perspective.

- Research shows that people are poor at detecting deception. The main reasons are that cues to deception are very scarce (objective cues), and that people's beliefs about cues to deception (subjective cues) are incorrect.
- *Statement Validity Analysis* and *Reality Monitoring* are two methods for analysing a statement's verbal content in order to detect deception. Scientific evaluation shows that none of these methods is perfect, but that they can be of help when assessing veracity.
- There is reason to be sceptical towards alternative methods such as Scientific Content Analysis, Voice Stress Analysis and Layered Voice Analysis, as these methods rest on very weak theoretical grounds, and lack empirical support.
- The Control Question Test (CQT) and the Guilty Knowledge Test (GKT) are the two most common tests within the domain of psychophysiological detection of deception. While both tests have been heavily criticized, they are both proven to have some discriminative value.

ESSAY/DISCUSSION QUESTIONS

1. The area of deception detection is not very well developed in terms of theory. However, a number of approaches have been suggested in order to predict behavioural differences between liars and truth tellers. Name and describe four such approaches, and reflect on their similarities and differences.

2. Research shows that people's deception detection performance is rather poor. How can this result be explained?

3. It is possible to identify two main techniques for analysing a statement's verbal content in order to detect deception. Describe these two methods and their reliability and accuracy.

4. Broadly speaking, there are two types of polygraph tests. Describe each type and their similarities and differences. Is either test a reliable instrument for detecting deception by offenders?

REFERENCES

Alonso-Quecuty, M.L. (1992). Deception detection and reality monitoring: a new answer to an old question?. In F. Lösel, D. Bender, & T. Bliesener (Eds). *Psychology and Law: International Perspectives* (pp. 328–332). Berlin: Walter de Gruyter.

Ben-Shakhar, G., Bar-Hillel, M., & Kremnitzer, M. (2002). Trial by polygraph: Reconsidering the use of the Guilty Knowledge Technique in court. *Law and Human Behavior, 26,* 527–541.

Ben-Shakhar, G. & Furedy, J.J. (1990). *Theories and applications in the detection of deception: A Psychophysiological and International Perspective.* New York: Springer-Verlag.

Bond Jr, C.F. & DePaulo, B.M. (2006). Accuracy of deception judgments. *Personality and Social Psychology Review, 10,* 214–234.

British Psychological Society (1986). The report of the working group on the use of the poly-graph in criminal investigations and personnel screening. *Bulletin of the British Psychological Society, 39,* 81–94.

British Psychological Society (2004). *A review of the current scientific status and fields of application of polygraphic deception detection.* Final Report from the BPS Working Party.

Bull, R. (1989). Can training enhance the detection of deception? In J. Yuille (Ed.). *Credibility assessment.* Deventer: Kluwer Academic.

Bull, R. (2004). Training to detect deception from behavioural cues: attempts and problems. In P.A. Granhag & L.A. Strömwall (Eds), *The detection of deception in forensic contexts* (pp. 251–268). Cambridge: Cambridge University Press.

Burgoon, J.K., Buller, D.B., & Guerrero, L.K. (1995). Interpersonal deception IX: Effects of social skills and nonverbal communication on deception success and detection accuracy. *Journal of Language and Social Psychology, 14,* 289–311.

Christianson, S.Å. & Merckelbach, H. (2004). Crime-related amnesia as a form of deception. In P.A. Granhag & L.A. Strömwall (Eds), *The detection of deception in forensic contexts* (pp. 195–225). Cambridge: Cambridge University Press.

Davies, G.M. (2001). Is it possible to discriminate true from false memories? In G.M. Davies & T. Dalgleish (Eds). *Recovered memories: Seeking the middle ground* (pp. 153–176). Chichester: John Wiley & Sons.

DePaulo, B.M. (1992). Nonverbal behavior and self-presentation. *Psychological Bulletin, 111,* 203–243.

DePaulo, B.M. & Kirkendol, S.E. (1989). The motivational impairment effect in the communication of deception. In J.C. Yuille (Ed.), *Credibility assessment* (pp. 51–70). Dordrecht, the Netherlands: Kluwer.

DePaulo, B.M., LeMay, C.S., & Epstein, J.A. (1991). Effects of importance of success and expectations for success on effectiveness at deceiving. *Personality and Social Psychology Bulletin, 17,* 14–24.

DePaulo, B.M., Lindsay, J.J., Malone, B.E., *et al.* (2003). Cues to deception. *Psychological Bulletin, 129,* 74–118.

DePaulo, R.M. & Morris, W.L. (2004). Discerning lies from truths: Behavioral cues to deception and the indirect pathway of intuition. In P.A. Granhag & L.A. Strömwall (Eds), *The detection of deception in forensic contexts* (pp. 15–40). Cambridge: Cambridge University Press.

Ekman, P. (2001). *Telling lies: Clues to deceit in the marketplace, politics and marriage.* New York: Norton.

Ekman P. & Friesen, W.V. (1972). Hand movements. *Journal of Communication, 22,* 353–374.

Elaad, E. (1990). Detection of guilty knowledge in real-life criminal investigations. *Journal of Applied Psychology, 75,* 521–529.

Elaad, E., Ginton, A., & Jungman, N. (1992). Detection measures in real-life criminal guilty knowledge tests. *Journal of Applied Psychology, 77,* 757–767.

Elaad, E., Ginton, A., & Shakhar, G. (1994). The effects of prior expectations and outcome knowledge on polygraph examiners' decision. *Journal of Behavioral Decision-Making, 7,* 279–292.

Eriksson, A. (in press). Charlatanry in forensic speech science: A problem to be taken seriously. *International Journal of Speech, Language and the Law.*

Faigman, D.L., Kaye, D., Saks, M.J., & Sanders, J. (Eds) (2002). *Modern scientific evidence: The law and science of expert testimony*, Vol. II (pp. 446–483). St. Paul, MN: West.

Fiedler, K., Schmid, J., & Stahl, T. (2002). What is the current truth about polygraph lie detection? *Basic and Applied Social Psychology, 24*, 313–324.

Fiedler, K. & Walka, I. (1993). Training lie detectors to use nonverbal cues instead of global heuristics. *Human Communication Research, 20*, 199–223.

Frank, M.G. & Feeley, T.H. (2003). To catch a liar: Challenges for research in lie detection training. *Journal of Applied Communication Research, 31*, 58–75.

Furedy, J.J. & Heslegrave, R.J. (1991). The forensic use of the polygraph: A psychophysiological analysis of current trends and future prospects. In J.R. Jennings, P.K. Ackles, & M.G. Coles (Eds), *Advances in psychophysiology*, Vol. 4 (pp. 157–189). Greenwich, CT: JAI Press.

Granhag, P.A. & Strömwall, L.A. (2004). Deception detection in forensic contexts: Intersections and future challenges. In P.A. Granhag & L.A. Strömwall (Eds), *The detection of deception in forensic contexts* (pp. 317–330). Cambridge: Cambridge University Press.

Granhag, P.A. & Vrij, A. (2005). Detecting deception. In N. Brewer & K. Williams (Eds). *Psychology & law: An empirical perspective* (pp. 43–92). New York: Guilford Press.

Grubin, D. & Madsen, L. (2005). Lie detection and the polygraph: A historical review. *The Journal of Forensic Psychiatry and Psychology, 16*, 357–369.

Grubin, D. & Madsen, L. (2006). Accuracy and utility of post-conviction polygraph testing of sex offenders. *British Journal of Psychiatry, 188*, 479–483.

Gudjonsson, G.H. (2003). *The Psychology of interrogations and confessions: A handbook.* Chichester: John Wiley & Sons.

Hartwig, M., Granhag, P.A., & Strömwall, L.A. (2007). Guilty and innocent suspects' strategies during police interrogations. *Psychology, Crime and Law, 13*, 213–227.

Hartwig, M., Granhag, P.A., Strömwall, L.A., & Kronkvist, O. (2006). Strategic use of evidence during police interviews: When training to detect deception works. *Law and Human Behavior, 30*, 603–619.

Hartwig, M., Granhag, P.A., Strömwall, L.A., & Vrij, A. (2004). Police officers' lie detection accuracy: Interrogating freely vs observing video. *Police Quarterly, 7*, 429–456.

Hira, S. & Furumitsu, I. (2002). Polygraphic examinations in Japan: Application of the guilty knowledge test in forensic investigations. *International Journal of Police Science and Management, 4*, 16–27.

Honts, C.R. (2004). The psychophysiological detection of deception. In P.A. Granhag & L.A. Strömwall (Eds), *The detection of deception in forensic contexts* (pp. 103–123). Cambridge: Cambridge University Press.

Honts, C.R. & Amato, S. (2002). Countermeasures. In M. Kleiner (Ed.), *Handbook of polygraph testing* (pp. 251–264). London: Academic.

Honts, C.R., Hodes, R.L., & Raskin, D.C. (1985). Effects of physical countermeasures on the physiological detection of deception. *Journal of Applied Psychology, 70*, 177–187.

Honts, C.R., Raskin, D.C., & Kircher, J.C. (1994). Mental and physical countermeasures reduce the accuracy of polygraph tests. *Journal of Applied Psychology, 79*, 252–259.

Iacono, W.G. & Lykken, D.T. (1997). The validity of the lie detector: Two surveys of scientific opinion. *Journal of Applied Psychology, 82*, 426–433.

Inbau, F.E., Reid, J.E., Buckley, J.P., & Jayne, B.C. (2001). *Criminal Interrogation and Confessions*. Gaithersburg: Aspen Publishers.

Johnson, M. K. & Raye, C. L. (1981). Reality monitoring. *Psychological Review*, 88, 67–85.

Kassin, S.M. (2004). True or false: 'I'd know a false confession if I saw one'. In P.A. Granhag & L.A. Strömwall (Eds), *The Detection of Deception in Forensic Contexts* (pp. 172–194). Cambridge: Cambridge University Press.

Kassin, S.M. (2005). On the psychology of confessions: Does innocence put innocents at risk? *American Psychologist, 60*, 215–228.

Kassin, S.M. & Fong, C. (1999). 'I'm innocent!': Effects of training on judgments of truth and deception in the interrogation room. *Law and Human Behavior, 23*, 499–16.

Köhnken, G. (2004). Statement Validity Analysis and the 'detection of the truth'. In P.A. Granhag & L.A. Strömwall (Eds), *The Detection of Deception in Forensic Contexts* (pp. 41–63). Cambridge: Cambridge University Press.

Lykken, D.T. (1959). The GSR in the detection of guilt. *Journal of Applied Psychology, 44*, 385–388.

Lykken, D.T. (1960). The validity of the guilty knowledge technique: The effects of faking. *Journal of Applied Psychology, 44*, 258–262.

Lykken, D.T. (1998). *A Tremor in the Blood: Uses and Abuses of the Lie Detector*. New York: Plenum Press.

MacLaren, V.V. (2001). A quantitative review of the Guilty Knowledge Test. *Journal of Applied Psychology, 86*, 674–683.

Madsen, L., Parsons, S., & Grubin, D. (2004). A preliminary study of the contribution of periodic polygraph testing to the treatment and supervision of sex offenders. *British Journal of Forensic Psychiatry and Psychology, 15*, 682–695.

Mann, S., Vrij, A., & Bull, R. (2004). Detecting true lies: Police officers' ability to detect suspects' lies. *Journal of Applied Psychology, 89*, 137–149.

Masip, J., Sporer, S.L., Garrido, E., & Herrero, C. (2005). The detection of deception with the Reality Monitoring approach: A review of the empirical evidence. *Psychology, Crime and Law, 11*, 99–122.

Miller, G.R. & Stiff, J.B. (1993). *Deceptive Communication*. Newbury Park: Sage Publications.

National Research Council (NRC) (2003). *The Polygraph and Lie Detection*. Washington, DC: National Academy Press.

Newman, M.L., Pennebaker, J.W., Berry, D.S., & Richards, J.M. (2003). Lying words: Predicting deception from linguistic styles. *Personality and Social Psychology Bulletin*, 29, 665–675.

Olsen, D.E., Harris, J.C., Capps, M.H., & Ansley, N. (1997). Computerized polygraph scoring system. *Journal of Forensic Sciences, 42*, 61–70.

Pennebaker, J.W. & King, L.A. (1999). Linguistic styles: Language use as an individual difference. *Journal of Personality and Social Psychology*, 77, 1296–1312.

Pollina, D.A., Dollins, A.B., Senter, S.M., Krapohl, D.J., & Ryan, A.H. (2004). Comparison of polygraph data obtained from individuals involved in mock crimes and actual criminal investigations. *Journal of Applied Psychology, 89*, 1099–1105.

Porter, S., Woodworth, M., & Birth, A. (2000). Truth, lies and videotape: An investigation of the ability of federal parole officers to detect deception. *Law and Human Behavior, 24*, 643–658.

Porter, S. & Yuille, J.C. (1996). The language of deceit: An investigation of the verbal clues to deception in the interrogation context. *Law and Human Behavior, 20*, 443–458.

Reid, John E. & Associates (2007). *The Reid Technique of interviewing and interrogation.* Retrieved 20 January 2007 from: www.reid.com.

Segrave, K. (2004). *Lie detectors: A social history.* Jefferson, NC: McFarland & Company.

Shearer, R.A. (1999). Statement Analysis Scan or Scam? *Skeptical Inquirer, 23,* May/June Issue.

Shipp, T. & Izdebski, K. (1981). Current evidence for the existence of laryngeal macrotremor and microtremor. *Journal of Forensic Science, 26,* 501–505.

Smith, N. (2001). *Reading between the lines: An evaluation of the scientific content analysis technique (SCAN).* London: Home Office – Policing and reducing crime.

Spence, S.A., Hunter M., Farrow T., *et al.* (2006). A cognitive neurobiological account of deception: Evidence from functional neuroimaging. In S. Zeki & O. Goodenough (Eds), *Law and the brain* (pp. 169–182). Oxford: Oxford University Press.

Sporer, S.L. (2004). Reality monitoring and detection of deception. In P.A. Granhag & L.A. Strömwall (Eds), *The detection of deception in forensic contexts* (pp. 64–102). Cambridge: Cambridge University Press.

Steller, M. & Köhnken, G. (1989). Criteria-Based Content Analysis. In D.C. Raskin (Ed.), *Psychological methods in criminal investigation and evidence* (pp. 217–245). New York, Springer-Verlag.

Strömwall, L.A., Granhag, P.A., & Hartwig, M. (2004). Practitioners' beliefs about deception. In P.A. Granhag & L.A. Strömwall (Eds). *The detection of deception in forensic contexts* (pp. 229–250). Cambridge: Cambridge University Press.

Sullivan, E. (2001). *The concise book of lying.* New York: Picador.

Trankell, A. (1963). *Vittnespsykologins arbetsmetoder.* Stockholm: Liber.

Undeutsch, U. (1967). Beurteilung der Glaubhaftigkeit von Aussagen. In U. Undeitsch (Ed.). *Handbuch der psychologie Vol. 11: Forensische psychologie* (pp. 26–181). Göttingen: Hogrefe.

Vrij, A. (2000). *Detecting lies and deceit: The psychology of lying and its implications for professional practice.* Chichester: John Wiley & Sons.

Vrij, A. (2003). We will protect your wife and child, but only if you confess. In P.J. van Koppen & S.D. Penrod (Eds), *Adversarial versus inquisitorial justice: Psychological perspectives on criminal justice systems* (pp. 55–79). New York, NJ: Kluwer Academic.

Vrij, A. (2004). Why professionals fail to catch liars and how they can improve. *Legal and Criminological Psychology, 9,* 159–181.

Vrij, A. (2005a). Criteria-Based Content Analysis: The first 37 studies. *Psychology, Public Policy and Law, 11,* 3–41.

Vrij, A. (2005b). Cooperation of liars and truth tellers. *Applied Cognitive Psychology, 19,* 39–50.

Vrij, A. (2008). *Detecting lies and deceit: Pitfalls and opportunities.* Chichester: John Wiley & Sons.

Vrij, A., Akehurst, L. Soukara, S., & Bull, R. (2004). Detecting deceit via analyses of verbal and nonverbal behavior in children and adults. *Human Communication Research, 30,* 8–41.

Vrij, A., Fisher, R., Mann, S., & Leal, S. (2006). Detecting deception by manipulating cognitive load. *Trends in Cognitive Science, 10,* 141–142.

Vrij, A. & Mann, S. (2004). Detecting deception: The benefit of looking at a combination of behavioral, auditory and speech content related cues in a systematic manner. *Group Decision and Negotiation, 13,* 61–79.

Vrij, A., Mann, S., Kristen, S., & Fisher, R.P. (2007). Cues to deception and ability to detect lies as a function of police interview styles. *Law and Human Behavior, 31,* 499–518.

Vrij, A. & Semin, G.R. (1996). Lie experts' beliefs about nonverbal indicators of deception. *Journal of Nonverbal Behavior, 20,* 65–80.

Zuckerman, M., DePaulo, B.M., & Rosenthal, R. (1981). Verbal and nonverbal communication of deception. In L. Berkowitz (Ed.), *Advances in experimental social psychology* (Vol. 14, pp. 1–59). New York: Academic Press.

ANNOTATED READING LIST

DePaulo, B.M., Lindsay, J.J., Malone, B.E., *et al.* (2003). Cues to deception. *Psychological Bulletin, 129,* 74–118. *Most recent and comprehensive meta-analysis of the research on cues to deception, highlighting how few cues are consistently reliable.*

Ekman, P. (2001). *Telling lies: Clues to deceit in the marketplace, politics and marriage.* New York: Norton. *Classic analysis of the process of deception written by an internationally acknowledged pioneer of the field.*

Granhag, P.A. & Strömwall, L.A. (Eds) (2004). *The detection of deception in forensic contexts.* Cambridge: Cambridge University Press. *Collection of papers by an international group of experts on various aspects of lying and deception.*

Granhag, P.A. & Vrij, A. (2005). Detecting deception. In N. Brewer & K. Williams (Eds). *Psychology and law: An empirical perspective* (pp. 43–92). New York: Guilford Press. *A useful recent review of the research literature written by the first author and Vrij.*

Vrij, A. (2008). *Detecting lies and deceit: Pitfalls and opportunities.* Chichester: John Wiley & Sons. *Aldert Vrij's book is probably the most comprehensive treatment of the research literature on lie detection.*

PART 3

THE TRIAL PROCESS

CHAPTER 7

JUDICIAL PROCESSES

Jacqueline M. Wheatcroft
Manchester Metropolitan University, United Kingdom

To many psychologists, the criminal justice system often seems remote and complex, even mystifying. Even its main aim – is it to uncover 'the truth' or construct a case against the guilty? – may seem confusing. This chapter examines the interface between psychology and law and the courts. It aims to provide an overview and understanding of the two principle legal systems that operate in different parts of the world and to examine the psychological processes that could influence decision making in the courtroom. Issues explored include the impact of different styles of questioning by advocates, pre-trial publicity and judicial pronouncements. In the UK and the US among other countries, judges and juries are central to the judicial process and the decisions taken. Research has explored how the composition, legal understanding and group dynamics of juries influence the verdicts they reach, and in systems that rely on judges and magistrates alone to pronounce on guilt, how they decide between the rival narratives of events offered by the prosecution and defence.

UNDERSTANDING THE JUSTICE SYSTEM

Adversarial versus Inquisitorial Systems of Justice

The two principal systems of justice in the Western world are the adversarial and inquisitorial systems. The **adversarial** system is based on the principles of common law, originating in England and now widely applied, both in the US and most Commonwealth countries. A trial under the adversarial system has been described by Damaska (1973) as structured proceedings involving a dispute between two sides that are in position of theoretical equality and where the court – whether judge, magistrate or jury – decides the outcome. In the UK, judges tend to be impartial umpires of procedure and are not involved in the investigation or preparation of cases or the evidence, although judges do sometimes decide *what* can be presented as evidence. Judges' main interests therefore lie in the fairness of the conduct of the trial rather than the outcome. According to the pure adversarial model, the judge plays a passive and disinterested role, merely ruling on legal technicalities when these are raised by one or other side. However, totally non-interventionist judges are somewhat mythical, particularly in civil or magistrates' courts where the judge may also become the trier of fact. More serious criminal matters are decided by juries, in the main consisting of laypersons without legal training but whose role and sworn duty is to "faithfully try the defendant and give a *true* verdict according to that evidence".

Conversely, in the **inquisitorial** approach practised in much of the European continent, judges are expected to arrive at the truth through their own investigations. Prior to trial, a full judicial investigation is conducted including interviewing witnesses and examining the defence case. In France, for example, this is done by the *juge d'instruction*, who is half magistrate, half police detective. Whether a case proceeds or not is decided by the judge and the trial itself is seen as a disinterested investigation rather than a dispute.

The major differences between the two systems (see Table 7.1 for summary) include when and how evidence is presented, and the role of the judge: theoretically passive in the adversarial system, but playing a leadership role both in terms of process and decision making in the inquisitorial system. However, in reality, neither system is wholly adversarial or totally inquisitorial. Several continental countries have introduced juries into inquisitorial processes, while in England and Wales, recent law reform, such as the right to silence and the need for magistrates to explain and justify their decisions, has led to inquisitorial elements being incorporated into the adversarial tradition.

SYSTEM	Mode	Evidence	Judicial role	Judicial interest
Adversarial	Dispute	At trial	Passive	Fairness of process
Inquisitorial	Investigation	Prior to trial	Leadership	Caseworthiness

Table 7.1: Key aspects of adversarial and inquisitorial systems of justice

Criminal versus Civil Cases

Both adversarial and inquisitorial systems distinguish between **civil** and **criminal** proceedings. The two processes typically differ in terms of **standards of proof** and rules of evidence. In England and Wales, in civil cases the general standard for a finding of guilty is on the *balance of probability*: *"if the evidence is such that the tribunal can say that we think it more probable than not the burden is discharged, but if the evidence is equal it is not"* (Eggleston, 1978, p. 129). This suggests an even balance, although would a probability of 0.501 suffice? In reality, this would not be sufficient when the overall impact of a guilty verdict upon the parties involved is taken into account. For example, in civil cases involving the custody of children, the courts have taken the view that any decisions should be taken with a burden of proof akin to that in criminal cases.

The criminal standard of proof requires *proof beyond reasonable doubt* (*Woolmington v. DPP,* 1935). It represents a much higher standard than its civil counterpart, yet still falls well short of scientific certainty. Definitions of the standard have been attempted and have often realized greater confusion than the standard itself. Lord Denning set the standard as: *"Proof beyond reasonable doubt does not mean proof beyond the shadow of a doubt . . . If the evidence against an individual is so strong that there is only a remote possibility in his favour . . . the case is proved beyond reasonable doubt, but nothing short of that will suffice"* (*Miller v. Minister of Pensions,* 1947). More recently, so long as the judge conveys the high degree of certainty required to the jury then that is thought to be satisfactory.

Associated with civil and criminal cases is the regulation of the process of proof through **rules of evidence,** which are designed to ensure a fair trial in either system. In civil cases the issues to be decided are typically those of liability and damages and since the introduction of the new Civil Procedure Rules in 1998, there has been a renewed emphasis on reducing cost, delay and complexity. Evidential issues may include issues of law and witness competence, and the weight to be attached to **expert evidence**. In criminal cases, the issue is one of guilt or innocence. The rules here cover styles of questioning, issues around hearsay and procedural rights, what the jury may hear and what use they can make of information in reaching their decision.

Magistrates' versus Crown Court

In England and Wales the great majority of criminal cases – some 95% – are heard in **Magistrates' Courts**. The least serious, known as '**summary**' offences, are tried by magistrates themselves and even those charged with more serious criminal offences, such as murder, manslaughter, rape and robbery, first appear in magistrates' court before passing to the **Crown Court** to be dealt with. Summary offences, such as common assault, must be tried in the Magistrates' Court, but '**either way**' offences, such as theft, can be tried either by magistrates or by jury in the Crown Court, dependent on the circumstances of each case and the wishes of the defendant.

The dynamics of being tried in Magistrates' Court are different to Crown Court in that the legal perception is that a defendant is more likely to be acquitted in the latter. However, such faith in juror decision making could well be misplaced according to research reviewed later in this chapter. In Magistrates' Court there is no separation between interpretation of the law and the finding of fact. Thus, magistrates may need to decide whether some evidence is admissible, but regardless of their decision, those sitting the case will have already heard the evidence. In Crown Court the judge decides upon the law and jury decides the facts. This might suggest that there is less room for bias in Crown Court procedures. Conversely, some lawyers have argued that precisely because juries are not allowed access to important evidence that they reach perverse decisions (see Taylor, 2004). Whether in the Crown Court or Magistrates' Court, decisions need to be reached on reliable evidence and it is on the reliability of such evidence that much psychological research has been conducted.

EVIDENCE IN COURT

The Impact of Appearance and Demeanour of Witness and Defendant on Decision-Making Processes

---

CASE STUDY

Convicted for a Speech Impediment?

Garry Coombe's downfall was his stutter. Charged with assaulting his wife, his speech impediment in court was mistaken for dishonesty. He was convicted after the magistrate did not believe his evidence because there was a noticeable tremor in his voice (Dick, 2006). Regardless of the legal facts or evidence presented at trial, Gary Coombe's case illustrates that there are effects of appearance and demeanour that may influence judicial assessments and impact upon the decision-making process.

Experimental research has shown that the attractiveness of a plaintiff is more likely to result in a favourable outcome for that complainant and accordingly such individuals would receive greater compensatory damages (Stephan & Corder-Tully, 1977). Even attractive defendants found guilty attract demonstrably less severe punishment, regardless of case type, than unattractive ones (Zebrowitz & McDonald, 1991). This influence upon what represents goodness is known as the 'halo effect' (Cooper, 1981) and suggests that judgments of attractive people may be more positive on a variety of dimensions. Feild (1979) conducted an analysis of the effects of victim and defendant case characteristics in relation to rape cases. Feild found an overall impact of attractiveness of the victim on trial outcome, but factors such as race, victim sexual experience, evidence strength and type of rape committed all moderated the effects of attractiveness, suggesting that the impact of attractiveness on jurors' decisions is far more complex than has previously been thought (see Memon, Vrij & Bull, 2003 for review).

Other characteristics, such as tearful remorse attracts fewer guilty verdicts and those defendants with an evident disability are more likely to receive the benefit of the doubt with regard to guilt, responsibility and sentence leniency. However, those who have a lower moral character (Hans & Vidmar, 1986) or previous convictions, recent or old (unless both recent and dissimilar to the current charge – Lloyd-Bostock, 2006), are more likely to be convicted.

Witness Credibility

The kinds of questioning styles used during cross-examination may influence the ways in which jurors perceive credibility. Wheatcroft, Wagstaff and Kebbell (2004) studied the effects of what they termed 'lawyerese' (i.e. the use of complex question forms) on the inferences made by those hearing the questioning, with regard to the accuracy and confidence of the witness. Mock jurors were most affected by observing the lawyerese with **negative feedback** style; judging the witness overall to be less accurate. Thus, implying the witness might be wrong through negative feedback may make observers doubt the accuracy of the witness' testimony (see Wheatcroft, Kebbell & Wagstaff, 2001). Research has also demonstrated that when mock jurors hear inconsistent recall testimony they perceive the eyewitness to be less accurate and credible (Berman, Narby & Cutler, 1995; Brewer *et al.*, 1999).

Research also suggests jurors believe confidence is a valid predictor of accuracy. Hence, many studies have demonstrated that jurors and jurists rely heavily upon the demeanour of the witness; if the witness appears to be confident, s/he will be considered more accurate (Cutler, Penrod & Dexter, 1990; Kassin, Rigby & Castillo, 1991; Leippe, Manion & Romanczyk, 1992; Lindsay, 1994; Sporer, 1993). Furthermore, Wheatcroft *et al.* found that, regardless of questioning style, presenting the testimony of the least confident witness first appeared to spuriously boost confidence and thereby perceived accuracy, in that witness' testimony. In this case, observers were possibly reliant upon their initial judgments and subsequently were unable to make sufficient adjustment upon hearing further witnesses (see Tversky & Kahneman, 1974 for details of such anchoring effects). Therefore, presentation *order* could have significant implication for demeanour judgments.

Overall, it seems that confident and likeable witnesses may be more likely to be believed than timid, unattractive or unsavoury ones. Thus, appropriate credit may not be given where it is due. Correspondingly, the drawing of false inferences from appearance and demeanour remains worryingly high. Moreover, commentators have previously overlooked the potential role of immediate situational factors, such as examination styles, within the courtroom process itself.

Styles of Examination and Cross-Examination by Lawyers

In court, every witness is subject to examination both by the party who has called the person as a witness and all the other parties who are legally represented at the trial. Examinations consist of **examination-in-chief**, **cross-examination**, re-examination, and possible examination by judge and/or magistrates (Murphy, 1994). Examination-in-chief is a procedure that rests upon the notion of gaining the trust of the court and jury in the witness; a witness' own counsel will encourage the witness to provide a free narrative account of events and importantly leading and suggestive questioning styles are disallowed. Cross-examination, however, has a different purpose: to establish witness creditworthiness. Thus, DuCann (1964) cites Lord Hanworth's statement: "*Cross-examination is a powerful and valuable weapon for the purpose of testing the veracity of a witness and the accuracy and completeness of his story*" (p. 95). Accordingly, a witness' knowledge of facts, impartiality, truthfulness, character, bias, unreliability, respect for oath and general demeanour can all be challenged at this point. Unsurprisingly, therefore, cross-examination strategies are built around the development of the most effective way to discredit a witness's account.

On the whole, cross-examination procedures have long been thought by the legal profession to be crucial for probing the accuracy of evidence obtained in the examination-in-chief, and to expose unreliable or dishonest witnesses (Stone, 1988). Hence, a firm rationale has developed in legal culture whereby **leading questions** may be permitted during cross-examination. Moreover, it is generally contended that asking questions containing false **presupposition** is a normal, useful, and effective procedure for verifying doubtful information and introducing new information (Hickey, 1993). Arguably then, the admissibility of leading questions is based upon the notion that they serve to calibrate or assess the memories of witnesses. However, leading questions are usually suggestive to a degree (e.g. "The car was black, wasn't it?"). Thus, such questioning aims to limit responses made to a two-alternative forced choice (i.e. yes/no), and to elicit a preferred answer in the context of 'yeah' saying (Harris, 1984). Consequently, serious concerns have been raised with regard to basic paradigms of justice and fairness in that lawyerese questions can suggest or compel responses (Brennan, 1995).

However, psychological research has raised serious doubts as to the impact of leading and presuppositional questions on witness accuracy. A number of studies have shown lawyerese question types to impede witness accuracy (Loftus, 1975; Kebbell & Giles, 2000 – see also Westcott, Chapter 8) and unwittingly provide obstructions to the truth (Perry *et al.*, 1995). As early as 1975, Loftus found that presupposition in a question could erroneously influence an answer given to a subsequent question regarding the presupposition (see also Holliday, Chapter 4). Furthermore, Perry *et al.* (1995) found that confusing lawyerese questions reduced accuracy for younger children and that negatives, double negatives, and multi-part questions posed the greatest problems for all age groups. Indeed, young or otherwise **vulnerable witnesses** are demonstrably exposed to greater influence from such questions (see also Westcott, Chapter 8). A real-life verbatim case extract illustrates the effect of yes/no leading questions and pre-supposition on an 11-year-old child's 'yeah' responses (see Case Study).

CASE STUDY

R v. D (Taylor, 2004)

The case of *R v. D* was heard in the Victorian County Court of Australia in 1995. A male child, who was 11 at the time of the trial, made a police statement at the age of eight, that his stepfather had sexually abused him between the ages of seven and eight. The boy alleged several incidents of abuse involving anal penetration by his stepfather. The accused was charged with three counts of penetration of a child under 10 years of age, two counts of indecent assault, and one count of a threat to kill. Cross-examination in this case centred heavily on revealing minor discrepancies in the child's evidence. Unsettling the witness to diminish confidence is a common strategy and in the series of questions outlined below the boy was repeatedly questioned in a way that can have important consequences on responses.

DEFENCE: You were also on that occasion [committal hearing] asked some
   questions about whether anything happened with his hands; remember that?
CHILD: Yes.
DEFENCE: On that occasion you said nothing about him spitting on his hands;
   is that right?
CHILD: Yes.
DEFENCE: You remember that, don't you?
CHILD: Yes.
DEFENCE: You remember saying nothing about that matter only *three* months ago?
CHILD: Yes.
DEFENCE: You were asked questions about that particular matter both by
   myself and [prosecutor] weren't you?
CHILD: Yes.
DEFENCE: You didn't say anything at all about spitting, did you?
CHILD: No.
DEFENCE: The reason why you didn't say anything about it [names child] was
   this, because it didn't happen, did it?
CHILD: It did so.
DEFENCE: You're just giving evidence, I suggest to you, from having read your
   statement, aren't you; only recently having read your statement?
CHILD: Yes, and stuff started materializing. I can remember stuff that I didn't
   remember before.

Similarly, Kebbell *et al.* (2001) examined 16 court cases involving witnesses
with learning difficulties and found that 84% of questions were designed to be
answered 'yes' or 'no'; 30% were leading questions, and 18% involved negatives.
In addition, other vulnerable witness studies, such as in cases of rape, have
described how the use of compound questions, rapid speech rate and antagonis-
tic tone can confuse and intimidate witnesses, impairing their ability to answer
questions clearly and competently (Ellison, 2001).

While questioning procedures are the accepted means of gaining evidence
from a witness, the preferred answer may clearly not necessarily be the most accurate. Research studies conducted into these question styles have demonstrated
that, in general, outcomes with respect to accuracy and the relationship between
confidence and accuracy (i.e. whether we can say that a confident witness is more
likely to be correct in what s/he is stating than a witness showing a lack of confidence in his or her statements) remain quite poor and pose major difficulties for
justice (Kebbell, Wagstaff & Covey, 1996; Kebbell & Giles, 2000; Wheatcroft,
Wagstaff & Kebbell, 2004; Wheatcroft & Wagstaff, 2003). Of course, if one
assumes that cross-examination of this kind tests the credibility of the witness to
the full (i.e. a witness who rejects all attempts to be led, must be accurate in what
he or she says), then, from the cross-examiner's point of view, there may be a
downside if the witness refuses to be led or comply with the presupposition.
Accordingly, some legal advisers have openly asserted that asking leading questions in cross-examination can be unwise and risk losing a case (Evans, 1995).

The Impact of Pre-Trial Publicity and Judicial Pronouncements upon Outcome

In high-profile cases, where there are no legal prohibitions on reporting, the public may gather information about the case through media reports. At this stage, they cannot know whether the information is accurate or reliable. Predictably, research demonstrates that those who hear such media reports about a case are more likely to believe a suspect is guilty (Kerr, 1995; Steblay *et al.*, 1999). In today's 24-hour news agenda, potential jurors can be repeatedly exposed to vivid and sometimes horrific images of crime. Ogloff & Vidmar (1994) examined the effects of print and television media in relation to prejudicial bias. The results again indicated that all media exposure had a prejudicial impact, but that the effects of television and print were particularly strong. Similarly, research has demonstrated an increase in guilty verdicts when mock jurors were exposed to negative pre-trial publicity (Hope, Memon & McGeorge, 2005). Negative pre-trial publicity then has a strong impact on trial outcome, at least for the accused (see Studebaker & Penrod, 1997 for review).

One reason for this is the biasing effects of **informational social influence**, i.e. the need to conform to sources of information other than our own because we believe others' interpretations are more accurate than our own (Cialdini, 1993). Material that arouses emotions can exercise a particularly powerful influence. Kramer, Kerr & Carroll (1990) asked three groups of jurors to watch a trial of a man accused of robbery. Prior to watching, one group were exposed to emotional publicity (i.e. a car matching the one used in the robbery struck and killed a seven-year-old girl), one group to factual publicity (i.e. extensive criminal record), and a third group, no publicity. Jurors who were given emotional publicity were subsequently biased to return significantly more guilty verdicts than those who received the adverse factual information. Furthermore, neither instruction nor deliberation strategies reduced the impact of either publicity type – indeed, deliberation was shown to strengthen publicity biases and illustrates the potential impact of social influence upon persuadability.

While judges can direct juries to disregard information, such directions might not necessarily be effective. In fact, they could even enhance jurors' attention by making such pronouncements (Fein, McCloskey & Tomlinson, 1997). A British judge, at the end of the trial, will sum up the case and give the jury instructions regarding law to consider during deliberation. The requirement for legal instruction stems from the fact that the jury are asked to decide whether a defendant is guilty according to the law rather than the truth of the evidence. However, jurors find instructions difficult to interpret, understand and apply, as they are written with the law rather than the layperson in mind (Steele & Thornburg, 1988). Research on the effects of jury instructions indicates that standard legal instructions can have adverse consequences for juror comprehension. For example, Alfini, Sales & Elwork (1982) used community group volunteers to observe a video of a civil personal injury case and were given, no instructions, standard instructions, or rewritten ones. The rewritten guidance was found to result in the best outcome. Severance & Loftus (1982) found similar results using criminal instructions. Response to research is painfully slow and, despite exposing juror difficulties since the 1970s, Dumas (2000) notes that standard instructions still tend to be written in dense, legal language.

Interestingly, however, Shaffer & Wheatman (2000) found that those with a dogmatic personality were more likely to apply instructions properly. The prospect of misunderstandings led lay jurors to tend to rely upon their own common sense and personal experiences as a guide, rather than assessments of the law. One commonly misunderstood direction is the proof required to satisfy the 'beyond reasonable doubt' criterion outlined above. Research suggests jurors have a tendency to apply the most stringent test – that of 100% certainty – which is unrealistic (Montgomery, 1998; Zander, 2000). Moreover, judges themselves have problems in identifying a percentage that would satisfy beyond reasonable doubt (Kagehiro, 1990). On the basis of research findings to date, pre-trial publicity should be kept to a minimum and judges should adopt jury-friendly versions of judicial directions, in order that jurors are better able to comprehend and accurately apply the information they receive.

JUDGE AS DECISION MAKER

Decision Making by Judges in the European Courts

In the civil courts in Britain and in the inquisitorial system of mainland Europe, judges rather than juries make decisions. Judges try to be impartial and derive their decisions purely from the law and the evidence. However, research on judicial decision making suggests this may not be the case. Wagenaar, Van Koppen & Crombag (1993) suggest that judges can be influenced by '**anchored narratives**'. According to Wagenaar *et al.*, '**anchors**' are common-sense rules that are generally expected to be true: unquestioned assumptions concerning people, behaviour, and ideas. These assumptions may be stereotypes that anchor any narrative to commonly held perceptions, such as 'once a thief always a thief' or 'drug abusers are always thieves' (Wagenaar, 1995). Such anchors, often embedded within legal decisions, are implicit rather than explicit. According to Wagenaar *et al.*, legal fact-finding is predominantly a psychological process and often lacks logic. Anchors support propositions or facts and are derived from general impressions of the world but are not necessarily correct. From this standpoint, proof in criminal cases may lack rigorous justification of the anchors upon which it is based.

The availability of anchors through 'common-sense' understandings demonstrates our lack of insight into the roots of our own decision making. Furthermore, a consensus need not be achieved, as all involved tend to share the common understanding in question. An example anchored in Dutch law is, 'police officers in the line of duty never lie'. This anchor presupposes that the statement of a single police officer is proof enough. In a case cited by Wagenaar *et al.*, a man was charged with illegally receiving unemployment benefits while he worked on an asparagus farm, the prosecutor successfully relied solely upon the statements of two police officers.

Spanish studies of past sentences also support the view that decisions are determined largely through systematic judgment biases (Fariña, Novo & Arce, 2002). Farina *et al.* considered 555 penal judgments from High Court and Criminal Courts in northwest Spain and estimated that anchoring drove 63.6% of those judgments. Therefore, cultural anchors can impact upon decision making and illuminate the reasons for inconsistent decisions.

An important component of a narrative is plausibility, which suggests "an internal coherence" (Jackson, 1988, p. 171). It is significant therefore that the aim of both parties in court is to put forward a plausible and credible account resembling what the judge and jury (i.e. in law, 'reasonable persons'), could believe. Plausibility could be sensitive to external anchors that activate relevant *schemata*: those integrated networks of knowledge, beliefs and expectations related to a particular subject (Canter *et al.*, 2002). Interestingly, Canter *et al.* found that plausibility levels were lower when statements did not follow a temporal sequence of events: "These processes relate both to 'internal' structural constituents of narratives, especially the order in which they are presented, and to 'external' stereotypes and belief systems on which an individual may draw to conceptualize and interpret particular components of the narrative" (Canter *et al.*, 2002, p. 261).

Anchored narratives are potential biasing factors in judicial decision making. Consequentially, in court, if decision makers have to choose between two narratives they are likely to choose the most plausible one (Baudet, Jhean-Larose & Legros, 1994). Moreover, should a witness fail to articulate a coherent series of events that is both plausible and anchored in the appropriate narrative for the listener, then that witness' story may carry little weight, irrespective of its truth value. However, for critical reason to occur judges' awareness needs to be raised (Perkins, 1989) and training provided, perhaps in raising awareness of the need for multiple anchor points (Plous, 1993) and source biasing. But do such biases apply to judicial decision making when groups of magistrates or judges are involved?

Decision Making by Groups of Magistrates or Judges: Group Dynamics

Research has demonstrated that magistrates' decision making is inconsistent and sometimes uninformed. For example, in the use of bail, limited information may be provided by the police which does not give the full picture to the courts (Doherty & East, 1985). One implication is that defendants may be unnecessarily remanded in custody and may be subsequently acquitted or given a non-custodial sentence. For the penal system, unnecessary detentions before trial add to the pressure on precious prison resources and force the penal authorities to release prisoners prematurely.

The gravest penalty available is the decision to impose an immediate custodial sentence, the average length of which has risen in the UK in recent years. In 1995 the average sentence for a man over 21 was 2.8 months compared to 2.6 months in 1990, while the corresponding figures for women were 2.3 and 2.4 months over the same period (Flood-Page & Mackie, 1998). It is unclear whether this increase reflected judgments derived from the facts of the cases, and that such increased punishment was warranted (Rumgay, 1995). Relatively little formal guidance exists to help judges and magistrates assess whether an offence is 'so serious that only a custodial sentence can be justified'. In Cox (1993) however, Lord Justice Taylor affirmed that a **right-thinking person's test** was the correct approach. However, the seriousness of an offence is a subjective judgment, which can differ between individuals and/or over time (Ashworth & Hough, 1996). Worryingly, past research has repeatedly revealed inconsistency in sentencing decisions concerning similar cases between different courts (Parker, Casburn & Turnbull, 1981), within the same court (Parker, Sumner & Jarvis, 1989), and by the same individuals (Ashworth *et al.*, 1984). Indeed, Flood-Page & Mackie (1998) examined current UK sentencing practice in magistrates' courts and concluded that, whilst past research had shown considerable differences in sentences applied: "since 1993 it is sentencing practice, not the legal framework that has changed" (p. 139). Therefore, the evolution and perpetuation of 'court-cultures' that routinize interactions and decision making could be invoked as an explanation for differences in magistrates' sentencing patterns.

Some influences on group decision making can be drawn from the literature on **conformity** to group pressure, where conformity increases significantly up to group sizes of three to four, but then plateaus and may even decline (Stang, 1976). Furthermore, **Social Impact Theory** specifies that we conform when the group is one we care about, when members are unanimous in thoughts or behaviour, and when the group size is three or more (Latané, 1981). Other significant psychological research into group processes suggests that **groupthink** (i.e. maintenance of group cohesiveness; Janis, 1982), **polarization** (i.e. making extreme decisions; Isenberg, 1986) and **social loafing** (Latané, Williams & Harkins, 1979) can all influence decision making. A bench of magistrates or judges is a small group consisting commonly of three people who interact with each other and are interdependent, in the sense that to fulfil their needs and goals, they must rely on each other (see Aronson, Wilson & Akert, 2005 for details). Thus, groups of judges or magistrates are not immune to bias, indeed they may be subject to additional pressures not experienced by judges sitting on their own.

JURIES AS DECISION MAKERS

The Impact of Selection and Profiling on Outcome

There are numerous aspects that pertain to both process and individual that might impact upon the outcome of jury decision making. However, with the jury room closed to scrutiny in the UK (see the Contempt of Court Act 1981), the extent of their impact remains the subject of constant attention by academics, psychologists and practitioners. In the absence of direct observation of juries, a rigorous debate rages in respect of the validity of jury research. Bornstein (1999), who conducted an analysis of jury simulation studies published in the first 20 years of *Law and Human Behavior*, identified a number of perceived weaknesses in simulations studies and asserted: "*these concerns are justified not only by fundamental principles governing the sound conduct of scientific research, but also by the desire to apply findings from simulation studies to understanding, and ultimately improving, the legal system*" (p. 2).

The principal concerns include the samples used in mock jury studies (i.e. undergraduates v. community adults), the research setting (i.e. laboratory v. courtroom), the trial medium (i.e. written summaries v. listening to an actual trial), the trial elements included (e.g. presence or absence of deliberation), the dependent variables used (e.g. dichotomous verdicts v. probability-of-guilt judgments), and the consequentiality of the task (i.e. hypothetical v. real decision) (Diamond, 1997; Konecni & Ebbesen, 1979). One obvious drawback with the use of mock juries, for example, is that the defendant's future is not at risk and so gravity and importance may well be lost (Darbyshire, 2001). The call for allowable juror research is subject to ongoing debate in the UK, although Zander (2005) has cautioned that such research might show "*an intolerably high degree of irrationality, prejudice, stupidity and other forms of undesirable conduct in the jury retiring room*" (p. 2) that might lead to calls for the abolition of juries.

Regardless, studies of selection and composition have shown that males are over-represented and non-whites underrepresented (Zander & Henderson, 1993) and that women and ethnic minorities are still minimized on juries (Lloyd-Bostock & Thomas, 1999). The system by which potential jurors are summoned and excused can impact upon **representativeness**. For example, Airs & Shaw (1999) found that, in England and Wales, 38% of potential jurors were excused for a variety of reasons and that only 34% were available for service. Additionally, non-registration was found to be highest for ethnic minorities, people aged between 20–24, and those living in rented accommodation. Thus, random electoral roll samples do not necessarily lead to representative population samples.

One of the main factors expected to influence a jury is the **evidence** (Kalven & Zeisel, 1966) and to a large extent this is probably still the case. However, Ellsworth (1993) comments that individual jurors draw different conclusions about the right verdict on the basis of exactly the same evidence; thus evidence alone is likely to be insufficient to produce a uniform verdict.

Studies examining the sex and age of jurors have also been found to influence decision making. For example, women are significantly more likely to convict on circumstantial evidence (Sealy & Cornish, 1973). In this study, females also gave 78% more initial guilty verdicts in cases of rape and 71% for murder cases whilst the corresponding rates for males was 53% and 50%, respectively. Nonetheless, upon further examination of the data it was found that this difference was between female and male blacks rather than whites, where no significant difference was present. However, Kemmelmeier (2005) continues to argue that race is a critical factor in white jurors' decision making. On the other hand, male jurors alone are more likely to impose harsher punishments, such as longer sentences on criminal defendants when committing rape, particularly when the female victim was attractive (Villemar & Hyde, 1983). Yet, increased levels of education have been shown to lead to a higher rate of acquittals by males (Mills & Bohannon, 1980). Such impact factors could be mediated by cognitive resource. For example, Hastie, Penrod and Pennington (1983) found that only 48% of case facts presented in testimonies were recalled by jurors with low education levels compared with 70% for those jurors with high levels of educational attainment. Case Study highlights some jury selection difficulties, although the interested reader is directed to Darbyshire (2001) for a full review of jury research up to 2001.

CASE STUDY

The Trials of Scott Dyleski and O.J. Simpson

"*Never forget, almost every case has been won or lost when the jury is sworn*"
                                         (Clarence Darrow, defence lawyer, 1936)

Juries decide thousands of cases each year. It is not surprising therefore that the jury system, where it operates throughout the world, is of central importance. Given this, jury selection services have become available, in the US for example, to those willing to pay the associated fees. These services tend to be based on social-psychological and behavioural principles in order to apply the most sympathetic jurors to particular cases.

One such case was that of Scott Dyleski, who at 17 was sentenced to life in prison in August 2006 without parole for the murder of Pamela Vitale, the wife of prominent Californian defence lawyer Daniel Horowitz, on 15 October 2005. Dyleski was convicted after the victim was found bludgeoned to death with a piece of crown moulding on the site of the couple's planned dream home. In such high profile cases finding jurors can be more difficult than usual and the courts may call hundreds of potential jurors in an attempt to find those who have not yet formed opinions. In Dyleski's case, Judge Barbara Zuniga called 200 jurors to the Contra Costa County Superior Court, but many more may have been called if so required. In similar fashion, more than 1000 jurors were summoned to Redwood City in the Scott Peterson trial during the same year.

In theory, large jury pools attempt to find people who are representative of the general population and exclude people with extreme views. However, 'in practice what you end up with is a jury that looks like the middle of a bell curve – it's not jury selection, it's a de-selection' (Rice, 2006). The 1995 O.J. Simpson trial famously publicized jury selection techniques and, whether classified as selection or de-selection, such methods were demonstrable through the **voir dire** process. Oral voir dire consists of follow-up questions to questionnaires completed by prospective jurors and questions the lawyer specifically wants to ask orally in order to observe juror responses. In the O.J. case, an adviser to the prosecution, Don Vinson, compiled the jury profile to include one African-American male, one Hispanic male, eight African-American females and two Caucasian females. The emphasis on African-American females came from voir dire questioning, which showed that these women were more tolerant of physical force within marriage, that every relationship has its troubles, and people do get slapped around – it just happens. Nevertheless, contrary to this view, Marcia Clark, the lead prosecutor in the case believed that these women would be more likely to have experienced domestic violence in the past and would judge O.J. more harshly than males.

What one can conclude is that jury selection is far from an exact science. The voir dire process of juror questioning might eliminate jurors whose opinions differ with either side but, in addition, and in accordance with much academic opinion outlined in this chapter, juries can be influenced by a range of factors.

Visher (1987) has argued that personal characteristics are insignificant in predicting trial outcome compared to the wider factors of witness credibility and other evidence. Yet, there is a body of research that counters such an assertion and suggests that it is inappropriate to expect jurors to negotiate the justice process in an unbiased manner. This includes less obvious aspects of judicial processes, such as the use of specialist language and complexity, which also impact in particular ways.

The Comprehension of Jurors of Complex Material and Legal Terminology

Law would not exist without its specialist use of language; its existence would fail if it were not for the close relationship between legal language and the legal system (Danet, 1984). As such, terminology embraced by the law and the legal system has two main characteristics: first, it is technical because it uses a specialized vocabulary and second, it is culturally bound because law is above all a social science (Terral, 2004). It is not surprising, therefore, that legal terminology can lead to collective misunderstanding by juries. For example, a study conducted by Bornstein *et al.* (2005) demonstrated that the two most important juror negative perceptions of the court system were trial complexity and making the decision. According to Horowitz, ForsterLee & Brolly (1996) jurors' perceptions of complexity fail to recognize that several evidential factors such as, volume to be processed, clarity, and comprehensibility, are relevant to the term and may further add to misconceptions.

Trials often involve complex material presented to juries in a haphazard and disorganized manner, which hampers juries in reaching an appropriate verdict (Bennett & Feldman, 1981). Instead, juries synthesize the information into an organized narrative that makes sense to *them* but this may be at variance with the perceptions of the court (Wiener *et al.*, 2002). Indeed, cognitive research would suggest that complex cases require greater amounts of cognitive work by jurors without previous experience of such tasks that could lead to overload. For example, Heuer & Penrod (1995) questioned real jurors who reported that they became progressively less confident in their verdict as the quantity of information increased, without additional instruction or other support. Thus, a positive correlation might be expected between cognitive overload and the employment of inappropriate *heuristics* (Gilovich, Griffin & Kahneman, 2001); excessive information might lead jurors to become confused, disengaged and seek the most available common-sense outcome. The testimony of expert witnesses might assist or conversely, skew comprehension. Cooper, Bennett and Sukel (1996) found that mock jurors in the US were more persuaded by high-level expert witnesses than less-expert witnesses, but only when the testimony was highly complex. These effects, observed in mock-juror studies, may be even greater in real trials, where the pressures on jurors are that much greater (Honess, Levi & Charman, 1998; Jackson, 1996).

Alternatives to Oral and Written Evidence: The Impact of CCTV

Apart from conventional forms of evidence such as **oral testimony** and **documentary evidence**, the courts increasingly have access to other sources of evidence, known as **real evidence**. Oral testimony generally consists of what the witness states from the witness box, or by written statement, or by live television link. Documentary evidence is normally presented as some writing or other form of communicating information, which today often includes tape or film. Real evidence is the name given to diverse forms of evidence that have in common the fact that they are observed and comprise of any material that enables inference through senses. For example, material objects, physical characteristics of persons or animals, witness demeanour, and views of objects incapable of being brought to court (i.e. tapes, sounds, films, including CCTV). Today, it is estimated that there is one CCTV camera for every 14 people in the UK (BBC News, 2006) and the use of CCTV images as police aids to the identification of offenders is one that has arguably become familiar to all (see Tim Valentine's chapter for further details).

One of the few studies to explore the impact of CCTV evidence is that of Chenery *et al.* (2001). They provided serving magistrates with criminal case details supplemented either by video depiction or a textual account. Magistrates consistently imposed more severe sentences on the basis of video evidence than in the text condition. Clearly, CCTV can communicate incidents graphically and directly in a way that produces far greater impact than a written statement (Davies, 2003). However, Davies & Noon (1991) found that as far as children's statements were concerned, CCTV testimony had less emotional impact upon the jury compared to live courtroom testimony. Overall, in a review of the impact of televised testimony Wilson & Davies (1999) concluded, *"Juries may show a preference for live witnesses but do not appear to allow that preference to influence their decision making"* (p. 249). Clearly, with increased use of recordings in the courtroom, further research on their impact is warranted.

Decision-Making Processes in Juries

The task of decision making for a jury is unenviable and compounded by the gravity of its importance. Nevertheless, it is necessary for the jury to evaluate the strength of evidence presented and make a decision (Vidmar, 2005). Psychological research into decision-making processes and juror ability suggest that social-cognitive factors may be influential, though there is the same concern about the applicability of analogue studies to the courts.

Jury members are more likely, than by a single judge, to be influenced by group processes that are activated during the deliberations that follow the trial. Many studies have explored the impact on juror discussions of a range of factors including individual differences of jury members and the layout of the courtroom (see Hastie, Penrod & Pennington, 1983 for a review). Group discussion tends to reinforce majority opinion; Meyers, Brashers & Hanner (2001) observed that the position that the majority of mock jurors favoured prior to group discussion became the final verdict in approximately 90% of occasions. In such circumstances, there is a danger of group polarization: groups make more extreme decisions in the direction of people's initial judgments. Views, however, tend to polarize less if the case for the prosecution is strong; those in favour of acquittal initially can be persuaded to convict (Arce, Fariña & Sabral, 1996). More recent research in the US has looked at the quality of deliberation (Gastil, Burkhalter & Black, 2007). A study of 267 real jurors found that on all measures of deliberative quality (i.e. examination of the facts and judicial instructions; listening and debating opinions) jurors deliberated at a high level of competence. Such work suggests that we need to learn more about the *actual* processes involved in jurors' decision making in groups.

Pennington & Hastie (1991) proposed an influential model of how individual jurors arrive at a decision: the **story model**. The model refers to an active, constructive comprehension process in which information is moulded into a coherent mental representation: the story (Pennington & Hastie, 1992). This process is hypothesized to occur for even the simplest discourse (Kintsch, 1988). However, research on discourse comprehension suggests that story chains have a higher order structure both when considering the discourse itself and when considering the listeners' or readers' mental representations of the discourse. Therefore, these representations are as important for the interpreter of information as for the conveyer. Stories are organized into units called episodes (Trabasso & Van den Broek, 1985) that represent attempts to apply meaning and thus plausibility to a series of statements or ideas. The resultant cognitive processing is central to decision making and includes a range of relevant cognitions made up of **scripts,** schemas and heuristics. Schemata, for example, have been identified to explain how people comprehend and remember a spoken or written story. For juries in particular, it has been argued that sense is made of the evidence by constructing *"their own stories of the case"* (Wiener *et al.*, 2002, p. 120), with obvious opportunities for bias and misunderstanding. The notion that humans instinctively need to make sense of information is central to the argument, as this hypothesized process can account for jurors making critical and devastating mistakes of judgment and interpretation. Understanding juror comprehension is at an early stage, but Pennington and Hastie's ideas continue to guide much research.

CONCLUSION

This chapter has highlighted psychological research on a number of important factors relevant to judicial processes. However, research into many issues is at an early stage and the translation into good practice must be cautious as a consequence. There are many issues, from the impact of inconsistency in testimony to the quality and quantity of group discussion where further exploration is warranted.

In some areas, however, results are much more clear-cut. It is clear that pre-trial publicity should be kept to a minimum. However, given that information exists and influences both judges and jurists, there is a vital need to explore further theoretical bases and why biasing effects occur. The most jury-friendly legal directions also require further clarification in order that jurors can more accurately apply and comprehend information. Further, one might assume that decision making for judges would be notably less difficult to achieve than for juries. However, anchored narrative work suggests that judges may need to develop critical reasoning and awareness skills, perhaps with the assistance of psychologists. Magistrate bias in decision making is also evident; signifying research into influential court culture is sorely needed. Small-group research points toward the requirement to learn more about the *actual* processes involved in jurors' decision making in groups with a focus on real-life studies.

Finally, the whole process of hearing evidence, processing information and making judgments in legal contexts is under-researched, but enough has emerged as to suggest that judicial decision making can be prone to bias in some circumstances. Effective research on these topics will require input from and the cooperation of   magistrates and judges in order to ask informed questions and where necessary, engineer change.

SUMMARY

- Psychologists have identified a number of important factors relevant to judicial processes. Many issues are at an early stage of research or are based on unrealistic legal assumptions and as a consequence, the application of research findings to actual court practice must be cautious.

- Further exploration is warranted in particular on the impact of inconsistency in testimony, the quality and quantity of group discussion, and the theoretical bases of informational influence and biasing effects upon judges and jurists.

More jury-friendly legal directions are also required in order that jurors can more accurately apply and comprehend information and instructions.

- The theory of anchored narratives suggests judges may need to develop critical reasoning and awareness skills, perhaps with help from psychologists.

- Magistrate decision making appears also to be influenced by extra-evidential factors, signifying the need for further research into court culture. Small-group research points toward the requirement to learn more about the *actual* processes involved in jurors' decision making in groups with a focus on real-life studies.

- The process of hearing evidence, processing information and making judgments in legal contexts is under-researched. Effective research on these topics will require input from and the cooperation of magistrates and judges in order to ask informed questions and where necessary, assist in developing fairer and more effective procedures.

ESSAY/DISCUSSION QUESTIONS

1. Discuss what psychological factors might influence evidence given in court.
2. Critically discuss the view that cross-examination is necessary to test witness accuracy and completeness.
3. Critically evaluate the effectiveness of judge and jury decision making.
4. Evaluate how jury composition and legal understandings of jurors might influence the verdicts they reach.

REFERENCES

Airs, J. & Shaw, A. (1999). Jury excusal and deferral. *Home Office Research Development and Statistics Directorate Report No. 102.*

Alfini, J., Sales, B., & Elwork, A. (1982). *Making jury instructions understandable.* Charlottesville, VA: Michie.

Arce, R., Fariña, F., & Sabral, J. (1996). From juror to jury decision making: A non-model approach. In G. Davies, S. Lloyd-Bostock, M. McMurran, & C. Wilson (Eds), *Psychology, law and criminal justice.* Berlin: de Gruyter.

Aronson, E., Wilson, T.D., & Akert, R.M. (2005). *Social psychology.* Upper Saddle River, NJ: Prentice-Hall.

Ashworth, A., Genders, E., Mansfield, G., Peay, J., & Player, E. (1984). *Sentencing in the Crown Court: Report of an exploratory study.* Oxford: Centre for Criminological Research.

Ashworth, A. & Hough, M. (1996). Sentencing and the climate of opinion. *Criminal Law Review,* 776–86.

Baudet, S., Jhean-Larose, S., & Legros, D. (1994). Coherence and truth: A cognitive model of propositional truth attribution. *International Journal of Psychology, 29,* 219–350.

BBC News (2006). Britain is a 'surveillance society'. Accessed at: http://news.bbc.co.uk/1/hi/uk/6108496.stm

Bennett, W.L. & Feldman, M. (1981). *Reconstructing reality in the courtroom.* London: Tavistock.

Berman, G.L., Narby, D.J., & Cutler, B.L. (1995). Effects of inconsistent statements on mock jurors' evaluations of the eyewitness, perceptions of defendant culpability and verdicts. *Law and Human Behavior, 19*, 79–88.

Bornstein, B.H. (1999). The ecological validity of jury simulations: is the jury still out? *Law and Human Behavior, 23*, 75–91.

Bornstein, B.H., Miller, M.K., Nemeth, R.J. *et al.* (2005). Jurors' reactions to jury duty: Perceptions of the system and potential stressors. *Behavioral Sciences and the Law, 23*, 321–346.

Brennan, M. (1995). The discourse of denial: Cross-examining child victim witnesses. Special issue: Laying down the law: Discourse analysis of legal institutions. *Journal of Pragmatics, 23*, 71–91.

Brewer, N., Potter, R., Fisher, R.P., Bond, N., & Luszcz, M.A. (1999). Beliefs and data on the relationship between consistency and accuracy of eyewitness testimony. *Applied Cognitive Psychology, 13*, 297–313.

Canter, D.V., Grieve, N., Nicol, C., & Benneworth, K. (2003). Narrative plausibility: The impact of sequence and anchoring. *Behavioral Sciences and the Law, 21*, 251–267.

Chenery, S., Henshaw, C., Parton, P., & Pease, K. (2001). Does CCTV Evidence Increase Sentence Severity. *Scottish Journal of Criminal Justice Studies, 7*(1).

Cialdini, R.B. (1993). *Influence: Science and practice* (3rd edn). New York: Harper Collins.

Civil Procedure Rules (1998).

Contempt of Court Act 1981.

Cooper, J., Bennett, E.A., & Sukel, H.L. (1996). Complex scientific testimony: How do jurors make decisions? *Law and Human Behavior, 20*, 379–394.

Cooper, W.H. (1981). Ubiquitous halo. *Psychological Bulletin, 90*, 218–244.

Cox (1993) 14 Cr App (S) 470.

Cutler, B.L., Penrod, S.D., & Dexter, H.R. (1990). Juror sensitivity to eyewitness identification evidence. *Law and Human Behavior, 14*, 185–191.

Damaska, M. (1973). Evidentiary boundaries to conviction and two models of criminal procedure: a comparative study. *University of Pennsylvania Law Review, 121*, 506.

Danet, B. (1984). Legal discourse. In Teun A. van Dijk, (Ed.), *Handbook of discourse analysis, Vol 1: Disciplines of discourse.* London: Academic Press.

Darbyshire, P. (2001). What can the English Legal System learn from Jury Research published up to 2001? Accessed at: http://www.kingston.ac.uk/~ku00596/elsres01.pdf

Davies, G.M. (2003). CCTV Identification in court and in the laboratory. *Forensic Update, 72*, 7–10.

Davies, G. & Noon, E. (1991). *An evaluation of the live link for child witnesses.* London: Home Office.

Diamond, S.S. (1997). Illuminations and shadows from jury simulations. *Law and Human Behavior, 21*, 561–571.

Dick, T. (2006). Court out: how slip of tongue meant justice wasn't done. *Sydney Morning Herald*, 3rd August 2006.

Doherty, M.J. & East, R. (1985). Bail decisions in Magistrates' Courts. *British Journal of Criminology, 25*, 251–266.

Dumas, B.K. (2000). Jury trials: Lay jurors, pattern jury instructions and comprehension issues. *Tennessee Law Review, 701.*

DuCann, R. (1964). *The art of the advocate.* Harmondsworth: Penguin.

Eggleston, R. (1983). *Evidence, proof and probability (Law in context)* (2nd edn). Butterworths Law: London.

Ellison, L. (2001). The Mosaic art? Cross-examination and the vulnerable witnesses. *Legal Studies, 21*(3), 353.

Ellsworth, P.C. (1993). Some steps between attitudes and verdicts. In R. Hastie (Ed.), *Inside the Juror: The psychology of juror decision making* (pp. 42–64). Cambridge: Cambridge University Press.

Evans, K. (1995). *Advocacy in court: A beginner's guide* (2nd edn). London: Blackstone.

Fariña, F., Novo, M., & Arce, R. (2002). Heuristics of anchorage in judicial decisions. *Psicothema, 14,* 39–46.

Feild, H.S. (1979). Rape trials and jurors' decisions: A psycholegal analysis of the effects of victim, defendant case characteristics. *Law and Human Behavior, 3,* 261–284.

Fein, S., McCloskey, A.L., & Tomlinson, T.M. (1997). Can the jury disregard that information? The use of suspicion to reduce the prejudicial effects of pre-trial publicity and inadmissible testimony. *Personality and Social Psychology Bulletin, 23,* 1215–1226.

Flood-Page, C. & Mackie, A. (1998). Sentencing practice: an examination of decisions in magistrates' courts and the Crown Court in the mid-1990s. *Home Office Research Study No. 180:* HMSO.

Gastil, J., Burkhalter, S., & Black, L.W. (2007). Do juries deliberate? A study of deliberation, individual difference, and group member satisfaction at a municipal courthouse. *Small Group Research, 38,* 337–359.

Gilovich, T., Griffin, D.W., & Kahneman, D. (Eds) (2001). *The Psychology of Judgement: Heuristics and biases.* New York: Cambridge University Press.

Hans, V.P. & Vidmar, N. (1986). *Judging the jury.* New York: Plenum Press.

Harris, S. (1984). Questions as a mode of control in magistrates' courts. *International Journal of Society and Language, 49,* 5–27.

Hastie, R., Penrod, S., & Pennington, N. (1983). *Inside the jury.* Cambridge, MA: Harvard University Press.

Heuer, L. & Penrod, S.D. (1995). Jury decision making in complex trials. In R. Bull & D. Carson (Eds), *Handbook of psychology in legal contexts.* Chichester: John Wiley & Sons.

Hickey, L. (1993). Presupposition under Cross-Examination. *International Journal for the Semiotics of Law, 1,* 89–109.

Honess, T.M., Levi, M., & Charman, E.A. (1998). Juror competence in processing complex information: Implications from a simulation of the Maxwell trial. *Criminal Law Review,* 763–773.

Hope, L., Memon, A., & McGeorge, P. (2005). Understanding pre-trial publicity: Predicisional distortion of evidence by mock jurors. *Journal of Experimental Psychology: Applied, 10,* 111–119.

Horowitz, I.A., ForsterLee, L., & Brolly, I. (1996). Effects of trial complexity on decision making. *Journal of Applied Psychology, 81,* 757–768.

Isenberg, D.J. (1986). Group polarization: A critical review and meta-analysis. *Journal of Personality and Social Psychology, 50,* 1141–1151.

Jackson, B. (1988). *Law, fact, and narrative coherence.* Merseyside, UK: Deborah Charles Publications.

Jackson, J. (1996). Juror decision making in the trial process. In G. Davies, S. Lloyd-Bostock, M. McMurran, & C. Wilson (Eds), *Psychology, law and criminal justice.* Berlin: De Gruyter.

Janis, I. (1982). Groupthink: *Psychological studies of policy decisions and fiascos,* (2nd edn). Boston: Houghlin Mifflin.

Kagehiro, D.K. (1990). Defining the standard to proof in jury instructions. *Psychological Science, 1,* 194.

Kalven, H. & Zeisel, H. (1966). *The American jury.* Boston, MA: Little Brown & Co.

Kassin, S.M., Rigby, S., & Castillo, S.R. (1991). The accuracy-confidence correlation in eyewitness testimony: limits and extension of the retrospective self-awareness effect. *Journal of Personality and Social Psychology, 61,* 698–707.

Kebbell, M.R. & Giles, D.C. (2000). Lawyers' questions and witness confidence: Some experimental influences of complicated lawyers' questions on witness confidence and accuracy. *The Journal of Psychology, 134,* 129–139.

Kebbell, M.R., Hatton, C., Johnson, S., & Caitriona, M.E. (2001). People with learning disabilities as witnesses in court: What questions should lawyers ask? *British Journal of Learning Disabilities, 29,* 98–102.

Kebbell, M.R., Wagstaff, G.F., & Covey, A.C. (1996). The influence of item difficulty on the relationship between eyewitness confidence and accuracy. *British Journal of Psychology, 87,* 653–662.

Kemmelmeier, M. (2005). The effects of race and social dominance orientation in simulated juror decision making. *Journal of Applied Social Psychology, 35,* 1030–1045.

Kerr, N.L. (1995). Social psychology in court: The case of prejudicial pre-trial publicity. In G.G. Brannigan & M.R. Merrens (Eds), *The social Psychologists: Research adventures* (pp. 247–262). New York: McGraw-Hill.

Kintsch, W. (1988). The role of knowledge in discourse comprehension: A construction-integration model. *Psychological Review, 95,* 163–182.

Konecni, V.J. & Ebbesen, E.B. (1979). External validity of research in legal psychology. *Law and Human Behavior, 3,* 39–70.

Kramer, G.P., Kerr, N.L., & Carroll, J.S. (1990). Pre-trial publicity, judicial remedies, and jury bias. *Law and Human Behavior, 14,* 409–438.

Latané, B., Williams, K., & Harkins, S. (1979). Social loafing. *Psychology Today, 110,* 104–106.

Leippe, M.R., Manion, A.P., & Romanczyk, A. (1992). Eyewitness persuasion: How and how well do fact finders judge the accuracy of adults' and children's memory reports? *Journal of Personality and Social Psychology, 63,* 181–197.

Lindsay, R.C.L. (1994). Expectations of eyewitness performance: Jurors verdicts do not follow from their beliefs. In D.F. Ross, J.D. Read, & M.P. Toglia (Eds), *Adult eyewitness testimony: Current trends and developments* (pp. 362–382). New York: Cambridge University Press.

Lloyd-Bostock, S. (2006). The effects on lay magistrates of hearing that the defendant is of 'good character', being left to speculate, or hearing that he has a previous conviction. *Criminal Law Review,* 189–212.

Lloyd-Bostock, S. & Thomas, C. (1999). Decline of the Little Parliament: Juries and jury reform in England and Wales. *Law and contemporary problems, 7,* 21.

Loftus, E. (1975). Leading Questions and the Eyewitness Report. *Cognitive Psychology, 7,* 560–572.

Memon, A., Vrij, A., & Bull, R. (2003). *Psychology and law: Truthfulness, accuracy and credibility.* Chichester: John Wiley & Sons.

Meyers, R.A., Brashers, D.E., & Hanner, J. (2001). Majority/minority influence: Identifying argumentative patterns and predicting argument-outcome links. *Journal of Communication, 50*, 3–30.

Miller v. Minister of Pensions [1947] 2 All ER 372 at 373.

Mills, C.J. & Bohannon, W.E. (1980). Juror characteristics: to what extent are they related to jury verdicts? *Judicature, 1*, 64.

Montgomery, J.W. (1998). The criminal standard of proof. *National Law Journal, 148*, 582.

Murphy, P. (1994). *Evidence and advocacy* (4th edn). London: Blackstone Press Ltd.

Ogloff, J.R.P. & Vidmar, N. (1994). The impact of pre-trial publicity on jurors: A study to compare the relative effects of television and print media in a child sex abuse case. *Law and Human Behavior, 18*, 507–525.

Parker, H., Casburn, M., & Turnbull, D. (1981). *Receiving juvenile justice: Adolescents and state care and control.* Oxford: Basil Blackwell.

Parker, H., Sumner, M., & Jarvis, G. (1989). *Unmasking the magistrates: The 'custody or not' decision in sentencing young offenders.* Milton Keynes: Open University Press.

Pennington, N. & Hastie, R. (1991). A cognitive theory of juror decision making: the story model. *Cardoza Law Review, 13*, 497.

Pennington, N. & Hastie, R. (1992). Explaining the Evidence: Tests of the Story Model for Juror Decision Making. *Journal of Personality and Social Psychology, 62*, 189–206.

Perkins, D.N. (1989). Reasoning as it is and could be: An empirical perspective. In D.M. Topping, D.C. Crowell, & V.N. Kobayaski (Eds), *Thinking Across cultures: The third international conference on thinking.* Hillsdale, NJ: LEA.

Perry, N., McAuliff, B., Tam, P., Claycomb, L., Dostal, C., & Flanagan, C. (1995). When lawyers question children: Is justice served? *Law and Human Behavior, 19*, 609–629.

Plous, S. (1993). *The psychology of judgment and decision making.* New York: McGraw-Hill.

Rice, J. (2006). In M. Krupnick (2006), Dyleski trial highlights jury selection difficulties. Accessed at: www.contracostatimes.com/mld/cctimes/email/news/15063386.htm.

Rumgay, J. (1995). Custodial decision making in a magistrates' court. *British Journal of Criminology, 35*, 201–217.

Sealy, A.P. & Cornish, W.R. (1973). Jurors and their verdicts. *Modern Law Review, 36*, 496.

Severance, L.J. & Loftus, E.F. (1982). Improving the ability of jurors to comprehend and apply criminal jury instructions. *Law and Society Review, 17*, 153–198.

Shaffer, D. & Wheatman, S. (2000). Does personality influence reactions to judicial instructions? *Psychology, Public Policy and Law, 6*, 655.

Sporer, S.L. (1993). Eyewitness identification accuracy, confidence, and decision times in simultaneous and sequential line-ups. *Journal of Applied Psychology, 78*, 22–33.

Stang, D.J. (1976). Group size effects on conformity. *Journal of Social Psychology, 98*, 175–181.

Steblay, N.M., Besirevic, J., Fulero, S.M., & Jimenez-Lorente, B. (1999). The effects of pre-trial publicity on juror verdicts: A meta-analytic review. *Law and Human Behavior, 21*, 283–297.

Steele, W.W. & Thornburg, E.G. (1988). Jury instructions: a persistent failure to communicate. *North Carolina Law Review, 67*, 77.

Stephan, C. & Corder-Tully, J. (1977). The influence of physical attractiveness of a plaintiff on the decisions of simulated jurors. *Journal of Social Psychology, 101*, 149–150.

Stone, M. (1988). *Cross-examination in criminal trials*. London: Butterworths.

Studebaker, C.A. & Penrod, S.D. (1997). Pretrial publicity: The media, the law, and common sense. *Psychology, Public Policy, and Law, 3*, 428–460.

Taylor, S.C. (2004). *Court licensed abuse: Patriarchal lore and the legal response to intra-familial sexual abuse of children*. New York: Peter Lang Publishing.

Terral, F. (2004). Cultural imprint of legal terms. *Meta, 49*, 876–890.

Trabasso, T. & Van den Broek, P. (1985). Causal thinking and the representation of narrative events. *Journal of Memory and Language, 24*, 612–630.

Tversky, A. & Kahneman, D. (1974). Judgment under uncertainty: Heuristics and biases. *Science, 185*, 1124–1131.

Vidmar, N. (2005). Expert evidence, the adversary system, and the jury. *American Journal of Public Health, 95*, 137–143.

Villemar, N. & Hyde, J. (1983). Effects of sex of defence attorney, sex of juror and attractiveness of the victim on mock juror decision making in a rape case. *Sex Roles, 9*, 879–889.

Visher, C.A. (1987). Juror decision making: The importance of evidence. *Law and Human Behavior, 11*, 1–17.

Wagenaar, W.A. (1995). Anchored narratives: A theory of judicial reasoning and its consequences. In G. Davies, S. Lloyd-Bostock, M. McMurran, & C. Wilson (Eds), *Psychology, law and criminal justice*. Berlin: de Gruyter.

Wagenaar, W.A., Van Koppen, P.J., & Crombag, H.F.M. (1993). *Anchored narratives: The psychology of criminal evidence*. Hemel Hempstead: Harvester Wheatsheaf.

Wheatcroft, J.M. & Wagstaff, G.F. (2003). The interface between psychology and law in the courtroom: Cross-examination. *Forensic Update, 75*, 8–18.

Wheatcroft, J., Kebbell, M., & Wagstaff, G. (2001). The influence of courtroom questioning style on eyewitness accuracy and confidence. *Forensic Update, 65*, 20–25.

Wheatcroft, J.M., Wagstaff, G.F., & Kebbell, M.R. (2004). The influence of courtroom questioning style on actual and perceived eyewitness confidence and accuracy. *Legal and Criminological Psychology, 9*, 83–101.

Wiener, R.L., Richmond, T.L., Seib, H.M. *et al.* (2002). The psychology of telling murder stories: Do we think in scripts, exemplars, or prototypes? *Behavioral Sciences and the Law, 20*, 119–139.

Wilson, J.C. & Davies, G.M. (1999). An evaluation of the use of video-taped evidence for juvenile witnesses in criminal courts in England and Wales. *European Journal on Criminal Policy and Research, 7*, 81–96.

Woolmington v. DPP (HL) [1935] AC 462.

Zander, M. (2000). The criminal standard of proof – how sure is sure? *National Law Journal, 150*, 1517.

Zander, M. (2005). Jury research and impropriety: A response to the Department of Constitutional Affairs' Consultation Paper. *(CP 04/05 March 2005)*.

Zander, M. & Henderson, P. (1993). *Crown Court Study*. The Royal Commission on Criminal Justice, Research Study No. 19: London: HMSO.

Zebrowitz, L.A. & McDonald, S. (1991). The impact of litigants' babyfacedness and attractiveness on adjudications in small claims courts. *Law and Human Behavior, 15*, 603–623.

ANNOTATED READING LIST

Ashworth, A. (1992). *Sentencing and criminal justice*. London: Weidenfeld & Nicolson. *The aim of the book is to examine English sentencing law in its context, drawing not only upon legislation and the decisions of the courts but also upon the findings of research and on theoretical justifications for punishment.*

Fariña, F., Novo, M., & Arce, R. (2002). Heuristics of anchorage in judicial decisions. *Psicothema, 14*(1), 39–46. *This study reviews judicial judgments to assess the impact of bias. Findings are discussed in terms of recommendations designed to mitigate bias.*

Hannibal, M. & Mountford, L. (2002). *The law of criminal and civil evidence: principles and practice*. Harlow: Pearson. *This major introduction to the law of both criminal and civil evidence develops understanding of contemporary law in a practical and academic way.*

Hastie, R. (Ed.) (1993). *Inside the juror: The psychology of juror decision making*. Cambridge: Cambridge University Press. Inside the Juror *presents interesting aspects of juror decision making that include facets drawn from social, cognitive, and behavioural psychology. Considers the validity of research in a comprehensive summary.*

Kaplan, M.F. & Martin, A.M. (2006). *Understanding world Jury systems through psychological research*. New York: Psychology Press. *Examines diverse jury systems in nations around the world and considers impact features upon jury selection, composition, functioning, processes, and trial outcomes.*

Wrightsman, L.S. (1999). *Judicial decision making. Is psychology relevant?* New York: Kluwer Academic/Plenum Publishers. *This book examines decision making by judges using contemporary concepts derived from a psychological viewpoint.*

CHAPTER 8

SAFEGUARDING WITNESSES

Helen L. Westcott
International Centre for Comparative Criminological Research,
The Open University, United Kingdom

Imagine being six years old and suddenly taken from your bath, in your own home, by a complete stranger. You are then driven around the city where you live for 20 minutes, subjected to two serious assaults, and abandoned in a lane before the stranger drives off. It is January and you are naked and freezing.

This is probably not the most comfortable scenario you would like to imagine, and perhaps you are feeling unhappy or even angry that you have been asked to put yourself in this position. However, the needs of children and vulnerable adults who *have* endured similar experiences – or other difficult personal circumstances – and later come to court to talk about them, are the concern of this chapter. How can *their* emotions, needs and welfare be accommodated? Specifically, we will examine here what steps can be taken to safeguard witnesses' well-being, without compromising the rights of the accused.

What do we mean by 'safeguard'? The term is increasingly important in child protection, in the UK at least. According to government guidance, 'safeguarding and promoting the welfare of children' refers to the "process of protecting children from abuse or neglect, preventing impairment of their health and development, and ensuring they are growing up in circumstances consistent with the provision of safe and effective care which is undertaken so as to enable children to have optimum life chances and enter adulthood successfully."[1]

Witnesses may be vulnerable due to their 'youth, incapacity or circumstances' (Youth Justice and Criminal Evidence (YJCE) Act 1999; see Chapter 5). Members of any of the following groups may therefore be considered vulnerable: children, elderly people, individuals with learning difficulties, physically impaired witnesses, victims of sexual assault, intimidated witnesses, those with mental health problems. Burton, Evans & Sanders (2006) 'conservatively' estimate that 24% of witnesses in their evaluation of the implementation of special measures[2] (see later discussion) were vulnerable or intimidated – two to three times the government's own estimate.

What, then, might safeguarding mean for vulnerable witnesses in the courtroom? First, safeguarding requires that the *stress of testifying is minimized* as much as possible. Second, the circumstance (or process) of giving evidence in court needs to be made *as effective* as possible for vulnerable witnesses. Finally, the *implications of the court experience* for witnesses as they move on to the rest of their lives need to be considered. In this chapter, we are going to address these issues through consideration of:

- witnesses' fears and perceptions about going to court
- preparing witnesses for court
- protecting witnesses at court; and
- challenging conventions.

If we reconsider our six-year-old child, what could we do to help her give an account of being abducted in court in a way that is least stressful and most helpful?

WITNESSES' FEARS AND PERCEPTIONS ABOUT GOING TO COURT

It is important that witnesses' fears and perceptions about going to court are acknowledged, since they can contribute directly as well as indirectly to the success or otherwise of a prosecution. If a witness has extreme fears, for example, that she will not be believed, or will not be treated fairly, then she may decide to withdraw her

---

[1] www.everychildmatters.gov.uk/socialcare/safeguarding, accessed 7 February 2007.

[2] Defined (Home Office, 2002) as "the measures specified in the YJCE Act 1999 which may be ordered in respect of some or all categories of eligible witness by means of a special measures direction" (Appendix A, p. 134).

complaint. Kelly, Lovett & Regan (2005) found that 14% of rape complainants declined to complete the initial process, another 14% withdrew at the investigative stage, and a further 2% withdrew at the prosecution and trial stages. Attrition figures in cases involving vulnerable witnesses portray a rather bleak picture (see Davies & Westcott, 2006, for a review). Most cases – around 70% – drop out at the initial stages of an investigation and prosecution. These witnesses have therefore *not* been able to provide their evidence to the court. If individuals have a poor experience of involvement with the criminal justice system, then it is legitimate to question how far they will be willing to become involved again in the future (e.g. Esam, 2002; Hamlyn *et al.*, 2004; Plotnikoff & Woolfson, 2004).

Studies of victims and witnesses have reported the following fears about participating in the investigative and prosecution process, and going to court (summarized in Box; see, for example, Harris & Grace, 1999; Kelly *et al.*, 2005; Sas *et al.*, 1995; Sas *et al.*, 1991).

Victims' and Witnesses' Fears about Participating in A Prosecution and/or Trial

Fear of harm by the abuser
Fear of rejection by the family
Fear of disbelief
Fear of others' reactions, e.g. carers being upset, professionals being insensitive
Fear of family break up, including their own removal from the family
Fear of embarrassment.

Additionally, the victim or witness may be feeling guilty, responsible, ashamed or intimidated (see Case Study, below). Family members may knowingly or unknowingly exert pressure on the witness to retract their statement (Sas *et al.*, 1991), or associates of the accused may actively seek to intimidate the witness to withdraw. Intimidation seems to be a particular problem facing vulnerable witnesses. Hamlyn *et al.* (2004) reported that 53% experienced some form of intimidation in the period leading to trial, coming primarily from the accused (36%) or from the accused's family (21%).

Witnesses' Experiences in Court

Although many victims and witnesses report such fears and apprehensions, they are not always borne out in practice (e.g. Gallagher & Pease, 2000; Kelly *et al.*, 2005; Sanders *et al.*, 1997; Westcott & Davies, 1996). However, many vulnerable witnesses *have* found the court experience to be extremely difficult, illustrated particularly in research with children (e.g. Plotnikoff & Woolfson, 2004; Wade, 2002; Wade & Westcott, 1997). Consider Case Study, which presents an extract from Mary's account.

CASE STUDY

Mary

I am 12 years old. The man next door, Uncle Bob, he and his wife were good friends of our family, he did sex things to me for about three years. All our family liked him and I did too. He was always very kind to me and used to babysit for us . . . I can't remember when it all began but he started doing things to me that I didn't like. At first I didn't understand what was happening and kept thinking I must be imagining things. I couldn't get him to stop although I asked him to. He made me feel like it was my fault and he told me nobody would believe me if I did say anything . . . one day when the teacher at school asked me what was the matter, it just all came out. She said she would tell my mum and then everything would be alright. My mum was really upset but she believed me . . . I tried not to think about going to court but one day my mum told me it was going to be next week.

We waited and then somebody came to tell me that I couldn't go into the television link room because it was being used by somebody else. They said I could give my evidence behind a screen but that meant I had to go into the courtroom. They said that if I wanted to wait for the television link we'd have to come back another day . . . I felt I had to go ahead with it that day. I don't think I would have ever gone through with it if I hadn't done it then.

The first barrister was okay but he didn't ask me much and I didn't always understand what he was saying . . . it was really embarrassing to say the details. I didn't tell them everything. I just couldn't. When the next barrister questioned me, she had a smiley face and made jokes with me. I began to think it wasn't going to be so bad. Then she seemed to change. She kept asking me about dates and times and I couldn't remember them exactly. I told her I could remember what had happened to me but not when. I didn't understand some of the long words she used . . . She called me a liar. I still don't understand half of what went on. I felt dirty. They made me feel like I didn't exist. If I had known how it was going to be like at court, I never would have gone through with it.
(Le Roy, undated, in Esam, 2002, pp. 309–310).

Mary's experience highlights a number of concerns about the treatment of vulnerable witnesses in the criminal courts, which we will return to throughout this chapter. As noted in the introduction, these concerns include the welfare of the witness, the effectiveness (or not) of their testimony and the implications of the experience for all involved. In particular, vulnerable witnesses are likely to raise issues in relation to cognitive, developmental and socio-emotional factors that have been previously considered in the interviewing of such witnesses (see Chapter 4). Some examples of these factors as they may apply to vulnerable witnesses are summarized in Box, but the extent of their influence on any particular witness, e.g. an elderly woman, a young man with learning difficulties, a traumatized rape victim, would need to be considered on an individual basis. Further reading, which will provide more detail pertaining to these factors, their implications for safeguarding vulnerable witnesses, as well as case examples, is suggested at the end of this chapter.

Cognitive, Developmental and Socio-Emotional Factors in Relation to Vulnerable Witnesses

Memory factors:[3] marked, negative, effect of delay on memory; problems with **source-monitoring** in relation to memories; susceptibility to **misinformation effects** on memory (e.g. through the influence of questioning); limited free recall; problems associated with script memory.

Language factors:[4] less developed vocabulary and understanding of complex grammatical structures; limited vocabulary for sexual offences; unfamiliarity with, and confusion caused by, the use of legalese; use of non-verbal communication systems.

Authority effects:[5] particular sensitivity to the need to give socially desirable responses; heightened susceptibility to leading questions; acquiescence and naysaying; reluctance to talk; fear and anxiety.

Stress Factors and Special Measures for Vulnerable Witnesses

Spencer & Flin (1993) presented a model that pulled together the particular stressors that can affect child witnesses, together with mediating factors and likely effects. This model predates the broader conception of a vulnerable witness, but remains a helpful summary of issues that have been discussed so far in this chapter. It is reproduced in Figure 8.1.

What can be done to address the issues highlighted in this model? In fact, a number of interventions are possible, and have been implemented since this model was conceptualized. In England and Wales, the Youth Justice and Criminal Evidence Act 1999 introduced a raft of special measures in order to facilitate the testimony of vulnerable witnesses. These stemmed from a government review entitled *Speaking Up For Justice* (Home Office, 1998) which argued that the rights of victims and witnesses were not being met within the criminal justice system as it currently operated. A number of these special measures in fact were already available to certain categories of witnesses, for example children, in certain categories of cases, for example sexual offences (Home Office, 1992). However, the 1999 Act, extended such measures to a broader range of 'vulnerable' witnesses and cases (Home Office, 2002). Box summarizes the special measures contained in the 1999 Act which required legislative change (rather than new practice development or administrative action).

---

[3] See, for example: Baker-Ward & Ornstein (2002); Powell & Thomson (2002); Saywitz (2002) and Holliday, Chapter 4.

[4] See, for example: Walker (1993, 1994); Brennan & Brennan (1988); Kennedy (1992).

[5] See, for example: Ceci, Ross & Toglia (1987); Goodman *et al.* (1991); Moston (1992); Moston & Engelberg (1992); Sanders *et al.* (1997) and Holliday, Chapter 4.

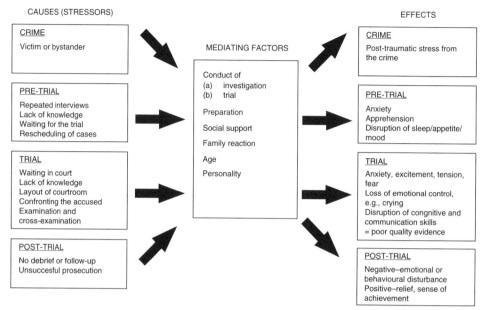

CAUSES (STRESSORS)

EFFECTS

MEDIATING FACTORS

Figure 8.1: Model of Stress Factors for Vulnerable Witnesses. Reproduced from Spencer & Flin, 1993, p. 364, with permission from Blackstone Press

In addition, restrictions on evidence and questions about the complainant's sexual behaviour were introduced, as well as the prohibition of cross-examination by the accused in person in certain offences (e.g. rape and sexual offences). Further, the value of professional support to witnesses, both pre-trial and at court, was more formally recognized than had previously been the case. Guidance on interviewing witnesses for the purposes of criminal proceedings – the *Memorandum of Good Practice* (Home Office, 1992) – was revised and expanded and published as *Achieving Best Evidence*[6] (Home Office, 2002; see Holliday, Chapter 4).

Summary of Special Measures in the YJCE Act 1999

Use of **screens** so that the witness is protected from being confronted by the defendant

Giving of evidence by **live link** (CCTV) from outside the courtroom

Giving of evidence in private – the press and public may be excluded (except for one named person to represent the press) in cases involving sexual offences or intimidation

Removal of wigs and gowns by barristers and the judge

Showing of **video-recorded evidence-in-chief**, cross-examination and re-examination

Questioning through the use of **intermediaries** and aids to communication.

---

[6] This guidance is currently under review again, and a revised version is being prepared.

The special measures listed in Box differ in the extent to which they have required change to law, procedure or practice in order to be implemented (Burton *et al.*, 2006). For example, removing the witness from the courtroom deviates from the assumed right of confrontation in person (Spencer & Flin, 1993), whereas removing wigs and gowns represents a more minor change to legal practice. Internationally, different approaches have been taken to implementing such measures for witnesses, depending upon whether the country's justice system is **adversarial** (**accusatorial**) or **inquisitorial**, and how vulnerable witnesses are already accommodated (e.g. Bottoms & Goodman, 1996; Cashmore, 2002; Spencer *et al.*, 1990). The special measures also differ in the extent to which they can be viewed as controversial, or challenging to the rights of the defendant, as in the use of video-recorded cross-examination or intermediaries. We will return to this debate in the final section, *Challenging Conventions*, below. For the purposes of this chapter, the special measures can be considered according to whether they apply *pre-* or *at* court. We will now move on to examine how they safeguard vulnerable witnesses in more detail, starting first with those measures that apply pre-court.

PREPARING WITNESSES FOR COURT

Preparation and Social Support In Practice

Preparation, and the provision of social support, are mediating factors in the model presented in Figure 8.1 above. That is, they can ameliorate the effects of pre-trial stressors if they are provided to vulnerable witnesses in the period before a court appearance – and hence safeguard the witness by reducing anxiety and promoting effective testimony. The revised guidance *Achieving Best Evidence* (Home Office, 2002) in fact argues that witnesses should be properly prepared and supported from the very beginning of their involvement with the criminal justice system, for example, preparation for the initial investigative interview (see Chapter 5). Research further suggests that perceiving such support to be available might help to reduce attrition in cases involving vulnerable witnesses (e.g. Kelly *et al.*, 2005).

What activities are incorporated into witness support and preparation? Box summarizes some different dimensions. *Which* support and preparation activities are actually provided, *by* whom and *to* whom, depends on local arrangements and the availability of resources (Murray, 1997; Plotnikoff & Woolfson, 1996). In brief, support and preparation activities are concerned with assessing the needs of the witness, providing support, liaising and communicating, and preparing for the trial (Home Office, 2002).

The development of support and preparation activities outlined in Box has stemmed mostly from work with child witnesses, and has not been without controversy. Opponents have been concerned that supporters may coach the child[7] or rehearse their testimony, a concern that has been fiercely denied. (A similar complaint has been

---

[7] Even to the point of making a false allegation.

Support and Preparation Activities Pre-Trial

Provision of emotional support and liaison with professionals providing therapy or counselling before trial

Provision of information and education, e.g. the *Young Witness Pack* (NSPCC/ChildLine, 1998)

Understanding and conveying the witnesses' views, wishes and concerns about testifying

Familiarization of the witness with the court and court procedures

Provision of a pre-trial visit to court

Liaison between the witness, family, friends and professionals

Communication with professionals who may have special expertise related to a witness's particular vulnerabilities, e.g. interpreters

---

levelled at those who engage with the child in therapy or counselling pre-trial.) It is nonetheless vitally important that supporters are aware of 'evidential boundaries' (Home Office, 2002, p. 88). They must not be a witness in the case and must not be given details of the case or of the witness's evidence. Further, they must not discuss the case or the witness' evidence as part of their activities. Should any indiscretions occur then it is likely that the witness' evidence will subsequently be compromised (see Holliday, Chapter 4).

Once a supporter has been identified for a vulnerable witness, their role pre-trial is to: 'seek the witness' views about giving their evidence and being at court; provide information about the criminal process and their role within it; support and general assistance [sic] to the witness to enable them to give their best evidence; liaise with others, as appropriate' (Home Office, 2002, p. 92). A great deal of the supporter's work may be 'behind the scenes', such as liaising and communicating with different agencies or authorities involved in the case about the witness' needs and preferences. Supporters may also accompany witnesses when they view a copy of their statement (which may involve seeing a video recording of the witness' investigative interview), and if they meet the prosecution counsel before the proceedings.

An increasing range of education and information materials is available for (mainly child) witnesses and their carers (see Home Office, 2002, Appendix Q). This includes written materials, models of courtrooms and videos about what it is like to give evidence (e.g. NSPCC, 2000). Materials for witnesses who have learning difficulties are also available, including the development of a 'virtual' courtroom (Cooke, 2001). *The Young Witness Pack* (NSPCC/ChildLine, 1998) is perhaps the most widely known preparation material in the UK; its contents are outlined in Box and give a glimpse of the range of people who may be involved in efforts to prepare a child for different types of court appearance.

The Young Witness Pack Materials

Let's Get Ready for Court: activity booklet for children aged 5–9 years

Tell Me More About Court: booklet for young witnesses aged 10–15 years

Inside a Courtroom: cardboard model of a courtroom with slot-in characters

Going to Court: information for Crown Court witnesses aged 13–17 years

Young Witnesses at the Magistrates' Court and the Youth Court: information for witnesses aged 9–17 years

Screens in Court: information for witnesses aged 9–17 years

Giving Evidence: What's it Really Like?: video for young witnesses

Your Child is a Witness: information for parents and carers

Preparing Young Witnesses for Court: booklet for child witness supporters.

Early evaluations of child witness support schemes were positive (Aldridge & Freshwater, 1993; Plotnikoff & Woolfson, 1995a, 1996), although a number of issues remain outstanding (especially regarding responsibility and resources for providing preparation, and witness access to such support; Plotnikoff & Woolfson, 2004). Young witnesses have themselves reported favourably on the materials and their supporters. For example:

The supporter came to my home and went through the books with me so that I knew what the TV link was all about. Then we had the court visit. We also talked about what would happen if I got upset or tired. I knew that I could ask if I wanted a break when I gave my evidence. (Fiona, 10)

I had a witness adviser just to help me out. He tells you everything, I had a tour of the court, he tells you who is going to be sitting where and obviously I felt a bit more at ease about what was going to happen. I got this support in both the Magistrates' Court and the Crown Court. (Colin, 16)

(Plotnikoff & Woolfson, 2004, p. 26)

Experimental Approaches to Preparing Child Witnesses

In essence, support and preparation activities are addressing the lack of knowledge (stressor), anxiety, and disruption of cognitive and communication skills (effects) experienced by vulnerable witnesses, as depicted in Figure 8.1. Although preparation activities are widely used, in fact empirical evaluation of the success of different components has not really been addressed (Murray, 1997). Developmental psychologists have also developed preparation programmes in experimental studies aimed at addressing the particular cognitive, developmental and socio-emotional factors that exist for vulnerable witnesses outlined in p. 187 (e.g. Saywitz *et al.*, 1993). These have included narrative elaboration, comprehension-monitoring and resistance training. *Narrative elaboration* was a successful technique for increasing the amount of detail recalled by children, by prompting them to talk about information relating to parti- cipants, setting, action, conversations and consequences, through the use of 'cue cards'. *Comprehension-monitoring training* helped children to identify questions they did not understand, and to ask adult interviewers for rephrasing. Finally, *resistance training* enabled children to identify and respond appropriately to (i.e. resist) mislead- ing questions put to them by interviewers. Evaluation of these techniques highlighted some unintended consequences (e.g. children becoming more reluctant to provide details) and they have yet to be considered in a genuine forensic context. Hence, although these experimental approaches have been found promising in empirical eval- uations, their practical utility remains untested.

PROTECTING WITNESSES AT COURT

Before moving on to consider safeguarding witnesses in the courtroom, read the case study of Sally, which introduces the use of information technology in the investigative and judicial process. This case study also highlights some of the other problematic issues which can arise when vulnerable witnesses testify in court.

CASE STUDY

Sally

Sally described herself as having been sexually abused by her stepfather from the age of 7. She eventually confided in her school teacher when she was 12. An inter- view was immediately arranged and conducted with Sally's mother sitting behind a one-way mirror, where she could see and hear the interview . . . During the interview Sally was preoccupied with the possible effects of her disclosure on her family and gave only a disjointed account of a single incident of abuse. However, a medical examination found physical signs consistent with her allegation and a prosecution followed. Sally's stepfather pleaded not guilty and at his trial the video recording of Sally's interview was used as her evidence-in-chief. She was then cross-examined and, questioned about there having been only one incident of abuse, related another incident. In his final summing up, defence counsel cast doubt on the initial allegation and the subsequent allegation in court, as follows:

The video interview:
All she said in the video interview, if it is true, is that there was one incident when her stepfather [attempted intercourse]. Now, if this man is perverted, you would

have expected some course of conduct wouldn't you? But according to her account there was only one occasion when he behaved indecently towards her.

The allegation made in court:
Out of the blue today came another allegation – that only weeks before the video was made he [indecently assaulted her] in front of her mother, who was also on the sofa. This is nonsense. It took us all by surprise, the prosecution included . . . She says now she didn't want to distress her mother. But she had already spoken of intercourse. It surely wouldn't have slipped her mind, especially if it happened only a few weeks before the video was made. Either it emphasizes the fragility of a child's mind, or the murky waters we are getting into.
Sally's stepfather was subsequently acquitted by the jury after a short deliberation.
(Wade & Westcott, 1997, pp. 58–59)

In this part of the chapter, special measures pertaining to the use of video-recorded evidence-in-chief, and cross-examination via live link, will be reviewed (Cashmore, 2002). The case studies of Sally and Mary both make reference to this technology. Their cases also pinpoint some of the problems that have accompanied implementation of these special measures. Sally's experience further highlights some of the challenges – 'murky waters' – which surround the appearance of vulnerable witnesses in formal courtroom settings. We will return to consider such challenges, for example cross-examination and the culture of the courtroom, below in the final part of the chapter. First, however, we will briefly revisit the topic of social support.

Social Support at Court

Previously, we considered how preparation and social support could be provided pre-trial. At court, more 'behind-the-scenes' work will be carried out by supporters, such as providing information for the plea and directions, hearing about the witness's requirements and preferred way of giving evidence. In addition, the 2002 Home Office guidance explicitly outlines the role of judges and magistrates in actively managing cases involving vulnerable witnesses, and in minimizing distress as far as possible (see also Scottish Executive, 2003a). That is to say, they must protect (we might say, safeguard) the interests of vulnerable and intimidated witnesses. In some cases, for example with young witnesses, the judge may be prepared to meet the witness beforehand to help 'demystify' the court process, although this does not appear to happen for a sizeable minority of vulnerable witnesses (Hamlyn *et al.*, 2004). Lawyers and the judge may also remove their wigs and gowns, if the witness would prefer; this practice almost doubled from 8% to 15% across the time periods pre- and post-special measures surveyed by Hamlyn *et al.* (2004).

They asked me if I wanted them to take their wigs off and that, and I said 'yes'. And they took them off, so they looked OK. (16-year-old male with mild learning disability)
(Sanders *et al.*, 1997, p. 65)

Finally, a court witness supporter may accompany witnesses when they testify, to reduce the witnesses' anxiety and stress, and enable them to give their best evidence. For example, someone from the Witness Service may sit in the 'live-link' room while a child provides evidence. The live link is the first special measure exploiting technology to have been introduced in England and Wales (via the Criminal Justice Act 1988), and we will now examine its use in more detail.

Screens and the Live Link

The principal aim of the live link, or closed-circuit television, in court is to remove the vulnerable witness from the intimidating and unfamiliar environment of the courtroom and to spare the witness from facing the defendant in court (Davies & Noon, 1991). Previously, screens had been used in court, and placed so that the witness was 'shielded' from the defendant, but remained in view of other people in the courtroom. They are still available today as one of the special measures for vulnerable witnesses who would prefer to give their testimony 'live' in the actual courtroom, but with a degree of protection. In fact, screens have the benefit (unlike live link) that they shield the witness from the defendant's view and appear to be popular with witnesses who use them (Burton et al., 2006). Hamlyn et al.'s survey (2004) suggests screens were used by 8% of vulnerable or intimidated witnesses. Some witnesses have spoken of valuing their 'day in court' and being able to speak publicly of their experiences – as a way of 'telling the world' what the defendant has done.

It was my mother or the police who said . . . I didn't want to go at the start. But then I was happy about going [to court]. When I knew it was to put him behind bars. (15-year-old autistic boy)

They asked me if I wanted to go to court and I said 'yes'. He had gone too far this time . . . I just wanted him to go down. (20-year-old woman with mild learning disability)

(Sanders et al., 1997, p. 37–38)

Screens are therefore one intervention that can promote effective testimony, while reducing stress for the witness.[8] If a witness uses the live link they are actually removed from the courtroom, whilst remaining in the court building. Two-way closed circuit television will connect the courtroom with another small room in which the witness sits (with a supporter if agreed). Using the live link, the witness can see who is speaking to them, whilst the witness's picture is relayed to the court. Again, the live link is attempting to reduce the witness's anxiety and promote their effective testimony by addressing socio-emotional factors.

Initial evaluations of use of the live link in the UK and Australia with child witnesses (Cashmore & De Haas, 1992; Davies & Noon, 1991; Murray, 1995) reflected a generally positive reception for the technology, especially on the part of

---

[8] Screens are also used in some cases involving 'non-vulnerable' witnesses, where the identity of the witness needs to be concealed.

those concerned to safeguard children's welfare. Many supporters felt live link enabled witnesses who otherwise would not have been able to testify to provide their evidence to the court. Witnesses themselves have reported as much (Hamlyn *et al.*, 2004):

If I was standing in a [witness] box, knowing me, if I saw [the defendant] I'd probably feel faint. I'd probably do summat. Or tell a lie. (Susie, 11 years)

I wanted to give [my evidence] that way. I couldn't face him. I couldn't see him. If I'd have had to see him, that would have been that. I wouldn't have been able to go in. [But] I felt safe, not having to see him. (Caitlin, 16 years)

(Wade, 2002, p. 224)

Researchers evaluating the live link noted that children using the system were rated as self-confident, and speaking fluently, and that audibility was rarely a problem (Davies & Noon, 1991). However, there were the inevitable teething problems, as well as a more fundamental opposition to the technology amongst some members of the legal profession (e.g. Davies & Noon, 1991; Murray, 1995). Teething problems centred around the success of the technology itself (e.g. the cameras being oversensitive to background noise; e.g. Plotnikoff & Woolfson, 2004; Sanders *et al.*, 1997), as well as some (possibly deliberate) misuses of the technology. These latter included, on one occasion, the whole screen in front of the child being filled with the eye of the defence barrister, and on others, defence barristers standing so that the defendant was in view behind them (Davies & Noon, 1991). One of the intentions of the live link is to enable witnesses to testify without seeing the defendant, as this is one of the biggest concerns reported by vulnerable witnesses anticipating their court appearance (e.g. Hamlyn *et al.*, 2004; Plotnikoff & Woolfson, 2004; Sanders *et al.*, 1997). A continuing practical problem remains the availability of live link, as illustrated in Mary's account (Case Study above). This is not an atypical experience and a sudden change of plan can be particularly alarming for vulnerable witnesses, especially if their preparation for court has been based around them testifying via live link (e.g. Plotnikoff & Woolfson, 2004).

More fundamental problems concerning 'resistance' to the technology have been reported by researchers. Davies & Noon (1991) noted that prosecution barristers were concerned that witnesses testifying via live link appeared more remote and had less of an impact on the jury. Perversely, witnesses *not* breaking down when testifying were seen as less likely to convince the jury of their account. Information collected at the time of the evaluation found no evidence to support such concerns (Davies & Noon, 1991), and the introduction of the 1999 Act in England and Wales with its assumption of special measures has rather superseded this debate – on paper at least.

Finally, it is important not to overlook the witnesses' experience of live link itself. Although it works well for many witnesses, some children have reported difficulties with the technology, in ways perhaps unanticipated at its introduction. For example, feeling like they were shut in a 'cupboard' (Plotnikoff & Woolfson, 2004), or struggling to adjust to the technology:

It were a bit funny . . . it weren't as if . . . people were talking to me straight face to face. It were . . . really funny. I couldn't hear them right . . . It were loud enough. It's just that they had to keep repeating it over and over again because I couldn't understand. I couldn't hear them right. (Lucy, 13 years)

(Wade, 2002, p. 225)

Awareness of such perceptions can be addressed in preparation, especially if the witness has a court visit and can practise using the technology. Another important issue for preparation includes making witnesses aware that the defendant will be able to see them via the live link (and watch their video-recorded interview; see below). Discovering this on the day has been reported as very disconcerting for witnesses and as negatively influencing their ability to testify.

It just felt horrible knowing he was watching that TV screen when I was saying [what he'd done to me]. He could be gloating over it and everything. (Ivy, 14 years)

When he saw me on the television it was really frightening thinking about [him seeing me] and I'm not seeing him. (Gemma, 9 years)

(Wade, 2002, p. 224)

Perhaps one of the most significant lessons from the introduction of live link has been that the *element of choice* about how to give their testimony is most important to witnesses (Cashmore & De Haas, 1992). Being able to decide whether or not to use the technology may be as important as the technology itself – which is why understanding witnesses' apprehensions and concerns, and their preferences for testifying, is such an important part of the supporter's role. The option of giving choice to children as to how to give their evidence is currently under consideration by the Ministry of Justice (see www.justice.gov.uk/docs/cjr-consult-young-witnesses.pdf).

Video-Recorded Evidence-In-Chief

As we have seen, the live link addresses mainly socio-emotional factors associated with testifying, although these may themselves impact on other cognitive factors outlined in Box. For example, stress at testifying may negatively affect a witness's recall of information (memory; Baker-Ward & Ornstein, 2002) and/or may exacerbate language factors (both comprehension and production; see Mary's comments in Case Study above). In 1989, Judge Pigot chaired a committee that evaluated the possibility for video technology to address other cognitive factors affecting child witnesses too (refer back to Box). The committee argued in its report (Pigot, 1989) that if children's initial interviews with police officers or social workers were recorded – at the early stages of a criminal investigation and/or child protection enquiry – then, this video recording of a child's account could replace the child's live evidence-in-chief at court. Further, Pigot argued that subsequent cross-examination could be video-recorded too (see Spencer & Flin, 1993, for a review). This would help the child in the following ways:

- *Memory:* the interview could be recorded soon after the child has made an allegation, or the investigating authority has received a referral, thus overcoming problems associated with the effect of delay on children's memory.

- *Language:* the interviewers should be trained to use developmentally appropriate language so that the child can understand the questions put to them (see case studies above).

- *Authority effects:* the interviews could take place in purpose-built interviewing suites with comfortable and non-threatening furnishings, and other facilities close by (i.e. to reduce stress).

Further, once the video interview(s) were completed, the child would be free to receive therapeutic services and would not need to attend trial at all (thus additionally addressing socio-emotional factors). At the time, the full Pigot proposals were considered too radical by the British government (Spencer & Flin,1993); however, video-recorded examination-in-chief for child witnesses of certain ages in specified sexual abuse offences was introduced in the Criminal Justice Act 1991 (Home Office, 1992). Following the publication of *Speaking Up for Justice* (Home Office, 1998; see above), the full Pigot proposals for the range of vulnerable witnesses was included in the Youth Justice and Criminal Evidence Act 1999. As we shall see in the last section of this chapter, however, video-recorded cross-examination appears to remain a 'bridge too far' for the government and judiciary.

Chapter 5 has reviewed the literature on practice in video-recorded interviews, and the guidance governing such interviews in the *Memorandum of Good Practice* (Home Office,1992) and *Achieving Best Evidence* (Home Office, 2002; see also Scottish Executive, 1993b). In brief, this literature shows that interviewers generally do include all the four proposed phases of interview, but struggle to ask sufficient open questions – asking too many specific and closed questions instead. Typically, the free narrative phase of the interview – when children have the opportunity to recall events in their own words, is brief and sometimes omitted (e.g. Davies *et al.*, 1995; Sternberg *et al.*, 2001; Westcott & Kynan, 2006; Westcott, Kynan & Few, 2006). The closure phase is also often poor or omitted.

As with live links, there were the inevitable technological teething problems following introduction of video-recorded evidence-in-chief, especially problems with hearing child witnesses, and with compatibility of recording equipment pre- and at court (Davies *et al.*, 1995). However, the Home Office evaluation of such interviews with children reported that generally the reforms had been welcomed by members of the judiciary, police and social services (Davies *et al.*, 1995), principally as a means of reducing stress for witnesses. Observations of children testifying in court, where their evidence-in-chief was either via video interview or live in court, showed no consistent differences, although both groups were anxious during live cross-examination. Again, there was some resistance amongst barristers, with prosecution barristers concerned (as with live link) that use of video-recorded evidence had a reduced impact on the jury, and defence barristers believing that witnesses would find it easier to lie and deceive if they were not physically present in the courtroom. Statistical analyses on prosecution and conviction rates conducted for the evaluation did not support either position (see also Burton *et al.*, 2006).

The presumption of the 1999 Act that video-recorded interviews will routinely be used in cases involving vulnerable witnesses has gone some way to 'over-riding' such resistance. As with live links, it is important to pause to consider witnesses' experiences of video interviews, especially at the point of trial. Practice with child witnesses has varied, so that some witnesses have seen their video-recorded interview ahead of trial as 'refreshing the witness' memory' – as if it was a written statement (Hamlyn *et al.*, 2004; Plotnikoff & Woolfson, 2004) – while others have not. Although most children have found it helpful to be reminded of what they said, many have found it distracting and distressing to see themselves on the video.

It was weird to see the video ahead of time – it didn't really seem like me. It helped refresh my memory about the things I couldn't remember clearly. I didn't like seeing the video again . . . it was weird . . . like when I had to describe everything that happened. It made me feel like I wanted to cry inside when I watched the video again. (Davina, 15)

It is distressing to relive it. You are looking at how I felt the day after the offence. (Paul, 15)

(Plotnikoff & Woolfson, 2004, p. 30)

Where children see the video for the first time at trial these feelings can be magnified.

Watching the video reminded me too much about what it was like before the trial. I only saw it once on the day of the trial. I felt sad listening to what happened to me. I thought my voice was very strange. It would've been a help to see it before. (Sheila, 9)

I didn't see my video before it was played to court. It was months before that I had been interviewed on the video. It felt very strange to watch the video. I have never had that feeling before. I thought that they'd all be laughing at me. It was difficult to concentrate on the video. (Hattie, 14)

(Plotnikoff & Woolfson, 2004, p. 31)

Preparation for the trial should consider the use of the video-recorded interview to refresh the witness' memory, and also should anticipate some of these emotions that may accompany its viewing.

Sally's case study (above) highlights one of the ways video-recorded evidence has been used by defence lawyers to cast doubt on children's testimony; practitioners involved at the early stage of investigations have been frustrated by the lengths that some courtroom counsel will go to either have video-recorded evidence excluded completely, or otherwise undermined (e.g. Department of Health, 1994; Davies *et al.*, 1995). We are now going to examine some of these frustrations in more detail, in the final part of this chapter.

CHALLENGING CONVENTIONS

Why would powerful, experienced authority figures – as defence barristers undoubtedly are – find the possibility of video-recorded evidence from vulnerable witnesses so troublesome? I would suggest that the reforms discussed in this chapter have been resisted because they challenge conventions: they aim to wrest some of the control away from the lawyers, and the legal setting, and they necessitate change to traditional ways of working that have operated largely unopposed for hundreds of years. Law is a self-referential system, ill-suited to consider the agendas of other systems such as psychology or welfare (e.g. Henderson, 2002; King & Piper, 1995; King & Trowell, 1992). Opening up such a system to outside scrutiny is therefore challenging for all involved and many have found that the prevailing legal culture often works to over-ride the spirit of the reforms intended to assist vulnerable witnesses (e.g. Davies & Noon, 1991; Davies *et al.*, 1995; Plotnikoff & Woolfson, 1995b). This is not to deny that progress has been made – as illustrated by the reforms discussed in this chapter. Hamlyn *et al.* (2004) found that witnesses using special measures were more likely to be satisfied with their experience, and less likely to experience anxiety. However, the inertia and resistance offered by the prevailing legal culture can be overwhelming (Westcott, 2006). Four examples of this inertia and resistance come easily to mind.

Delay

Despite a number of targeted reforms and practice directions, delays in the processing of cases involving vulnerable witnesses remain endemic (e.g. Plotnikoff & Woolfson, 1995b, 2004). Typically, a child will wait approximately 10–12 months for their case to come to court. Such delays have a negative impact on the child's memory (for the event and for their video-recorded evidence), as well as influencing socio-emotional development as their lives move on in the pre-trial period. The problem is also acute for witnesses with learning difficulties.

Video-Recorded Cross-Examination

Despite the inclusion of relevant legislation in the 1999 YJCE Act to permit video-recorded cross-examination, it is now apparent that the judiciary has resisted its introduction to the extent that plans for implementation have been abandoned by the government. As with video-recorded evidence-in-chief, video-recorded cross-examination would have addressed all three categories of factors outlined in Box: memory, language and authority to the benefit of vulnerable witnesses.

Intermediaries

Practitioners have reported successes using skilled interpreters in investigative interviews with children who have multiple impairments, including no verbal communication (e.g. Marchant & Page, 1992). However, plans for the use of trained communicators and intermediaries with vulnerable witnesses have also not progressed smoothly, but a national 'role-out' of the intermediaries scheme for England and Wales is expected in 2008. The use of intermediaries as interlocutors between witness and barrister/judge is perhaps the *most* witness-centred of all the proposed reforms. It is also probably the most unpalatable to the legal profession, who regard their right to *personally* question witnesses as fundamental (e.g. Spencer & Flin, 1993). However, the literature is rife with examples of how poorly in many (or even most) cases lawyers actually conduct such questioning, whether this is motivated by their tactics to win their case, or results from their ignorance of the psychology of questioning (e.g. Henderson, 2002; Walker, 1993,1994).

Cross-Examination

Commentators on the cross-examination of child witnesses have produced extensive analyses documenting their concerns about the implications of cross-examination practice for both witnesses' welfare (e.g. Westcott & Page, 2002), and for effectively eliciting witnesses' accounts of events (e.g. Zajac, Gross & Hayne, 2003; see Blackwell-Young, Chapter 9). For example,

People with Down's Syndrome in particular tend to be particularly sensitive to negative emotion. They therefore sometimes respond to what they perceive as aggression (e.g. 'tough' questioning) by attempting to appease the questioner, which can lead to suggestibility and contradictory testimony. Thus in [particular case] the result of two days' questioning was a mass of contradictions with which the defence barrister regaled the victim. As a result of this one of the jurors burst into tears.

(Sanders *et al.*, 1997, p. 76–7)

British lawyers seem to be extremely concerned with the dangers of leading questions being posed by social workers, doctors or police officers during the early stages of a criminal investigation. Paradoxically, they do not seem to be the least bit concerned about their own use of leading questions in cross-examination and the effects this may have on the quality of a child's evidence. The characteristics of a typical interview conducted during cross-examination appear to violate all the principles of best practice, with the predicted outcome of maximizing the risk of contaminating the evidence.

(Spencer & Flin, 1993, p. 307)

   Manipulative, unkind or offensive cross-examination can have devastating consequences on the witness' self-esteem, and on the effectiveness of their testimony (see Sally's case study above). Guidance from the Home Office (2002) and the Scottish Executive (2003b) clearly states that the court has a duty to have regard to the welfare of witnesses, and that inappropriate questioning can be harmful: "responsible practitioners consider carefully the . . . tone, content and manner of questioning to be employed" (Scottish Executive, 2003b, p. 6). And of course, a skilled barrister does not have to demean a witness in order to make their point. However, given the 'hallowed' status of cross-examination as "the greatest legal engine ever invented for the discovery of truth"[9] (Wigmore, cited in Spencer & Flin, 1993, p. 270) this will remain a real hurdle for vulnerable witnesses and their supporters to overcome. It is also repeatedly reported as one of most distressing (e.g. Hamlyn *et al.*, 2004; Plotnikoff & Woolfson, 2004; Sanders *et al.*, 1997; Sas *et al.*, 1991).

---

[9] Readers may be interested to know that Wigmore previously compares the role of cross-examination to that of torture in society before extolling its virtues!

Protecting Witnesses and Testing Their Evidence

The use of video-recorded cross-examination and intermediaries, and the practice of cross-examination, highlight clearly the tension between testing witnesses' evidence in court, and prioritizing their needs and welfare. Of course, the defendant has a right to a fair trial, and the duty of the court is to ensure that this occurs. However, 'murky waters' arise when we confuse *substantive* and *formal* equality between defendant and witness:

[It] is necessary to put learning disabled victims, like other victims, on as equal a footing with the defendant as possible. This requires adopting a stance of 'substantive' as distinct from 'formal' equality . . . To subject an intelligent defendant and a learning disabled victim to identical complex questioning is not to treat them equally, except in the most artificial 'formal' sense. Truly equal treatment would ensure that the victim is as able to understand the proceedings as the defendant. The same applies to coping with the intimidating nature of the court and its personnel. Thus it is on the basis of this substantive equality criterion that thought needs to be given to the conduct of trials, intervention in questioning by the judge, and the use of screens, video-recorded interviews, closed circuit TV, and so forth.

(Sanders *et al.*, 1997, p. 81–2)

In this chapter, we have seen how reforms have tried to progress *substantive* equality for vulnerable witnesses through special measures; however, experiences such as delays, cross-examination and the associated stress can moderate the success of special measures in practice so that, from the witness' perspective, *formal* equality is what results. Further, some of this poor practice can be most detrimental to witnesses' perceptions of the criminal justice process, their welfare post-court, and have lasting implications for certain witnesses (e.g. Goodman *et al.*, 1992; Hamlyn *et al.*, 2004; Sas *et al.*, 1991, 1995).

Hamlyn *et al.* (2004) found that vulnerable and intimidated witnesses remain less satisfied than all witnesses with their overall experience, and Burton *et al.* (2006) report a very patchy picture of implementation of the special measures. Vulnerable witnesses are being identified too late in the process to benefit from special measures, with the Crown Prosecution Service often applying for special measures on the day of trial itself (too late, and not part of the witness' preparation). Video-recorded interviews are being used for only a minority of the appropriate vulnerable witnesses, and preparation (e.g. pre-trial visits) is often not offered. Burton *et al.* (2006) describe the situation as one of 'significant unmet need' (p. vii), and highlight problems with the investigative and pre-trial processes as well as court. If we are truly to safeguard vulnerable individuals, then we have to aim to achieve substantive equality between defendant and witness – and be prepared to challenge conventional priorities, policies and practices in order to achieve this goal.

SUMMARY

- Most witnesses find testifying at court a stressful experience, particularly where a witness is vulnerable by reason of age or mental or physical disability and/or a victim of crime.

- Among the fears of child witnesses going to court are suffering harm from defendants or their associates; rejection and the break-up of the family and being disbelieved or embarrassed when giving evidence.

- In recent years, the courts in England and Wales have introduced a variety of Special Measures to assist witnesses in giving their best evidence while still preserving the adversarial nature of the trial process.

- Special Measures include the provision of video-recorded evidence-in-chief; the use of a CCTV link to enable the witness to testify from outside the courtroom, social support within the courtroom and the use of an intermediary to assist a witness with communication difficulties.

- Action on these issues needs to be matched by measures to tackle delays and postponements in hearing cases at court and a more proactive approach to overly aggressive cross-examination.

- Recognition of the needs of vulnerable witnesses is widespread within countries which share our common law tradition and there have been many experiments involving procedural change. However, the essentially adversarial nature of this legal process makes substantive equality for the vulnerable victim an elusive goal.

ESSAY/DISCUSSION QUESTIONS

1. What makes victims and witnesses vulnerable? How have special measures addressed the needs of vulnerable witnesses?

2. Discuss the concept of 'safeguarding' in relation to the reception of testimony from vulnerable witnesses.

3. Have recent attempts to safeguard witnesses in criminal courts in England and Wales gone far enough to meet their needs?

4. Discuss the statement that 'normal procedures which create formal equality between defendant and victim often create substantive inequality when the victim is vulnerable' (Sanders *et al.*, 1997, p. 87).

5. To what extent can the needs of vulnerable witnesses and the rights of defendants be reconciled at court?

REFERENCES

Aldridge, J. & Freshwater, K. (1993). The preparation of the child witnesses. *Tolley's Journal of Child Law*, 5, 25–28.

Baker-Ward, L. & Ornstein, P.A. (2002). Cognitive underpinnings of children's testimony. In H.L. Westcott, G.M. Davies, & R.H.C. Bull (Eds), *Children's Testimony: A Handbook of Psychological research and forensic practice*. Chichester: John Wiley & Sons.

Bottoms, B. & Goodman, G.S. (1996). *International perspectives on child abuse and children's testimony: Psychological research and law*. Thousand Oaks, CA: Sage Publications.

Brennan, M. & Brennan, R.E. (1988). *Strange language: Child victims under cross-examination.* Wagga Wagga, NSW: Riverina Murray Institute of Higher Education.

Burton, M., Evans, R., & Sanders, A. (2006). *Are special measures for vulnerable and intimidated witnesses working? Evidence from the criminal justice agencies.* London: Home Office (Home Office Online Report 01/06).

Cashmore, J. (2002). Innovative procedures for child witnesses. In H.L. Westcott, G.M. Davies, & R.H.C. Bull (Eds), *Children's testimony: A handbook of psychological research and forensic practice.* Chichester: John Wiley & Sons.

Cashmore, J. & De Haas, N. (1992). *The use of closed-circuit television for child witnesses in the ACT.* A Report for the Australian Law Reform Commission and the Australian Capital Territory Magistrates Court.

Ceci, S.J., Ross, D.F., & Toglia, M.P. (1987). Suggestibility of children's memory: Psycho-legal implications. *Journal of Experimental Psychology: General, 116,* 38–49.

Cooke, P. (2001).The virtual courtroom: A view of justice. *Ann Craft Trust Bulletin, 35,* 2–5.

Davies, G.M. & Noon, E. (1991). *An evaluation of the live link for child witnesses.* London: Home Office.

Davies, G.M. & Westcott, H.L. (2006). Preventing withdrawal of complaints and psychological support for victims. In M.R. Kebbell & G.M. Davies (Eds), *Practical psychology for forensic investigations and prosecutions.* Chichester: John Wiley & Sons.

Davies, G.M., Wilson, C., Mitchell, R., & Milsom, J. (1995). *Videotaping children's evidence: An evaluation.* London: Home Office.

Department of Health (1994). *The child, the court and the video: A study of the implementation of the Memorandum of Good Practice on video interviewing of child witnesses.* London: Department of Health Social Services Inspectorate.

Esam, B. (2002). Young witnesses: Still no justice. In H.L. Westcott, G.M. Davies, & R.H.C. Bull (Eds), *Children's testimony: A handbook of psychological research and forensic practice.* Chichester: John Wiley & Sons.

Gallagher, B. & Pease, K. (2000). *Understanding the attrition of child abuse and neglect cases in the criminal justice system.* Unpublished Report to the ESRC (R000236891).

Goodman, G.S., Taub, E.P., Jones, D.P.H. *et al.* (1992). Testifying in criminal court: emotional effects on child sexual assault victims. *Monographs of the Society for Research in Child Development,* 57 (Serial no. 229).

Hamlyn, B., Phelps, A., Turtle, J., & Sattar, G. (2004). *Are special measures working? evidence from surveys of vulnerable and intimidated witnesses.* London: Home Office (Home Office Research Study 283).

Harris, J. & Grace, S. (1999). *A question of evidence? Investigating and prosecuting rape in the 1990s.* London: Home Office (HO Research Study 196).

Henderson, E. (2002). Persuading and controlling: The theory of cross-examination in relation to children. In H.L. Westcott, G.M. Davies, & R.H.C. Bull (Eds), *Children's testimony: A handbook of psychological research and forensic practice.* Chichester: John Wiley & Sons.

Home Office (1992). *The memorandum of good practice on video recorded interviews with child witnesses for criminal proceedings.* London: Home Office.

Home Office (1998). *Speaking up for justice: Report of the interdepartmental working group on the treatment of vulnerable and intimidated witnesses in the criminal justice system.* London: Home Office.

Home Office (2002). *Achieving best evidence in criminal proceedings: Guidance for vulnerable or intimidated witnesses, including children.* London: Home Office Communication Directorate.

Kelly, L., Lovett, J., & Regan, L. (2005). *A gap or a chasm? Attrition in reported rape cases.* London: Home Office RDS (Home Office Research Study 293).

Kennedy, M. (1992). Not the only way to communicate: A challenge to voice in child protection work. *Child Abuse Review, 1,* 169–177.

King, M. & Piper, C. (1995). *How the law thinks about children* (2nd edn). Aldershot: Arena.

King, M. & Trowell, J. (1992). *Children's welfare and the law: The limits of legal intervention.* London: Sage Publications.

Marchant,R. & Page, M. (1992). *Bridging the gap: Child protection work with children with multiple disabilities.* London: NSPCC.

Moston, S. (1992). Social support and children's eyewitness testimony. In H. Dent & R. Flin (Eds), *Children as witnesses.* Chichester: John Wiley & Sons.

Moston, S. & Engelberg, T. (1992). The effects of social support on children's eyewitness testimony. *Applied Cognitive Psychology, 6,* 61–76.

Murray, K. (1995). *Live television link: An evaluation of its use by child witnesses in Scottish criminal trials.* Edinburgh: HMSO.

Murray, K. (1997). *Preparing child witnesses for court.* Edinburgh: The Stationery Office.

NSPCC (2000). *Giving evidence – What's it really like?* London: NSPCC.

NSPCC/ChildLine (1998). *The young witness pack.* London: NSPCC.

Pigot, T. (1989). *Report of the advisory group on video evidence.* London: Home Office.

Plotnikoff, J. & Woolfson, R. (1995a). *The child witness pack – An evaluation. Research Findings No. 29:* London: Home Office Research and Planning Unit.

Plotnikoff, J. & Woolfson, R. (1995b). *Prosecuting child abuse: An evaluation of the government's speedy progress policy.* London: Blackstone Press.

Plotnikoff,J. & Woolfson, R. (1996). Evaluation of witness service support for child witnesses. In Victim Support (Ed), *Children in court.* London: Victim Support.

Plotnikoff, J. & Woolfson, R. (2004). *In their own words: The experiences of 50 young witnesses in criminal proceedings.* London: NSPCC.

Powell, M. & Thomson, D. (2002). Children's memories for repeated events. In H.L. Westcott, G.M. Davies, & R.H.C. Bull (Eds), *Children's testimony: A handbook of psychological research and forensic practice.* Chichester: John Wiley & Sons.

Sanders, A. Creaton, J., Bird, S., & Weber, L. (1997). *Victims with learning disabilities: negotiating the criminal justice system.* Oxford: University of Oxford Centre for Criminological Research.

Sas, L.D., Cunningham, A.H., Hurley, P., Dick, T., & Farnsworth, A. (1995). *Tipping the balance to tell the secret: Public discovery of child sexual abuse.* London, Ontario: London Family Court Clinic, Child Witness Project.

Sas, L.D., Hurley, P., Hatch, A. *et al.* (1991). *Three years after the verdict: A longitudinal study of the social and psychological adjustment of child witnesses referred to the child witness project.* London, Ontario: London Family Court Clinic, Child Witness Project.

Saywitz, K.J. (2002). Developmental underpinnings of children's testimony. In H.L. Westcott, G.M. Davies, & R.H.C. Bull (Eds), *Children's testimony: A handbook of psychological research and forensic practice.* Chichester: John Wiley & Sons.

Saywitz, K.J., Nathanson, R., Snyder, L., & Lamphear, V. (1993). *Preparing children for the investigative and judicial process: Improving communication, memory and emotional resiliency*. Final Report to the National Center on Child Abuse and Neglect (Grant No. 90CA1179).

Scottish Executive (2003a). *Lord Justice General's memorandum on child witnesses. Appendix to guidance on the questioning of children in court*. Edinburgh: The Stationery Office.

Scottish Executive (2003b). *Guidance on the questioning of children in court*. Edinburgh: The Stationery Office.

Spencer, J.R. & Flin, R.H. (1993). *The evidence of children: The law and the psychology* (2nd edn). London: Blackstone Press.

Spencer, J.R., Nicholson, G., Flin, R., & Bull, R. (1990). *Children's evidence in legal proceedings: An international perspective*. Cambridge: Cambridge University Faculty of Law.

Sternberg, K.J., Lamb, M.E., Davies, G.M., & Westcott, H.L. (2001). The Memorandum of Good Practice: Theory versus application. *Child Abuse & Neglect, 25*, 669–681.

Wade, A. (2002). New measures and new challenges: Children's experiences of the court process. In H.L. Westcott, G.M. Davies, & R.H.C. Bull (Eds), *Children's testimony: A handbook of psychological research and forensic practice*. Chichester: John Wiley & Sons.

Wade, A. & Westcott, H.L. (1997). No easy answers: Children's perspectives on investigative interviews. In H.L. Westcott & J. Jones (Eds), *Perspectives on the Memorandum: Policy, practice and research in investigative interviewing*. Aldershot: Arena.

Walker, A.G. (1993). Questioning young children in court: A linguistic case study. *Law and Human Behavior, 17*, 59–81.

Walker, A.G. (1994). *Handbook on questioning children: A linguistic perspective*. Washington: ABA Center on Children and the Law.

Westcott, H.L. (2006). Child witness testimony: What do we know and where are we going? *Child and Family Law Quarterly, 18*, 175–190.

Westcott, H.L. & Davies, G.M. (1996). Sexually abused children's and young people's perspectives on investigative interviews. *British Journal of Social Work, 26*, 451–474.

Westcott, H.L. & Kynan, S. (2006). Interviewer practice in investigative interviews for suspected child sexual abuse. *Psychology, Crime and Law, 12*, 367–382.

Westcott, H.L., Kynan, S., & Few, C. (2006). Improving the quality of investigative interviews for suspected child abuse: A case study. *Psychology, Crime and Law, 12*, 77–96.

Westcott, H.L. & Page, M. (2002). Cross-examination, sexual abuse and child witness identity. *Child Abuse Review, 11*, 13–152.

Zajac, R., Gross, J., & Hayne, H. (2003). Asked and answered: Questioning children in the courtroom. *Psychiatry, Psychology and Law, 10*, 199–209.

ANNOTATED FURTHER READING

Burton, M., Evans, R., & Sanders, A. (2006). *Are special measures for vulnerable and intimidated witnesses working? Evidence from the criminal justice agencies*. London: Home Office (Home Office Online Report 01/06). *Report of a multi-method research project carried out both before and after implementation of special measures. Reports on the extent to which the measures were working in practice; contains observations on 'cultural changes' required, and makes recommendations for future attention.*

Hamlyn, B., Phelps, A., Turtle, J., & Sattar,G. (2004). *Are special Measures working? Evidence from surveys of vulnerable and intimidated witnesses.* London: Home Office (Home Office Research Study 283). *Report of a research project that surveyed vulnerable witnesses' experiences of special measures before and after implementation of the new provisions.*

Kelly, L., Lovett, J., & Regan, L. (2005). *A gap or a chasm? Attrition in reported rape cases.* London: Home Office RDS (Home Office Research Study 293). *Report of a research project that examined over 2000 rape cases and explored victims' perceptions and experiences of the criminal justice system. Provides a breakdown of attrition rates in these cases, and makes detailed recommendations.*

Plotnikoff, J. & Woolfson, R. (2004). *In their own words: The experiences of 50 young witnesses in criminal proceedings.* London: NSPCC. *Report of a research project that interviewed 50 young witnesses about all aspects of their pre-trial and court experience. Includes detailed discussion of special measures, especially video-recorded interviews, live link, and pre-trial preparation and support.*

Sanders, A., Creaton, J., Bird, S., & Weber, L. (1997). *Victims with learning disabilities: Negotiating the criminal justice system.* Oxford: University of Oxford Centre for Criminological Research. *Report of a research project that examined 76 cases involving learning disabled victims. A step-by-step analysis of particular problems that these victims encountered at each stage of the investigative and prosecution process.*

Westcott, H.L., Davies, G.M., & Bull, R.H.C. (Eds) (2002). *Children's testimony: A handbook of psychological research and forensic practice.* Chichester: John Wiley & Sons. *A comprehensive edited collection that covers a range of issues pertaining to child witnesses: cognitive and developmental underpinnings; memory and interviewing; court issues; and alternative perspectives on children's testimony. Includes reviews and a glossary of relevant terminology featured in the book.*

CHAPTER 9

WITNESS EVIDENCE

Julie Blackwell-Young
Newman University College,
Birmingham, United Kingdom

Witnesses are crucial to the criminal justice system (Kebbell & Milne, 1998; Rand, 1975; Wells & Olson, 2003). They provide information about what happened and descriptions of the perpetrators, which aid the police in finding those responsible. Witnesses play a vital role in the courtroom in giving their first-hand accounts of the incident which the judge or jury will use in deciding whether the defendants are guilty or not guilty. However, there is evidence that witnesses are not as reliable as the criminal justice system would like to believe. For example, in the US, studies of innocent persons wrongly convicted of serious crimes who have been subsequently exonerated by new DNA evidence have found that in over 75% of cases, faulty eyewitness testimony was the main contributor to the original guilty verdict (Wells & Olson, 2003).

Psychologists have been investigating the problems of memory since Ebbinghaus (1885) and the implications of confident but inaccurate witness memory were highlighted by Münsterberg as early as 1908 (Münsterberg, 1908). However, it was not until the 1970s that researchers began to seriously study memory in a forensic context. Since then, much research has been devoted to finding out what makes eyewitness memory inaccurate and what can be done to improve its accuracy.

This chapter explores what has been discovered about the psychological factors influencing evidence and what can be done to ensure that witnesses give as accurate testimony as possible. We begin by introducing some crucial distinctions in research on eyewitness memory: between the different stages of the memory process – encoding, storage and retrieval – and between estimator and system variables. We then go on to consider research on the role of witness factors such as age, mental ability and confidence in determining witness credibility. This is followed by a discussion of recent research on the impact of two important factors influencing the encoding stage eyewitness memory: drug and alcohol intoxication and the presence of a weapon. We then consider how memory may become distorted during the storage phase by reading accounts or speaking to others about the critical event before considering how questioning procedures can impact on the reliability of the account the witness provides at court. It is important that witnesses provide as accurate an account as possible and much psychological research has gone into finding out what can affect witness evidence.

THE MEMORY PROCESS

Test Your Own Memory

People tend to believe that our memories are like video recorders that faithfully record the things that we do and replay them back perfectly later (Haber & Haber, 2000). Take a few seconds to think about what you have done so far today. The chances are you think that you have a perfect memory for what happened. How well do you think you will remember these events in one week's time? How about three months later? One year later? Think about the last time you went out with someone else, for example to the cinema. If you were to ask them what happened that day, would they remember things exactly the same way that you do? Try it and see what happens.

It is generally agreed that there are three main stages to memory:

- **Encoding/**Acquisition – this is when the information first goes into our memories;
- **Storage/**Retention – this is when we keep the information in our memories to recall later;
- **Retrieval** – this is when we release the information in our memories, perhaps as a response to questioning.

Problems can occur in each of these three stages. For example, if not enough attention is paid to what is going on in the *encoding* stage, then events may not be encoded properly. During the *storage* phase, new relevant information may be encountered: witnesses might read a news report about the incident, which can affect their original memory, or if the information is stored for a long time the natural processes of forgetting could further degrade the memory. Finally, in the *retrieval* stage, the information can undergo further changes: the way questions are asked can distort the original memory or the stressful circumstance may prevent accurate recall (many readers will be familiar with the problems of retrieving information under examination conditions!).

Psychologists distinguish between two types of retrieval: **recall** and **recognition.** *Recognition* is where, for example, a witness may take part in an identification parade (or 'line-up') or be shown an article of clothing that was allegedly worn by the perpetrator and asked if they have seen it before. The *recall* equivalent of these tasks would be to ask the witness to describe the suspect's appearance or what they were wearing. Recall is usually considered to be more difficult because it involves more stages of processing: not only verification but also retrieval (Kebbell & Wagstaff, 1999). There are also two principle types of recall: **free recall** and **cued recall.** In *free recall* witnesses are simply asked an *open-ended question* such as "Tell me what happened" and is allowed to give their own account of the event without interference or interruption. Free recall tends to be very accurate, but rarely complete, because people leave details out, particularly those they don't consider important. *Cued recall* involves question and answer. The person answering the questions is cued as to what kind of information is required by the question: we ask questions about specific aspects of the event and get specific answers in return. This means that the person asking the questions gets the information they want, but the questions are biased towards the questioner's conception of what happened. As discussed later, this can lead to problems with the accuracy of the answers given.

It can be argued though, that being a witness to a crime is such an unusual event that it is likely to be better retained in memory than other, routine, events. There is some evidence to support this. Studies comparing recall of bizarre or usual sentences usually show that the bizarre are remembered better than usual sentences (McDaniel, DeLosh & Merritt, 2000). Studies conducted on actual crimes have also suggested that these are better remembered than might be expected, given the problems of memory described above (Leippe, 1995). Yuille & Cutshall (1986) investigated the memory of witnesses to a real armed robbery. Some 13 eyewitnesses were interviewed immediately after the event and again four or five months later. Yuille and Cutshall found that despite the delay of several months, the witnesses showed no appreciable drop in accuracy from what they had said immediately after the shooting. Yuille and Cutshall suggested this could be due to the uniqueness of the event witnessed or because these witnesses were actually part of the event, not seeing something as an impartial observer like most memory research. Both factors could have helped encode and preserve the memory better. Inevitably, with real-life events, experimental control is not perfect: the participants were self-selected volunteers. Perhaps the witnesses who remembered the event less well decided not to participate in the study.

An important distinction when considering factors influencing witness memory is that between **estimator variables** and **system variables** first outlined by Wells (1978).

Wells emphasized that researchers focused on *estimator variables*: variables that are not under the control of the criminal justice system. These include the lighting conditions, the personality and character of the witness, their alcohol level, their confidence and the presence of a weapon. These variables cannot be controlled as they are part of the witness's experience and we can only estimate their impact on a witness's accuracy. Wells contrasted such estimator variables with system variables. *System variables* are under the control of the criminal justice system, for example, how line-ups are conducted, the way in which questions are asked and levels of support given to witnesses at interview or in court (see Valentine, Chapter 3). The research which has been conducted on system variables allows psychologists to give guidance to criminal justice professionals on how to adjust procedures and practice to improve the quality of evidence that witnesses can provide. An example of this is the **Cognitive Interview** developed by psychologists based on psychological theories about memory and social interaction which has been shown to lead to more accurate information being given by witnesses. (Fisher, 1995; see Holliday, Chapter 4). This means that despite the unpredictable circumstances witnesses experience during criminal acts, there is much that can be done by the legal system to try and ensure witnesses provide their most accurate account of such events.

Wells *et al.* (2000) have suggested that psychologists are making a valuable contribution to the criminal justice system, through the development of guidelines for police officers and other investigators. Examples include **Achieving Best Evidence** (Home Office, 2002), guidelines for the safeguarding and interviewing of child witnesses in England and Wales (see Holliday, Chapter 4), and guidelines endorsed by the Attorney General for the proper conduct of **line-ups** and **photo-spreads** in the US (Wells *et al.*, 2001; see also Valentine, Chapter 3).

Koriat & Goldsmith (1994) emphasize that the outcome of research on memory in the laboratory and real life may lead to very different outcomes. Real-life research often shows much better memory performance than laboratory studies. Koriat and Goldsmith suggest that is it important to consider what is being measured in the different studies that have been conducted. When investigating real-life situations it can be very difficult to know exactly what happened unless good quality **CCTV** or video footage is available. For this reason, a great deal of eyewitness research has been done in laboratory settings where careful control can be achieved. However, this has been criticized as not providing an accurate guide to the real world where often events are much more ambiguous and stressful and a variety of additional factors may impact on memory (Egeth, 1993; Yuille & Cutshall, 1986). Such issues need to be borne in mind when reading the experiments described in this chapter and any journal articles on the subject. Three core issues will now be explored: witness credibility and factors that influence this; witness reliability, and state and post-event influences.

WITNESS CREDIBILITY

In England and Wales as in many other legislatures, it is the duty of the prosecution or defence to decide which witnesses should be called to give evidence on their behalf. They must decide whether a witness is credible enough to appear in court. However, it is the jury (in the Crown Court in England and Wales) or magistrates or judges in other court systems, who have the final word over the credibility of the witness. One way the court can determine this is to examine the consistency of one witness's statements over time and how the statement fits the facts collected from other sources, such as CCTV or forensic evidence. When the witness is questioned in court, how consistent is this with what they said during the earlier police interview? In addition to considering the actual testimony, judges and juries use other factors, such as the personal attributes of the witness in making judgements about **credibility**.

There are many factors that can impact on perceived credibility. People make credibility judgments all the time, for instance, when watching a celebrity endorsing a product in a TV commercial. Among the factors explored by psychologists as influencing credibility are age, mental impairment and confidence.

Age

One factor that people consider is the age of the witness. Research suggests that witnesses from each end of the age spectrum may be less reliable on average than those in between. For example, elderly witnesses and young children were found to be poorer at identifying strangers accurately than other age groups (Pozzulo & Lindsay, 1998; Wells & Olson, 2003).

Dodson & Krueger (2006) investigated whether older people (60–79 years of age) were more likely to suffer from memory distortion than younger adults (17–23 years of age). They showed a video and then asked questions, some of which referred to events that had not actually happened in the video. The participants were also asked to give indications of how certain they were of their answers. They found that both older and younger people were equally likely to respond incorrectly to questions that asked about events that had not actually happened. However, the older adults were more confident when making their incorrect responses. This adds to the literature which suggests that when witnesses are confident in their memories, this does not automatically mean they are more accurate than somebody who is less confident. Judges and jurors are more likely to believe a confident witness, but as with some elderly witnesses, confidence is not necessarily a good guide to accuracy (Shaw, McClure & Dykstra, 2007).

Cognitive factors can also cause some older witnesses to be less reliable than younger adults. As people age, their cognitive functions begin to decline (Albert *et al.*, 1995). Their perceptual abilities get worse – sight and hearing – as well as their ability to encode, store and retrieve information from memory. If information is not encoded then it cannot be retrieved later. Kensinger *et al.* (2005) found that older adults as a group were less effective than younger adults at remembering peripheral details of emotional scenes, even when given instructions that they would have their memories assessed and should try to remember as much as possible. Yarmey & Kent (1980) found that younger adults were better at giving a verbal account of an event when compared to older adults. Older mock witnesses also appear more susceptible to **post-event misinformation** (Mitchell, Johnson & Mather, 2003).

Not all studies have found differences between the performances of older and younger adult witnesses. Yarmey and Kent found no differences in identification ability and Adams-Price (1992) found that older (60–75 years old) and younger adults (20–35 years old) performed similarly in a recall task, both on **central detail** and **peripheral detail**. However, Adams-Price found a weaker relationship between confidence and accuracy in older compared to younger adults. In sum, most recent research suggests that older adults do not perform as well as younger adults and are more susceptible to misinformation and more likely to be confident in wrong answers.

So how do police officers perceive the credibility of older witnesses? Wright & Holliday (2005) found that police officers tended to consider witnesses over the age of 60 to be less reliable and less thorough than witnesses below 60. See, Hoffman & Wood (2001) found that participants judged a younger female witness (aged 28) to be more competent and so more accurate than an elderly female witness (aged 82) but the elderly witness was considered more honest. In general, potential jurors also appear to believe that older witnesses are invariably less competent.

A similar prejudice extends toward children's evidence in many legal systems. Until recently for instance, judges in England and Wales were mandated to give special warnings to the jury when considering the evidence of a child witness (Judicial Studies Board, 2006) because the testimony of children was seen as unreliable. However, since research has been focused on child witnesses, we now know that children are not inevitably unreliable as witnesses. A quick-thinking 10-year-old provided such a precise description of her abductor and the vehicle he drove that police were able to trace the car and arrest and convict the owner (see case history below).

CASE STUDY

A Remarkable Witness

The B9002 Cabrach to Lumsden road winds its way through some of the most lonely and inhospitable moorland in Scotland. On 23 June 1986, a tourist venturing along this road was surprised to come across a 10-year-old girl, dazed, bleeding and half-naked, standing beside a culvert. The girl was rushed to hospital in Aberdeen where she was found to have multiple fractures of the skull, cheek and jaw consistent with being hit repeatedly with a large stone. She had also been sexually assaulted.

A police officer stayed with the girl day and night as she slowly recovered and began to tell of her ordeal. She told police she had been abducted at knifepoint, driven to the lonely spot where she was found where she was attacked and left for dead. Shortly beforehand, her teacher had told her class to always try and remember the appearance of strangers who approached them in suspicious circumstances. Within two days, the police officer had elicited enough information to issue a description: 'A well-built man, about 5'7" tall, clean-shaven with dark centre-parted greasy hair'. She also reported that he had worn a sweatshirt with a distinctive oil-rig logo on the pocket. There was also a very precise description of the seat covers of the car which police were able to link to a mudflap, tyre marks and paint fragments found at the scene to identify the vehicle concerned. It was a mass-produced Datsun saloon, but the child's description of the seats marked it out as one of just 700 Special Edition models imported into the UK, of which just nine were registered locally.

The first vehicle checked belonged to Colin Findlay, an oil-rig worker, currently working off-shore. In his drive was a Datsun saloon missing a mudflap. In his wardrobe the police found a sodden bundle of clothing, including the sweatshirt with the distinctive logo. Within a week of the crime, police flew out to an oil platform in the North Sea to arrest Findlay who pleaded guilty at trial to attempted rape and assault of the young girl.

Talking point: The critical role of the police officer who stayed with the young girl as she recovered from her ordeal. What questions might you have asked and how would you have framed them so as to elicit the maximum amount of useful and accurate information?

(adapted from Davies, Stephenson-Robb & Flin, 1988).

In the US, the majority of child witnesses are called to court to give evidence in child sexual abuse cases (Goodman, 2005). Goodman reports that in these cases, children are often questioned as to their credibility. It is often argued that because their memories are not mature, children are very susceptible to suggestion and to making up events and reporting crimes that have not been committed. The classic research in this area was undertaken by Stephen Ceci with various colleagues in the 1990s. Ceci & Bruck (1993) define **suggestibility** as "the degree to which children's encoding, storage, retrieval and reporting of events can be influenced by a range of social and psychological factors" (p. 404). Ceci and Bruck suggest that there are a range of cognitive and social factors which may lead young children to be suggestible. These include memory function, linguistic competence, knowledge, belief in the credibility of adults asking the questions, repeated questioning, and style of questioning (see Holliday, Chapter 4 for a description of these studies). Stephen Ceci has been responsible for the most innovative and interesting research on the suggestibility of children, including the famous 'Sam Stone' study.

CASE STUDY

Sam Stone Pays a Visit to the Nursery

In a now classic study, Leichtman & Ceci (1995) investigated the effects of suggestive questioning and stereotyping on young children's reports of an event when a man named "Sam Stone" paid a brief visit to the children's day centre (nursery). The children were aged between 3 and 6 years and were allocated to one of four groups: first, a *control* group who were not given any information about his visit beforehand and second, a *stereotype* group who were read repeated stories illustrating the supposed clumsiness of Sam Stone, in the weeks leading up to his visit. Both these groups were subsequently interviewed four times in a non-suggestive

(Continued)

way over the next 10 weeks concerning Sam's visit. A third *suggestion* group who were not given any stereotype information about Sam's clumsiness, but were again interviewed four times in the 10-week period, but with suggestive questions which implied that Sam had ripped a book and soiled a teddy bear. A fourth, *stereotype and suggestion* group were read the stereotypic stories beforehand *and* interviewed four times with suggestive questions. In the final phase, all the children received a fifth interview in which they were asked first, to give a free recall about what had happened and second, asked specific but neutral questions by a trained interviewer concerning whether Sam had damaged the book or the teddy bear.

Those in the *control* group gave generally highly accurate accounts and did not implicate Sam in damaging either the book or the teddy. In the *stereotype*-only group, no children spontaneously reported damage by Sam to the book or teddy, but some 42% of the youngest children agreed that he had when questioned, with 11% maintaining this claim when gently challenged; the figures for the 5–6-year-olds were roughly half those of the younger participants. For the *suggestion*-only group, some 52% of the 3–4-year-olds and 38% of the 5–6-year-olds agreed when questioned that Sam had damaged the book and/or the teddy bear and again 12% of the youngest group continued to maintain this claim when challenged (compared to 10% for the older children). However, it was the combination of *stereotype and suggestion* which proved the most lethal to accuracy. Here, some 72% of the youngest group and 21% continued to insist that Sam had damaged the book or teddy, even when gently challenged. The figures for the 5–6-year-olds were more accurate, but 11% still continued to maintain the misbehaviour had taken place when challenged. Many children in this condition did not stop at acceding to the suggestions but also spontaneously embellished their responses with false details (Sam took the teddy into the bathroom and soaked it in hot water before smearing it with crayon).

Talking point: What are the potential implications of this study for investigators involved in assessing allegations of child sexual or physical abuse?

Finally Leichtman and Ceci showed videotapes of the children describing Sam's actions to various groups of child protection professionals to see if they could distinguish between the accurate and inaccurate accounts on the basis of the child's statement alone. Performance in this informal test was essentially at chance; overall, they rated the accurate account as the least credible and the most inaccurate account as the most credible!

Talking point: What questions, if any, could the experts have asked the children to try to establish more accurately which children were telling the truth and which were relying on false memories?

In his research, Ceci was also able to persuade children that they had been party to events which had never occurred. Ceci *et al.* (1994) asked children to think about a series of events, both true and not true, for example whether they had ever caught their finger in a mousetrap and had to go to hospital to get it removed, which was an event that none of the children had experienced. Forty-four per cent of the 3-4-year-olds and 25% of the 5-6-year-olds falsely reported that events had happened to them when initially asked. The children were continually asked about these events over a period of 10 weeks and by the end 58% of the children were agreeing that one of the false events had happened to them. The accounts the children gave were very vivid and 27% of the children refused to change their minds even when told by the researchers and their parents that the events had never happened. Again, professionals were unable to distinguish between the accurate and inaccurate accounts.

However, other research suggests that it is actually quite difficult to suggest successfully to children that they have taken part in fictitious events involving themselves being touched inappropriately, particularly older children. Pezdek & Roe (1997) conducted an experiment with 4-year-olds and 10-year-olds where they tried to change the children's memories about touching or **implant memories** about touching. They found that it was possible to change an existing memory by suggestion but that it was difficult to plant a memory of touching that had not occurred or to remove a memory of touching that had actually happened (see also Leippe, Romanczyk & Manion, 1991).

However, the legal system and the public at large still have concerns about child witnesses. Leippe, Manion & Romanczyk (1992) found that mock jurors judged adult witnesses to be more accurate and believable than child witnesses even when both groups performed at the same accuracy levels. Melinder *et al.* (2004) asked professionals about their views of child witnesses in Norway and found that police and psychiatrists tended to be quite positive in their beliefs about children's capabilities, but that defence attorneys and psychologists were much more negative.

Goodman (2005) suggests though, that research is still at an early stage with regard to the strength of children's memories. She writes:

children's memory and suggestibility depend on what children are asked about, on individual differences among children, on what transpires before a forensic interview begins, on the retrieval cues and context at the time of interview, on the delay since the event, and on the strength of particular memories. (Goodman, 2005; p. 874)

Therefore, as with the elderly, there are no hard-and-fast rules that can be applied regarding the credibility of an individual child witness. However, the way vulnerable witnesses such as children and the elderly are questioned about their evidence is considered to be very important in terms of whether the witness is likely to make errors in their account. Questioning will be covered in more detail later in the chapter.

Learning Disabilities

Criminal justice system professionals generally believe that witnesses with learning disabilities are not good eyewitnesses to crime and as a result, crimes against those with such disabilities are often not taken to court (Green, 2001; Gudjonsson, Murphy & Clare, 2000; Kebbell & Hatton, 1999). The reasons for these difficulties include the belief that the memory function of those with such disabilities is impaired relative to others. Such witnesses are often thought to be less effective at encoding, storage and retrieval from memory, thus making their testimony unreliable (Kebbell & Wagstaff, 1999).

The perception of credibility for those with a learning disability is further diminished when they are also children (Peled, Iarocci & Connolly, 2004). This can be particularly problematic as children with learning disabilities can often behave less maturely than other children of comparable age, a factor that has been found to be important when juries judge child witnesses. Peled *et al.* (2004) showed that credibility bias against those with learning disabilities was such that mock witnesses rated a 15-year-old witness, who was said to operate intellectually at the level of a typical 10 year-old, was perceived as less credible than a 10-year-old witness of average ability, although cognitively both would be performing at the same level. Stobbs & Kebbell (2003) also showed that when people believed a written **transcript** came from the evidence of someone with mild learning disabilities, they did not consider the evidence to be as strong as those who read the same transcript and believed it came from someone of average abilities.

However, Kebbell & Hatton (1999), in their review of the literature regarding witnesses with learning disabilities (termed mental retardation in the US literature), found that whilst the memory of those with such disabilities may suffer from some deficits compared to other people, procedures employed by the criminal justice system exaggerated their difficulties. For example, the styles of questions used in court cause problems for the general adult population and even greater problems for those witnesses with some degree of mental impairment. This can be made worse by the acquiescence bias displayed by such witnesses who are much more likely to answer "yes" to questions of which they are unsure resulting in their evidence seeming contradictory and unreliable. Witnesses with learning disabilities give the most accurate answers to open-ended questions that encourage free recall, such as "Tell me what happened on Monday morning" but their answers are not necessarily as complete as for typical witnesses. However, these types of questions are not widely used within the courtroom, particularly in cross examination. What all this suggests is that witnesses with learning disabilities may be capable of being reliable, credible witnesses but that the processes within the criminal justice system serve to highlight and exacerbate the problems that this group may have, thus making them appear less reliable witnesses than they could be (see Westcott, Chapter 8).

Mental Illness

Mental illness is another factor that may affect the credibility of a witness. A report in New South Wales, Australia, claimed that those with mental illness are not taken seriously when reporting crimes and may even be perceived as fabricating complaints (Karras *et al.*, 2006). Research suggests that certain mental illnesses like depression are associated with impairments of memory. Burt, Zember & Niederehe (1995) conducted a **meta-analysis** which examined studies that had been conducted on the relationship between depression and memory and found that both recall and recognition memory are impaired in people with depression. However, whether depression causes memory impairment is not clear from the literature and the levels of memory impairment will also differ from person to person. For example, younger people with depression seem to experience greater memory impairment than older people. Burt *et al.* also found memory impairments in people with schizophrenia but not in people who only had substance abuse issues or anxiety disorders. There does seem to be an indication that people with depression are better at remembering negative events and Burt *et al.* suggest that this bias may be mood related. The implications of this for eyewitness memory are less clear cut. However, it has also been suggested that people with depression are less likely to attend to events and so fail to encode them well and may also have less motivation to rehearse and recall such information, leading to lowered memory performance overall (Kebbell & Wagstaff, 1999). Overall, there is very little literature on mental illness and its effects on witnesses (Maizel *et al.*, 2001) and further research is required.

Confidence

As indicated earlier, the legal system and the general public tend to believe that confident witnesses are accurate (Leippe, Manion & Romanczyk, 1992; Wells *et al.*, 2000). However, as noted in the discussion of elderly witnesses, this is not always the case. Shaw & Zerr (2003) showed that if people put a lot of effort into remembering (e.g. in a courtroom situation) then they tend to feel more confident in their accounts, but this does not necessarily reflect greater accuracy in what was said. Shaw (1996) also found that when people were forced to choose answers, they often had greater confidence in those answers when questioned later, even when the original answers were incorrect. It is suggested that people tend to be generally over-confident in their own abilities, which can cause difficulties when it comes to giving evidence in criminal proceedings (Bornstein & Zickafoose, 1999). The relationship between confidence and accuracy is a complicated one, which can be affected by a number of factors (Luus & Wells, 1994). There is some evidence that high confidence judgments at an identity parade are likely to be accurate (Sporer *et al.*, 1995). But the judgments must be made at the time of choice; giving witnesses positive feedback subsequent to the parade can inflate confidence irrespective of the actual accuracy (Wells, Olson & Charman, 2003; see Valentine, Chapter 3).

One method often used by those involved in the criminal justice system to infer confidence from the way in which people speak. In the 1970s, distinctions were made between **powerful** and **powerless** types of speech. Initially these were thought to operate on gender lines (e.g. Lakoff, 1975) but later O'Barr (1982) noted that this was not necessarily the case, although it is argued that women and low status men are more likely to use powerless speech.

According to Gibbons (2003) *powerful* speakers tend to use variation in their speech, both in terms of volume and intonation, to repeat phrases, are not afraid of using silence but will also interrupt, are fluent and coherent in their speech and do not use common expressions of agreement such as 'yeah'. Those who use a *powerless* speech style tend to hesitate and show uncertainty; they also use deferential forms of address – 'sir' – and use phrases such as 'would you mind if . . .' .

Research has shown that in court situations in particular, those using more powerful forms of speech are considered more credible (Erikson *et al.*, 1978; O'Barr, 1982; Tiermsa, 1999). More recently Ruva & Bryant (2004) also found that adults who used a powerless form of speech were considered less credible than adults who used a more powerful form of speech, but that form of speech was not associated with credibility for child witnesses. This suggests that jurors may formulate different rules for children compared to adults in terms of how they are expected to speak in court.

Do The Findings of Psychological Research Reflect Legal Conceptions of Credibility?

The legal system has definite ideas about what constitutes a credible witness. Credible witnesses are 100% accurate, have enough emotion to seem genuine but not so much as to appear hysterical and display confidence. However, psychology tells us that witnesses who fall short of these ideals are not necessarily poor witnesses.

For example, just because a witness is wrong on some details does not necessarily mean that they will be wrong on other details. Bell & Loftus (1989) showed that witnesses who gave more detail (even when this detail was not relevant) were considered to have enhanced credibility, a better memory and to have paid more attention (see also Borckardt, Sproghe & Nash, 2003). Psychological research on memory shows that our memory for peripheral information (e.g. details at the edges of our vision) can be impaired but our memory for the central facts of what happened is still very accurate, particularly for emotional events (Christianson, 1992; Kensinger *et al.*, 2005).

Emotional witnesses can also be seen as less credible. Wessel *et al.* (2006) showed that lay people (who might expect to serve on a jury) were influenced by emotion in their judgments of credibility, but that legal professionals (such as judges) were not. Kaufmann *et al.* (2003) had an actress deliver testimony concerning a rape in one of three emotional states: congruent (despair and sobbing); neutral (no emotion); and incongruent (positive and pleasant). The results showed that those who saw the neutral and incongruent states rated the witness as less credible than those who saw the congruent state, but the participants maintained they were making credibility decisions solely on the content of the evidence. Kaufmann *et al.* (2003) point out that this throws up two issues. First, that people are unaware that they are making judgments based on the emotion of the witness and secondly, that different people may react very differently to the same situation. The work of Amanda Konradi (e.g. 1999), for example, reports that rape victims will attempt in court to inhibit emotion to present a reasoned case, but the evidence above suggests this may count against them in the eyes of some jurors.

WITNESS RELIABILITY AND WITNESS STATE

As well as our perceptions about witness credibility there are also other factors that might impact on a witness's reliability. This section considers drugs, alcohol, stress and the presence of weapons and their impact on memory.

Drugs and Alcohol

Surprisingly little research appears to have been done on the effect of drugs on witness evidence, despite their ubiquity in Western society. In one study, Yuille *et al.* (1998) showed that there was a temporary effect of marijuana on memory but that after a

week's delay, those who had used marijuana were performing as well as those participants who did not. This would suggest that in the court situation, marijuana use at the
time of the crime would not be a problem for witness evidence. However, it can be
assumed that any drugs that have an effect on perception may lead to issues with the
encoding of events and the consequent quality of memory that can be retrieved.

More work has been done on the effects of alcohol, but the results are far from
clear-cut. Yuille & Tollestrup (1990) conducted a **staged theft** and some of those
involved were given alcohol. Their results showed that those given alcohol recalled less
when questioned immediately, and recalled less and were less accurate after a one-week
delay. However, Ober & Stillman (1988) found that alcoholics were no more susceptible to misleading influences than non-alcoholics.

Assefi & Garry (2003) raised the question as to whether the effects of alcohol on
memory may not be due directly to the alcohol itself, but rather people's expectations.
In their study, some participants were given tonic water but were told that it was an
alcoholic drink. Such participants were more likely to be influenced by misleading
information during questioning than those who knew they were only drinking tonic
water. This suggests that the belief of the participants was critical in influencing their
performance. However, Clifasefi, Takarangi & Bergman (2006) using a similar procedure to mask the presence or absence of alcohol in a drink, still found significant
impairments in perception of an unexpected event. Participants watched a film of a
person in a gorilla costume turning up in the middle of basketball practice (see Simons
& Chabris, 1999). Those who had drunk alcohol were less likely to notice the gorilla
compared to those who had drunk just tonic water (18% v. 46%); whether or not the
person thought they had been given alcohol made no difference to the results.

Stress and Weapon Focus

High levels of stress have been suggested to have a negative effect on a witness's ability
to encode information at the time of the crime. As discussed earlier, if information is
not encoded properly then the witness will not be able to recall that information at a
later stage in court. A survey of forensic psychology experts published in 2001, found
that 60% of the experts agreed that the statement "high levels of stress impair the accuracy of eyewitness testimony" (Kassin *et al.*, 2001, p. 408) was reliable enough for psychologists to testify about it in court with 98% saying that this opinion was based on
"published, peer-reviewed, scientific research" (Kassin *et al.*, 2001, p. 407).

However, the relationship between stress and eyewitness evidence is quite complex
and high levels of stress do not automatically create problems for the witness. One reason may be that witnesses will focus on some aspects of the scene (usually the central
ones) and ignore others (Christianson, 1992; Kebbell & Wagstaff, 1999). This can
mean that some information is recalled very well whereas other aspects can be less
accurate. However, as noted earlier, the legal system requires witnesses to be able to
recall peripheral as well as central details and a failure to do so can have an adverse
effect on a witness' credibility.

According to Yuille & Cutshall's (1986) account of an actual case, witnesses who
were very stressed were also very accurate, in fact more accurate than less stressed witnesses. However, the authors do acknowledge that those who were highly stressed were

also more directly involved in the incident, so there is a confounding variable there. A review by Christianson (1992) also supported the view that high levels of stress are not problematic when it comes to witness performance.

However, a recent meta-analysis on the area of stress and witness memory suggests that high levels of stress do adversely impact on witness recall, with adults being affected more than children, and participants performing worse when being asked questions about the event than when allowed to give a free recall (Deffenbacher *et al.*, 2004). These findings would suggest that the traditional police and court experience of being questioned about the crime would have a detrimental impact on witness performance. Deffenbacher *et al.* point to the ethical difficulties of inducing high levels of stress within an experimental paradigm and suggest that individual differences may play an important role in modulating stress effects.

Linked to high stress is the phenomenon of weapon focus. It has been widely demonstrated in the literature that when a weapon is produced in an eyewitness scenario, participants tend to focus on the weapon rather than other aspects of the incident (Kebbell & Wagstaff, 1999). In particular, research has tended to concentrate on how the presence of a weapon leads to poorer recall of the weapon-holder's face. A meta-analysis of the research in 1992 showed that the presence of a weapon led to lower line-up identification accuracy and a lower ability to describe the features of the perpetrator (Steblay, 1992). This finding was consistent across different methods of investigating the effect e.g. type of participant, type of stimulus and different arousal levels. In a survey of forensic psychology experts published in 2001, 87% felt that the weapon focus effect was reliable enough for psychologists to testify about it in court with 97% saying that this opinion was based on "published, peer-reviewed, scientific research" (Kassin, *et al.*, 2001, p. 407).

Recent research has tried to find out why the weapon focus effect occurs. The most common view is that people focus on the weapon, to the exclusion of peripheral detail such as the appearance of the perpetrator, in line with Easterbrook's cue-utilization hypothesis (Easterbrook, 1959). There have been two main explanations put forward for this narrowing of attention. The first is that the threat of the object is responsible and the second that the unusualness of the object is the main factor. Contrary to the threat interpretation, lower arousal levels still result in a weapon focus effect (Steblay, 1992) and higher levels of threat do not necessarily increase the strength of the effect (Pickel, 1998, 1999).

There is evidence that unusualness can in itself induce a report pattern consistent with weapon focus. Pickel (1998, 1999) showed that participants' recall of a robbery in a hairdressers was lower when the robber produced an unusual object (a handgun or a whole frozen chicken) than when he held an object that might be expected to be part of the scene (scissors or a wallet). The raw chicken was unlikely to be threatening, but still resulted in lower recall for the robber's appearance. The unusualness effect also means that people tend to be better able to give descriptions of unusual objects when compared to descriptions of neutral objects in scenes, indicating that the weapon focus effect is due to concentrating on the weapon (Pickel, Ross & Truelove, 2006).

Fahsing, Ask & Granhag (2004) studied real-life bank robberies in Norway. They had CCTV footage of the robberies and so were able to compare the witnesses' evidence with what actually happened. One of the things that they investigated was the effect of a weapon on testimony. All their robbers had some kind of weapon, either a knife or a firearm. Fahsing *et al.* found that the type of weapon used was important with a larger negative effect on the completeness of witness descriptions when the weapon used was a firearm compared to a knife. However, the information that was given was more accurate. It must be noted, however, that because of an absence of robberies within the sample where a weapon was not used, it is not possible to draw strong conclusions about the impact of a weapon as such on witness testimony.

Pickel *et al.* (2006) also have demonstrated that weapon focus does not have to be automatic. They demonstrated that participants who have been informed about the effect can actively over-ride it and concentrate on other aspects of the scene, for example the perpetrator. This is also supported by Fahsing *et al.*'s findings that bank tellers gave better descriptions than bystander witnesses which Fahsing *et al.* suggest might be due to the bank clerks having received witness training. Hulse and Memon (2006) also failed to find a weapon focus effect with police officers.

Post-Incident Influences

After the crime has occurred things can still happen to the witness that might have an impact on their memory. These are known as post-incident or post-event influences. Often these are matters that the criminal justice system has control over: system variables in Wells' terms, such as when and how witnesses are interviewed. In this section the impact of delay, stereotyping, questioning style and exposure to other people's accounts on witness recall are discussed.

Delay

Witnesses can often be called to give their evidence in court months or even years after witnessing an event. There are increasing reports, particularly in North America, of cases coming to court concerning incidents that have happened many years previously. Haber & Haber (1998) for example, give details of a case where two sisters approached the police about the murder of their younger sister 35 years before. The legal system therefore has to come to some decisions about what to do with cases like this, particularly where there is no statute of limitations, which means that the case can still be pursued many years after the event. Haber & Haber (1998) suggest a number of issues that need to be taken into account including whether the witness's memory could have been tainted by other people or other information. In an experimental study, Poole & White (1995) re-tested participants in a study two years after initially testing their recall for a contrived incident. They found that, after two years, adults were less accurate in their recall. Delays of even four weeks have been found to lead to lower levels of correct recall (Rae Tuckey & Brewer, 2003). Overall, however, there is evidence that real-life events that have a strong emotional impact are generally well recalled even after extended periods of time (see review in Porter *et al.*, 2003).

There may also be some circumstances under which memories may resurface after long delays as 'recovered memories'. The existence and reliability of recovered memories continues to be hotly debated within the literature (Porter *et al.*, 2003). One area where this debate has caused particular controversy is when allegations of childhood sexual abuse are made at a much later date: when the victim is an adult and recovers such a memory in therapy. Many clinical psychologists believe that such **recovered memories** are the result of patients repressing or dissociating threatening memories from childhood, concepts derived from the ideas of Freud and Janet respectively (Brewin & Andrews, 1998). Cognitive psychologists on the other hand query whether we can truly 'recover' memories that have been previously forgotten or whether such memories are actually false memories, perhaps derived from suggestions in therapy. Initially, experts tended to be entrenched on one side or the other; today there has been a move to the middle ground, conceding that it is possible to recover memories for events previously forgotten but also to create false memories in adults (Davies & Dalgleish, 2001). Certainly, complete forgetting and then recovery of emotionally-charged events appears rare; indeed people usually have robust memories of **emotional events** (Magner & Parkinson, 2001; see Clifford, Chapter 10 for more coverage of this topic).

There are a number of theories as to why recall can become difficult after time. One theory suggests that our memories simply decay over time; however, there is little direct empirical evidence for this (Eysenck & Keane, 2005). More and better evidence exists that memories may be interfered with, both by pre-existing attitudes and beliefs – **stereotypes** – and by new information about the event subsequently acquired from others – discussing the event with other witnesses. These types of interference are discussed below.

Stereotyping and Partisanship

In a now classic study, Bartlett (1932) showed that when people pass on a story to other people, the information contained in the story increasingly conforms to what in our culture we would expect to happen. It has been suggested that this is because the people providing the account want to give one which is easily understood by other people and one way of doing this is by the use of stereotypes (Lyons & Kashima, 2006). Stereotypes are an easy cultural shorthand for people to understand concepts and so the use of stereotypes should result in a shared understanding of what the person is saying. It is also suggested that stereotypes are activated when our cognitive load is high, that is when we have a lot of information to process, again as a processing shortcut (Van Knippenberg, Dijksterhuis & Vermeulen, 1999).

If we think about a witness scenario then we might, for example, expect a robbery to involve a weapon and so we might report having seen a gun when in fact there was no gun present. Van Knippenberg *et al.* (1999) showed that our beliefs can lead to us remembering negative but stereotype consistent information about an offender under high cognitive load conditions. The work of Rae Tuckey & Brewer (2003) also provide support for schema consistent information being less susceptible to decay over extended time periods and schema inconsistent information – the presence of a skull on a lecturer's desk – being less likely to be remembered (Brewer & Treyens, 1981).

Witnesses usually want to be helpful to the investigation and will have come forward voluntarily to give their accounts because they wish to see justice done. However, this can be problematic as witnesses may alter their accounts in order to fit in with what they think will be helpful (Evans, 1995) or what they have learned from other people (Gabbert, Memon & Wright, 2006). This is not necessarily done knowingly, however, it can impact negatively on the case if, in court, parts of the witness's account are shown to be incorrect.

Witnesses are often questioned on a number of occasions. There is a concern that this repeated questioning along with any deterioration of memory over time can lead to mistakes in eyewitnesses' accounts. However, there is actually evidence that repeated interviewing can serve to maintain and even improve memory over time: a phenomenon known as **hypermnesia**. Dunning & Stern (1992) review evidence for *hypermnesia*, even if there is a delay of one week before the first interview. However, these reviewers go on to note that while there is evidence for a hypermnesia effect with free recall, as questioning becomes more constrained, so the effect disappears (Dunning & Stern, 1992). This may be because of problems with the types of questions that are often used and this issue is discussed further below.

Questioning

Factors like delay and interference can degrade recall, but does this mean that the material is permanently lost from memory? This is another area of continuing debate within the psychology of memory. Tulving (1974) has argued that much material we are unable spontaneously to recall still exists in memory and can be elicited, provided the original cues used to encode material can be reinstated. Whether this **cue-dependent theory of memory** can account for all forgetting is debatable, but there is plenty of evidence that optimizing the **retrieval environment** through appropriate questioning techniques can make a real difference to the amount and accuracy of information given by witnesses (see Holliday, Chapter 4).

A great deal of research has been conducted on how different types of questioning can impact on witness evidence. Perhaps the best-known study is that of Loftus & Palmer (1974) who manipulated the wording in a question. Participants observed a series of filmed collisions between vehicles. After each film, they were asked about the speed of the vehicles. For some participants, the question was "About how fast were the cars going when they *smashed* into each other?" For others: "About how fast were the cars going when they *contacted* each other?" Those in the *contacted* condition estimated speed at 31.8 mph compared to 40.5 mph for those in the *smashed* condition. Thus, the way the question was worded strongly influenced the answer the witnesses gave.

Badly worded questions, complex sentences, ambiguous questions and difficult vocabulary are all potentially problematic for witnesses. Problems over the wording of questions can give rise to error both during police witness interviews and equally importantly, at court (Kebbell & Johnson, 2000; Roebers & Schneider, 2000; Wheatcroft, Wagstaff & Kebbell, 2004; see Wheatcroft, Chapter 7). These forms of questions can make it difficult for the witness to work out what the questioner is asking and so influence the answer provided. Negatives ('is it not true to say the perpetrator wore a black coat?') and double negatives ('it is the case, is it not, that the perpetrator did not wear a black coat?') are particularly difficult for witnesses if confined to a 'yes' or 'no' answer by the lawyer at court. When leading questions ('you would agree that the perpetrator wore a black coat?') are asked, they can persuade an uncertain witness to agree with the questioner's view, particularly under a high-pressure situation such as a courtroom or police station (Gudjonsson, 1984; Roebers & Schneider, 2000). An interviewer who jumps between topics will force the witness to shift between different aspects of the event being remembered, which is not conducive to good recall (Fisher & Geiselman, 1992) and can affect the witness' credibility with the jury.

These types of questions are particularly frequent in the stressful arena of the courtroom (e.g. Kebbell, Deprez & Wagstaff, 2003) and can lead to problems when witnesses attempt to give their best evidence. Zajac and Hayne (2003) found that using these questioning techniques with child witnesses resulted in children changing their responses, making them less accurate. This links to the issue of credibility discussed earlier, as children who change their testimony whilst being cross-examined are likely to be seen as less credible. Children and vulnerable adult witnesses can also be influenced by factors such as the stress of the situation, the presence of other people and the authority of the person asking the questions (see Westcott, Chapter 8).

The idea that the way in which questions are asked can subsequently affect the responses given by the witnesses has substantial support in the literature and has led to changes in how child witnesses are questioned by police in the UK (Davies & Westcott, 1999; see Holliday, Chapter 4). It is argued that this should also lead to changes in how witnesses are questioned in court (Kebbell *et al.*, 2003), but any move to constrain lawyers over the questions they ask could be seen as an attack on the adversarial principle of justice (see Wheatcroft, Chapter 7). Generally speaking, free recall is considered to produce the most accurate evidence, though this may be incomplete; as questions become more constraining then accuracy tends to decrease (Kebbell & Wagstaff, 1999).

Misinformation can be conveyed by questions, but can also arise from hearing or reading other people's accounts of the crime. Witnesses may discuss the crime with each other, friends and family. They may also hear or read accounts of the crime in the media. There is concern what effect this post-event information can have on the memory of a witness. As discussed above, our stereotypes and the types of language used can all influence someone's recall of an event. In their survey of undergraduates who had been witnesses to a serious crime, Paterson & Kemp (2006a) found that only 14% of the overall sample had witnessed an event on their own and that out of those who had co-witnessed an event, 86% discussed the event with other co-witnesses. Therefore, the majority of crimes are witnessed by more than one person and the majority of these witnesses will discuss what they saw with someone else who was there.

Paterson & Kemp (2006b) also experimentally manipulated how post-event information was provided. Participants were variously exposed to misinformation in the form of: leading questions, a newspaper report, discussion with a co-witness or indirectly finding out from a co-witness. They reported that obtaining the misleading information from co-witnesses (no matter whether direct or indirect) lead to a larger misinformation effect than leading questions or reading a newspaper report. Magner, Markham & Barnett (1996) also reported that reading a misleading account by someone else did not lead to more witness errors, but reading their own previous account did lead to better evidence. In England and Wales, the Criminal Evidence Act 2003 allows witnesses to refresh their memory from their previous statements prior to testifying, a practice supported by Magner *et al.*'s findings (see Holliday, Chapter 4 for more on the theory of misleading post-event information).

CONCLUSION

This chapter has described a variety of factors that can influence the perceived and actual credibility of a witness and how inappropriate questioning techniques can lead to witnesses making mistakes. However, witnesses are not automatically unreliable; there is much that can be done to promote good evidence both by the police and the courts. It is the forensic psychologist's role to investigate issues which lead to accurate as well as inaccurate accounts and to assist the criminal justice system in interpreting research findings for the benefit of all parties.

SUMMARY

- This chapter has examined recent research on the psychological factors influencing the reliability of witness evidence and what can be done to ensure that such evidence is as reliable as possible.
- Research on eyewitness memory has looked at sources of potential distortion at all three stages of the memory – encoding, storage and retrieval.
- As regards sources of distortion, Wells has drawn an important distinction between estimator and system variables; the investigator can only control system variables.
- As regards witness credibility, research has demonstrated the influence of such factors as witness age, mental state and confidence on accuracy.
- During the encoding phase of memory, recent research has underlined the importance of drug and alcohol intoxication and the presence of a weapon on the quality of subsequent memories.
- During the storage phase, research shows that reading accounts of the crime or speaking to other witnesses seriously distort testimony at trial.
- In the retrieval phase, the choice of questioning procedures can have a positive or negative impact on the account offered by the witness in evidence.
- Accurate and complete witness evidence remains central to the criminal justice system and it is important that the results of relevant psychological research are taken into account in developing effective investigative and judicial procedures.

ESSAY/DISCUSSION QUESTIONS

1. Eyewitness memory can be affected by all stages of memory. Describe these stages, giving examples of factors which can influence the accuracy of eyewitness memory. Which stage has the most adverse effect on memory and why?
2. Discuss the importance of the distinction between 'system' and 'estimator' variables for eyewitness testimony.

3. Consider the strengths and vulnerabilities of eyewitness testimony over the life span.

4. Describe how the level of stress of a witness' experiences influences how effectively they are able to first observe and later report eyewitness events.

REFERENCES

Adams-Price, C. (1992). Eyewitness memory and aging: Predictors of accuracy in recall and person recognition. *Psychology and Aging, 7*, 602–608.

Albert, M., Jones, K., Savage, C., *et al.* (1995). Predictors of cognitive change in older persons: MacArthur studies of successful aging. *Psychology and Aging, 10*, 578–589.

Assefi, S.L. & Garry, M. (2003). Absolute memory distortions: alcohol placebos influence the misinformation effect. *Psychological Science. 14*, 77–80.

Bartlett, F.C. (1932). *Remembering*. Cambridge: Cambridge University Press.

Bell, B.E. & Loftus, E.F. (1989). Trivial persuasion in the courtroom: The power of (a few) minor details. *Journal of Personality and Social Psychology, 56*, 669–679.

Borckardt, J.J., Sproghe, E., & Nash, M. (2003). Effects of the inclusion and refutation of peripheral details on eyewitness credibility. *Journal of Applied Social Psychology, 33*, 2187–2197.

Bornstein, B.H. & Zickafoose, D.J. (1999). "I know I know it, I know I saw it": The stability of the confidence-accuracy relationship across domains. *Journal of Experimental Psychology: Applied, 5*, 76–88.

Brewer, W.F. & Treyens, J.C. (1981). Role of schemata in memory for places. *Cognitive Psychology, 13*, 207–230.

Brewin, C.R. & Andrews, B. (1998). Recovered memories of trauma: Phenomenology and cognitive mechanisms. *Clinical Psychology Review, 4*, 949–970.

Burt, D.B., Zember, M.J., & Niederehe, G. (1995). Depression and memory impairment: A meta-analysis of the association, its pattern, and specificity. *Psychological Bulletin, 17*, 285–305.

Ceci, S.J. & Bruck, M. (1993). Suggestibility and the child witness: A historical review and synthesis. *Psychological Bulleting, 113*, 403–439.

Ceci, S.J., Loftus, E.F., Leichtman, M.D., & Bruck, M. (1994). The role of source misattributions in the creation of false beliefs among preschoolers. *International Journal of Clinical and Experimental Hypnosis, 62*, 304–320.

Christianson, S-A. (1992). Emotional stress and eyewitness memory: A critical review. *Psychological Bulletin, 112*, 284–309.

Clifasefi, S.L., Takarangi, M.K.T., & Bergman, J.S. (2006). Blind drunk: The effects of alcohol on inattentional blindness. *Applied Cognitive Psychology, 20*, 697–704.

Davies, G.M. & Dalgleish, T. (2001). Introduction. In G.M. Davies & T. Dalgleish (Eds), *Recovered memories: Seeking the middle ground* (pp. xiii–xvi). Chichester: John Wiley & Sons.

Davies, G.M., Stevenson-Robb, Y., & Flin, R. (1998). Tales out of school: Children's memory for an unexpected event. In M. Gruneberg, P. Morris, & R. Sykes (Eds), *Practical aspects of memory*. Chichester: John Wiley & Sons.

Davies, G.M. & Westcott, H.L. (1999). *Interviewing children under the Memorandum of Good Practice: A research review*. London: Home Office.

Deffenbacher, K.A., Bornstein, B.H., Penrod, S.D., & McGurty, E.K. (2004). A meta-analytic review of the effects of high stress on eyewitness memory. *Law and Human Behavior, 28,* 687–706.

Dodson, C.S. & Krueger, L.E. (2006). I misremember it well: Why older adults are unreliable eyewitnesses. *Psychonomic Bulletin and Review, 13,* 770–775.

Dunning, D. & Stern, L.B. (1992). Examining the generality of eyewitness hypermnesia: A close look at time delay and question type. *Applied Cognitive Psychology, 6,* 643–657.

Easterbrook, J.A. (1959). The effect of emotion on cue utilization and the organization. *Psychological Review, 66,* 183–201.

Ebbinghaus, H.E. (1885/1964). *Memory: A contribution to experimental psychology.* New York: Dover.

Egeth, H.E. (1993). What do we not know about eyewitness identification? *American Psychologist, 48,* 577–580.

Erickson, B., Lind, E.A., Johnson, B.C., & O'Barr, W.M. (1978). Speech style and impression formation in a court setting: Effects of 'powerful' and 'powerless' speech. *Journal of Experimental Social Psychology, 14,* 266–279.

Evans, K. (1995). *Advocacy in court: A beginner's guide.* Oxford: Blackstone Press.

Eysenck, M.W. & Keane, M.T. (2005). *Cognitive psychology: A student's handbook.* Hove: Psychology Press.

Fahsing, I.A., Ask, K., & Granhag, P.A. (2004). The man behind the mask: Accuracy and predictors of eyewitness offender descriptions. *Journal of Applied Psychology, 89,* 722–729.

Fisher, R.P. (1995). Interviewing victims and witnesses and crime. *Psychology, Public Policy and Law, 1,* 732–764.

Fisher, R.P. & Geiselman, R.E. (1992). *Memory enhancing techniques for investigative interviewing: The Cognitive Interview.* Springfield, IL: Thomas.

Gabbert, F., Memon, A., & Wright, D.B. (2006). Memory conformity: Disentangling the steps toward influence during a discussion. *Psychonomic Bulletin and Review, 13,* 480–485.

Gibbons, J. (2003). *Forensic linguistics: An introduction to language in the justice system.* Oxford: Blackwell Publishing.

Goodman, G.S. (2005). Wailing babies in her wake. *American Psychologist, 60,* 872–881.

Green, G. (2001) Vulnerability of witnesses with learning disabilities: Preparing to give evidence against a perpetrator of sexual abuse. *British Journal of Learning Disabilities, 29,* 103–109.

Gudjonsson, G.H. (1984). A new scale of interrogative suggestibility. *Personality and Individual Differences, 5,* 303–306.

Gudjonsson, G.H., Murphy, G.H., & Clare, I.C.H. (2000). Assessing the capacity of people with intellectual disabilities to be witnesses in court. *Psychological Medicine, 30,* 307–314.

Haber, L. & Haber, R.N. (1998). Criteria for judging the admissibility of eyewitness testimony of long past events. *Psychology, Public Policy and Law, 4,* 1135–1159.

Haber, R.N & Haber, L. (2000). Experiencing, remembering and reporting events. *Psychology, Public Policy and Law, 6,* 1057–1097.

Home Office (2002). *Achieving best evidence in criminal Proceedings: Guidance for vulnerable or intimidated witnesses, Including Children.* London: Home Office Communication Directorate.

Hulse, L.M. & Memon, A. (2006). Fatal impact? The effects of emotional arousal and weapon presence on police officers' memories for a simulated crime. *Legal and Criminological Psychology, 11,* 313–325.

Judicial Studies Board, (2006). *Evidence*. Retrieved from: http://www.jsboard.co.uk/criminal_law/cbb/mf_04.htm#19.

Karras, M., McCarron, E., Gray, A., & Ardasinski, S. (2006). *On the edge of justice: The Legal Needs of people with a mental illness in NSW*. Sydney: Law and Justice Foundation of NSW.

Kassin, S.M., Tubb, V.A., Hosch, H.M., & Memon, A. (2001). On the 'general acceptance' of eyewitness testimony research: A new survey of the experts. *American Psychologist, 56*, 405–416.

Kaufmann, G., Drevland, G.C.B., Wessel, E. *et al*. (2003). The importance of being earnest: Displayed emotions and witness credibility. *Applied Cognitive Psychology, 17*, 21–34.

Kebbell, M.R., Deprez, S., & Wagstaff, G.F. (2003). The direct and cross-examination of complainants and defendants in rape trials: A quantitative analysis of question type. *Psychology, Crime and Law, 9*, 49–59.

Kebbell, M.R. & Hatton, C. (1999). People with mental retardation as witnesses in court: A review. *Mental Retardation, 37*, 179–187.

Kebbell, M.R. & Johnson, S.D. (2000). The influence of lawyers' questions on witness confidence and accuracy. *Law and Human Behavior, 24*, 629–641.

Kebbell, M.R. & Milne, R. (1998). Police officers' perceptions of eyewitness factors in forensic investigations: A survey. *Journal of Social Psychology, 138*, 323–330.

Kebbell, M.R. & Wagstaff, G.F. (1999). *Face value: Evaluating the accuracy of eyewitness information*. London: Home Office.

Kensinger, E.A., Piguet, O., Krendle, A.C., & Corkin, S. (2005). Memory for contextual details: Effects of emotion and aging. *Psychology and Aging, 20*, 241–250.

Konradi, A. (1999). "I don't have to be afraid of you": Rape survivors' emotion management in court. *Symbolic Interaction, 22*, 45–77.

Koriat, A. & Goldsmith, M. (1994). Memory in naturalistic and laboratory contexts: Distinguishing the accuracy-oriented and quantity-oriented approaches to memory assessment. *Journal of Experimental Psychology: General, 123*, 297–315.

Lakoff, R. (1975). *Language and woman's place*. New York: Harper & Row.

Leichtman, M.D. & Ceci, S.J. (1995). The effects of stereotypes and suggestions on preschoolers' reports. *Developmental Psychology, 31*, 568–578.

Leippe, M.R. (1995). The case for expert testimony about eyewitness memory. *Psychology, Public Policy and Law, 1*, 909–959.

Leippe, M.R., Manion, A.P., & Romanczyk, A. (1992). Eyewitness persuasion: How and how well do fact finders judge the accuracy of adults' and children's memory reports? *Journal of Personality and Social Psychology, 63*, 181–197.

Leippe, M.R., Romanczyk, A., & Manion, A.P. (1991). Eyewitness memory for a touching experience: Accuracy differences between child and adult witnesses. *Journal of Applied Psychology, 76*, 367–379.

Loftus, E.F. & Palmer, J.C. (1974). Reconstruction of automobile destruction. *Journal of Verbal Learning and Verbal Behavior, 13*, 585–589.

Luus, C.A. & Wells, G.L. (1994). The malleability of eyewitness confidence: Co-witness and perseverance effects. *Journal of Applied Psychology, 79*, 714–723.

Lyons, A. & Kashima, Y. (2006). Maintaining stereotypes in communication: Investigating memory biases and coherence-seeking in storytelling. *Asian Journal of Social Psychology, 9*, 59–71.

Magner, E., Markham, R., & Barnett, C. (1996). Would reading an account of an event refresh your memory? *Journal of Applied Psychology, 81*, 769–776.

Magner, E. & Parkinson, P. (2001). Recovered memories: The legal dilemmas. In G.M. Davies & T. Dalgleish (Eds), *Recovered memories: Seeking the middle ground* (pp. 51–68). Chichester: John Wiley & Sons.

Maizel, S., Abramowitz, M.Z., Itzchaky, S. *et al.* (2001). The fitness of the mental patient to be a witness. *Medicine and Law, 20*, 85–92.

McDaniel, M.A., DeLosh, E.L., & Merritt, P.S. (2000). Order information and retrieval distinctiveness: Recall of common versus bizarre material. *Journal of Experimental Psychology: Learning, Memory, and Cognition, 26*, 1045–1056.

Melinder, A.A., Goodman, G.S. Eilertsen, D.E., & Magnussen, S. (2004). Beliefs about child witnesses: A survey of professionals. *Psychology, Crime and Law, 10*, 347–365.

Mitchell, K.J., Johnson, M.K., & Mather, M. (2003). Source monitoring and suggestibility to misinformation: adult age-related differences. *Applied Cognitive Psychology, 17*, 107–119.

Münsterberg, H. (1908). *On the witness stand: Essays on psychology and crime.* New York: Clark Boardman.

O'Barr, W.M. (1982). *Linguistic evidence: Language, power and strategy in the courtroom.* London: Academic Press.

Ober, B.A. & Stillman, R.C. (1988). Memory in chronic alcoholics: Effects of inconsistent versus consistent information. *Addictive Behaviors, 13*, 11–15.

Paterson, H.M. & Kemp, R.I. (2006a). Co-witness talk: A survey of eyewitness discussion. *Psychology, Crime and Law, 12*, 181–191.

Paterson, H.M. & Kemp, R.I. (2006b). Comparing methods of encountering post-event information: The power of co-witness suggestion. *Applied Cognitive Psychology, 20*, 1083–1099.

Peled, M., Iarocci, G., & Connolly, D.A. (2004). Eyewitness testimony and perceived credibility of youth with mild intellectual disability. *Journal of Intellectual Disability Research, 48*, 699–703.

Pezdek, K. & Roe, C. (1997). The suggestibility of children's memory for being touched: Planting, erasing, and changing memories. *Law and Human Behavior, 21*, 95–106.

Pickel, K.L. (1998). Unusualness and threat as possible causes of 'weapon focus'. *Memory, 6*, 277–295.

Pickel, K.L. (1999). The influence of context on the 'weapon focus' effect. *Law and Human Behavior, 22*, 299–311.

Pickel, K.L., Ross, S.J., & Truelove, R.S. (2006). Do weapons automatically capture attention? *Applied Cognitive Psychology, 20*, 871–893.

Poole, D.A. & White, L.T. (1995). Effects of question repetition on the eyewitness testimony of children and adults. *Developmental Psychology, 27*, 975–986.

Porter, S., Campbell, M.A., Birt, A.R., & Woodworth, M.T. (2003). "He said, she said": A psychological perspective on historical memory evidence in the courtroom. *Canadian Psychology, 44*, 190–206.

Pozzulo, J.D. & Lindsay, R.C.L. (1998). Identification accuracy of children versus adults: A meta-analysis. *Law and Human Behavior, 22*, 549–570.

Rae Tuckey, M. & Brewer, N. (2003). The influence of schemas, stimulus ambiguity, and interview schedule on eyewitness memory over time. *Journal of Experimental Psychology: Applied, 9*, 101–118.

Rand (1975). *The Criminal investigation process*. (Rand Corporation Tech. Rep. R-1777, 1-3). Santa Monica, CA: Rand Corporation.

Roebers, C.M. & Schneider, W. (2000). The impact of misleading questions on eyewitness memory in children and adults. *Applied Cognitive Psychology, 14*, 509–526.

Ruva, C.L. & Bryant, J.B. (2004). The impact of age, speech style, and question form on perceptions of witness credibility and trial outcome. *Journal of Applied Social Psychology, 34*, 1919–1944.

See, S.T.K., Hoffman, H.G., & Wood, T.L. (2001). Perceptions of an old female eyewitness: Is the older eyewitness believable? *Psychology and Aging, 16*, 346–350.

Shaw, J.S. (1996). Increases in eyewitness confidence resulting from post-event questioning. *Journal of Experimental Psychology: Applied, 2*, 126–146.

Shaw, J.S., McClure, K.A., & Dykstra, J.A. (2007). Eyewitness confidence from the witnessed event through trial. In M.P. Toglia, J.D. Read, D.F. Ross, & R.C.L. Lindsay (Eds), *Handbook of eyewitness psychology. Volume 1: Memory for events* (pp. 371–400). Mahwah, NJ: Erlbaum.

Shaw, J.S. & Zerr, T.K. (2003). Extra effort during memory retrieval may be associated with increases in eyewitness confidence. *Law and Human Behavior, 27*, 315–329.

Simons, D.J. & Chabris, C.F. (1999). Gorillas in our midst: Sustained inattentional blindness for dynamic events. *Perception, 28*, 1059–1074.

Sporer, S.L., Penrod, S., Read, D., & Cutler, B. (1995). Choosing, confidence and accuracy: A meta-analysis of the confident-accuracy relation in eyewitness identification studies. *Psychological Bulletin, 118*, 315–327.

Steblay, N.M. (1992). A meta-analytic review of the weapon focus effect. *Law and Human Behavior, 16*, 413–424.

Stobbs, G. & Kebbell, M.R. (2003). Jurors' perception of witnesses with intellectual disabilities and the influence of expert evidence. *Journal of Applied Research in Intellectual Disabilities, 16*, 107–114.

Tiersma, P.M. (1999). *Legal language*. Chicago: University of Chicago Press.

Tulving E. 1974. Cue dependent forgetting. *American Scientist, 62*, 74–82.

Van Knippenberg, A.D, Dijksterhuis, A.P., & Vermeulen, D. (1999). Judgement and memory of a criminal act: The effects of stereotypes and cognitive load. *European Journal of Social Psychology, 29*, 191–210.

Wells G.L. (1978). Applied eyewitness testimony research: System variables and estimator variables. *Journal of Personality and Social Psychology, 36*, 1546–1557.

Wells, G.L. & Olson, E.A. (2003). Eyewitness testimony. *Annual Review of Psychology, 54*, 277–295.

Wells, G.L., Olson, E.A., & Charman, S.D. (2003). Distorted retrospective eyewitness reports as functions of feedback and delay. *Journal of Experimental Psychology: Applied, 9*, 42–52.

Wells, G.L., Malpass, R.S., Lindsay, R.C.L., Fisher, R.P., Turtle, J.W., & Fulero, S.M. (2000). From the lab to the police station: A successful application of eyewitness research. *American Psychologist, 55*, 581–598.

Wessel, E., Drevland, G.C.B., Eilertsen, D.E., & Magnussen, S. (2006). Credibility of the emotional witness: A study of ratings by court judges. *Law and Human Behavior, 30*, 221–230.

Wheatcroft, J.M., Wagstaff, G.F., & Kebbell, M.R. (2004). The influence of courtroom questioning style on actual and perceived eyewitness confidence and accuracy. *Legal and Criminological Psychology, 9*, 83–101.

Wright, A.M. & Holliday, R.E. (2005). Police officers' perceptions of older eyewitnesses. *Legal and Criminological Psychology, 10,* 211–223.

Yarmey, A.D. & Kent, J. (1980). Eyewitness identification by elderly and young adults. *Law and Human Behavior, 4,* 359–371.

Yuille, J.C. & Cutshall, J.L. (1986). A case study of eyewitness memory of a crime. *Journal of Applied Psychology, 71,* 291–301.

Yuille, J.C. & Tollestrup, P.A. (1990). Some effects of alcohol in eyewitness memory. *Journal of Applied Psychology, 75,* 268–273.

Yuille, J.C., Trollestrup, P.A., Marxsen, D. *et al.* (1998). An exploration on the effects of marijuana on eyewitness memory. *International Journal of Law and Psychiatry, 21,* 117–128.

Zajac, R. & Hayne, H. (2003). I don't think that's what really happened: The effect of cross-examination on the accuracy of children's reports. *Journal of Experimental Psychology: Applied, 9,* 187–193.

ANNOTATED READING LIST

Ainsworth, P.B. (1998). *Psychology, law and eyewitness testimony.* Chichester: John Wiley & Sons. *Covers a number of issues described in this chapter such as theories of memory, child witnesses, as well as the use – and misuse – of hypnosis.*

Davies, G.M. & Dalgleish, T. (Eds) (2001). *Recovered memories: Seeking the middle ground.* Chichester: John Wiley & Sons. *A useful discussion of the recovered memories topic which considers all sides of the debate.*

Kebbell, M.R. & Wagstaff, G.F. (1999). *Face value? Factors that influence eyewitness accuracy.* London: Home Office. *Originally written for police officers, this booklet provides a readable and introductory account of the issues that could impact on eyewitnesses and their evidence.*

Loftus, E.F. (1996). *Eyewitness testimony* (2nd edn). Harvard: Harvard University Press. *Although published a number of years ago, this book is still a very accessible introduction to many of the themes discussed in this chapter.*

Milne, R. & Bull, R. (1999). *Investigative interviewing: Psychology and practice.* Chichester: John Wiley & Sons. *This book focuses psychological research on how to interview suspects, victims and witnesses to achieve the best quality evidence.*

Westcott, H.L., Davies, G.M., & Bull, R. (Eds) (2002). *Children's testimony: A handbook of psychological research and forensic practice.* Chichester: John Wiley & Sons. *This book concentrates on children's testimony and covers a range of topics from the development of memory to how court professionals deal with child witnesses.*

10

ROLE OF THE EXPERT WITNESS

Brian R. Clifford
University of Aberdeen, Scotland

The use of expert witnesses by the court is not a modern phenomenon. Such witnesses have been employed since at least the fourteenth century (Wigmore, 1978), and experts appearing for the rival parties to a dispute since about the eighteenth century (Miller & Allen, 1998). While the legal purpose of engaging such witnesses has always been the same – to provide expertise that the triers of fact do not possess – the ground rules for their admissibility has undergone constant revision.

In this chapter we will focus on three controversial forensic psychology areas: mistaken identification, child witnesses and sexual abuse cases, and recovered memories, and explore the possible roles that expert witnesses can play in their resolution. We will see how the role of the expert witness has expanded, and note that there are differences in the acceptance of expert testimony in different countries and in different legal systems. At base, however, it will be argued that it is the quality of the science that experts rely upon in giving testimony that is at issue. It will be concluded that expert witnesses have the potential to aid the trial process but that realizing this potential is not a simple or settled matter within the psychological community.

THE EVOLUTION OF THE EXPERT WITNESS

Historically it can be seen that courts initially preferred experts who testified about non-human factors rather than human factors; then later, experts who testified about human physical states rather than mental states. When experts concerning mental states were accepted, the courts preferred experts who testified about abnormal mental states rather than normal mental states. Within this, courts preferred psychiatric experts over clinical psychology experts because the former were grounded in medical science. Only lately have the courts come to accept experts whose expertise lies in experimental investigations of normal states of mind, who study memory, perception and language. Until fairly recently such normal human processes were held to be within the knowledge and experience of the jury, the triers of fact, thus requiring no expert opinion to clarify or inform their rational decision-making roles (see Clifford, 2003; Mackay, Colman & Thornton, 1999).

This evolution of the type of expert acceptable to the court can be traced in both the **adversarial** and **inquisitorial** court systems, although, historically, the inquisitorial system has employed experts for longer than the adversarial system (Spencer, 1998).

While the US, UK, Australia, New Zealand and Canada all employ the adversarial method of trial, the use of normal-mental-state experts varies quite markedly among these countries (see Kapardis 1997 for an excellent account of the admissibility of expert testimony in each of these jurisdictions). As an example, expert testimony has been much more prevalent in the US than the UK. In fact, since *Jenkins v. U.S.* (1962) the general rule has been that *every* psychologist is a potential witness and must be prepared to interact with the legal system unless they have ethical grounds not to do so.

Yet the use of experts in the US is much more formalized and codified than in the UK. In the United States, the admissibility of experts is governed by landmark cases such as Frye[1] (1923) and later Daubert[2] (1993), which specify the conditions that must be met to allow an expert to testify. However, the judge in both the UK and the US jurisdictions is the ultimate 'gatekeeper' of whether or not expert testimony is allowable.

Specifically, four questions should be asked by the judge: (a) can the theory used to form an opinion be tested? (b) have the findings been subjected to peer review? (c) is there a measurable error rate for the findings? and (d) are the theories or methods generally accepted within the expert's community?

If deemed admissible, whatever form the experts' opinion takes, on whatever subject matter, while the aim of that testimony is to aid the triers of fact in coming to a reasoned and reasonable decision, the expert must not trespass upon the 'ultimate issue'. This stipulation prohibits any witness from giving his or her opinion about a

---

[1] Frye: Before Daubert (1993) most courts in the US decided to admit or exclude expert testimony on the bases of the Frye test. This test stipulated that scientific testimony was admissible only if it was based on a theory or research findings that had "general acceptance in the particular field in which it belongs" (*Frye v. United States*, 1923, p. 1014).

[2] The *Daubert* ruling (*Daubert v. Merrell Dow Pharmaceuticals, Inc.* (1993)) superseded Frye, by stressing not only general acceptance but the broader question of whether the testimony offered would be based on information that was not only relevant but also reliable and valid, and obtained through sound scientific methods.

matter if it is the very question on which the court is called to determine i.e. the fact at issue – for example, *was* the child sexually abused? Is *this* witness reliable? This fine line between addressing the ultimate issue but not giving an opinion on it lies at the heart of much of the controversy concerning the role of the expert witness.

WHO IS AN EXPERT?

To give best evidence the expert must be qualified by education, training, experience, skill and knowledge. Their area of expertise must fit with the issue at trial. The database to which they make recourse must be sufficiently valid and reliable to allow definitive statements, opinions, conclusions, and assertions under both direct and cross-examination, or in the face of counter-experts. Lastly, the expert must be prepared to get involved in the adversarial process in which their scientific credentials, objectivity and expertise can be attacked by counsel less concerned with either truth or justice than with asserting his or her client's position and using any and all means – fair or foul – to have it prevail. The courtroom is the arena of choice of the barrister, not the expert. The barrister knows the rules of the game, what the game is, and how best to play that game, the expert does not.

Haward (1981) lists the main roles an expert may perform as clinician, experimentalist, **actuary** or adviser. Within these classifications an expert witness can give testimony in open court, or they may provide expert reports or opinions to be presented in court, or after trial, but before sentencing, but not actually appear as a witness. Experts may also act as adviser to counsel faced with the other side's expert. Clearly then, there are gradations of 'being an expert'. In addition, the expert may be appointed by the court, especially in the inquisitorial system, or instructed by either the prosecution or the defence, in the adversarial system. This chapter will deal mainly with the role of the expert in the adversarial system, who appears as a witness at trial, either for the defence or the prosecution in criminal cases, or for the **plaintiff** or the defence in civil cases.

Depending upon the type of case: criminal or civil; the legal system: adversarial or inquisitorial; and their area of expertise: clinical or experimental, an expert may be called upon to talk (a) directly to a fact or consideration at issue, such as competence to stand trial, hyper suggestibility, 'of sound mind', or (b) perform an educative function such as discussing factors that could cause a witness to be unreliable, a victim to be vulnerable to suggestion, or explain why an abused child could be asymptomatic, i.e. show no signs of abuse, delayed disclosing the abuse, or recanted on one or more occasions. If the experts are asked to perform the first type of role they almost certainly will have examined the defendant and, as such, the expertise will be that of a psychologist, clinician or therapist. If asked to perform the latter role, the expert will not have interacted with the defendant, victim or witness, and the expertise will be that of a researcher or experimental psychologist. As we will see the epistemological, or knowledge base, of these two types of testimony are said to be in conflict and opposed.

Irrespective of the expert's area of expertise, clinical or scientific, a critical consideration is the reliability and validity of the knowledge base that the expert will rely upon to underpin his or her testimony. As we go through the role of the expert in certain controversial areas we will note the central importance of knowledge base reliability and

---

CASE STUDY

H.M.A. v. Campbell, Steele & Gray

Appeal Court, High Court of Justiciary, Edinburgh 2004

Case: Murder

Expert Witness: Professor Brian R. Clifford

Expert Role: Experimentalist

In 2001 I received a call from the Scottish Criminal Cases Review Commission enquiring if I would be interested in acting as an expert witness in the third appeal of Campbell, Steele and Gray who were convicted on murder charges in the so-called ice-cream wars in Glasgow in 1984. The appeal aspect I was approached about concerned independent, verbatim-identical, recall by several policemen of a number of supra-span (i.e. exceeding short-term memory capacity) utterances allegedly made by the appellants, under various time delays and verbal interference conditions. At base this was a psycholinguistic issue on which, by publication, training, experience and education (PhD in Psycholinguistics; MSc in Artificial Intelligence and Natural Language Processing), I was qualified to offer an expert opinion.

I decided that while extant psycholinguistic theory and data was applicable to the issue of the possibility of verbatim recall under specific conditions of the case, novel, case-relevant data would be more compelling. I thus ran four experiments in which I manipulated mental set, various delay intervals and verbal interference conditions to ascertain if the degree of memory exhibited by the various police personnel in the case under appeal was probable. In the event not one of my 224 participants were able to recall what all four police officers averred they did. Given that these new data replicated known limits of short-term verbatim memory, and meshed with accepted theory in psycholinguistics, the Appeal judges concluded "In our view, the new evidence is of such significance that the verdicts of the jury, having been returned in ignorance of it, must be regarded as miscarriages of justice."

---

relevance and how issues of **ecological validity**, generalizability, internal and external validity and replicability keep appearing.

To ensure 'fitness for purpose' any expert witness must be an active researcher, who reads the relevant literature carefully, critically and comprehensively, and has a reasoned grasp of the issues that could be raised by the parties to the dispute to which they have been summoned. Experts will have decided beforehand those fields that appear to be related to, but, de facto, are distinct from, their areas of expertise, and into which they will not stray or be induced to offer speculation.

CONTROVERSY: MISTAKEN IDENTIFICATION

Known cases of mistaken identification (Scheck, Neufeld & Dwyer, 2000) imply the need for expert witnesses. Many exonerations, pardons or setting aside of previous convictions clearly indicate that something is amiss with this class of evidence, especially if it is the only evidence being brought before a jury. Many of the issues in identification evidence are covered by Valentine in Chapter 3 of this book.

The law appreciates the potential problems of identification evidence. In the UK, the Devlin Report (1976) concluded that if a case was brought where the sole evidence was identification evidence then such a case "should not proceed". Certain notable exceptions, however, were instanced, such as rape, where the victim may be the only witness present, with no other forensic evidence available. Following the Devlin report a landmark ruling in the Appeal Court (*R v. Turnbull*, 1976) made a 'Turnbull warning' mandatory in all cases involving disputed identification evidence (see Chapter 3 by Valentine).

The importance of eyewitness evidence and identification in criminal trials cannot be over-emphasized. Such evidence is among the most common and influential forms of testimony (Leippe, 1995; Loftus, 1983; Woocher, 1977) and frequently is the primary evidence against the defendant in up to 80 000 trials in the US per year (e.g. Goldstein, Chance & Schneller, 1989). It is compelling evidence to the jury and the more certain, credible and reliable the identification is portrayed to be, the stronger the impact it has (Leippe, 1980, 1995).

Eyewitnessing is not easy. Most eyewitness situations are likely to fall under the class of a complex event, because it is likely to be dynamic (rather than static), arousing (rather than innocuous) and perceptually dense (rather than sparse). A victim/witness is likely to be interrogated on numerous occasions by other victims/witnesses, friends, acquaintances, and the police, thus storage is likely to be repeatedly activated and then re-stored. Recent evidence indicates that co-witnesses can manipulate the memories of fellow witnesses. (e.g. Gabbert, Memon & Allen, 2003; Meade & Roediger, 2002). At the retrieval stage, when explicit identification procedures are employed, we know that there are procedural variables such as the nature of the line-up and the communication of feedback which can precipitate faulty identification and enhance confidence (e.g. Wells & Olson, 2003).

The experimental psychologist would contend that a great many factors (see Clifford, 1979) and estimator and system variables (see Valentine, this volume; Wells, 1978) are unknown to the lay person (jurors) and should be brought to their attention to ensure that justice is done.

There is another line of reasoning, however, that would drive an alternative conclusion. This line would concede that (a) we can agree that memory comprises encoding, storage and retrieval components (see Holliday, Chapter 4), and (b) various system and estimator variables can impinge on one or more of these stages to reduce the veracity of memory (see Blackwell-Young, Chapter 9). However, just what phases, and to what degree we can never know, and certainly not in the case of a particular witness/victim in a particular case that is being tried. By offering expert testimony against this background of uncertainty, such testimony may unjustifiably increase scepticism on the part of jurors where it is not merited.

In addition, to what extent do controlled laboratory studies generalize to real-life crimes? How often should a finding replicate before it is regarded as a 'fact'? What if a finding replicates but in one case the variable's **effect size** (magnitude) is large (0.8 or above), in another medium (0.6) and in a third only small (0.2)? And how do we weigh all the known (and possibly larger unknown) studies that have not replicated the effect?

Over and above factors that may or may not have been operational, and effects that may or may not be present in a particular case, there is another consideration. Experimental psychology is largely predicated upon group means, with overlap between the **distributions**. What this means in practice is that while an experimental group as a whole may perform 'better' than a control group, any one member of the experimental group may, in fact, perform more poorly than any one member of the 'poorer' group. More concretely, if we find that 70% of an experimental group give an incorrect identification under condition x, how do we know that the particular witness in the particular case currently being tried, that involves condition x, falls into the 70% category and not the 30% category? We just cannot possibly know. How, then, can we possibly seek to educate the jury when what we may be doing is rendering them more sceptical than they need to be in the particular case at hand. If this line of reasoning is adopted then expert testimony may be more prejudicial than **probative** (see Ebbesen & Konecni, 1996).

And yet, as concerned citizens, we must be concerned by the findings of the Innocence Project (http://www.innocenceproject.org) that began in the US in 1992, but now has offshoots worldwide. This project, which uses post-conviction DNA testing to prove innocence, had in December 2006, served to exonerate 188 wrongfully convicted persons. In the majority of these cases eyewitness evidence is asserted to be a leading cause of the convictions.

But do the courts really need expert witnesses to educate the jury in such matters? In the US case of *Neil v. Biggers* (1972) the argument was made that in cases where identification evidence played a part, judges should always instruct the jury to consider:

1. The opportunity to view the perpetrator;
2. The length of time between the crime taking place and later identification;
3. The level of certainty shown by the witness;
4. The degree of attention given by the witness;
5. The accuracy of prior descriptions offered of the perpetrator.

Following the case of *State v. Warren* (1981) two further factors were added:

6. The emotional state of the witness at the crime scene;
7. Whether the witness has seen the perpetrator before.

Now while these indicators of good identification have a common sense aura about them, (and in fact are very similar to the 'Turnbull warnings' in the UK – see Valentine, Chapter 3), in truth every one of the issues has been shown empirically to be problematic (e.g. Wells & Murray, 1983).

Where life (as in many states in America) and liberty are at stake, justice demands something over and above intuitive insights that may lack empirical foundations. If judicial instruction is not the answer, expert testimony may be the solution. However, because of the constantly shifting, refining and nuancing database that would underpin such testimony, testifying experts must be very circumspect as to what they will be prepared to testify about, and to what extent they will be prepared to present conditional, probabilistic, contextualized statements, rather than definitive, singular and certain opinions. The expert's true role is education, not advocacy or partisanship. (e.g. Miller & Allen, 1998). Relevant testimony will explain the general principles relevant to the case, data relied upon in coming to a conclusion, and why these data were relied upon, and finally the lines of reasoning used to get from these data to the conclusion being offered.

Both the US (see Yarmey, 2003) and the UK (PACE, 1984, 2005) have implemented guidelines for identification evidence and any deviations from these guidelines or protocols can and perhaps should be raised in court and would be a legitimate area of expert testimony.

As indicated above, one of the major concerns with using expert testimony in cases involving identification evidence is the possibility that such testimony will increase the general level of scepticism concerning all such evidence, where in fact such scepticism may not be justified in a particular case. Two fairly recent studies have looked at this scepticism issue and, additionally, the possibility that such testimony can increase juror sensitivity to factors causing bias and thus unreliability in identification.

In a study by Devenport *et al.* (2002), 800 mock jurors viewed a video-taped trial that included information about a line-up identification procedure. **Suggestiveness** of the identification procedure varied in terms of foil selection bias, instruction bias (being told that the perpetrator may or may not be present, or not being told this) and presentation bias (**simultaneous line-ups** being categorized as biased, **sequential line-ups** as unbiased). The researchers were interested in the degree to which expert testimony would sensitize mock jurors to these three separate factors affecting line-up suggestiveness. They found that initially jurors were sensitive to foil selection bias, but not to instruction bias or presentation bias. The presentation of expert testimony served to enhanced sensitivity to instruction bias. Importantly, there was little evidence for expert testimony creating an overall sceptical attitude to identification evidence as indicated by **culpability** and verdict measures. This study is important because it indicates that expert testimony can enhance jurors' sensitivity to factors influencing identification conditions without overly increasing juror scepticism of the witness' identification.

The second study was conducted by Leippe *et al.* (2004). In two experiments 453 mock jurors read a murder trial transcript that either included or did not include general expert testimony about eyewitness memory. The expert testimony was given either before the evidence in the case, or after the evidence was presented. The judge's final instructions to the jury either did or did not remind the jury of the expert's testimony. Leippe *et al.* found that expert testimony decreased perception of guilt and eyewitness believability *if* it followed the evidence *and* was mentioned by the judge but not if it preceded the evidence and was not mentioned by the judge. This was the case whether the prosecution case was moderately weak or moderately strong. The fact that the timing of the expert testimony was critical, and that it needed to be supported by the judge's reminding, serves to rule out the fear that presentation of expert eyewitness testimony would have the effect of increasing scepticism about eyewitness evidence per se, whether justified or not in the specific case at hand.

These two studies taken together indicate that the introduction of expert testimony does not 'colour' the jurors' verdicts in a gross way by increasing global scepticism of all eyewitness testimony and identification. Rather they indicate that both general (Leippe, *et al.*, 2004) and more specific expert testimony (Devenport *et al.*, 2002) can be beneficial in enhancing sensitivity to critical aspects of bias depending on its timing and support within the overall trial.

CONTROVERSY: RELIABILITY OF CHILDREN'S TESTIMONY

Children's testimony has always been a problem for the law (Spencer & Flin, 1990). Originally, in England and Wales, **corroboration** and demonstrable understanding of truthfulness were required. With the increase in crime levels and the veritable explosion of child sexual abuse cases worldwide, the law's perception, in some countries, of the child witness/victim has changed. Increasingly children have begun to have their voices both heard and believed.

Just as this right was being recognized, however, research was appearing that children could be shown to be especially suggestible and that they could be made to assert things that were deliberately instilled in, or subtly suggested to, them via strategic questioning protocols and tactical questions of a **leading** and **closed** nature (e.g. Ceci & Bruck, 1993, 1995; see Holliday, Chapter 4).

Experts in the child witnessing domain, just as in the other domains discussed in this chapter, are, therefore, confronted with an apparently less than cohesive and consensual database of research findings. On the one hand, children, even very young children, can exhibit reliable and accurate memories for traumatic and non-traumatic events (e.g. Goodman & Paz-Alonso, 2006). On the other hand, children have been shown to answer nonsensical questions such as "which is heavier, white or red?" (e.g. Waterman, Blades & Spencer, 2002). However, adults as well as children can show **compliance**.

Adults answer in the affirmative when asked if, for example, they remember seeing on television the El-Al Boeing 747 crashing into the apartment building in Amsterdam, when no such film footage exists (Crombarg, Wagenaar & Van Koppen, 1996). This so-called 'crashing memory' phenomenon has been demonstrated for non-existing footage of Diana's car crash (Ost *et al.*, 2002), and the sinking of the Estonian ferry, in which 900 lives were lost (Granhag, Stromwall & Billings, 2003). Recent research has shown that the number of adults falsely recalling seeing non-existing footage drops as the nature of the question changes from being ambiguous, through being specific high-suggestive, to being specific low-suggestive to being, eventually, neutral (Smeets *et al.*, 2006).

Thus, it is not surprising to find in the child literature that they can come to believe, for example, that they were lost in a mall when no such event occurred (e.g. Loftus & Pickrell 1995). As we will see, the resolution of this conflicting database of child studies can be achieved by looking at the nature of the questioning rather than focusing on the nature of the respondent. Children are no different in many respects from adults: both can be shown to be suggestible, **malleable**, susceptible to misleading information, and persuaded by verbal feedback.

Nonetheless, adults have many concerns about children's memories, and especially memories of a traumatic nature. They are unaware of the various stages of memory development and how this can impact on reliability and credibility of free recall, cued recall, recognition and facial identification. Jurors need to be made aware that the supposed generally poorer memories of children, relative to adults, are based upon experimentation that employed abstract, non-ego-involving stimuli. When material is concrete, age-appropriate and relevant, then children's memories can be shown to be very good indeed (e.g. Fivush, 2002).

Conversely jurors need also to be made aware that children are susceptible to suggestion, whether subtle or overt, that source monitoring (correctly identifying the source of their memories) is weaker in children than in adults (e.g. Lindsay, 2002) and that these two factors can come together to produce bizarre testimony (e.g. Ceci & Bruck, 1995).

A key insight then in forensic testimony involving children is that it is not so much the child's memory that is at issue but rather the questioning strategy and tactics that have led up to the testimony. Criminal justice systems in some countries have recognized the importance of appropriate questioning of child witnesses/victims to the extent that guidelines have been produced. While only guidelines, serious deviation from them can result in cases not proceeding, being thrown out, or appealed. Of special note here in the UK are the *Memorandum of Good Practice* (MOG, 1992) and its revised edition *Achieving Best Evidence* (ABE, 2002). These guidelines represent a summary of best practice in interviewing, designed to ensure reliable testimony from children or vulnerable adults (see Holliday, Chapter 4). Where these guidelines have been ignored or flouted, this becomes a legitimate area of expert witness comment.

Child Sexual Abuse (CSA) Cases

We have seen how, in 'everyday' witnessing situations, the reliability of some children's testimony can be considered problematic. It is much more problematic when the child alleges sexual abuse. In child sexual abuse (CSA) cases there are frequently different types of expert, different sets of data and different starting points reflecting different assumptions and theories of experts.

Berliner (1998) argues that expert testimony is necessary in such cases because fact finders have little knowledge of the nature of CSA (e.g. Morison & Greene, 1992), and are sceptical about abuse. In other words, the prevailing norm is negativity concerning the credibility of children's testimony in such matters (e.g. Goodman, 1984; Raitt & Zeedyk, 2003).

To offset this negative bias American researchers have suggested that one of two types of expert testimony can be given. One is what Walker & Monahan (1987) call social framework testimony. This type of testimony provides a framework or background context based on conclusions from psychological research designed to inform jurors of something they did not already know, or disabuse them of common but erroneous misconceptions concerning the nature of sexual abuse, reaction of victims, and the ways trauma can affect memory. A second type of testimony, often referred to as substantive testimony, is where the expert specifically opines that the child in the case has been abused or exhibits the characteristics commonly found in sexually abused children.

All countries and jurisdictions are concerned with the trespass of experts on the 'ultimate issue' although differences are seen in terms of what is permissible. Legally, in the US, social framework testimony is frequently allowed: substantive testimony is frequently disallowed, because it is a direct comment upon credibility (e.g. *United States v. Whitted*, 1993).

Scientifically, substantive testimony causes concerns for experimental psychologists because many researchers assert that the data that underpin such testimony are unscientific, psychometrically weak (i.e. lacking either validity or reliability, or both), and are based on subjective opinion rather than objective fact. As Berliner (1998) notes, there is no empirical evidence that clinicians reliably arrive at the same conclusions from identical data sets. Indeed McAnulty (1993) goes further and asserts that the scientific bases for expert opinion of a substantive nature about sexual abuse may not be sufficiently valid and reliable for admission in court.

Scientific support for the notion of a unique or universal response **symptomology** in CSA is lacking (Berliner, 1998). As an example Kendall-Tackett, Williams & Finkelhor (1993) found no one symptom was present in more than half of sexually abused children. In addition, symptoms frequently found in abused children (anxiety, depression, low self-esteem) are also found in non-abused children, and thus can have **aetiologies** other than CSA. This would also be predicted from base-rate considerations – i.e. the naturally occurring frequency of anxiety, depression, etc. in the general population (Melton, 1994).

Because CSA is multifaceted, varying in nature, intensity, duration and frequency it is not surprising that several models and associated checklists have been developed. One is the child sexual abuse accommodation syndrome (CSAAS: Summit, 1983) but deemed not to be a medically accepted scientific concept in *Bussey J. v. Commonwealth* (1985). Others are the child sexual abuse syndrome (CSAS: Sgroi, 1982); post-traumatic stress disorder (PTSD: Walker, 1990), and the traumagenic model (Finkelhor & Browne, 1985). However, as Fisher (1995; Fisher & Whiting, 1998) points out these are all symptom-based models derived from therapeutic contexts that have not been tested scientifically to form the basis of diagnosing whether CSA has occurred. As Fisher & Whiting (1998) state, few if any empirical studies testing the validity of checklists based on these theoretical models have been reported. Summit (1992) specifically asserts that the CSAAS is a clinical opinion not a scientific instrument, and the cause and effect relationship between factors themselves and actual abuse is generally obscure.

In the light of the ultimate issue question, the most the expert can say, following the checking of the child's behaviour against the various syndrome checklists, is that the evidence is 'consistent with' or 'indicative of' CSA having taken place. This may satisfy the law, but it does not satisfy the scientist because such phrases attempt to do by connotation (implication) what cannot be done by denotation (demonstration) (Lawlor, 1998). While such phraseology apparently avoids commenting upon the ultimate issue, it is designed to leave the impression that CSA has been detected, which is unwarranted by the facts. 'Consistent with' and 'indicative of' ignore the issue of *equifinality* (the fact that the same set of symptoms can have different causes) and *equicausality* (the fact that the same cause – abuse – can have a multitude of different effects) (Baker, 1969).

In the US, symptom-based, substantive, testimony appears more allowable when it is used to rebut the defence case (Myers, 1993). Thus, where a defence is mounted that

(1) the allegedly abused child does not exhibit behaviours and emotions commonly thought to be associated with an abused child, therefore (2) the child was not abused, thus (3) the defendant is innocent, substantive testimony can be offered to support the allegation of abuse. Known symptomology of CSA can be presented to explain that asymptomatic behaviour, non-spontaneity, delay in reporting, gradual disclosure, refusal to report, and even recantation are all recognized symptoms of CSA. From the scientists' point of view, however, such evidence used in this way is still unacceptable – bad science is always bad science, irrespective of its intent.

While symptom checklists are the most prevalent form of evidence given by experts in substantive testimony, other techniques have also been deployed but are equally questionable scientifically. For example **anatomically-correct dolls** (ACD) suffer from what Fisher and Whiting (1998) call the problem of *definitive differentiation*: both abused and non-abused children demonstrate sexuality in doll play (e.g. Dawson, Vaughan & Wagner, 1991). Additionally, because of the lack of psychometric evidence for the reliability and validity of ACDs, their use cannot be regarded as a valid assessment of the presence of sexual abuse.

A completely different technique, which focuses on the verbal content of a child's utterances, is **Statement Validity Analysis** (SVA), presented as a reliable and valid criterion-based method for assessing the credibility of children's allegations of sexual abuse (e.g. Raskin & Esplin, 1991).

The SVA generally, and the criterion-based content analysis (CBCA) part specifically, has been subjected to empirical test (e.g. Esplin, Boychuk & Raskin, 1988; Steller, 1989; Yuille, 1988). However, inter-rater reliability doubts (e.g. Anson, Golding & Gully, 1993), and the finding of plausible criteria in objectively implausible accounts (Lamb *et al.*, 1997), raise questions over the psychometric reliability and practical use of this technique for corroborating sexual abuse allegations. Indeed, Vrij (2005) after conducting a qualitative review of the first 37 studies in CBCA concluded "It is argued that SVA evaluations are not accurate enough to be admitted as expert scientific evidence in criminal courts" (p. 3). Following a later study, in which a quantitative approach was taken, the same researcher concluded "we failed to uncover the underlying theoretical principles of CBCA scores . . . a lack of theoretical foundation . . . makes it unclear what the possibilities and restrictions of the instrument are" (Vrij & Mann, 2006, p. 347).

It would appear then that most substantive testimony lacks empirically based psychometric foundations. Fisher & Whiting (1998) stress that the expert witness must avoid the employment of clinically relevant, but diagnostically unsubstantiated techniques for assessing symptoms of CSA. An expert must not confuse clinical judgment with scientific fact, thereby potentially slipping from educator to advocate.

How Effective Is Expert Testimony in CSA Cases?

Crowley, O'Callaghan & Ball (1994) looked at the impact of social framework-type testimony. They presented a video-taped simulation of a trial in which an expert testified about delayed disclosure, memory, suggestibility and **reality monitoring**. The mock jurors who heard the expert testifying rated the child witness as higher on memory ability, reality monitoring, and resistance to suggestion. However there was no relation to verdict.

Kovera & Borgida (1998) reported a study in which they presented participants with a three and a half hour video of a simulated child sexual abuse trial, in which the alleged abused child was played by either an 8-year-old or a 14-year-old actress. They compared the effects of (1) social framework testimony, (2) substantive testimony that was 'concretized' with a hypothetical example closely related to the trial, and (3) a no-expert testimony condition. The substance of the expert testimony concerned the typical set of victim reactions to sexual abuse, and, in young children, their frequent lack of knowledge to communicate effectively about their abusive experiences due to their age. They found that the no-expert testimony condition resulted in a higher conviction rate of the defendant when the witness was 14, than when the child was eight. However, the child witness' age did not influence conviction rate when jurors were presented with either type of expert testimony. The researchers concluded that both expert-testimony conditions – general and specific – served to correct jurors' perception of counter-intuitive behavioural reactions to abuse, exhibited by the younger child, as indications of fabrications, compared to the no-expert testimony condition.

From these two studies it can be concluded that expert testimony of both the social framework and substantive kind can effect an educative function, by correcting misperceptions that jurors may have about such things as anxiety, hesitation, and clarity of description in a sexually abused child.

CASE STUDY

State v. Michaels 1988, 1993

Case: Sexual abuse of children, Wee Care Day Nursery, New Jersey

Expert: Eileen Treacy

Expert role: Substantive testimony

In 1988 Treacy gave testimony consisting of both background information (social context testimony) and child-specific statements (substantive testimony). Based on analysis of pre-trial interviews and behaviour described by relatives of the children, together with the children's court testimony, Treacy testified that the children's testimony and conduct were consistent with child sexual abuse. She went on to define 'consistent with' as "having a high degree of correlation, over 0.6 in numerical terms, and a probability" (*State v. Michaels*, 1993, p. 501). The jury convicted Michaels of abusing 19 children and sentenced her to 47 years.

In 1993 an appeal court overturned the decision on the grounds that Treacy's "testimony constituted nothing less that substantive evidence of defendant's guilt" (p. 501). This was based on *State v. J.Q.* (1993) where it was decided that while an expert witness could describe symptoms found in victims of CSA to aid jurors in evaluating specific defences (*State v. J.Q.*, 1993, p. 1197) they could not offer the opinion that abuse had, in fact, occurred.

A question you may like to ask yourself is where did Treacy get the figure of 0.6 from?

Controversy: Recovered Memories

As Schacter, Norman & Koutstaal (1977) point out, the recovered memory debate is the most passionately contested battle that has ever been waged about the nature of human memory, and has involved a clash of **paradigms** as between clinicians and experimentalists. However, the debate is far from being parochial: it has touched the lives of thousands of families across the globe and the emotional stakes for all involved are huge.

Consequently, the false/recovered memory debate has been frequently acrimonious and emotional, generating more heat than light (e.g. Lindsay & Read, 1994, 1997). And yet at base the fundamental issue or issues *seem* simple: the veridicality – truthfulness – of human memory (Conway, 1997); memory, trauma and suggestibility (Yapko, 1997); and forgetting, distortion and accuracy (Schacter *et al.* 1997). In reality each of the named issues is the tip of a very large iceberg adrift in an ocean of ignorance. The recovered/false memory debate is beautifully captured by Donald Rumsfeld's (2002) homily " . . . there are known knowns . . . there are known unknowns . . . but there are also unknown unknowns".

We know that child sexual abuse is a significant problem within society – 5% to 33% in girls, 3% to 30% in boys (Finkelhor, 1987; Ghate & Spencer, 1995; Hall & Lloyd, 1989; Herman, 1981), and estimates of suppressed memories range between 20% and 40% in a sample of adults who report CSA (Elliot, 1997; Epstein & Bottoms, 2002; Melchert, 1996; Melchert & Parker, 1997). We know that traumatic memories are formed in some ways that are different from normal memories (Cahill *et al.*, 1994; Christianson, 1992; Van der Kolk & Saporta, 1993). We know that **disassociation** can be used defensively, giving rise to **amnesia** that can dissipate at a later date (Briere & Conte, 1993; Hornstein, 1992). But we also know that memory can be both highly reliable and unreliable, and can be influenced by suggestion, discussion, and by misinformation (Ceci & Bruck, 1993, 1995; Rich, 1990; see Holliday, Chapter 4).

When we move from the known knowns to the troublesome known unknowns we tend to move from objective fact to subjective inference. As an example we know that traumatic experiences can be encoded somewhat differently from non-traumatic experiences (e.g. Christianson, 1992; Horowitz & Reidbord, 1992), being more vivid and integrated than more routine memories. However, while there has been an attempt to subsume CSA under the PTSD umbrella, post-traumatic stress disorder is characterized by flash-backs, while recovered memories of sexual abuse are characterized by no recollection until recovery. Why do these two types of traumatic memory operate so differently? We must admit we don't know.

Given there is no valid way to distinguish between a genuine memory and a confabulated or illusory memory, without external corroboration, and that the existence of a true memory and its accuracy are conceptually distinct, we must again conclude that we don't know how to verify a memory account in the absence of external verification.

Specifically within the recovered memory arena, we must accept that the combination of a vulnerable client and a theoretically-driven therapist is a potentially lethal concoction, pregnant with possibilities for 'recovered' or 'false' memory. But can people be led to believe that they have been abused when in reality they have not? Case examples of virtually impossible forms of abuse, such as alien abduction, that are vividly remembered make it clear that the answer is 'yes' (e.g. Baker, 1992; French, 2003; Gardner, 1992).

But what of the supposedly documented case studies of recovered memory? Surely they testify to the reality of the occurrence? Well not quite in the view of many sceptics. The scientific validity of such cases is hotly disputed. Demonstration of true recovered memories requires evidence of the abuse having taken place, intermittent forgetting of the event, and eventual recovery of the event in the absence of any other way of gaining knowledge of the abuse (Schooler, Ambada & Bendiksen, 1997; Wright, Ost & French, 2006). As Wright *et al.* (2006) indicate, a less stringent set of criteria underlie the supposed 101 corroborated cases compiled by Cheit (2005) (http://www.brown.edu/Departments/Taubman_Center/Recovmem/arch_crit.html). To ensure inclusion in the Cheit archive the case must have 'strong corroboration', such as confession, guilty pleas or self-incriminating statements; testimony from other witnesses; or 'significant' circumstantial evidence. A guilty verdict can also ensure inclusion, but, of course, other factors could play a role in achieving such a verdict.

To illustrate the debate we will highlight a case (Corwin & Olafson, 1997) that appears in both Cheit's (2005) and Schooler *et al.*'s (1997) archives. This case is argued to be one of the clearest and most unambiguous examples of recovered memory – the so-called Jane Doe case. Corwin first interviewed Jane when she was six years old. At the time the child's biological and divorced parents were going through an acrimonious custody dispute and Jane was living with her mother. Jane's father and stepmother claimed that Jane's mother was sexually and physically abusing the child, and Corwin was brought in to evaluate these allegations. In the last of three video-taped interviews Jane told Corwin that her mother "rubbed her finger up my vagina" in the bath and that her mother had burned her feet. Corwin concluded that sexual and physical abuse had occurred and custody was granted to the father. Eleven years later Corwin again interviewed Jane, who by now seemed to have repressed the memory of sexual abuse. Upon showing her the earlier videotapes, Jane came to remember how her mother had sexually abused her.

However, even with this case, that passed both Schooler's more stringent criteria (forgetting and then remembering the abusive episode), and despite being endorsed by several key memory researchers, Loftus & Guyer (2002a, b) point out that there are good grounds for raising doubts about its validity. Despite this case being presented as concrete proof of the validity of repressed memory (and later recovery) in *State of Rhode Island v. Quattrocchi* (1998), Loftus and Guyer contend that the claim of recovered memory in this case is founded upon a type of corroboration that is highly unreliable and invalid. Loftus doubts whether the clinical evaluation method used for assessing the abuse allegation would pass the 'junk' science test set out by the US Supreme Court in *Daubert v. Merrill Dow*.

Fundamentally in this case there was no external corroborative evidence of sexual abuse. Rather Corwin's evaluation served as corroboration. To the extent that such evaluation lacked reliability, validity and objectivity upon which the scientific claim was made, then the evaluation is an opinion, not a fact. It is merely subjective clinical judgment. Loftus & Guyer (2002b) go on to say that clinical evaluations of abuse allegations in general do not have the desired indications of reliability necessary for corroborating scientific theories.

Against this wall of ignorance some experimental psychologists have been trying to chip away at both logical and practical aspects of the recovery debate. Logically for a case of recovered memory to have credence there must have been an original memory that was then lost, and then subsequently recovered. One line of attack by sceptical cognitive psychologists is to question the reality of the actual forgetting of memories that are later recovered. A study by Merckelbach *et al.*, (2006) is informative. They began by asked participants to recall any childhood memories that they could remember. In the next phase, just one hour or two days after this explicit remembering phase, the participants were asked if they had thought about certain specific events recently. These events including both events they had recalled in phase one, and other, previously unrecalled, events. Many participants reported not having thought about previously recalled events for years – despite having just recalled them one hour or two days before.

Interestingly, Merckelbach *et al.* went on to run the same experiment with participants who had either 'continuous' or 'recovered' memories of CSA. They found that those who had 'recovered' memories of CSA were more likely to forget remembering the recent events recalled than 'continuous' memory participants. If it is simply the case that people who testify to recovered memory forget what they have remembered more frequently than those who remember CSA episodes continuously, then the 'recovered' memory debate drops away – or at least part of it does. Therapeutic **iatrogenic** issues, whereby therapy produces the breeding ground for suggestion, remain, but 'recovered' memory falls back into the study of memory per se.

However, Raitt & Zeedyk (2003) argue that to approach the recovered memory debate from a purely scientific memory perspective is flawed. Such an approach, focused as it is on memory processes only, tends to treat abuse (the thing recovered) as a background societal context rather than as one of the components central to understanding the syndrome and its symptoms. This immediately contrasts experimentalists with clinicians (researchers with therapists). Therapists argue that the use of decontextualizing methods (experiments) to investigate decontextualized processes (memory) cannot provide the kinds of insights that are necessary to understand the more complex aspects of (recovered) memory.

We have met this confrontation before in the controversy over the reliability and credibility of children's testimony – between those who treat the problem (clinicians) and those who study the problem (experimental researchers). At base there is a difference in orientation. Therapists do not seek a simple objective truth; researchers do. Therapists are not concerned with the veracity of the precipitating memory; researchers are. Therapists take the memory as a given and ask what impact does that memory have; researchers ask is the memory real? The law, and justice, requires to know what the reality is in this domain. Did abuse take place? Does the victim have a true, accurate memory of actual abuse that can act as strong evidence of its occurrence? Can that memory be forgotten and then later be recovered? Because a defendant's life, liberty or reputation is at stake the law requires answers to these questions.

What role exists for the expert witness who appears in such cases? Clearly the role will be a complex one. A clinician may be asked to offer an opinion on the probability of the recovered memory actually being true, probably by a hypothetical, but close-to-case, line of argument. They may be drawn into statements such as 'consistent with' but we have already seen that such statements try to do by implication what cannot be done directly in court. If the expert is an experimentalist she/he could be asked to educate the jury as to possible mechanisms of lost but later recovered memory. To many researchers, to offer more than this is to slip into advocacy and partisanship.

On the basis of their review of the existing research literature, Wright *et al.* (2006) argue, firstly, that newly remembered recovered memories of past trauma are sometimes accurate, sometimes inaccurate or a mixture of both; secondly, much of what is recalled cannot be confirmed or disconfirmed; and thirdly, because of the two previous points, reports of trauma based on recovered memories are not reliable enough to be the sole basis for legal decisions.

The way forward in this most controversial area of expert testimony may be that suggested by Brewin & Andrews (1997) in their discussion of repression – the assumed mechanism of recovered memories. They argue there must be a dialogue between clinicians and experimentalists. Both parties must accept that causal and **intentional explanations** have equal value in understanding human behaviour. They must accept that while their respective data may be very different, nonetheless, both can be regarded as equally valuable in explaining mental states. If this dialogue takes place, then an overly narrow view of what is 'scientific' may be broadened and the phenomenon of recovered memory more quickly understood. The expert witness would then have a more solid base upon which to offer testimony.

WHAT CAN THE EXPERT WITNESS TELL THE COURT?

To date I have indicated that expert witnesses have increasingly aided the court in reaching decisions. However, the willingness and openness to experts testifying about normal human processes has been hard won, and is more prevalent in some jurisdictions, for example, the US, than in others, such as the UK. Today experts who offer testimony in areas of abnormality such as brain damage and mental impairment are generally welcome in **civil** and **criminal** courts because the nature and sequelae of, for example, closed-head injuries, do not fall within the common knowledge and experience of the jury. Likewise, mental impairment leading to heightened suggestibility, and PTSD (now recognized by the DSM-IV Revision) with its well documented syndromal characteristics, fall outside juries' competence. Thus such expert evidence has been admitted by the courts within the UK and other western common law countries as well as in the US, as it is recognized that such testimony can educate and sensitize the jury or the court as to the likely outcomes of such conditions and thus guide their decision making.

These areas are, in general, non-contentious in most jurisdictions. However, the latest acceptance of expert evidence in such areas as have been discussed in this chapter, have traditionally been regarded as falling within the discretion of the jury, particularly in the UK. Expert testimony in what has been called here normal-mental-state cases is designed to increase awareness of jurors to matters they may not have considered, to correct long-held but perhaps erroneous assumptions and preconceptions, thus allowing them to reach better decisions and thus serve justice better. These are the true roles of the expert witness in such cases.

Alongside the debate between psychology and law about the appropriateness of psychologists appearing as experts in courts of law, psychologists have been arguing among themselves whether such a role is indeed appropriate, given the state of psychological knowledge. This internal debate has surfaced periodically in several special issues of leading journals, for example, *Law and Human Behavior* (1986), *American Psychologist* (1993) and *Expert Evidence* (1996/7). Such public debates have had a very positive impact on the quality and relevance of forensic research. However, they have not settled the issue of whether, or how, experimental psychologists should appear as expert witnesses.

Opponents of experimentally-based psychological expert testimony frequently argue that such testimony is little better than common sense, dressed up as scientific fact. However it is much more than this. Several studies have shown that the knowledge eyewitness experts agree upon differs markedly from the views held by legal personnel and potential jurors. This has been demonstrated in, for example, Canada, (Yarmey & Jones, 1983), the US (Benton *et al.*, 2006; Kassin, Ellsworth & Smith, 1989; Kassin *et al.*, 2001), Australia (McConkey & Roche, 1989), and in the UK (Noon & Hollin, 1987).Thus there is a **prima facie** case that the knowledge experts in the field would bring to the court differs from the knowledge (beliefs) that they would find there.

However, there are a number of strident and dissenting voices to this conclusion. Ebbesen & Konecni (1996) make the point that in all the cited surveys of experts, and non-expert but legally relevant, participants, the apparent consistency of the experts' views, and their disagreements with non-experts, would likely be eliminated if the surveys had given a response option of 'don't know'. This is Ebbesen and Konecni's main point: most findings are inconsistent, inapplicable or invalid because either experimental procedures or measures used to study various relationships are not well tied to legal procedures, or particular findings are not well substantiated. In addition, they argue that knowledge about, for example, memory is so complex that any honest presentation of this knowledge to a court would only serve to confuse rather than improve the jury decision-making process. These authors argue that where expert evidence has been admitted it is because the courts have been misled about the validity, consistency and generalizability of the research in the area due to the legal system's lack of understanding about the nature of science, and partly because researchers have been overconfident in their own expertise.

While Clifford (1997) broadly agreed with their position but argued that they over-stated their case, Yarmey (1997, 2001) disagreed with their assertions, pointing out that a great number of findings upon which experts would be prepared to offer testimony are reliable and consistent.

This lack of consensus persists to the current day. DNA exonerations show wrongful convictions exist, and that many of these cases involve erroneous eyewitness statements or identifications. Many psychologists believe they know why these errors occur and are prepared to testify as to what they know. Other psychologists believe they know, in general, why errors arise, but not in particular cases, and thus are not prepared to testify in a specific case. All, however, are keen that jurors should be educated as to the ways that human frailties can impact on veracity; all are concerned to 'give psychology away' to bring about this education. Some believe that raising the issues in the media, to which the lay person (prospective juror) will be exposed, is the way forward. Others believe that focusing upon system variables can best serve the cause of justice. Yet others feel that appearing as an expert witness is the most direct and focused way to serve justice. All agree that communication between law and psychology should be applauded, encouraged and increased. Education of both legal personnel about psychology and psychologists about law should continue and expand. In this vein, the relative merits of court appointed, versus party-appointed, experts require closer study and more research.

Only slowly is the law coming to realize that the lay person's beliefs and understandings in many fields may be misguided, biased, unexamined, and, frankly wrong. To the extent that they are so, then, for justice to prevail, these misconceptions and misapprehensions have to be addressed at trial and experts may be best placed to address them.

But are judges not better placed to educate the jury as to the misconceptions that lay people may have about basic human processes, social interactional persuasions, and contextual effects on performance and behaviour? The *Daubert* (1993) ruling clearly places the judge as 'gatekeeper' of the admissibility of scientific and non-scientific testimony. In effect they ask the judge to 'think like a scientist' in order to prohibit junk science but to allow reliable science into the courtroom. But is the judge capable of this level of discrimination? While highly educated, they cannot be expected to be at the forefront of knowledge in the ever-expanding and evolving frontiers of scientific knowledge and methodology.

So, pre-trial, the judge is placed in an impossible situation. Dahir *et al.* (2005) in a survey of US judges found that they neither understood nor applied the more technical *Daubert* guidelines. What about during the trial? In both the US and the UK stress has been placed on the judge's instruction to the jury concerning key aspects of the case being tried. Thus, for example, it is argued that judges' instructions to juries about the dangers of identification evidence, or more precisely, the indicants of reliable identification, are held to be sufficient to sensitize the jury as to the issues concerning this most venerable but vulnerable form of evidence. Yet we know from research in the US that jurors often fail to understand judges' instructions (e.g. Cutler, Dexter & Penrod, 1990); that they fail to apply them when they do understand them; and the supposed indicants of reliable identification are far from infallible (e.g. Brigham, Wasserman & Meissner, 1999; Wells & Murray, 1983).

In the light of these qualifications, and the increased pace of knowledge production, there can be little doubt that expert witnessing will continue to grow in all areas of jurisprudence and in all systems of adjudication (see Faigman & Monahan, 2005; Huff, 2002).

CONCLUSION

Unreliable expert evidence can put justice in jeopardy. In 2006, American scientists announced that they had found strong evidence that sudden infant death syndrome (cot death) was caused by a genetic disorder. This contrasts strongly with the assertion made in court by a highly respected and distinguished expert witness, Professor Sir Roy Meadow, that one cot death is a tragedy, two is suspicious, and three is murder, and that there is only a 1:73 million chance that two children in the same family would die of cot death (*R. v. Cannings*, 2002). Angela Canning's conviction for murdering her two baby sons was overturned by the Court of Appeal in 2003.

Expert evidence is admitted to provide expertise that fact finders do not have. The aim of such admittance is to assist them to reach the right decision. Only the expert who is asked to act as such can decide if he or she is sufficiently schooled, skilled and knowledgeable to fulfil that role. It is a judgment call – but a call of such magnitude that it should not be made lightly or without a great deal of thought and consideration. Ceci & Hembrooke (1998) may well be right when they assert that the quality of justice may be diminished without expert witnesses, but, conversely, such witnessing must be ethical, moral, reliable, relevant and admissible if it is to serve such lofty ideals.

SUMMARY

- Expert witnesses have been employed by the courts for several centuries, but psychologists are a relatively recent innovation. The role played by the expert psychologist can be that of clinician, experimentalist, actuary or adviser. Whatever the role, the expert must be qualified by education, training, experience, skill and knowledge.

- The major debate over the acceptance of expert witnesses is the nature and quality of the research which the expert would draw upon to offer testimony. In the case of normal mental state issues, the law believes the jury is sufficiently competent, but international studies suggest they may not be. In addition, it has been argued that judges' instructions are insufficient safeguards.

- It has been demonstrated that expert psychological testimony can enlighten juries as to problems in identification procedures while not creating an unjustified scepticism in overall witness testimony. Equally, it can dispel misconceptions about child abuse, and its behavioural symptoms. Recovered memory cases often reveal a conflict between clinical and experimental approaches to cognition.

- Within the wider psychological community, debate concerns the relative probative value of clinical judgment versus scientific fact. Within experimental psychology, there is concern over the reliability, validity, generalizability and hence, applicability of laboratory-based findings to real-life forensic issues.

- Cutting across all the areas surveyed is the emphasis on the role of the expert psychologist being one of education and information provision, rather than advocacy or partisanship. Overall, sound, research-based, expert witnessing has the power to enhance the quality of justice, while unsound, opinion-based, testimony can only diminish it.

ESSAY/DISCUSSION QUESTIONS

1. Select any one area of potential legal dispute and then identify the database that would be addressed by an expert called to give evidence in the case. How reliable and valid is that database?

2. How should psychology best address the transparency doctrine formulated by *R. v. Turner* (1975) that non-disordered behaviour is fully transparent and therefore not in need of explanation or clarification by experts?

3. Are researchers and clinicians inevitably and irredeemably confrontational and conflicting?

4. How could an expert approach the problem of definitive differentiation in either cases of possible mistaken identification or CSA?

5. Should experimental psychologists *ever* act as expert witnesses? Give reasons for your answer.

REFERENCES

Anson, D.A., Golding, S.L., & Gully, K.J. (1993). Child sexual abuse allegations: Reliability of criteria-based content analysis. *Law and Human Behaviour, 17,* 331–341.

Baker, F. (1969). Review of general systems concepts and their relevance for medical care. *Systematics, 7,* 209–229.

Baker, R. (1992). *Hidden memories.* Buffalo, NY: Prometheus Books.

Benton, T.R., Ross, D.F., Bradshaw, E., Thomas, W.N., & Bradshaw, G.S. (2006). Eyewitness memory is still not common sense: Comparing jurors, judges and law enforcement to eyewitness experts. *Applied Cognitive Psychology, 20,* 115–129.

Berliner, L. (1998). The use of expert testimony in child sexual abuse cases: In S.J. Ceci & H. Hembrooke (Eds), *Expert witnesses in child abuse cases* (pp.11–27). Washington, DC: American Psychological Association.

Brewin, C.R. & Andrews, B. (1997). Reasoning about repression: inferences from clinical and experimental data. In M.A. Conway (Ed.), *Recovered memories and false memories* (pp.192–205). Oxford: Oxford University Press.

Briere, J. & Conte, J. (1993). Self-reported amnesia for abuse in adults molested as children. *Journal of Traumatic Stress, 6,* 21–31.

Brigham, J.C., Wasserman, A.W., & Meissner, C.A. (1999). Disputed eyewitness identification evidence: Important legal and scientific issues. *Court Review, 36,* 12–25.

Bussey J. v. Commonwealth (1985). Appellee Supreme Court. Sept. 6 697 S.W. 2d 139 (Ky. 1985)

Cahill, L., Prins, B., Weber, M., & McGaugh, J. (1994). B-adrenergic activation and memory for emotional events. *Nature, 371,* 702–704.

Ceci, S.J. & Bruck, M. (1993). The suggestibility of children's recollections: An historical review and synthesis. *Psychological Bulletin, 113,* 403–439.

Ceci, S.J. & Bruck, M. (1995). *Jeopardy in the courtroom: A scientific analysis of children's testimony.* Washington, DC: American Psychological Association.

Ceci, S.J. & Hembrooke, H. (1998). Introduction. In S.J. Ceci & H. Hembrooke, (Eds), *Expert witnesses in child abuse cases* (pp. 1–8). Washington DC: American Psychological Association.

Cheit, R.E. (2005). The archive: 101 corroborated cases of recovered memory. Retrieved 10 December 2006 from: http://tinyurl.com/42yj7.

Christianson, S-A. (1992). Emotional stress and eyewitness memory: A critical review. *Psychological Bulletin, 112*, 284–309.

Clifford, B.R. (1979). The relevance of psychological investigation to legal issues in testimony and identification. *Criminal Law Review*, March, 153–163.

Clifford, B.R. (1997). A commentary on Ebbesen and Konecni's eyewitness memory research: Probative v. prejudicial value. *Expert Evidence, 6*, 140–143.

Clifford, B.R. (2003). Forensic psychology. In R. Bayne & I. Horton (Eds), *Applied psychology* (pp.67–78). London: Sage.

Conway, M.A. (1997). Introduction: What are memories? In M.A. Conway (Ed.), *Recovered memories and false memories* (pp.1–22). Oxford: Oxford University Press.

Corwin, D.L. & Olafson, E. (1997). Videotaped discovery of a reportedly unrecallable memory of child sexual abuse: Comparison with a childhood interview videotaped 11 years before. *Child Maltreatment, 2*, 91–112.

Crombag, H.F.M., Wagenaar, W.A., & van Koppen, P.J. (1996). Crash monitoring and the problem of 'source monitoring'. *Applied Cognitive Psychology, 10*, 95–104.

Crowley, M.J., O'Callaghan, M.G., & Ball, P.G. (1994). The judicial impact of psychological expert testimony in a simulated child sexual abuse trial. *Law and Human Behaviour, 18*, 89–105.

Cutler, B.L., Dexter, H.R., & Penrod, S.D. (1990). Non adversarial methods for sensitising jurors to eyewitness evidence. *Journal of Applied Social Psychology, 20*, 1197–1207.

Dahir, V.B., Richardson, J.T., Ginsburg, G.P., Gatowski, S.J., Dobbin, S.A., & Merlino, M.L. (2005). Judicial application of Daubert to psychological syndrome and profile evidence. *Psychology, Public Policy and Law, 14*, 62–82.

Daubert (1993). *Daubert v. Merrell Dow Pharmaceuticals Inc.* 509 U.S., 113 S.Ct. 2786 1993

Dawson, B., Vaughan, A.R., & Wagner, W.G. (1991). Normal responses to sexually anatomically detailed dolls. *Journal of Family Violence, 7*, 135–152.

Devenport, J.L., Stinson, V., Cutler, B.L., & Kravitz, D.A. (2002). How effective are the cross examination and expert testimony safeguards? Juror's perceptions of the suggestiveness and fairness of biased line-up procedures. *Journal of Applied Psychology, 87*, 1042–1054.

Devlin, Lord P. (1976). *Report to the secretery of state for the Home Department of the departmental committee on evidence of identification in criminal cases.* London: HMSO.

Ebbesen, E.B. & Konecni, V.J. (1996). Eyewitness memory research: Probative v. prejudicial value. *Expert Evidence, 5*, (1&2), 2–28.

Elliot, D.M. (1997). Traumatic events: Prevalence and delayed recall in the general population. *Journal of Consulting and Clinical Psychology, 65*, 811–820.

Epstein, M.A. & Bottoms, B.L. (2002). Explaining the forgetting and recovery of abuse and trauma memories: Possible mechanisms. *Child Maltreatment, 7*, 210–225.

Esplin, P.W., Boychuk, T., & Raskin, D.C. (1988). *A field validity study of Criteria-Based Content Analysis for children's statements in sexual abuse cases.* Paper presented at the NATO Advanced Study Institute on Credibility Assessment, Matatea, Italy.

Faigman, D.L. & Monahan, J. (2005). Psychological evidence at the dawn of the law's scientific age. *Annual Review of Psychology*, 56, 631–659.

Finkelhor, D. (1987). The trauma of child sexual abuse: Two models. *Journal of Interpersonal Violence*, 2, 348–366.

Finkelhor, D. & Browne, A. (1985). The traumatic impact of child sexual abuse: A conceptualisation. *American Journal of Orthopsychiatry*, 55, 530–541.

Fisher, C.B. (1995). The American Psychological Association's ethics code and the validation of sexual abuse in day-care settings. *Psychology, Public Policy and Law*, 1, 461–468.

Fisher, C.B. & Whiting, K.A. (1998). How valid are child sexual abuse validations? In S.J. Ceci & H. Hembrooke (Eds), *Expert Witnessing in Child Sexual Abuse Cases* (pp. 159–184). Washington, DC: American Psychological Association.

Fivush, R. (2002). The development of autobiographical memory. In H. Westcott, G. Davies, & R.H.C. Bull (Eds), *Children's testimony: A handbook of psychological research and forensic practice* (pp. 55–68). Chichester: John Wiley & Sons.

French, C.C. (2003). Fantastic memories. *Journal of Consciousness Studies*, 10, 153–174.

Frye (1923). *Frye v. United States* 293 F.1013 (D. C. Cir. 1023)

Gabbert, F., Memon, A., & Allen, K. (2003). Memory conformity: Can eyewitnesses influence each other's memory for an event. *Applied Cognitive Psychology*, 17, 533–544.

Gardner, R. (1992). *True and false accusations of child abuse*. Cresskill, NY: Creative Therapeutics.

Ghate, D. & Spencer, L. (1995). *The prevalence of child sexual abuse in Britain: A feasibility study for a large-scale national survey of the general population*. London: HMSO.

Goldstein, A.G., Chance, J.E., & Schneller, G.R. (1989). Frequency of eyewitness identification in criminal cases: a survey of prosecutors. *Bulletin of the Psychonomic Society*, 27, 71–74.

Goodman, G.S. (1984). Children's testimony in historical perspective. *Journal of Social Issues*, 40, 9–31.

Goodman, G.S. & Paz-Alonso, P.M. (2006). Trauma and Memory: Normal versus special memory mechanisms. In B. Utti, N. Ohta, & A.L. Siegenthales (Eds), *Memory and emotion: Interdisciplinary perspectives* (pp. 233–258). Oxford: Blackwell Publishing.

Granhag, P.A., Stromwall, L., & Billings, J. (2003). I'll never forget the sinking ferry: how social influence makes false memories surface. In M. Vanderhallen, G. Vervaeke, P.J. van Koppen, & J. Goethals (Eds), *Much ado about crime: Chapters on psychology and crime* (pp. 129–140). Politeia: Brussels.

Hall, L. & Lloyd, S. (1989). *Surviving child sexual abuse: A handbook for helping women challenge their past*. Lewes, UK: The Falmer Press.

Haward, L.R.C. (1981). *Forensic psychology*. London: Batsford.

Herman, J.L. (1981). *Father–daughter incest*. Cambridge MA: Harvard University Press.

Home Office (1992). *Memorandum of good practice on video recording interviews with child witnesses for criminal proceedings*. Home Office & Department of Health. London: HMSO.

Home Office (2002). *Achieving best evidence in criminal proceedings: Guidance for vulnerable or intimidated witnesses including children*. London: Home Office Communication Directorate.

Hornstein, G. (1992). The return of the repressed. *American Psychologist*, 47, 254–263.

Horowitz, M. & Reidbord, S. (1992). Memory, emotion and response to trauma. In S. Christianson (Ed.), *The Handbook of emotion and memory: Research and theory* (pp. 343–358). Hillsdale, NJ: Erlbaum.

Huff, C.R. (2002). Wrongful conviction and public policy: The American Society of Criminology 2001 presidential address. *Criminology*, *40*, 1, 1–18.

Innocence Project (1992). Retrieved December 2006 from: http://www.innocenceproject.org/about/.

Jenkins v. U.S. (1962). 307 F.2d 637 1962.

Kapardis, A. (1997). *Psychology and law: A critical introduction*. Cambridge: Cambridge University Press.

Kassin, S.M., Ellsworth, P.C., & Smith, V.L. (1989). The general acceptance of psychological research on eyewitness testimony: A survey of the experts. *American Psychologist*, *44*, 1089–1098.

Kassin, S.M., Tubb, V.A., Hosch, H.M., & Memon, A. (2001). On the general acceptance of eyewitness testimony research: A new survey of the experts. *American Psychologist*, *56*, 405–416.

Kendall-Tackett, K.A., Williams, L.M., & Finkelhor, D. (1993). Impact of sexual abuse on children: A review and synthesis of recent empirical studies. *Psychological Bulletin*, *113*, 164–180.

Kovera, M.B. & Borgida, E. (1998). Expert scientific testimony on child witnesses in the age of Daubert. In S.J. Ceci & H. Hembrooke (Eds), *Expert witnessing in child abuse cases* (pp. 185–215). Washington, DC: American Psychological Association.

Lamb, M.E., Stemberg, K.N.J., Esplin, P.W., Hershkowitz, I., Orbach, Y., & Hovay, M. (1997). Criterion based content analysis: A field validation study. *Child Abuse and Neglect*, *21*, 255–264.

Lawlor, R.J. (1998). The expert witness in child sexual abuse cases: A clinician's view. In S.J. Ceci & H. Hembrooke (Eds), *Expert witnessing in child abuse cases* (pp. 105–122). Washington, DC: American Psychological Association.

Leippe, M.R. (1980). Effects of integrative memorial and cognitive processes on the correspondence of eyewitness accuracy and confidence. *Law and Human Behavior*, *4*, 261–274.

Leippe, M.R. (1995). The case for expert testimony about eyewitness memory. *Psychology, Public Policy and Law*, *1*, 909–959.

Leippe, M.R., Eisenstadt, D., Rauch, S.M., & Seib H.M. (2004). Timing of eyewitness expert testimony, jurors' need for cognition and case strength as determinants of trial verdicts. *Journal of Applied Psychology*, *89*, 524–541.

Lindsay, D.S. (2002). Children's source monitoring. In H. Westcott, G.M. Davies & R.H.C. Bull (Eds), *Children's testimony: A handbook of psychological research and forensic practice* (pp. 83–98). Chichester: John Wiley & Sons.

Lindsay, D.S. & Read, D.J. (1994). Psychotherapy and memories of child sexual abuse: A cognitive perspective. *Applied Cognitive Psychology*, *8*, 281–338.

Lindsay, D.S. & Read, D.J. (1997). 'Memory work' and recovered memories of childhood sexual abuse: Scientific evidence and public, professional and personal issues. *Psychology, Public Policy and Law*, *1*, 845–908.

Loftus, E.F. (1983). Silence is not golden. *American Psychologist*, *38*, 564–572.

Loftus, E.F. & Guyer, M.J. (2002a). Who abused Jane Doe? The hazards of the single case history. Part 1. *Skeptical Inquirer*, *26*, 3, May/June. Retrieved November 2006 from: http://www.csicop.org/si/2002-05/jane-doe.html.

Loftus, E.F. & Guyer, M.J. (2002b). Who abused Jane Doe? The hazards of the single case history. Part 2. *Skeptical Inquirer*, *26*, 4, July/August. Retrieved November 2006 from: http://www.csicop.org/si/2002-07/jane-doe.html.

Loftus, E.F. & Pickrell, J.E. (1995). The formation of false memories. *Psychiatric Annals*, 25, 720–725.

Mackay, R.D., Colman, A.M., & Thornton, P. (1999). The admissibility of expert psychological and psychiatric testimony. In A. Heaton-Armstrong, E. Shepherd, & D. Wolchover (Eds), *Analysing witness testimony: A guide for legal practitioners and other professionals* (pp. 321–33). London: Blackstone Press.

McAnulty, R.D. (1993). Expert psychological testimony in cases of alleged child sexual abuse. *Archives of Sexual Behaviour*, 22, 311–324.

McConkey, K.M. & Roche, S.M. (1989). Knowledge of eyewitness testimony. *Australian Psychologist*, 24, 337–384.

Meade, M.J. & Roediger, H.L. (2002). Explorations in the social contagion of memory. *Memory and Cognition*, 30, 995–1009.

Melchert, T.P. (1996). Childhood memory and history of different forms of abuse. *Professional Psychology: Research and Practice*, 27, 438–446.

Melchert, T.P. & Parker, R.L. (1997). Different forms of childhood abuse and memory. *Child Abuse and Neglect*, 21, 125–135.

Melton, G.B. (1994). Doing justice and doing good: Conflicts for mental health professionals. *The Future of Children*, 4, 102–118.

Merckelbach H., Smeets, T., Geraerts, E. *et al.* (2006). I haven't thought about this for years! Dating recent recalls of vivid memories. *Applied Cognitive Psychology*, 20, 33–42.

Miller, J.S. & Allen, R.J. (1998). The expert as an educator. In S.J. Ceci & H. Hembrooke (Eds), *Expert witnesses in child abuse cases* (pp.137–155). Washington, DC: American Psychological Association.

Morison, S. & Greene, E. (1992). Juror and expert knowledge of child sexual abuse. *Child Abuse and Neglect*, 16, 595–613.

Myers, J.E.B. (1993). Expert testimony regarding child sexual abuse. *Child Abuse and Neglect*, 17, 175–185.

Neil v. Biggers (1972). 409 U.S. 188 1972.

Noon, E. & Hollin, C.R. (1987). Lay knowledge of eyewitness behaviour: A British survey. *Applied Cognitive Psychology*, 1, 143–153.

Ost, J., Vrij, A., Costall, A., & Bull, R. (2002). Crashing memories and reality monitoring: distinguishing between perception, imagination and 'false memories'. *Applied Cognitive Psychology*, 16, 125–134.

PACE (1984, 2005). Police and Criminal Evidence Act 1984, updated Codes of Practice 2005. British Home Office. London: HMSO.

R. v. Cannings (2004). EWCA Crim 1 (19 January 2004).

Raitt, F.E. & Zeedyk, M.S. (2003). False memory syndrome: Undermining the credibility of complainants in sexual offences. *International Journal of Law and Psychiatry*, 26, 453–471.

Raskin, D.C. & Esplin, P.W. (1991). Assessment of children's statements of sexual abuse. In J. Doris (Ed.), *The suggestibility of children's memory: Implications for eyewitness testimony* (pp. 172–176). Washington, DC: American Psychological Association.

Rich, C. (1990). Accuracy of adult's reports of abuse in childhood. *American Journal of Psychiatry*, 147, 1389.

Rumsfeld, D. (2002). DoD News Briefing – Secretary Rumsfeld and Gen. Myers. Retrieved January 2007 from: http://www.defenselink.mil/Transcripts/Transcript.aspx?TranscriptID = 2636

Schacter, D.L., Norman, K.A., & Koutstaal, W. (1997). The recovered memories debate: a cognitive neuroscience perspective. In M.A. Conway (Ed.), *Recovered memories and false memories* (pp. 63–99). Oxford: Oxford University Press.

Scheck, B., Neufeld, P., & Dwyer, J. (2000). *Actual innocence.* New York: Doubleday.

Schooler, J.W., Ambada, A., & Bendiksen, M. (1997). A cognitive corroborative case study approach for investigating discovered memories of sexual abuse. In J.D. Read & D.S. Lindsay (Eds), *Recollections of trauma: Scientific research and clinical practices* (pp. 379–388). New York: Plenum.

Sgroi, S.M. (1982). *Handbook of clinical intervention in child sexual abuse.* Lexington, MA: Lexington Books.

Smeets, T., Jelicic, M., Peters, M.J.V. *et. al.* (2006). 'Of course I remember seeing that film' – how ambiguous questions generate crashing memories. *Applied Cognitive Psychology,* 20, 779–789.

Spencer, J.R. (1998). The role of experts in the common law and the civil law: A comparison. In S.J. Ceci & H. Hembrooke (Eds), *Expert witnesses in child abuse cases* (pp. 29–59). Washington, DC: American Psychological Association.

Spencer, J.R. & Flin, R. (1990). *The evidence of children: The law and the psychology.* London: Blackstock Press.

State v. J.Q. (1993). 617 A.2d 1196 (N.J. 1993).

State v. Michaels (1993). 625 A.2d 489 (N.J. Superior Ct. App. Div.) 1993; 136 N.J. 299, 642, A.2d. 1372 1994; 642 A.2d. 1372 (N.J.)1994.

State of Rhode Island v. Quattrocchi (1998). March 24 Case: No. P.92-3759.

State v. Warren (1981). 230 Kan 385 [635 P.2d. 1236 1243, 23 A.L.R. 4th 1070].

Steller, M. (1989). Recent developments in statement analysis. In J.C. Yuille (Ed.), *Credibility assessment* (pp. 135–154). London: Kluwer.

Summit, R. (1983). The child sexual abuse accommodation syndrome. *Child Abuse and Neglect,* 7, 177–192.

Summit, R. (1992). Abuse of the child sexual abuse accommodation syndrome. *Journal of Child Sexual Abuse,* 1, 153–161.

United States v. Whitted (1993). 994 F.2d. 444 (8th Cir.).

Van der Kolk, B. & Saporta, J. (1993). Biological responses to psychic trauma. In J. Wilson & B. Raphael (Eds), *International handbook of traumatic stress syndromes* (pp. 25–34). New York: Plenum.

Vrij, A. (2005). Criteria-based content analysis: a qualitative review of the first 37 studies. *Psychology, Public Policy and Law,* 11, 3–41.

Vrij, A. & Mann, S. (2006). Criteria-based content analysis: An empirical test of its underlying processes. *Psychology, Crime and Law,* 12, 337–349.

Walker, L.E. (1990). Psychological assessment of sexually abused children for legal evaluation and expert witness testimony. *Professional Psychology: Research and Practice,* 21, 344–353.

Walker, L.E. & Monahan, J. (1987). Social frameworks: A new use of social science in law. *Virginia Law Review,* 73, 559–598.

Waterman, A., Blades, M., & Spencer, C. (2002). How and why do children respond to nonsensical questions? In H. Westcott, G.M. Davies, & R.H.C. Bull (Eds), *Children's testimony: A handbook of psychological research and forensic practice* (pp. 147–159). Chichester: John Wiley & Sons.

Wells, G.L. (1978). Applied eyewitness testimony research: system variables and estimator variables. *Journal of Personality and Social Psychology, 36,* 1546–1557.

Wells, G.L. & Murray, D.M. (1983). What can psychology say about the *Neil v. Biggers* criteria for judging eyewitness accuracy? *Journal of Applied Psychology, 68,* 347–362.

Wells, G.L. & Olson, E. (2003). Eyewitness identification. *Annual Review of Psychology, 54,* 277–295.

Wigmore, J.H. (1978). *Evidence in trials at common law.* Boston: Little Brown.

Woocher, F.D. (1977). Did your eyes deceive you? Expert psychological testimony on the vulnerability of eyewitness identification. *Stanford Law Review, 29,* 969–1030.

Wright, D.B., Ost, J., & French, C.C. (2006). Recovered and false memories. *The Psychologist, 19,* 352–355.

Yapko, M. (1997). The troublesome unknowns about trauma and recovered memories. In M.A. Conway (Ed.), *Recovered memories and false memories* (pp. 23–33). Oxford: Oxford University Press.

Yarmey, A.D. (1997). Probative v. prejudicial value of eyewitness memory research. *Expert Evidence, 5,* 89–97.

Yarmey, A.D. (2001). Expert testimony: Does eyewitness memory research have probative value for the courts? *Canadian Psychology. 42,* 2, 92–100.

Yarmey, A.D. (2003). Eyewitness identification guidelines and recommendations for identification procedures in the United States and Canada. *Canadian Psychology, 44,* 181–189.

Yarmey, A.D. & Jones, H.P.T. (1983). Is the psychology of eyewitness identification a matter of common sense? In S. Lloyd-Bostock & B.R. Clifford (Eds), *Evaluating witness evidence* (pp. 18–40). Chichester: John Wiley & Sons.

Yuille, J. C. (1988). The systematic assessment of children's testimony. *Canadian Psychology, 29,* 247–262.

ANNOTATED READING LIST

Brewer, N. (2006). Uses and abuses of eyewitness identification confidence. *Legal and Criminological Psychology, 11,* 3–23. *This paper nicely exemplifies the nature of the database that an expert, testifying about the reliability of an eyewitness, would make recourse to. It has been argued in the past that the correlation between confidence and accuracy is either weak or non-existent. This recent paper suggests otherwise. This paper is thus an example of the ever-changing database to which experts make recourse.*

Bruck, M. (1998). The trials and tribulations of a novice expert witness. In S.J. Ceci & H. Hembrooke (Eds), *Expert Witnesses in child abuse cases.* (pp. 85–104). Washington, DC: American Psychological Association. *A heart-felt personal account of an expert's first appearance in a court, with an 'unfriendly' cross-examining barrister.*

Ceci, S.J. & Hembrooke, H. (Eds) (1998). *Expert witnesses in child abuse cases.* Washington, DC: American Psychological Association. *An excellent text that focuses upon child sexual abuse and the possible roles of experts. It also touches on certain aspects of false/recovered memories.*

Conway, M.A. (Ed.) (1997). *Recovered memories and false memories.* Oxford: Oxford University Press. *A scholarly approach to the debates surrounding false/recovered memories.*

Faigman, D.L. & Monahan, J. (2005). Psychological evidence at the dawn of the law's scientific age. *Annual Review of Psychology, 56*, 631–659. *This paper argues that psychology is on its way to being used as authority to create a general legal rule, as evidence to determine a specific fact, and as a framework to provide context.*

Mackay, R.D., Coleman, A.M., & Thornton, P. (1999). The admissibility of expert psychological and psychiatric testimony. In A Heaton-Armstrong, E. Shepherd, & D. Wolchover (Eds), *Analysing witness testimony: A guide for legal practitioners and other professionals* (pp. 321–334). London: Blackstone Press. *This chapter maps out the increasing acceptance in English law of expert testimony in the face of the Turner rule and the transparency assumption (R. v. Turner [1975] QB 834).*

Wright, D.B. (2006). Causal and associative hypotheses in psychology. *Psychology, Public Policy and Law, 12*, 190–213. *This article points out that the conclusions that can be reached from studies employing causal and associative hypotheses differ. This distinction is very important in CSA cases and all would-be experts should appreciate the difference.*

PART 4

AFTER SENTENCING

11

WHAT'S THE POINT OF SENTENCING?

PSYCHOLOGICAL ASPECTS OF CRIME AND PUNISHMENT

James McGuire
University of Liverpool, United Kingdom

The process of sentencing is probably familiar to most people. For the majority, this is likely to have derived from pervasive media attention devoted to 'law and order' issues and to courtroom decisions. But a sizeable proportion experience direct personal contact with the legal system; in the UK it has been estimated that almost one-third of the population will be convicted of a criminal offence at some point in their lives.

This chapter examines several aspects of sentencing with reference to psychological research. The opening section of the chapter takes us into the field of penology – the study of legal punishments. It outlines what are generally considered to be the main objectives of sentencing, and the rationales underpinning them in each case. These objectives include *retribution, incapacitation, deterrence, rehabilitation,* and *restoration.* To the extent that sentencing is intended to achieve certain socially desirable effects, mainly in terms of its impact on those made subject to it, the second section of the chapter reviews research findings relevant to this. Is it possible to reduce rates of recidivism (a pattern of repeated criminality) amongst persistent offenders? Research clearly shows that the nature of a sentence is much less important in this respect than what happens during the course of it. Alongside other professions, psychologists have made significant contributions to this area in a number of ways: for example, in terms of identifying *risk factors* for recurrent involvement in crime; in designing and implementing methods of working with frequently convicted offenders; and in evaluating the outcomes of psychosocial interventions. The final, brief section of the chapter considers the somewhat paradoxical situation in which psychology finds itself in relation to the practice of criminal justice.

THE SENTENCE OF THE COURT

Individuals found guilty of committing crimes[1] can expect to be sentenced by the courts. This has been standard practice in many countries for several hundred years. Broadly speaking, there is a rough correspondence between the seriousness of crimes committed and the severity of sentences imposed. Where there are marked departures from this – mainly when sentences are deemed too lenient – controversy often erupts. Centuries of accumulated experience notwithstanding, many aspects of the process remain poorly understood. Until recently some of them had not been very searchingly examined.

This chapter approaches the nature and the outcomes of sentencing from a psychological perspective, and outlines the roles that psychologists may play in the different stages of sentencing decisions; though generally with reference to what happens *after* those decisions have been made. Other chapters have addressed earlier stages of the legal process, such as police investigation and the presentation of evidence in court. For the criminal courts, at least at present, the culmination of the legal process is the finding of guilt or innocence and the passing of sentence.

The word 'sentence' derives (via Middle English and Old French) from the Latin word *sententia,* meaning a feeling or opinion communicated by someone to others. This captures something crucial about it: other than in highly exceptional circumstances, sentencing is a public process. Magistrates, judges and others engaged in it are reflecting and embodying the community's distaste, perhaps revulsion, regarding something someone has done. Hence sentencing is often considered to serve a primarily *expressive* function: it conveys to the offender the public's reaction to his or her conduct in the criminal offence.

---

1 There is no universally agreed definition of the word 'crime' and present space does not permit discussion of the complexities within this. As used here the term refers simply to the breaking of the criminal law (however that is formulated in a given jurisdiction at a given time). For more extended discussion see McGuire (2004a) and Jame (Chapter 1).

Penology is the study of legal punishment and of how it is administered. This occurs within that segment of criminal justice usually referred to as the *penal system*, a term loosely denoting the arrangement of courts, prisons, probation, youth justice and allied agencies within society. Since these arrangements have developed in stepwise fashion over very many years, to call the end-product a 'system' may be, as Ashworth (2005, p. 67) has remarked, ". . . merely a convenience and an aspiration" rather than an accurate description.

Potentially, psychology has a significant contribution to make at numerous places within this 'system' and although the number of psychologists directly employed within it is still low relative to other professions, it has been steadily expanding in recent years. Since the process of sentencing should entail an understanding of why someone acted as he or she did, and that process is also intended to reduce the chances of similar actions recurring, psychology should perhaps be playing a far more influential role than has been the case so far. For arguably, if this does not sound too grandiose, the operation of law is in one sense a form of applied psychology.

THE OBJECTIVES OF SENTENCING

Within the criminal law and specifically within penology, sentencing has been conceptualized as serving a number of distinct but interconnected and overlapping purposes. The core of them is the idea of punishment, the signalling of society's displeasure concerning what the offender has done, by the imposition of a penalty. But this apparently straightforward idea conceals a number of underlying complexities. The following outline borrows from several texts addressing this issue (Ashworth, 2005; Duff & Garland, 1994; Easton & Piper, 2005; Miethe & Lu, 2005). Although there is no definitive consensus on these matters, sentencing is currently thought to perform five main kinds of function.

Retribution and Desert

From one perspective, society responds to offenders by punishing them purely and simply because it has to. While there are various nuances within this, the reasoning that underpins the concept of retribution is as follows. There is a fundamental principle at stake when an individual acts against society by breaking its laws. The harm caused by such actions gives society an automatic right, indeed an obligation, to inflict pain on the offender in response. Conversely, so the argument continues, the offender also has a right to be punished. Retributive action corrects an imbalance created by the offences, by rectifying the wrong the offender has done; a concept that informs the familiar notion of 'just deserts'.

The origins of this idea can be traced back to ancient Judeo-Christian texts enunciating the 'law of retaliation' or *lex talionis*, where punishment corresponds to the crime both in its severity and its type ('an eye for an eye'). Such a viewpoint underpins practices that are still applied in some countries where pain is inflicted on the law-breaker commensurate with that inflicted on the original victims. But the modern conceptual framework for this is usually attributed to the eighteenth-century German philosopher Immanuel Kant, who argued that in committing a crime, an offender gains an unfair advantage over those who have adhered to the law. Under the general political obligation that binds individuals to each other and to the state, there is a necessary reciprocity; punishment then restores a proper balance between the offender and the rest of society. He or she owes and must repay a debt to law-abiding members of the community (Murphy, 1994).

A more recent reformulation of this is contained in the idea of *censure*, or expression and attribution of blame. Sentencing serves a reprobative function, and to be just it should be based on the principle of proportionality between the amount of harm done and the amount of punishment dispensed (Von Hirsch *et al.*, 1994).

Overall the philosophy of retribution is not concerned with instrumental effects or outcomes. Punishment is viewed as ". . . intrinsically appropriate" (Duff & Garland, 1994, p. 7) and the cycle of crime and official response is, as it were, a closed loop. But as we will see below the idea of retribution can also be combined with other elements whereby sentences can be designed to accomplish a number of goals simultaneously.

Incapacitation

In almost complete contrast, incapacitation refers to the possibility of crime control by removing offenders from circumstances where they are likely to commit crimes; by restricting their freedom to act. The most palpable means of doing this in contemporary societies is through imprisonment, or detention in other locked-up residential settings (ranging from children's homes to high security hospitals). Thereby, offenders are 'taken out of circulation': they are removed from society and from situations in which they have opportunities to take vehicles, break into houses, sell drugs or get into fights (though unfortunately as we know, some of these activities continue in prison). Apart from physical incarceration, liberty can be restricted to varying degrees in community penalties also. This is achieved, for example, by night curfews or electronically monitored home confinement; by exclusion from a neighbourhood where previous crimes were committed; or by a requirement to attend for supervision at specified times. There is wide civic endorsement of the principle that persons who have inflicted serious or repeated harm upon others (or in some instances upon themselves) should be restrained in some way, encapsulated in frequently heard phrases such as 'public protection' and 'community safety'.

But the idea of incapacitation has a similarly ancient history to that of retribution. In the distant past, individuals might have been exiled or banished from their communities. Not so long ago, a parallel of this was practised in the transportation of many thousands of offenders from the UK to Australia. In medieval Europe, the use of bodily restraints such as stocks and pillories, and that most durable symbol of penal confinement – the ball and chain – was designed to incapacitate as well as to punish in other ways. Whilst modern methods of doing this are less overtly physical, the net effect is similar in seeking to control the offender's scope for antisocial action.

Deterrence

A third declared intention that drives the sentencing process is that it should alter criminal behaviour by attaching negative consequences to it. This is the paradigmatic example of what is entitled the *utilitarian* or *consequentialist* rationale for punishment as a response to crime (Walker, 1991). It is founded on the idea that legal sanctions will have an impact on individuals made subject to them. This set of expectations is sometimes referred to as **deterrence theory** (or occasionally deterrence doctrine) and it is probably the most widely taken-for-granted purpose of sentencing.

Deterrent effects can be sub-divided with respect to different scales of intended outcomes. One basic, conventional distinction is that between *specific* and *general* deterrence. The former refers to the impact of punishment on the individual made subject to it: theoretically, when someone is punished for committing a crime, he or she should be less likely to do it again. The latter refers to the wider effect this is expected to have on others and on the community as a whole. If committing crimes is known to be punished, the public-at-large should be less likely to do it, as they have observed that it will result in unpleasantness for them. These are useful conceptual distinctions, but in everyday reality there is likely to be a complex interplay between specific and general deterrent effects (Stafford & Warr, 1993).

Penologists have recognized that the objective features of sentencing are probably less important to prospective offenders than its subjective or perceptual features (Gibbs, 1986). *Objective* properties are those that might be recorded by the police or by a government statistician, showing, for example, rates of detection, arrest, or subsequent imprisonment for different types of crime. *Subjective* or perceptual properties are those which are meaningful to an individual offender, who may be wholly uninformed concerning criminal statistics but is probably conscious of peers who have escaped arrest, or who have been arrested, for specific misdemeanours. The real operative factors in everyday decision making by anyone considering an offence are likely to be immediate personal knowledge rather than official databases.

There are several features of sentences that may be considered from either objective or subjective standpoints: certainty, celerity, and severity. **Certainty** refers to the likelihood of legal punishment as a result of committing a crime; **celerity,** to the amount of time that lapses between an offence being committed and an official sanction being imposed; **severity,** to the magnitude of a punishment or the estimated amount of pain or discomfort a convicted offender would endure. Defined objectively, certainty refers to the proportion of crimes of a specific type that result in formal punishment; subjectively, however, it reflects individual offenders' estimates of the chances of being caught. To draw an everyday parallel, just as most people preparing to drive off in their cars think an accident is unlikely to happen to them (though they may be distantly aware of statistics concerning such a risk), so most individuals contemplating a crime tend to discount measured probabilities and focus on the details of their own actions and circumstances. Penologists have discovered that it is changes in the perceived features of sanctions that are more likely to influence the behaviour of individuals inclined to break the law (Von Hirsch *et al.*, 1999).

Rehabilitation

Retribution, incapacitation and deterrence are often in themselves believed to promote a further effect, that of *rehabilitating* the offender. The individual's recognition of how society perceives his or her actions, conjoined with the unpleasantness of losing liberty or enduring other effects of punishment, will encourage him or her to become reformed and to desist from criminal acts. Thus some penologists consider that rehabilitation is integrally achieved *through* retributive and deterrent effects.

Others, however, take the view that the sentence of the court should incorporate procedures explicitly designed to support rehabilitation. The latter might include, for example, remedial education, employment training, various types of psychotherapy where indicated, developing awareness of victims, or participation in specially designed programmes for the reduction of offending behaviour. Each of these will (potentially) reduce both the alienation that many offenders already experience and the additional stigmatization induced by the sentencing process, while also enhancing the individual's prospects of becoming a more fully-fledged citizen and a law-abiding member of the community.

It is with reference to this that psychology has perhaps had its farthest-reaching influence on practices in the criminal justice system in recent years. The model that informs such work begins with the observation that some kinds of individual differences are reliably associated with risks of repeated involvement in crime. These *risk factors* derive not from variations in personality traits, as was hypothesized at an earlier stage, but in a range of other variables. They include patterns of criminal associates, antisocial attitudes, a tendency towards impulsiveness, poor emotional self-regulation, and deficits in a number of social, cognitive, and problem-solving skills (Andrews & Bonta, 2003; McGuire, 2004a). Identification of these risk factors led to the proposal that if they could be successfully remedied by psychosocial interventions, individuals might be less likely to commit further offences as a result. There is now substantial evidence to support such proposals and some of the key findings in this area will be described later in this chapter.

Restoration and Reparation

A fifth and relatively novel perspective on punishment has emerged over approximately the last 25 years, influenced in part by a steadily growing recognition of the rights and needs of crime victims. One application of this in some countries has been the provision to victims of opportunities to make 'impact statements' in court that might influence the deliberations of sentencers (Ashworth, 2005).

But the more innovative development has been influenced by approaches to crime taken in some non-Western societies. This has introduced the concept of *restorative justice*, of attempted reconciliation between offenders and victims, with the former making direct reparations to the latter where possible, as traditionally occurred amongst some indigenous communities in various parts of the world. The fundamental principle here is the repair of the damage done to the victim and community by the commission of the offence. But it takes a direction quite different from the punitive sanctions customary in a retributive approach. It may entail a variety of elements, including the acknowledgement by the offender or his or her responsibility for the offence, the offering of an apology, or making of direct restitution in some manner settled jointly between victims, offenders and other interested parties.

In several jurisdictions an extensive application of restorative models has occurred in which special arrangements have been made to include all relevant parties – the victim, the offender, their families, and community representatives – in collective decision making to agree a response to the offender's actions. From early initiatives in New Zealand and

Australia these procedures have been piloted in many other countries, although to date they have remained on the margins of other longer established sentencing procedures. Evaluation of such projects has typically shown that they produce higher levels of satisfaction for victims than the more impersonal proceedings of formal court hearings.

The various philosophies of punishment can be combined, so that a single sentence might represent an attempt to achieve several objectives at once. In some circumstances judges may enunciate this, indicating how they arrived at a given sentence by designating portions of it intended to serve different penal purposes (Ashworth, 2005, p. 73). The prevailing sentencing framework for England and Wales, the Criminal Justice Act of 2003, specifies the purposes of sentencing in a way that makes explicit the possibility of integrating different judicial purposes in a single sentencing decision (Taylor, Wasik & Leng, 2004), in a manner characterized by Ashworth (2005, p. 74) as a "pick-and-mix" approach. Details of the types and severity of sentences that can be applied to different offences are set out in a series of documents produced by the Sentencing Guidelines Council (2007), which also provides advice on clarifying the objectives of sentences (available on the Council's website). For Magistrates' Courts, sentencing decisions are accompanied by a **Sentencing Reasons Form** on which the bench stipulates the 'main points' of the sentence imposed.

The legal framework of courts, their sentencing powers, the sentencing options available to them, and many other features of criminal justice vary considerably between different countries and are subject to change over time. It is advisable for any psychologist working in the penal system to become familiar with the principal features of the context in which he or she is working. Numerous textbooks, websites and other information sources exist to facilitate this in virtually every country and there are also integrative volumes summarizing key attributes of criminal justice taking a comparative, international approach (e.g. Newman, Bouloukos & Cohen, 2001).

THE IMPACT OF SENTENCING

Is it possible to answer the question posed in the title of this chapter, and draw any firm conclusions about the usefulness of sentencing? As outlined earlier, to the extent that sentencing might have a solely retributive or 'non-consequentialist' purpose, its application does not involve an appeal to direct empirical testing, since there is no primary concern with outcome effects. If its purpose is meant to be expressive and symbolic, then as Garland (1990) has argued, those who seek to evaluate its effectiveness have somehow missed the point.

Other declared objectives of sentencing are potentially testable in principle, but there are variations in the extent to which doing so would be feasible in practice. To evaluate general deterrence, for example, societies are scarcely likely to embark on large-scale experiments in which they temporarily suspend their laws for hypothesis-testing purposes. This reluctance may lead us to conclude that it is the existence of criminal sanctions that holds society together; that it is only the general deterrent effect of the portfolio of state punishments that restrains citizens from more or less constantly violating each other's interests.

However, a partial test of general deterrence might be adduced from other sources. One is observation of what occurs when there is a breakdown of 'law and order' in society, for example during episodes of civil unrest. History is replete with relevant examples, and indeed rates of many crimes often do rise sharply during such episodes. When social order disintegrates, however, so many changes are happening in parallel that it is problematic to attribute the resultant 'lawlessness' to any one of them. In less extreme situations, it can be difficult to discern the role of criminal justice agencies as a component of the observed changes and their impact appears to be marginal. For example, following the downfall of communism in the then Soviet Union in the early 1990s and the social liberalization that ensued, there was a 50% rise in crime rates in a period of just two years (Gilinskiy, 2006).[2] But this was almost certainly a function of many influences, involving simultaneous economic, political and social change. The network of police and courts continued to operate in the same manner through this period, but had no observable restraining effect on a trend that was driven by other factors.

Perhaps more surprisingly, even when the police are not available to arrest wrong-doers – because they are on strike – there is no convincing evidence of upward surges in crime. There was a 'rash of crimes' following a one-day police strike in Montreal in 1969 (Clark, 1977), but apart from this instance other studies of industrial action by police do not support what has been called the 'thin blue line' hypothesis. There were public riots during a longer strike in Boston in 1919 but analysis suggests these events were about to happen in any case and would have done whether or not the police had gone on strike (White, 1988). Pfuhl (1983) analysed crime-rate data for police strikes in 11 US cities during the 1970s. Strikes ranged in duration from three to 30 days. While there were increases in rates of some crimes in some locations, in the majority there were no changes at all. Similarly, following a police strike in Finland in 1976 no upsurge in crime nor other social upheaval occurred (Makinen & Takala, 1980). Thus, our predilections notwithstanding, there is no overall pattern supportive of police presence as a major deterrent against crime.

A third type of evidence that calls into question the assumption of a general deterrent effect of sentencing emerges from studies of the death penalty. The usage of this most serious of sanctions is a highly emotive issue regardless of its exact outcomes. But the rationale for applying capital punishment is almost universally based on its expected deterrent effects. Amongst the 71 countries that still retained its use up to the year 2001, ". . . the most common political justification is the belief that it has a unique general deterrent capacity to save further innocent lives or reduce significantly other capital offences" (Hood, 2002, p. 209). However, systematic research has failed to find that the availability of the death penalty as a sentencing option has any clear suppressant effect on rates of the most serious crimes such as homicide. In a global survey conducted on behalf of the United Nations, Hood (2002) allocated different countries (or their constituent member states) to discrete categories according to their pattern of usage of capital punishment over a 40-year period. Some countries or states retained the use of the sentence throughout that epoch. Others had either not used it throughout the same

---

[2] Recorded crimes per 100 000 population rose from 1242 in 1990 to 1856 in 1992.

period, or at some point had formally abolished its use. Of specific interest, the US had an interlude when execution was not used (1967–1976, as a result of a moratorium and subsequent rulings by the Supreme Court), following which its use was resumed in 37 of the 50 states.

Examination of patterns of homicide and other capital crimes under these different jurisdictions yields no evidence that capital punishment is associated with reductions in their rate of occurrence. Even in Texas, "... by far the most active death penalty state" (Sorensen *et al.*, 1999, p. 483), analysis of crime statistics for the period 1984–1997 has found no relationship between the execution rate and the murder rate.

There are other sound reasons for suggesting that the presence of criminal sanctions is not necessarily the fundamental force that holds back a tide of lawbreaking on a daily basis. Firstly from an 'instrumental' standpoint, the majority of individuals obtained reward and satisfaction from their everyday involvement in routine, socially accepted activities in the domains of family, work and leisure. These entail deep and significant personal investment for virtually everyone, and whilst the patterning of this may be uneven and may sometimes present individuals with formidable challenges, in behavioural terms such activities are the source of a steady flow of positive reinforcement. Arguably, it is when such reinforcement schedules are substantially weakened (for example, through inconsistent parenting, family breakdown, school failure, unemployment, or specific aversive experiences) that individuals are susceptible to following other routes towards achieving goals. Several major criminological theories (e.g. *strain*, *differential association*, and *social learning* theories) are founded on these types of observations (McGuire, 2004a).

Secondly, there are clear 'normative' factors influencing individuals' self-regulation of their own conduct in society. Tyler (2006) has adduced strong evidence to suggest that the everyday law-abiding behaviour of most people is a function of their endorsement of the law and perception of its operation as legitimate, rather than their fear of detection and punishment. Tyler conducted a series of structured interviews with a random sample of 1575 respondents in Chicago, 804 of whom were re-interviewed one year later. Participants were asked about their experience and perceptions of the law, the extent of any contacts with the police or courts and various factors potentially linked to their behaviour. The key influence underpinning most individuals' adherence to lawful behaviour was their commitment to doing so, arising partly from personal morality and partly from beliefs in the appropriateness of laws. Thus where the law is perceived to have legitimacy, that is, where its rationale is considered sound and its operation perceived as fair, most citizens regularly and willingly act in accordance with it. Where individuals disagree with laws or experience their enactment as unjust, their compliance is reduced; some laws may then be difficult, even impossible, to enforce, *despite* the availability of punitive sanctions.

With reference to other penal philosophies it is possible to collect data that can subject them to outcome tests. This applies, for example, to incapacitation. Criminologists have constructed elaborate models for the evaluation of its crime-preventive effects. Doing so entails a type of modelling process, for example projecting from data on the numbers of dwellings broken into by the average burglar in a year, and estimating the number of crimes that would be prevented by sentencing larger numbers of house burglars to imprisonment. While the logic of this appears straightforward, the effects of incapacitation are much weaker than we might have supposed, and it proves a proportionately very expensive method of reducing crime. For example, applying such a model to England and Wales, Tarling (1993) concluded that even if the prison population were to be increased by 25%, the net effect on the rate of crime would be a decrease of just 1%. Similar conclusions were reached following time-series analysis of crime trends and imprisonment rates in California (Zimring & Hawkins, 1994).

The Effects of Criminal Sanctions

'Crime and punishment' are inextricably linked in our culture and within everyday discourse and public expectations. Notwithstanding the range of penal philosophies reviewed above, the presumed individual deterrent function of the sentence is arguably pivotal in perceptions of the process as a whole. "Whichever sentencing principles are used to decide the exact form and amount of punishment, there is a widespread assumption that the resulting punishment *will* deter the convicted offender from re-offending, or potential offenders from offending" (Easton & Piper, 2005, p. 101, italics in original). Given the central place allotted to punitive sanctions in the legal systems of the world, does the available evidence justify these ubiquitously held expectations that individuals will be deterred from future offending by the experience of official punishment? Several types of evidence indicate that these expectations are very badly misplaced.

If punitive sanctions reliably achieved individual or specific deterrence, it would be not unreasonable to expect the following. We might expect that there would be a relationship between the experience of punishment and what individuals say in relation to their behaviour as a result. We might expect there to be an association between the severity of sentences and recidivism outcomes, when other variables are held equal, with heavier penalties leading to larger effects. We might anticipate that in specially designed studies where some offenders are dealt with more severely, they would go on to commit fewer crimes. In a pattern that might at first appear counter-intuitive, none of these expectations is supported by the evidence that has been collected to date.

The first type of evidence is derived from what individuals say has had an impact on them and has influenced them to change their behaviour (where that occurred) after being arrested for offences such as theft or substance abuse. Klemke (1982) interviewed young people some time after their first arrest to explore levels of subsequent involvement in offending. Individuals who had desisted from offending were very unlikely to attribute this to any deterrent effect of their contacts with the criminal justice system. Of course, some researchers would regard self-report data of this kind as a rather weak form of evidence, given variables such as impression management, fear of arrest and other factors potentially at work.

A second type of evidence is likely to be regarded as more robust, being based on officially recorded statistics: patterns of re-conviction following different types of sentences, usually involving very large samples. These data are of particular interest as they allow comparisons to be made between *actual* offence rates and those that would be *expected*, based on predictions made by using a specially designed scale to assess risk of re-offending, derived from information on individuals' previous criminal histories. The **Offender Group Reconviction Scale** (now in Version 2: OGRS-2) was developed for this purpose, but when Lloyd, Mair & Hough (1994) and later Kershaw (1999) used it to compare the impact of different types of sentences (e.g. imprisonment versus community penalties), they found that rates of recidivism two years later were virtually identical. Patterns of subsequent criminality appeared wholly unaffected by the type of punishment imposed. There was no evidence that the more severe sanction had any suppressant or punitive effect. Similarly, in a large-scale review for the Solicitor General of Canada, integrating data from 23 studies and with an aggregate sample of 68 248, Gendreau, Goggin & Cullen (1999) found no clear relationship between the lengths of prison sentences and rates of subsequent recidivism, once other differences between samples were taken into account.

But perhaps the strongest kind of test of the deterrence hypothesis comes from specially designed experiments in which the intervention consists of 'enhanced' (i.e. harsher) punishments whilst the comparison sample receives 'business as usual' in the criminal justice system. There have been numerous studies of this type, and they more or less uniformly show that the net effects of dealing with offenders in this way are either absent (the effect size is zero) or actually negative; that is, people 'got worse' and committed more crimes (Gendreau *et al.*, 2001; and see McGuire, 2004a).

If we accept this evidence and conclude that deterrent effects are either very weak, simply non-existent, or actually harmful, we may be left with what looks like a paradox. Most people assume that the unpleasantness of being punished for doing something is likely to reduce our chances of doing it. Behavioural psychology has demonstrated the power of reinforcement and punishment in shaping patterns of human behaviour. But research in that field has also shown that for punishment to work efficiently, certain conditions have to be met. For example in order to be effective, it should be virtually certain to happen and should follow swiftly on the problem behaviour to be reduced. These circumstances are rarely if ever met in the criminal justice system, and other evidence suggests that individuals on the verge of committing crimes are unlikely to be thinking in any detailed way about the possible negative consequences of their actions (McGuire, 2004a).

REDUCING OFFENDING BEHAVIOUR THROUGH PSYCHOSOCIAL INTERVENTIONS

Fortunately there are other approaches to addressing the problem of offender recidivism at the individual level that have emerged as more effective than official sanctions. This field of activity is sometimes denoted as **tertiary prevention** (Gendreau & Andrews, 1990) as it focuses on adjudicated offenders – those who have been convicted of crimes and duly sentenced.[3] More colloquially, drawing on the title of a journal paper by Martinson (1974) which famously drew negative conclusions regarding early evidence on offender rehabilitation, it is often referred to simply as 'What Works'.

The discussion of this within social science is often very hard to separate from moral, political and philosophical dimensions of the same issue. For many people, their opinions

---

[3] This is sometimes contrasted with primary prevention, which is focused on long-term developmental family- and community-based initiatives (see for example Farrington & Welsh, 2007) and secondary prevention, which focuses on work with groups considered to be already 'at risk' of involvement in delinquency (see for example Goldstein, 2002).

concerning how society should deal with offenders are influenced by their broader beliefs on other social questions. In journalistic terms this is sometimes called the 'law-and-order' debate, and it can be very difficult to distinguish the relevant empirical evidence from other aspects of it, and decide how that evidence could be used realistically to inform the administration of justice. There has been continuing controversy over whether it is possible to change the behaviour of those who have been persistently involved in crime.

However, the systematic study of criminal sentencing and of the treatment of offenders took a sizeable stride forward some years ago when several review studies were published based on the application of statistical integration or **meta-analysis** of research findings. Since its initial use in the field of criminal justice in 1985, this approach has been employed in a number of reviews of treatment-outcome studies with offenders (Wilson, 2001). By late 2007, a total of 65 meta-analyses of tertiary-level offender treatment had been published. While much research remains to be done, the cumulative findings of this work provide some firm indications concerning which approaches to working with offenders are most likely to yield intended outcomes in terms of reduced criminal recidivism.

The Evidence Base

The majority of the reviews conducted in this field, and the bulk of the primary research on which they are based, originate from North America, although data from many countries are encompassed within them. Several have been conducted in Europe, and these have been reviewed separately, as a validation or generalizability test of the American results (Redondo, Sánchez-Meca & Garrido, 2002). Most are published in the English language, but in the largest review so far conducted (Pearson, Lipton & Cleland, 1997), contacts were made with 14 non-English speaking countries and more than 300 reports were obtained in languages other than English.

Not surprisingly given that most crimes are committed by men, the overwhelming majority of the primary studies deals with male offenders. In one of the largest meta-analyses, carried out by Lipsey (1992, 1995), only 3% of published studies focused exclusively on samples of female offenders. With regard to age, roughly two-thirds of the reviews focus on interventions with adolescent or young adult offenders in the age range 14 to 21 years. This covers the peak age for delinquency in most countries. The remaining studies are either concerned exclusively with adults, or include offenders across a wide range of ages. Concerning ethnicity, while many studies provide data on the proportions of offenders from different ethnic groups, the pattern of this is variable and it is not consistently recorded. However given the over-representation of minority communities under criminal justice jurisdiction in many countries, these findings are based on populations containing a broad mixture in terms of ethnicity.

Research in this area involves experts from many disciplines. Some reviewers have coded the professional backgrounds of those who undertook the primary studies. For example, Lipsey & Wilson (1998) reviewed 200 reports on the outcomes of work with serious and violent young offenders. Amongst these studies, they found that 29% of the senior authors were from psychology and 19% from criminology. For a further 28% of the studies, no main discipline was identifiable. Other backgrounds represented to varying degrees included sociology, education, psychiatry, political science, and social work.

Findings of the Reviews

The first meta-analysis published in this field was an evaluation of the impact of institutionally-based interventions for juvenile offenders. Garrett (1985) surveyed 111 studies conducted in the period 1960–1984, describing residential treatment programmes. Altogether, 13 055 individuals with a mean age of 15.8 years were participants in these studies. Since then, several meta-analyses have been conducted covering a wide range of interventions with young offenders, including community as well as residential settings. Other reviews have focused on specific types of offence (driving while intoxicated, violence, sexual assault, substance abuse). Several have focused on different types of punitive sanctions, such as intermediate punishment and 'scared straight' interventions, correctional boot camps, and outdoor-pursuit, wilderness-challenge schemes.

The focus in other reviews has been on the relative impact of different intervention methods. Reviews have dealt with educational and vocational programmes; with the impact of specially designed socio-therapeutic prison regimes in Germany; and with the effects of therapeutic communities defined in broader terms. There is a meta-analysis on the importance of addressing cognition as a mediating variable in behavioural change, several on the effectiveness of structured cognitive-behavioural programmes, and others of family-based interventions and school-based interventions respectively. Meta-analysis has also been used to synthesize findings from evaluations of restorative justice and victim-offender mediation.

Moderator variables, including (as we saw earlier) the impact of age, gender and ethnicity and the importance of staff skills and other aspects of organizational practices, have also been reviewed in this way. Table 11.1 shows the numbers of meta-analytic reviews addressing different topics, though it should be noted that this listing represents the prime area of interest in each case and many of the reviews focus on more than one type of issue.

- Young offenders 12
- Cognitive-behavioural methods 7
- Sex offenders 6
- Deterrence/Sanctions 5
- European studies 5
- Family interventions 4
- Restorative justice/mediation 4
- Substance-abuse 3
- CDATE project (all studies) 2
- Educational/vocational 2
- School-based interventions 2
- Cognitive vs. non-cognitive 1
- Drink-driving 1
- Violence/domestic violence 1
- Principles of Human Service 1
- Skills training 1
- Relapse prevention 1
- Personality disorder 1
- Therapeutic communities 1
- Age as a moderator 1
- Gender as a moderator 1
- Ethnicity as a moderator 1
- Staff skills & practice 1
- Treatment integrity 1

Table 11.1: Numbers of meta-analyses focused on different populations or issues (total 65 reviews)

In meta-analysis, the principal outcome of interest is known as the **effect size**. This can be represented in various ways, but the function in each case is the same: to provide a measure of the extent of any difference between 'experimental' and 'control' conditions in an intervention study. There are different methods of calculating effect sizes, and given the complexities of meta-analysis, some researchers have been critical of it. McGuire (2004a) provides an overview of these issues, and of how effect sizes can be interpreted and compared.

The overall finding from meta-analysis of offender treatment sharply contradicts the once commonly repeated assertion that 'nothing works' (Hollin, 2001; McGuire, 2004a). The impact of psychosocial interventions on criminal recidivism is on average positive, that is, it is associated with a net reduction in re-offending rates in experimental relative to comparison samples. However, the average effect taken across a broad spectrum of different types of treatment or intervention is relatively modest. Expressed as a correlation coefficient, it is estimated on average to be approximately 0.10. This average finding obtained from the meta-analyses corresponds to recidivism rates of 45% for experimental groups, and 55% for control groups, respectively. Though this figure is low, it is statistically significant and it compares reasonably well with effects found in many other fields. Some healthcare interventions that are generally regarded as producing worthwhile benefits have lower mean treatment effects. But crucially, when different sub-groups of studies are compared, the variations between them show some consistent patterns that prove to be much more informative in illuminating aspects of intervention associated with higher rates of success.

There are some notable trends within the meta-analytic findings, but the following can be highlighted as emerging most clearly. On average, it has been found that effect sizes are larger for adolescent and for adult offenders than for those in what is usually called the 'young adult' age range (15–18). On balance, with other factors held equal, community-based interventions have larger effect sizes than those delivered in institutions: the ratio of relative effect sizes obtained has ranged from approximately 1.33/1 to as high as 1.75/1. There are some complex interaction effects between criminal justice settings, types of interventions, and their quality of delivery. The best-designed services have their optimal benefit when provided in a non-custodial location. But even well designed interventions can have zero, possibly even negative effects if the quality of delivery is poor.

There is now a widespread consensus that it is possible to maximize effect sizes by combining a number of elements in offender programmes (Andrews, 2001; Gendreau, 1996; Hollin, 1999). Effective interventions are thought to possess certain common features which Andrews and his colleagues (Andrews *et al.*, 1990), in an early but highly influential review, called 'principles of human service', or alternatively formulated as the *Risk-Needs-Responsivity* (RNR) model (Andrews, Bonta & Wormith, 2006). When Andrews and his associates pinpointed those features that contributed separately to enhancing effect size, they found that the combination of them produced an additive effect. Interventions that possessed these features yielded an average reduction in recidivism rates of 53%. So although the mean effect size across all studies is not especially large, when interventions are appropriately designed and delivered it is possible to secure much larger effects.

A selection of effect sizes is displayed in Figure 11.1. This shows the extent of variation derived from different types of interventions. If it were the case that 'nothing works', this graph would be rather simple: the horizontal bars would be absent or

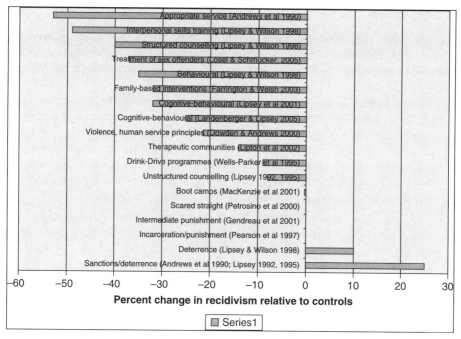

Figure 11.1: Selected Effect Sizes for Psychosocial Interventions

minimal, and closely clustered around the vertical zero effect size line. In fact there are some markedly divergent outcomes. As discussed in the earlier part of this chapter, deterrent sanctions overall have nil or even negative effects (they are associated with net increases in recidivism). Some interventions have positive but rather weak effects, whereas others have effects that are both statistically and practically meaningful in terms of reductions in rates of re-offending.

Probably the most widely disseminated innovation flowing from the above findings has been the synthesis of methods and materials into a number of pre-arranged formats known as **programmes**. This word sounds sinister to some people as it conjures up images of a rigid and insensitive method of working. But strictly defined, a programme consists simply of a planned sequence of learning opportunities (McGuire, 2001). Used in criminal justice settings, its general objective is to reduce participants' subsequent criminal recidivism. Within that context, the typical programme is a pre-arranged set of activities, with clearly stated objectives, entailing a number of elements inter-connected according to a planned design, which can be reproduced on successive occasions.

The largest single part played by psychologists in translating research findings into practice has been in designing structured programmes for use in this way (see Hollin & Palmer, 2006). Most such programmes currently employed in the criminal justice system use methods derived from cognitive social learning theory and are known as **cognitive-behavioural** interventions. While this is far from being the only theoretical option available, to date it has been most consistent in yielding positive outcomes. Programmes of this type are usually supported by a specially prepared manual.

Messages for Effective Practice

Expert reviewers agree that there are certain features of criminal justice interventions that maximize the likelihood of securing a practical, meaningful impact in terms of reduced re-offending. The major findings that arise from this include the following:

- *Theory and evidence base.* Intervention efforts are more likely to succeed if they are based on a theory of criminal behaviour that is conceptually sound and has good empirical support. This provides a rationale for the methods that are used and the 'vehicle of change' considered to be at work when an individual participates in the programme. This might be accomplished, for example, by learning new skills, changing attitudes, improving ability to communicate, increasing self-knowledge, solving problems, or overcoming bad feelings.

- *Risk level.* It is generally regarded as good practice to assess risk levels and allocate individuals to different levels of service accordingly. Risk assessment is usually based on information about an individual's criminal history, such as the age at which he or she was first convicted of a crime, and the total number of convictions to date. The most intensive types of intervention should be reserved for those offenders assessed as posing the highest risk of re-offending; individuals estimated as posing a low risk should not be exposed to such interventions. This has been called the *risk principle* (Andrews & Bonta, 2003).

- *Risk-need factors as targets of change.* Research on the emergence of delinquency suggests that certain patterns of social interaction, social or cognitive skills, attitudes, the influence of delinquent peer groups, and other factors are associated with its onset and maintenance. If work with offenders is to make a difference to their prospects of re-offending, those variables should be its targets of change; they are factors that need to be addressed to alter offending and are therefore entitled **criminogenic needs**. Given their susceptibility to change they are sometimes called **dynamic risk factors** and there are strong reasons for prioritizing them in rehabilitation services.

- *Multiple targets.* Given the multiple factors known to contribute to criminal activity, there is virtual unanimity amongst researchers that more effective interventions will comprise a number of ingredients, addressed at a range of the aforementioned risks. Interventions that successfully do this are called **multimodal**. For example, working with a group of persistent young offenders might involve training them in social skills, learning self-control of impulses, and providing support for these changes through a mentoring scheme.

- *Responsivity.* There are certain methods or approaches that have a superior record in engaging, motivating and helping participants in criminal justice interventions to change (Andrews, 2001; Gendreau & Andrews, 1990; McMurran, 2002). There are two aspects of this. First, rehabilitative efforts will work better if they have clear, concrete objectives, their contents are structured, and there is a focus on activity and the acquisition of skills. Personnel involved in providing this should possess high quality interpersonal skills and foster supportive, collaborative relationships within clearly explained boundaries (*general responsivity*). Second, it is vital to adapt intervention strategies to accommodate diversity amongst participants with respect to age, gender, ethnicity, language, and learning styles (*specific responsivity*).

- *Integrity.* Lipsey (1995) and other meta-analysts have noted that intervention services appear to work better when they are being actively researched. Regular collection of data on how an intervention is delivered sustains its clarity of purpose, and its adherence to the methods it was intended to deploy. This feature is called the *integrity* or *fidelity* of an intervention (Bernfeld, 2001; Hollin, 1995) and in the best intervention services it is regularly monitored and checked.

To provide the most favourable conditions for the delivery of the above kinds of services, many other ingredients should be in place, for example, to ensure the validity of the assessment methods used, and the thoroughness of monitoring and evaluation procedures, alongside larger-scale strategies for managing the implementation of services within the provider agency (for fuller discussion, see Andrews, 2001).

Examples of Effective Interventions

There are some variations, but also important overlaps, between the kinds of interventions shown to have the largest impact on young and adult offenders respectively. For young offenders who have committed more serious offences, applying results from his own meta-analysis Lipsey (1995) recommended that intervention programmes generally need to be provided for a duration of not less than six months, with a minimum of two contacts per week. On the basis of several reviews, several methods have emerged as more likely to be effective for working with this group (Dowden & Andrews, 1999; Lipsey & Wilson, 1998):

EFFECTIVE INTERVENTIONS

- **Interpersonal skills training.** This consists of a series of exercises designed to improve participants' skills in interacting with others. Working in a small group, individuals identify situations in which they are not sure how to act, or which they sometimes mishandle, for example giving into pressure applied by others. Suitable ways of managing the situation are discussed, then practised using role play, plus practice and feedback.

- **Behavioural interventions.** In work with offenders this has included contingency contracts, where individual offenders and their supervisors compose a list of problem behaviours and a system of rewards for progress in modifying them. Behavioural training procedures such as modelling and graduated practice form part of many other types of interventions.

- **Cognitive skills training.** There are several programmes of this type. Most consist of a series of structured sessions, each containing exercises designed to help participants acquire or develop their abilities in the domain of thinking about and solving everyday (usually interpersonal) problems. Typical material includes work on putting an everyday problem into words, gathering

---

(Continued)

information about it, generating possible solutions, linking means and ends, anticipating consequences, making decisions, and allied skills.

- **Structured individual counselling.** In its most widely used format, counselling is a relatively unstructured activity, in which the counsellor acts in a person-centred, non-directive manner, allowing the client to take the lead. This can be valuable for a number of purposes, but it has not emerged as an effective means of reducing offender recidivism. In order for it to work in that context, research suggests it needs to be more directive and structured, and based on a 'reality therapy' or 'problem-solving' framework.

- **Teaching family homes.** These are residential units or group homes in which specially trained adults work in pairs as 'teaching parents'. Their role is to develop positive working alliances with residents, impart a range of social and self-management skills, and provide counselling and advocacy services. Young people can continue to attend school and return to their homes-of-origin at weekends.

The largest effect sizes published so far have been obtained from *Functional Family Therapy*, *Parenting Wisely*, family empowerment, and similar therapeutic approaches which involve working with young offenders and their families. The most elaborate approach is *Multi-Systemic Therapy* (MST) which comprises work with the young person, his or her family and school staff (Henggeler *et al.*, 1998).

For adult offenders, as mentioned earlier average effect sizes are generally lower than for those at the younger age range. Nevertheless results are meaningful in practice, and comparable patterns emerge in respect of the types of intervention most likely to work. With this age group, with the exception of domestic violence programmes, family-based work is uncommon and interventions are almost exclusively conducted with individuals themselves, though often employing a group format.

- The best-validated and most widely disseminated approaches involve 'manualized' cognitive-behavioural programmes focused on risk factors for criminal recidivism (Lipsey, Chapman & Landenberger 2001; Lipton *et al.*, 2002a; Tong & Farrington, 2004; Wilson, Bouffard & MacKenzie, 2005). Variants of the approach have been well supported primarily for individuals with mixed patterns of offending that may include property, violent, and substance-related crimes (Hollin, 2001; McGuire, 2006; Motiuk & Serin, 2001).

- Specially designed programmes with additional components have been developed for adults who have committed violent offences. This may include a focus on anger control, modulation of moods, and recognition and self-management of risk (Bush, 1995; Henning & Frueh, 1996). While there have been some very strong findings from anger management programmes, such as those of Dowden, Blanchette and Serin (1999) who reported an 86% reduction in violent re-offending over a 3-year follow-up with high-risk prisoners in Canada, in other instances treatment gains have been very marginal and more research is need on the appropriateness of allocation to this type of programme and the related issue of 'readiness to change'.

- For men who have committed domestic violence offences, to achieve successful outcomes further sessions need to be included examining perceptions of male and female roles, beliefs concerning responsibility for actions, or concepts of masculinity (Dobash & Dobash, 2000).

- Still further ingredients are added in work with individuals who have committed sexual offences, the vast majority of whom are male. In addition to cognitive and social skills training and similar activities, these interventions usually also include a focus on deviant sexual arousal, cognitive distortions, empathy training and other sessions designed to address the established risk factors for this kind of offence. The precise contents may vary further according to specific types of offence, differentiated mainly by whether victims are children or adult women (Marshall *et al.*, 2006).

- For offenders with lengthy histories of substance abuse, therapeutic communities have been shown to be beneficial. These may be located in institutions or in the wider community and there are several different models on which they can be based (Lipton *et al.*, 2002b). Other multi-modal, integrated programmes containing several ingredients have also demonstrated good effects for reducing substance misuse (Springer, McNeece & Arnold, 2003).

Many of the above programmes, and the majority that are in most widespread use, are delivered in a group format, which has potential advantages in terms of including larger numbers of participants, achieving greater cost-efficiency in services, and also in generating additional 'change factors' that can enhance the effects of some of the methods employed (Bieling, McCabe & Antony, 2006). However, a large proportion of the work done with many people who have broken the law takes place on an individual basis. The following two published case studies illustrate applications of psychologically-based methods to the reduction of different types of offending behaviour.

CASE STUDY

'Diane'

Aust (1987) described working alongside a psychologist in order to help Diane, a young woman given a suspended prison sentence and placed on probation after a series of shoplifting offences. Assessment indicated that she had committed numerous shop thefts and despite having been arrested and sentenced on several previous occasions, felt unable to control her urges to steal, which had been a feature of her life since the age of 16. She described a cycle of elation and compulsion when in shops but at other times suffered from depressed moods. Diane had two children and was now expecting a third, and was highly distressed by the imminent prospect, should she re-offend, of giving birth to her child in prison.

Diane, her probation officer and the psychologist worked out an intervention plan to help her overcome her compulsive stealing. This had two main components. One was **covert sensitization**, a behaviour therapy procedure that in Diane's case entailed recording an audiotape in which she told herself the story of being arrested, with all its dreaded consequences. The power of this was such that she simply had to

(Continued)

look at it rather than listen to it in order for it to have its effects. The second was practice of several techniques of **self-management,** which included a range of actions such as drawing the attention of staff whenever she went shopping, for example, by asking them to show her where an item was; keeping receipts as a record of purchases; avoided wearing clothes in which she could conceal items; and using a large, transparent carrier bag. While she implemented these changes, she also joined gym sessions, which helped raise her self-esteem and underlying moods, providing an alternative to the 'buzz' of shoplifting. At her subsequent appearance in court, the judge deferred sentence for six months to allow her to work on this plan; at the end of this period, she had successfully avoided shop theft and gained a new equilibrium in having reduced her impulses and replaced them with new patterns of behaviour. It is interesting to place this study in the context of research carried out by Carroll & Weaver (1986) who found remarkably different patterns of cognitions amongst a group of 'expert' shoplifters as compared with a 'novice' group.

CASE STUDY

Working with a very different type of offence, but also employing behavioural methods, Marshall (2006) has described a treatment programme carried out with Bill, a 38-year-old lorry driver who had convictions for sexual offences against children. Over a period of 20 years he had molested eight girls aged between 6 and 10 years old. He was given early release from prison on condition that he attend for treatment at a community-based clinic. Bill's history showed a pattern of sexual fantasies concerning younger girls, and of failure in his relationships with females closer to his age, feeling he had been humiliated in these encounters. As an only child who had grown up in an isolated rural area, his development was characterized by very limited social contacts and more extensive assessment showed negative attitudes towards women, some distortions in his views of children whom he saw as submissive but also as provocative, and an undervaluing of himself. Assessment by phallometry (penile plethysmograph or PPG) showed a pattern of strongest arousal to children but some evidence of arousal to adult women.

Intervention with Bill involved a multi-faceted programme that focused on a series of areas including reduction of his sexual interest in children. This was approached by means of a combination of **olfactory aversion therapy,** in which he learned to associate sexual arousal to children with a foul odour in a series of 40 conditioning trials over a four-week period; and **directed masturbation** associated with images of adult women. These interventions were accompanied by a separate series of sessions of cognitive restructuring, designed to address attitudes and beliefs he held that were supportive of offending. The treatment programme proved to be effective in altering both Bill's sexual preferences and his habitual thoughts and feelings and a follow-up over two years indicated that the changes were sustained. By that point in time, he had developed a stable relationship with an adult female partner.

Psychological Contributions to Offender Assessment and Management

Forensic psychologists working in prisons, probation or youth justice settings have progressively extended their roles from their previous 'niche' focused more-or-less exclusively on assessment and allocation, to a broader function in which they now contribute to risk assessment, delivery of interventions at the individual level, design and evaluation of programmes, report-writing, and research on all of these issues.

In recent years the **risk-need-responsivity** framework has been used to construct a number of more complex in-depth assessment instruments for prediction of future involvement in crime. Several scales now exist for combined assessment of *static* and *dynamic* risk factors. The former refers to factors that are fixed at a given point in time (for example, an individual's age on first appearance in court). The latter refers to influences that fluctuate over time and are also potentially susceptible to change through intervention (for example, antisocial attitudes or problem-solving skills). Probably the best-known example of an assessment combining this spectrum of variables is the **Level of Service/Case Management Inventory** (*LS/CMI*; Andrews, Bonta & Wormith, 2004). However, there are numerous specialized methods of carrying out this work for general case-management purposes (for an overview, see Hollin 2002). This type of approach, based on amalgamation of variables is widely perceived as having more practical value than any single theoretical model. In addition to yielding predictions of the likelihood of re-offending, these approaches also generate information that can be applied in risk management, identifying target areas on which psychologists and other criminal justice staff can focus in their work with individual offenders.

There are also numerous specialized methods for undertaking risk assessment with reference to specific types of offence, such as violence, sexual offending, and domestic violence; and for assessment of mental disorders that have been shown to be associated with criminal conduct, most notably, psychopathy or antisocial personality disorder. Given the seriousness of crimes committed by some individuals who have enduring personality difficulties such as patterns of callousness or irresponsibility, the use of these types of assessments has attracted a great deal of attention, and also controversy with regard to the accuracy of the methods, and the ethical issues raised by their use (McGuire, 2004b).

Psychologically based research and other approaches in criminology linked to it have made enormous strides over approximately the last two decades, with respect to developing an understanding of: the factors that contribute to criminal behaviour, the traditional and entrenched practices that have no impact on it, and methods that can genuinely help reduce the chances of its recurrence. None of this has achieved a state of perfection of course, but the advances made have been significant nevertheless. Given this accumulated knowledge base, coupled with the level of public and governmental concern over crime, there remains a surprisingly large gap between this acquired information and everyday practice in many criminal justice agencies. The widespread perception that seeking to understand individual factors in crime implies that psychologists believe those are the *only* factors takes a very long time to dissipate. Apart from further research and knowledge accumulation then, a sizeable challenge remains in translating available findings judiciously into practice, and convincing other concerned parties that psychology has something valuable to offer in this field.

SUMMARY

- The principal objectives of sentencing in courts of law are: retribution/desert, incapacitation, deterrence, rehabilitation, and restoration/reparation. The rationale for each has been discussed.
- An overview has been provided of the effects of penal sentences and of the evidence for sanctions and deterrence.
- An outline of the evidence has been provided of the impact of psychosocial interventions on criminal behaviour, including a summary of the findings of 66 meta-analytic reviews.
- The implications for practice in criminal justice and allied agencies are surveyed.
- Illustrations of the types of interventions that have been shown to be effective in reducing offending behaviour are provided, including group programmes and individual case studies.
- Some of the current psychological contributions to offender assessment and management are briefly described.

ESSAY/DISCUSSION QUESTIONS

1. Summarize the main arguments for the use of punishment as the principal component of society's response to criminal offending. Explain whether, in your view, some approaches to this have a sounder basis than others.

2. Evaluate evidence concerning the extent to which those who have repeatedly broken the criminal law can be 'rehabilitated' using psychosocial interventions. Give your views on whether this evidence might be of interest to policy makers in criminal justice.

3. Psychological research on offending and how to reduce it has tended to focus on serious crimes such as violence and sexual assault, or on the links between crime and mental disorder. Do you consider that this is the case? If so, what in your view are the reasons for it and are they justifiable?

4. Briefly survey current applications of psychological knowledge in the penal system and roles psychologists play within it. Propose possible extensions to these applications and roles, and provide appropriate justifications for them.

REFERENCES

Andrews, D.A. (2001). Principles of effective correctional programs. In L.L. Motiuk & R.C. Serin (Eds), *Compendium 2000 on effective correctional programming*. Ottawa: Correctional Service Canada.

Andrews, D.A. & Bonta, J. (2006). *The psychology of criminal conduct* (4th edn). Cincinnati, OH: Anderson Publishing Co.

Andrews, D.A., Bonta, J., & Wormith, J.S. (2004). *Level of service/case management inventory (LS/CMI)*. Toronto: Multi-Health Systems.

Andrews, D.A., Bonta, J., & Wormith, J.S. (2006). The recent past and near future of risk and/or need assessment. *Crime and Delinquency*, *52*, 7–27.

Andrews, D.A., Zinger, I., Hoge, R.D. *et al*. (1990). Does correctional treatment work? A clinically relevant and psychologically informed meta-analysis. *Criminology*, *28*, 369–404.

Ashworth, A. (2005). *Sentencing and criminal justice* (4th edn). Cambridge: Cambridge University Press.

Aust, A. (1987). Gaining control of compulsive shop theft. *National Association of Probation Officers' Journal*, 145–146.

Bernfeld, G.A. (2001). The struggle for treatment integrity in a 'dis-integrated' service delivery system. In G.A. Bernfeld, D.P. Farrington, & A.W. Leschied (Eds), *Offender rehabilitation in practice: Implementing and evaluating effective programs*. Chichester: John Wiley & Sons.

Bieling, P.J., McCabe, R.E., & Antony, M.M. (2006). *Cognitive-Behavioral Therapy in Groups*. New York, NY: Guilford Press.

Bush, J. (1995). Teaching self-risk-management to violent offenders. In J. McGuire (Ed.), *What works: Reducing reoffending: Guidelines from research and practice*. Chichester: John Wiley & Sons.

Carroll, J. & Weaver, F. (1986). Shoplifters' perceptions of crime opportunities: a process-tracing study. In D.B. Cornish & R.V. Clarke (Eds), *The reasoning criminal: Rational choice perspectives on offending*. New York, NY: Springer-Verlag.

Clark, G. (1977). What happens when the police strike? In R.M. Ayres & T.L. Wheelen (Eds), *Collective bargaining in the public sector: Selected readings in law enforcement*. Alexandria, VA: International Association of Chiefs of Police.

Dobash, R.E. & Dobash, R P. (2000). Evaluating criminal justice interventions for domestic violence. *Crime and Delinquency*, *46*, 252–270.

Dowden, C. & Andrews, D.A. (1999). What works in young offender treatment: a meta-analysis. *Forum on Corrections Research*, *11*, 21–24.

Dowden, C., Blanchette, K., & Serin, R.C. (1999). Anger management programming for federal male inmates: An effective intervention. *Research Report R-82*. Ottawa, ON: Correctional Service of Canada.

Duff, R.A. & Garland, D. (Eds) (1994). *A reader on punishment*. Oxford: Oxford University Press.

Easton, S. & Piper, C. (2005). *Sentencing and punishment: The quest for justice*. Oxford: Oxford University Press.

Farrington, D.P. & Welsh, B.C. (2007). *Saving children from a life of crime: Early risk factors and effective interventions*. New York, NY: Oxford University Press.

Garland, D. (1990). *Punishment and modern society: A study in social theory*. Oxford: Clarendon Press.

Garrett, C.G. (1985). Effects of residential treatment on adjudicated delinquents: A meta-analysis. *Journal of Research in Crime and Delinquency*, *22*, 287–308.

Gendreau, P. (1996). Offender rehabilitation: What we know and what needs to be done. *Criminal Justice and Behavior*, *23*, 144–161.

Gendreau, P. & Andrews, D.A. (1990). Tertiary prevention: what the meta-analyses of the offender treatment literature tell us about 'what works'. *Canadian Journal of Criminology*, *32*, 173–184.

Gendreau, P., Goggin, C., & Cullen, F.T. (1999). *The effects of prison sentences on recidivism*. Report to the Corrections Research and Development and Aboriginal Policy Branch. Ottawa: Solicitor General of Canada.

Gendreau, P., Goggin, C., Cullen, F.T., & Paparozzi, M. (2001). The effects of community sanctions and incarceration on recidivism. In L.L. Motiuk & R.C. Serin (Eds), *Compendium 2000 on effective correctional programming*. Ottawa: Correctional Service Canada.

Gibbs, J.P. (1986). Deterrence theory and research. In G.B. Melton (Ed.), *The law as a behavioral instrument: Nebraska symposium on motivation 1985*. Lincoln/London: University of Nebraska Press.

Gilinskiy, Y. (2006). Crime in contemporary Russia. *European Journal of Criminology*, 3, 259–292.

Goldstein, A.P. (2002). Low-level aggression: Definition, escalation, intervention. In J. McGuire (Ed.), *Offender rehabilitation and treatment: Effective programmes and policies to reduce re-offending*. Chichester: John Wiley & Sons.

Henggeler, S.W., Schoenwald, S.K., Borduin, C.M. *et al.* (1998). *Multisystemic treatment of antisocial behavior in children and adolescents*. New York, NY: Guilford Press.

Henning, K.R. & Frueh, B.C. (1996). Cognitive-behavioral treatment of incarcerated offenders: An evaluation of the Vermont Department of Corrections' Cognitive Self-Change Program. *Criminal Justice and Behavior*, 23, 523–542.

Hollin, C.R. (1995). The meaning and implications of program integrity. In J. McGuire (Ed.), *What works: Reducing reoffending: Guidelines from research and practice*. Chichester: John Wiley & Sons.

Hollin, C.R. (1999). Treatment programmes for offenders: Meta-analysis, 'what works', and beyond. *International Journal of Law and Psychiatry*, 22, 361–371.

Hollin, C.R. (2001). To treat or not to treat? An historical perspective. In C.R. Hollin (Ed.), *Handbook of offender assessment and treatment*. Chichester: John Wiley & Sons.

Hollin, C.R. (2002). Risk-needs assessment and allocation to offender programmes. In J. McGuire (Ed.), *Offender rehabilitation and treatment: Effective programmes and policies to reduce re-offending*. Chichester: John Wiley & Sons.

Hollin, C.R. & Palmer, E.J. (Eds) (2006). *Offending behaviour programmes: Development, application, and controversies*. Chichester: John Wiley & Sons.

Hood, R. (2002). *The death penalty: A worldwide perspective* (3rd edn). Oxford: Oxford University Press.

Kershaw, C. (1999). *Reconviction of offenders sentenced or released from prison in 1994*. Research Findings No. 90. London: Home Office Research, Development and Statistics Directorate.

Klemke, L.W. (1982). Reassessment of Cameron's apprehension-termination of shoplifting finding. *California Sociologist*, 5, 88–95.

Lipsey, M.W. (1992). Juvenile delinquency treatment: A meta-analytic inquiry into the variability of effects. In T. Cook, D. Cooper, H. Corday, *et al.* (Eds), *Meta-analysis for explanation: A casebook*. New York, NY: Russell Sage Foundation.

Lipsey, M.W. (1995). What do we learn from 400 studies on the effectiveness of treatment with juvenile delinquents? In J. McGuire (Ed.), *What works: Reducing re-offending: Guidelines from research and practice*. Chichester: John Wiley & Sons.

Lipsey, M.W., Chapman, G.L., & Landenberger, N.A. (2001). Cognitive-behavioral programs for offenders. *Annals of the American Academy of Political and Social Science*, 578, 144–157.

Lipsey, M.W. & Wilson, D.B. (1998). Effective intervention for serious juvenile offenders: A synthesis of research. In R. Loeber & D.P. Farrington (Eds), *Serious & violent juvenile offenders: Risk factors and successful interventions*. Thousand Oaks, CA: Sage Publications.

Lipton, D.S., Pearson, F.S., Cleland, C.M., & Yee, D. (2002a). The effects of therapeutic communities and milieu therapy on recidivism. In J. McGuire (Ed.), *Offender rehabilitation and treatment: Effective programmes and policies to reduce re-offending.* Chichester: John Wiley & Sons.

Lipton, D.S., Pearson, F.S., Cleland, C.M., & Yee, D. (2002b). The effectiveness of cognitive-behavioural treatment methods on recidivism. In J. McGuire (Ed.), *Offender rehabilitation and treatment: Effective programmes and policies to reduce re-offending.* Chichester: John Wiley & Sons.

Lloyd, C., Mair, G., & Hough, M. (1994). *Explaining reconviction rates: A critical analysis.* Home Office Research Study No. 136. London: HMSO.

Makinen, T. & Takala, H. (1980). 1976 police strike in Finland. In R. Hauge (Ed.), *Policing Scandinavia.* Oslo: Universitetsforlaget.

Marshall, W.L. (2006). Olfactory aversion and directed masturbation in the modification of deviant sexual preferences: A case study of a child molester. *Clinical Case Studies, 5,* 3–14.

Marshall, W.L., Fernandez, Y.M., Marshall, L.E., & Serran, G.A. (2006). *Sexual offender treatment: Controversial issues.* Chichester: John Wiley & Sons.

Martinson, R. (1974). What works? – Questions and answers about prison reform. *The Public Interest, 10,* 22–54.

McGuire, J. (2001). Defining correctional programs. In L.L. Motiuk & R.C. Serin (Eds), *Compendium 2000 on effective correctional programming.* Ottawa: Correctional Service Canada.

McGuire, J. (2004a). *Understanding psychology and crime: Perspectives on theory and action.* Maidenhead: Open University Press/McGraw-Hill Education.

McGuire, J. (2004b). Minimising harm in violence risk assessments: Practical solutions to ethical problems? *Health, Risk and Society, 6,* 327–345.

McGuire, J. (2006). General offending behaviour programmes. In C.R. Hollin & E.J. Palmer (Eds), *Offending behaviour programmes: Development, application, and controversies.* Chichester: John Wiley & Sons.

McMurran, M. (Ed.) (2002). *Motivating offenders to change: A guide to enhancing engagement in therapy.* Chichester: John Wiley & Sons.

Miethe, T.D. & Lu, H. (2005). *Punishment: A comparative historical perspective.* Cambridge: Cambridge University Press.

Motiuk, L.L. & Serin, R.C. (Eds) (2001). *Compendium 2000 on effective correctional programming.* Ottawa: Correctional Service Canada.

Murphy, J.G. (1994). Marxism and retribution. In R.A. Duff & D. Garland (Eds), *A reader on punishment.* Oxford: Oxford University Press.

Newman, G., Bouloukos, A.C., & Cohen, D. (Eds) (2001). *World factbook of criminal justice systems.* Washington, DC: Department of Justice. Available from web-site: http://www.ojp.usdoj.gov/bjs/pub/ascii/wfbcjhon.txt

Pearson, F.S., Lipton, D.S., & Cleland, C.M. (1997). *Rehabilitative Programs in Adult Corrections: CDATE Meta-analyses.* Paper presented at the Annual Meeting of the American Society of Criminology, San Diego, November.

Pfuhl, E.H. (1983). Police strikes and conventional crime – a look at the data. *Criminology, 21,* 489–503.

Redondo, S., Sánchez-Meca, J., & Garrido, V. (2002). Crime treatment in Europe: A review of outcome studies. In J. McGuire (Ed.), *Offender rehabilitation and treatment: Effective programmes and policies to reduce re-offending*. Chichester: John Wiley & Sons.

Sentencing Guidelines Council (2007). *Compendium of guideline judgments* (3rd edn). London: Sentencing Guidelines Council. http://www.sentencing-guidelines.gov.uk/

Sorensen, J., Wrinkle, R., Brewer, V., & Marquart, J. (1999). Capital punishment and deterrence: Examining the effect of executions on rates of murder in Texas. *Crime and Delinquency, 45,* 481–493.

Springer, D.W., McNeece, C.A., & Arnold, E.M. (2002). *Substance abuse treatment for criminal offenders: An evidence-based guide for practitioners*. Washington, DC: American Psychological Association.

Stafford, M.C. & Warr, M. (1993). A reconceptualisation of general and specific deterrence. *Journal of Research on Crime and Delinquency, 30,* 123–135.

Tarling, R. (1993). *Analysing crime: data, models and interpretations*. London: Home Office.

Taylor, R., Wasik, M., & Leng, R. (2005). *Blackstone's guide to the Criminal Justice Act 2003*. Oxford: Oxford University Press.

Tong, L.S.J. & Farrington, D.P. (2006). How effective is the 'Reasoning and Rehabilitation' programme in reducing re-offending? A meta-analysis of evaluations in three countries. *Psychology, Crime and Law, 12,* 3–24.

Tyler, T.R. (2006). *Why people obey the law*. Princeton, NJ: Princeton University Press.

Von Hirsch, A. (1994). Censure and proportionality. In R.A. Duff & D. Garland (Eds), *A reader on punishment*. Oxford: Oxford University Press.

Von Hirsch, A., Bottoms, A.E., Burney, E., & Wikström, P.O. (1999). *Criminal deterrence and sentencing severity: An analysis of recent research*. Oxford: Hart Publishing.

Walker, N. (1991). *Why Punish? Theories of punishment reassessed*. Oxford: Oxford University Press.

White, J.R. (1988). Violence during the 1919 Boston police strike: An analysis of the crime control myth. *Criminal Justice Review, 13,* 61–68.

Wilson, D.B. (2001). Meta-analytic methods for criminology. *Annals of the American Academy of Political and Social Science, 578,* 71–89.

Wilson, D.B., Bouffard, L.A., & Mackenzie, D.L. (2005). A quantitative review of structured, group-oriented, cognitive-behavioral programs for offenders. *Criminal Justice and Behavior, 32,* 172–204.

Zimring, F.E. & Hawkins, G. (1994). The growth of imprisonment in California. *British Journal of Criminology, 34,* (Special Issue), 83–96.

ANNOTATED READING LIST

Andrews, D.A. & Bonta, J. (2003). *The psychology of criminal conduct*. Cincinnati, OH: Andersen Publishing; Blackburn, R. (1993). *The psychology of criminal conduct*. Chichester: John Wiley & Sons; McGuire, J. (2004). *Understanding psychology and crime: Perspectives on theory and action*, Maidenhead: Open University Press/McGraw-Hill Education; Hollin, C.R. (2007). Criminological psychology. In M. Maguire, R. Morgan, & R. Reiner (Eds), *The Oxford handbook of criminology* (4th edn), pp. 43–77. Oxford: Oxford University Press.

These sources provide recent and more extensive introductions to the relationships between psychology and crime in general.

Ashworth, A. (2005). *Sentencing and criminal justice.* Oxford: Oxford University Press; and Easton, S. & Piper, C. (2005). *Sentencing and punishment: The quest for justice.* Oxford: Oxford University Press. *Both books provide more detailed background on the law with particular reference to sentencing and punishment (though primarily focused on England and Wales).*

McGuire, J. (Ed.) (2002). *Offender rehabilitation and treatment: Effective practice and policies to reduce re-offending.* Chichester: John Wiley & Sons. *A full description of research, concerning psychosocial interventions to reduce offending behaviour.*

Miethe, T.D. & Lu, H. (2005). *Punishment: A comparative historical perspective.* Cambridge: Cambridge University Press. *An in-depth discussion of the history, and numerous other aspects of punishment.*

Tyler, T.R. (2006). *Why people obey the law.* Princeton: Princeton University Press. *An overview of research on the relationship between punishment and other factors mediating law-abiding behaviour.*

12

PSYCHOLOGICAL SKILLS IN WORKING WITH OFFENDERS

Ruth Hatcher

School of Psychology: Forensic Section, University of Leicester, United Kingdom

During the latter quarter of the twentieth century, the 'What Works' movement contributed a plethora of evidence to those working with correctional services regarding the effectiveness of different ways of working with offenders. Perhaps the most influential volume of evidence has come from a number of collective reviews of a large number of studies, using a method for integrating research findings known as *meta-analysis*. These evaluations have advanced our knowledge concerning the components of interventions most effective in reducing recidivistic behaviour and have been particular influential in shaping modern day correctional service provision. As a consequence, offending behaviour programmes, and the associated practice of risk assessment, are now commonplace within many correctional services of the world, including those within the UK, Europe, Australasia, and North America.

Andrews *et al.*'s (1990) meta-analysis of intervention evaluation studies is perhaps one of the most prominent of the What Works papers to date. Within this and subsequent publications, Andrews and colleagues founded the evidence-based principles of risk, need and responsivity of offender programming, which have since been particularly influential on the design and implementation of offending behaviour programmes. These shall each be discussed in turn.

The risk principle dictates that to impact on offending behaviour the level of intervention received by an offender should depend on the level of risk that s/he poses. Offenders assessed to be high risk cases should, therefore, receive a greater level of intervention than offenders who are lower risk. Clearly then, accurate assessments of risk are necessary to allocate offenders to individually appropriate levels of intervention.

Whilst the risk principle is concerned with the dosage of programming, the need principle determines the treatment targets interventions should intervene upon. Andrews & Bonta (1994) make the distinction between general issues, problems, or needs which may be generally present within the offenders' lives, and those which are linked to their offending behaviour. The need principle proposes that to reduce recidivistic behaviour, interventions should target only those needs (or risk factors) which contribute to offending behaviour. Such factors have been termed 'criminogenic' needs.

The third principle, responsivity, is concerned with how the intervention is delivered to the offender. The responsivity principle states that more effective programmes are those which successfully match the style and methods of delivery to the learning styles of the attendees. The issue of responsivity will be discussed in more detail in the second half of this chapter. For now, we will look into the theory and practice of risk and need assessment in more detail before considering some examples of such tools commonly used by correctional services today.

RISK ASSESSMENT

Risk assessment within offender management operates on much the same principles as risk assessment within other fields. When you apply for insurance, for example, the insuring company generally requests particular information about you and your personal circumstances. This information is used by the company to judge the likelihood of the outcome they are insuring against occurring. In general, the higher the likelihood of the outcome or, to put it another way, the more risky it is for the company to insure you, the more expensive your premium will be. Consider the cost of a car insurance premium, for example. A 35-year-old driver with 15 years of driving experience, no motoring convictions, and no previous car insurance claims would be able to obtain a lower insurance quote than a 21-year-old with two years' driving experience, a conviction for driving over the speed limit and a previous insurance claim to cover repairs to the vehicle acquired in an accident involving the car and a lamp post! It is easy to see that the likelihood of a future claim is higher in the second scenario than the first: the driver has less experience of driving, has displayed risky driving behaviour and has a history of crashing the car. The insurance premium is thus adjusted to reflect the higher risk to the insurance company of having to finance a future claim.

In much the same manner, the risk assessment of offenders draws on information about offenders and their circumstances in order to reach judgments about their likely future behaviour. Such assessments may consider how likely an offender is to reoffend, be reconvicted, or cause harm to others. The choice of which future behaviour is the subject of the prediction will depend on the purpose of the assessment.

The efficacy of risk assessment, then, rests on the ability to accurately predict future behaviour. Prediction, however, is not an exact science. If we recall our insurance illustration for a moment: a life insurance company will use information relating to our age, current health status, lifestyle, family medical history, and, maybe at some point in the future, our DNA to determine the probability of future serious illness or premature death. The premium is then calculated on this perceived risk. It is perhaps obvious, however, that such information will not allow for the prediction of more idiosyncratic threats to health, such as being hit by a bus or struck by lightening. In much the same way, an assessment of offender risk of reconviction or harm is open to the same inaccuracies.

Figure 12.1 overleaf presents the four potential outcomes in relation to prediction. When an event is predicted to occur, it then can either occur (outcome one) or not (outcome two). Likewise when an event is predicted to not occur, it then can either occur (outcome three) or not (outcome four). The consequences of incorrect prediction (outcomes two and three) can be rather unpalatable. For example, in the case of offender recidivism prediction, an offender deemed by the risk assessment as unlikely to reoffend could, on the basis of that prediction, be given a non-custodial sentence or released from incarceration. If the prediction is incorrect and the offender does recidivate (i.e. outcome three) the previous decisions, predicated on the incorrect risk assessment, will inevitably impact on society creating real and unwelcome consequences. At the individual level, the subsequent offending behaviour creates additional victims and the associated distress of victimization whilst society is also affected by the monetary costs of the administration of further investigation and justice.

A false positive outcome is also undesirable: an offender's application for parole may be rejected on the basis of a risk assessment that predicts future offending behaviour. If the risk assessment was incorrect and the offender would not have reoffended on release (i.e. outcome two), it could be argued that the faulty assessment had contributed to an infringement of the detained individual's human rights and the squandering of public money spent on continued imprisonment. In all risk assessments, then, the overarching aim is to maximize the proportion of correct predictions whilst minimizing the false positives and false negatives.

Methods of Assessing Risk

Whilst there are a multitude of ways of determining an individual's level of risk, these tend to fall broadly into two categories: clinical and actuarial risk assessments. Clinical risk assessment, as the name implies, draws on the clinical skills of the assessor to evaluate the offender's risk level. Hence, clinical assessment involves the observation of, and the collection of background information on, the offender by professionals. The clinician utilizes the information gleaned from such observations, alongside their experience and training, to guide the formulation of the risk prediction. Originating from

		Prediction	
		Reoffend	Not-reoffend
Actual Event	Reoffend	Outcome 1 Correct prediction (true positive)	Outcome 3 Incorrect prediction (false negative)
	Not-reoffend	Outcome 2 Incorrect prediction (false positive)	Outcome 4 Correct prediction (true negative)

Figure 12.1: Possible outcomes in risk assessment

the medical field (Monahan, 1981), this practice can be construed as a diagnostic assessment of risk (Howells & Hollin, 1989).

Actuarial prediction is really quite different. Actuarial methods typically employ statistical **algorithms,** or equations, to generate risk scores from specific items of information. These scores can be construed as estimated likelihoods of the occurrence of the event of interest or can be categorized into risk bands such as low, medium, and high risk. The algorithms utilized within actuarial prediction are generally determined through large cohort longitudinal research projects assessing the factors associated with the risky behaviour or event in question. The resultant assessments are hence derived through the comparison of the individual's risk predictors against the amassed knowledge of a similar sample's outcomes.

Both clinical and actuarial assessments draw on a range of data points. These data can be static (or historic factors), such as the offenders' number of previous convictions, their age, and their gender. Such factors are termed static as they are not amenable to change through intervention or otherwise. Furthermore, both types of assessment can also utilize dynamic, or theoretically changeable, factors such as social (employment status, the nature of peer relationships) or behavioural (levels of impulsivity, attitudes to crime) measures. Hence the choice of information used by the two kinds of assessment can overlap partially or indeed fully; it is the employment of this information that differs between the clinical and actuarial prediction fields.

A longstanding debate within the field of psychology has centred on the comparative merits of these two methods of risk assessment. Advocates of the clinical method argue that the generalization of information from a group to an individual is in itself problematic (Dingwall, 1989). Others have claimed that actuarial methods oversimplify the complexity of factors involved in an offender's decision to reoffend or cause harm (Grubin, 1997; Grubin & Wingate, 1996; Litwack, 2001) and fail to attend to idiosyncrasies which might be highly predictive. In contrast, Grove & Meehl (1996) have argued that actuarial risk assessment "involves a formal, algorithmic, objective procedure (e.g. equation) to reach the decision" (p. 293) whilst clinical prediction "relies on an informal, 'in the head', impressionistic, subjective conclusion, reached (somehow) by a human clinical judge" (p. 294). This view was predicated on the findings of their meta-analysis which compared the predictive accuracy of both methods and concluded in favour of actuarial assessments. This view is now generally accepted (Howe, 1994; Milner & Campbell, 1985; Quinsey *et al.*, 1993). Moreover some authors have gone so far as to propose the 'complete replacement' of clinical assessments with actuarial measures (Quinsey *et al.*, 1998). Others have proposed that such statements are too hasty. Douglas, Cox & Webster (1999) argue that:

the actuarial method, while useful, is not a panacea, and that it has limitations in the risk assessment field. The function of actuarial prediction methods is simply that – prediction. Risk assessment as conceived here is broader than prediction. Prediction is a necessary first step. Yet risk management and prevention are equally necessary steps. Once a person is defined as high risk, it is in everyone's best interest to suggest means by which such risk can be attenuated. (p. 155)

The authors endorse a combination of clinical and actuarial methods into an 'empirically validated, structured clinical assessment' (p. 157) of risk and need. Such tools draw on the expertise of professionals' decisions and allow them to highlight idiosyncrasies which may impact on risk, whilst also providing an empirically derived and validated risk score or banding. Indeed the combination of clinical assessment with actuarial methods, it has been argued, can play an important role in identifying the factors which contribute to the outcome of interest (Limandri & Sheridan, 1995). As such, the development of structured clinical judgment, sometimes referred to as third generation tools, allows for the objective assessment of risk whilst also supplying an empirically derived and individualized profile of criminogenic needs. In the next section of this chapter, we will examine some of the more commonly used assessment tools.

Risk and Need Instruments for Offenders

Within England and Wales, the prison population has been growing over recent years and, at the time of writing, is rapidly approaching the 80 000 figure. An additional 150 000 convicted offenders are serving their sentences in the community under the supervision of the Probation Service. The crimes that these individuals have committed cover the full spectrum from benefit fraud and shoplifting to the more heinous crimes of sexual assault, manslaughter and murder and, hence, at the point of contact with prison and probation services, they will have varying levels of risk and need. Risk and need instruments can therefore be used to determine the risks that offenders pose to themselves, others, and society, and to decide how the risks and needs are best managed by the correctional services. Indeed, the key principle of offender management within the recently established England and Wales **National Offender Management Service** (NOMS) is that "resources should follow risk" (National Offender Management Service, 2006, p. 22). This rule of offender management echoes the earlier message of Andrews and colleagues in their discussion of the 'risk principle', which, if you remember, stated that higher risk individuals should receive longer and more intensive interventions than those of lower risk. The operational consequence of these principles is that the levels of containment, supervision, and intervention imposed on an offender are determined by their risk of reoffending, risk of harm, and level of need, all of which can be derived though the utilization of risk and need assessment tools.

In practice then, risk and need assessment tools are often administered prior to sentencing to inform decisions on the requirements placed on the offender as part of their sentence. For example, the court may decide that the potential risk of harm to others an offender poses, coupled with their high risk of reconviction, is too high to allow a community penalty and hence sentence them to a period of imprisonment. Or, it may feel that a medium risk of reoffending can be mediated by attendance at an rehabilitative offending behaviour programme within the community. Furthermore, community agencies may use the outcomes of risk and need assessments to inform the detail of offenders' sentence plans, parole decisions, and risk management plans within custody or on release into the community. Case Study presents an example of how risk assessment information can be used to inform decisions within prison settings. It also highlights the need not only to ensure useful and accurate assessments but also to ensure that the outcomes of such assessments are taken seriously and used to inform decisions about the management of offenders.

CASE STUDY

The Death of Zahid Mubarek

Consider the potentially volatile setting of a prison. Risk assessment can be used to minimize the risk of harm posed by a prisoner to other prisoners or staff. For example, when an individual's risk assessment indicates that they pose a risk to staff, their management plan can be adapted to include provision to manage this risk – they might only be allowed out of their cell when two or more prison officers are there. Likewise such assessments can identify whether an offender poses a risk to other prisoners based, for example, on offence history or ethnicity. Such information can be used by prison staff to inform cell allocation, for example. The high-profile and tragic case of Zahid Mubarek, murdered whilst sleeping in his own cell by his cellmate, Robert Stewart, is an example of the consequences of ignoring the outcome of, or, as in this case, failing to conduct, such assessments. The report of the inquiry into the death of Zahid Mubarek (House of Commons, 2006), states that Robert Stewart was known to have strong racist views, a history of violent behaviour and possible mental health problems. Despite this information being known by some of the prison officers within the prison, Stewart was placed in a cell with Mubarek, a teenager of Asian origin. The inquiry into this case concluded that

the history of Stewart's management within the prison system . . . reveals a number of missed opportunities . . . his history within the prison system should have resulted in some thought being given to his suitability to share a cell . . . We can only speculate about what would have happened if Stewart's potential dangerousness had been properly addressed . . . it is likely that he would have been assessed as posing a risk to the safety of other prisoners and as someone who was unsuitable to share a cell. So the opportunity . . . to manage him in a way which might have resulted in him not eventually sharing a cell with Zahid was missed. (House of Commons, 2006, p. 178)

Since this tragic incident, the prison service has introduced and evaluated the 'cell-sharing risk assessment form'. This is now completed as part of the reception process into the prison in an attempt to reduce the possibility of such events in the future. At the time of the inquiry, however, the training provided for the completion of these assessments was lacking and the report questioned "whether this initial assessment results in an accurate predictor of risk" (House of Commons, 2006, p. 500). It seems then that despite steps forward within this field of risk assessment, there is still some way to go.

The following three examples describe assessment tools used commonly within correctional services. These tools are general in nature and hence aim to predict, or derive treatment targets in relation to, recidivism or reconviction per se as opposed to than any particular type or classification of reoffending behaviour.

The Offender Group Reconviction Scale (OGRS: Copas & Marshall, 1998; OGRS2: Taylor, 1999)

The Offender Group Reconviction Scale (OGRS: Copas & Marshall, 1998) is a purely actuarial risk of reconviction instrument developed within England and Wales. OGRS, and its latest incarnation which incorporates the prediction of sexual and violent offences (OGRS2: Taylor, 1999), calculates from a small number of criminal history and demographic items, the probability that an offender will be reconvicted within the following two years.

The development of OGRS and OGRS2 was based on a study of 44 000 offenders discharged from prison or sentenced to a community penalty in the 1990s. The sample's subsequent two-year reconviction history was elicited from a national database and used to assess the predictive utility of a range of static data points. Those that proved to be efficient in predicting reconviction were incorporated into the OGRS algorithm, which produces a risk of reconviction score of between 0 and 100. The data used within OGRS2 to predict reconviction are presented in Figure 12.2.

The OGRS instrument has become widely used within correctional services within the UK; the ease and speed of the tool has ensured its practicality. The OGRS instrument has been criticized, however, for focusing solely on static and historic criminal history and demographic variables at the expense of more dynamic social and behavioural items. As such the tool acts exclusively as a risk of reconviction estimator and hence does not provide any assessment of offender need.

---

1. Offender age at time of sentence
2. Gender
3. Number of custodial sentences as a youth
4. Current offence type
5. Age at current conviction
6. Age at first conviction
7. The Copas rate variable (the rate at which the offender has been convicted)
8. History of burglary offences
9. History of breach (of community orders)

Figure 12.2: Variables used within OGRS2 to predict risk of reconviction (Taylor, 1999)

Level of Service Inventory-Revised (LSI-R: Andrews & Bonta, 1995)

The LSI-R is a 54-item risk and need assessment instrument designed originally utilizing Canadian data (Andrews, 1982) and has been used extensively with a variety of offender samples within Europe and North America. This tool not only provides an assessment of the risk of reoffending but also information relating to the treatment needs of the assessed offender. The items of the LSI-R, which comprise both static and dynamic factors, produce scores relating to 10 sub-components. These sub-components provide information relating to the offender's needs within the domains of criminal history, education/employment, finances, family/marital, accommodation, leisure/recreation, companions, alcohol/drug problems, emotional/personal, and attitude/orientations. These domain scores are also weighted according to how efficiently previous research has shown them to predict reconviction to produce a composite score. The composite score hence represents the likelihood of future offending. Lower scores represent a lower prevalence of criminogenic risk factors and hence a lower risk of future offending.

Hollin & Palmer (2003) have described the LSI-R as "an effective and efficient assessment instrument for needs-risk assessment with offenders". Indeed research findings attest to the validity and reliability of the assessment tool with the general offender population (Raynor, 2007), in relation to females (Coulson, Nutbrown & Giulekas, 1993), minority ethnic groups (Schlager & Simourd, 2007), violent (Hollin & Palmer, 2003), sex (Simourd & Malcolm, 1998), and young offenders (Shields, 1993; Shields & Simourd, 1991).

The Offender Assessment System (OASys)

The turn of the twenty-first century saw the ambitious development and subsequent implementation of a new risk and needs assessment tool within the prison and probation services of England and Wales. Prior to the development of the Offender Assessment System (OASys), the prison and probation services within England and Wales were using a range of risk prediction tools, including ACE (Assessment, Case management and Evaluation instrument: Roberts *et al.*, 1996), OGRS2, and LSI-R. The provision of a common tool which could be used across prison and probation environments, it was argued, would allow for continued assessment and evaluation throughout the correctional services system (now known as the National Offender Management System or NOMS).

The tool itself can be completed manually, but is now increasingly used in its electronic form, through file review and offender interviews utilizing static and dynamic risk factors. As such OASys is a structured clinical assessment tool. The main criticism of OASys is the time required to complete a full assessment. The Home Office (2003, cited in Raynor, 2007) has estimated that a full OASys assessment can take two and a half hours compared to the LSI-R, which can take as little as 10 minutes (Raynor, 1997, cited in Raynor, 2007). The payback for this resource outlay is the richness of data which OASys produces. These data are contained within the five components of OASys, which are summarized in Figure 12.3.

The first of these components, which comprises the main section of OASys, consists of the assessment of 12 different offending related factors (see Figure 12.3). Similar to the LSI-R, the scores obtained for each section are weighted and summed to provide the overall risk of reconviction score. As can be seen from Figure 12.3 below, however, the OASys tool provides more than just a risk of reconviction score. The second section provides an analysis of risk of serious harm, defined as "a risk which is life-threatening and/or traumatic, and from which recovery, whether physical or

1. Risk of reconviction and offending-related factors
    a. Offending information
    b. Analysis of offences
    c. Accommodation
    d. Education, training and employability
    e. Financial management and income
    f. Relationships
    g. Lifestyle and associates
    h. Drug misuse
    i. Alcohol misuse
    j. Emotional well-being
    k. Thinking and behaviour
    l. Attitudes
2. Risk of serious harm, risks to the individual and other risks
3. OASys summary sheet
4. Sentence planning
5. Self-assessment

Figure 12.3: The components of the OASys risk and need assessment tool (Moore, 2006)

psychological, can be expected to be difficult or impossible" (OASys manual, n.d., cited in Howard, Clark & Garnham, 2006, p 7), through the evaluation of actuarial, social and personal factors. The output from this section, therefore, is intended to inform the employment of risk management procedures. The summary sheet and sentence planning sections of OASys are also designed to aid practitioners use the individual's identified risk and need factors to inform the management and supervision of the offender. Finally, OASys has provision for offenders to complete a Self-Assessment Questionnaire providing the opportunity for criminal justice professionals to gain insight into the offenders' views of their needs. A recent evaluation of the Self-Assessment Questionnaires of over 100 000 offenders concluded that offenders tended to be more optimistic about their chances of desisting from crime than their OASys assessment would predict and less likely than practitioners to identify problem areas in their lives (Moore, 2007).

Although the development and implementation of OASys has suffered from delays and, at the time of writing, is not yet fully functional in all areas (Raynor, 2007), it has received positive acclaim: "OASys is a very comprehensive and strongly research-based assessment instrument, informed by detailed study of others including LSI-R and ACE" (Raynor, 2007, p. 135). Indeed OASys, which has been adopted for use outside England and Wales (Bunton & Morphew, 2007), has been subject to an extensive piloting process which has refined and improved the tool in line with the ongoing research. An evaluation of the ability of OASys to accurately predict reconviction reported that it outperformed ACE and LSI-R assessments but was not as predictive as the purely actuarial OGRS2 instrument (Howard, Clark & Garnham, 2006). The possibility of combining OGRS and OASys in order to improve the prediction of reconviction is, at the time of writing, being considered by the OASys Data, Evaluation and Analysis Team (O-DEAT: Howard, 2006).

Risk and Need Instruments for Violent Offenders

In the way in which we can use risk assessments to determine the likelihood of any type of reoffending, we can also used tools to predict the risk of certain types of future offending. Violent offending is one such offence we might like to predict, given the damaging effects this behaviour can have on its victims. According to the British Crime Survey, there were 1 025 500 violent offences against the person within England and Wales during the year commencing July 2006, representing approximately one-fifth of all crime during this period, with the most serious offences (homicide, attempted murder, serious wounding, and so on) totalling 18 500 offences (Moley et al., 2007). When violent offenders are reprimanded it is helpful to be able to assess how likely they are to reoffend in a violent manner and what their level of criminogenic need is, to inform decisions relating to their sentencing and management. For example, an offender who has a history of violent offending and harbours strong negative views against a certain sector of society would be managed in a different way to an individual who, after consuming large amounts of alcohol, offended violently towards a partner. It is hence necessary to assess, for each individual, the presence of factors which indicate repeat violent behaviour, and the triggers of that potential behaviour. One tool that does exactly this is the HCR-20.

HCR-20 (Historical, Clinical, Risk Management-20: Webster *et al.*, 1997)

The HCR-20 is a risk assessment instrument that incorporates structured clinical judgments to provide an assessment of future violent behaviour amongst civil psychiatric, forensic, and criminal justice populations. Cooke (2000) has stated that the HCR-20 is "the best known, and best researched, empirically-based guide to risk assessment" (p. 155). The tool consists of 20 items: 10 historical, five clinical, and five risk management factors (see Figure 12.4). Indeed the tool takes its name from the initial letter of each of these domains – HCR – and the number of items that comprise the tool – 20. The HCR-20 currently in use is the second version, which was developed following careful consideration of the empirical literature and subsequently amended in the light of evidence from the clinical experience of early trials. The use of consultation with forensic clinicians in the development and refinement of the tool is seen positive: "as such, the HCR-20 is an attempt to merge science and practice by offering an instrument that can be integrated into clinical practice but also is empirically based and testable" (Douglas, Guy & Weir, 2006; p. 4).

The HCR-20 tool has been shown to be predictive of inpatient violence by civil psychiatric clients (Klassen, 1999) as well as violent crime by the same population on release from hospital (Douglas & Webster, 1999). Research on forensic populations, both community- and prison-based, also attests to its predictive ability in relation to violence (Douglas & Webster, 1999; Strand *et al.*, 1999; Wintrup, 1999). Indeed, the authors of the HCR-20 tool periodically maintain an annotated list of research papers which assess the utility of the HCR-20 with a range of populations both civil and criminal. The latest update contained in the region of 100 studies reporting on the usefulness of this violence risk and need tool (Douglas, Guy & Weir, 2006).

Historical items	**Clinical items**
1. Previous Violence	1. Lack of Insight
2. Young Age at First Violent Incident	2. Negative Attitudes
3. Relationship Instability	3. Active Symptoms of Major Mental Illness
4. Employment Problems	4. Impulsivity
5. Substance Use Problems	5. Unresponsive to Treatment
6. Major Mental Illness	**Risk Management items**
7. Psychopathy	1. Plans Lack Feasibility
8. Early Maladjustment	2. Exposure to Destabilizers
9. Personality Disorder	3. Lack of Personal Support
10. Prior Supervision Failure	4. Noncompliance with Remediation Attempts
	5. Stress

Figure 12.4: The components of the HCR-20 (Webster *et al.*, 1997)

Risk and Need Instruments for Sex Offenders

Sex offending represents a small but significant proportion of all crime. In England and Wales, the British Crime Survey recently reported, in a one-year period, approximately 56 000 crime of a sexual nature from a total of just over 5 million crimes (Moley *et al.*, 2007). Similar statistics are available in the US; in the year 2005, approximately 44 160 households, out of a total of approximately 114 million, had members who experienced sexual assault of some kind (Klaus, 2007). When reading and digesting these statistics, it is apt to remember that official figures are considered to underestimate the true prevalence of sex offences – some individuals are reluctant, feel too ashamed, or unable to report such crimes. Even allowing for this, however, it seems that sex offences represent a small fraction of all crimes committed. Nevertheless, correctional services still need to be equipped with the tools to assess the risk and need of the perpetrators of this type of offence.

The term 'sex offending' encompasses a wide variety of different behaviours with varying levels of severity – from stranger rape and child sexual assault, through the collection of child abuse images and **grooming** behaviour, to indecent exposure and **voyeurism**. As such, those individuals deemed by their behaviour to be 'sex offenders' are not homogenous in nature but will present to correctional agencies with very different risk and need profiles. Given this alongside the destructive effects of sex offending, the reduction and prevention of such violence should be the ultimate goal of risk and need assessment. The identification of dynamic risk factors, which inform targets for treatment and the content of management plans, and the assessment sexual recidivism risk, are therefore the aims of sex offender risk and need tools. One such tool, the Structured Assessment of Risk and Need (SARN), was developed empirically using the sex offender literature and is used alongside the England and Wales Prison Service's Sex Offender Treatment Programme (SOTP) to inform the intervention work of those on the programme.

Risk Matrix 2000 (RM2000: Thornton *et al.*, 2003) and *Structured Assessment of Risk and Need* (SARN: Thornton, 2002)

The SARN initially measures static risk through the use of the Risk Matrix 2000, a purely actuarial risk tool (Thornton *et al.*, 2003). Based on the earlier Structured Anchored Clinical Judgement (Thornton, 1997) and Static 99 (Hanson & Thornton, 1999) tools, the Risk Matrix 2000 uses a two-step process to determine the offender's judged risk banding (low, medium, high, or very high). Step one provides an initial assessment of risk level through the evaluation of the number of sex offence sentences, the number of any criminal offence sentences, and the offender's age on release from prison. The second step considers the presence of aggravating factors and adjusts the initial assessed risk level, if needed. The presence of two or more of factors results in the increase of the initial risk level by one unit. Level two risk factors are: a male victim in any previous sex offence, a stranger victim in any previous sex offence, any non-contact sex offence, having never been married.

Once the Risk Matrix 2000 banding has been determined, the second step of the SARN assesses the presence or absence of 16 dynamic risk factors which, through empirical research, have been linked to sex offender recidivism (Thornton, 2002).

These risk factors are grouped across four domains: sexual interests, distorted attitudes, social and emotional functioning, and self-management. The 16 factors are scored twice: first in relation to its relevance to the offender's offence chain and second their life generally. Utilizing psychometric data, personal history information, interview material and file review each factor is rated as 0 (not present), 1 (present but not a central characteristic), or 2 (a central characteristic). Any factor that receives a score of 2 both for the offence chain and the offender's general life is designated as a relevant treatment need for that particular offender. This tool, therefore, provides a risk score in conjunction with a needs profile that can be utilized within treatment planning.

Webster *et al.* (2006), mindful that the clinical scoring of the 16 risk factors may vary between assessors, have conducted an evaluation of the inter-rater reliability of the SARN. Using two pools of assessors, the authors found that experienced, or 'expert', raters showed greater levels of reliability than less experienced raters. The authors argue that in the field of sex offending, where the offenders often display denial and minimization to confuse and manipulate assessors, very high levels of reliability are perhaps unattainable. The finding that reliability is further weakened when less experienced or poorly trained assessors are used brings the authors to conclude that:

it is not appropriate to use the SARN framework to make quantitative predictions about risk of reoffending. It is our view, however, that the studies reported in this paper support the use of the SARN as an instrument for guiding clinical assessment of treatment need. Provisos for its use to this end are as follows: users of the SARN should have demonstrated reasonable inter-rater reliability before conducting assessments without supervision, the SARN should be applied wherever possible by experienced psychologists rather than trainee-level staff, and the use of the SARN should continue to be monitored and evaluated (Webster et al., 2006, p. 451).

Mentally Disordered Offenders

Within England and Wales, there are over 3300 mentally disordered offenders currently detained within hospitals (Home Office, 2007). In line with prison populations these numbers have slowly increased, year on year, for the past 10 years (Home Office, 2007). The Mental Health Act (1983) specifies four categories of mental disorder: mental illness, such as anxiety disorder and schizophrenia, arrested or incomplete development of the mind (mental impairment), psychopathic disorder, and any other disorder or disability of the mind. Of those currently detailed, 74% have been diagnosed as having a mental illness and 13% as suffering from psychopathic disorder (Home Office, 2007). The remainder have been diagnosed with co-morbid conditions or severe mental impairment (Home Office, 2007).

There is a common misconception (perhaps fuelled by certain sections of the media) that all mentally disordered individuals are dangerous individuals who consequently present a risk of harm to the general population. Furthermore this viewpoint seems to place the cause of this assumed dangerousness at the door of the mental disorder itself. Such a position, however, fails to consider those members of the population, who are diagnosed with a mental disorder but are law-abiding citizens and present no risk of harm to the public. At the same time, this stance assumes that the correlates of danger-ousness in the non-disordered criminal population are inherently different to those in the disordered criminal population.

Research within this field has historically, to some degree, concurred with these assumptions, choosing to focus on clinical or psychopathological factors in their inves-tigations of risk amongst the mentally disordered. Meta-analytical research in this field, however, has found that "the major predictors of recidivism were the same for mentally disordered offenders as for non-disordered offenders . . . clinical variables showed the smallest effect sizes" (Bonta, Law & Hanson, 1998, p. 123). On the basis of such conclusions, there is a call for a shift away from clinical or psychopathological variables, to an investigation of the role social psychological and criminological factors play in the relationship between mental disorder and recidivism.

There is one type of mental disorder which perhaps has a closer link within offend-ing behaviour than others. Psychopathy, defined by the Mental Health Act (1983) as "a persistent disorder or disability of mind (whether or not including significant impairment of intelligence) which results in abnormally aggressive or seriously irresponsible conduct on the part of the person concerned" is, by definition, closely linked with offending behaviour. Within England and Wales, a recently established Dangerous people with Severe Personality Disorder (DSPD) programme aims to protect the public from such dangerous people and provide appropriate support and treatment to these individuals to improve their mental health outcomes. The DSPD programme, at the time of writing, has four pilot units within secure settings assessing and treating people who meet the DSPD criteria of having a high or very high OASys (or risk of reconviction) score and a severe personality disorder. A severe personality disorder is defined by the DSPD programme as one characterized by two or more personality dis-orders and/or a high score on the Psychopathy Checklist Revised (PCL-R).

Psychopathy Checklist-Revised (PCL-R: Hare, 1991)

Designed to guide clinical assessment, the PCL-R provides a framework for diagnosis of psychopathic disorder. As such it is not strictly a risk assessment tool but has been found to predict violent recidivism among adult (Hart, Hare & Forth, 1994; Serin, 1991; Serin, Peters & Barbaree, 1990) and young (Forth, Hart & Hare, 1990) male offenders. Based on the work of Cleckley (1964), Hare conducted an empirically based assessment of the clinical factors that comprise psychopathy (Hare, 1980). The resultant checklist and its later revision (Hare, 1991) is now used widely within the forensic and clinical fields and has been described as the "gold standard for the diagnosis of psychopathy worldwide" (Morana, Arboleda-Flórez & Câmara, 2005, p. 2).

The 20 items of the PCL-R cover demographic, criminological, social and psycho-logical domains (see Figure 12.5) and the presence or absence of these are determined through interview, file and case history review. Each item is scored either 0 (not evident in the record of the offender), 1 (some but not complete evidence), or 2 (the character-istic is definitely present). The maximum possible score is hence 40. The cut-off score for a diagnosis of psychopathy has been the subject of debate within forensic psychol-ogy and psychiatry circles. Hare (1991) recommends that only those individuals who score at, or above, 30 should be deemed to be psychopathic. This high number was set

1. Superficial charm

2. Grandiose sense of self-worth

3. Need for stimulation/easily bored

4. Pathological lying

5. Manipulative

6. Lack of remorse or guilt

7. No emotional depth

8. Callous

9. Parasitic lifestyle

10. Poor behavioural control

11. Promiscuous sexual behaviour

12. Early behaviour problems

13. Lack of long term planning

14. Impulsive

15. Irresponsible

16. Failure to accept responsibility for own actions

17. Frequent marital failures

18. Delinquent as a juvenile

19. Poor record on probation or other conditional releases

20. Versatile as a criminal

Figure 12.5: Items within the PCL-R (Hare, 1991)

in order to reduce the number of false positive within the psychopathic group. Rice & Harris (1995), however, reported that the validity of the tool is maximized when the cut-off score of 25 is applied and furthermore different cut offs have been used depending on the population under review (Morana, Arboleda-Fólrez & Câmara, 2005).

The DSPD programme, which spans the Ministry of Justice and the Department of Health, has secured funding for a programme of research and evaluation which seeks to improve knowledge relating to the causes of personality disorder and the effectiveness of assessments and interventions within these individuals. A recent Ministry of Justice publication assessing the utility of currently available risk assessment tools for future violent and sex reoffending is one such early example of this research (Coid et al., 2007). This research has provisionally estimated that 15% of offenders within the secure estate currently meet the DSPD criteria, a statistic which justifies the ongoing resourcing of work within this field. In addition, it has provided evidence of the efficacy of existing risk assessments, with OGRS2 outperforming the PCL-R and HCR-20 in the prediction of future recidivism amongst DSPD offenders. Further research into the risk and needs of this population is ongoing and should, over the coming years, improve how correctional services manage the risk of dangerous personality disordered offenders in the protection of public.

Summary

As has been described within this section, the method of assessing risk in relation to offender recidivism has been, and continues to be, the subject of much debate. Actuarial tools seem to be more reliable in predicting future outcomes than clinical judgment alone, but they are not sensitive to idiosyncratic evidence in the way a clinician would be and also provide little detail about the needs of the assessed offender. In light of this, there has been a move in recent years to develop structured tools which combine actuarial and clinical methods of assessment. These 'third generation' assessment tools provide not only judgment as to the risk the individual poses, but also rich needs information which informs subsequent rehabilitative work with the offender. The remaining sections of this chapter will focus on the type of rehabilitative work that is currently untaken with offenders.

TREATMENT DELIVERY

The number of offending behaviour programmes available to practitioners for use with offenders continues to grow apace. An illustration of this can be seen within the correctional services of England and Wales. Within this jurisdiction, the components of effective practice identified by meta-analytic reviews of programme evaluations have been formalized into a set of programme accreditation principles (see Figure 12.6). The latest report from the England and Wales Correctional Services Accreditation Panel (CSAP), the role of which is to assess programmes and provide accredited status to those which satisfy all criteria, describes 36 programmes that have provisional or full accreditation for use within either the Prison or Probation Services (CSAP, 2006). Manualized programmes have now been developed for a wide range of offenders: violent including domestically violent, sex including Internet sex offenders, drink-impaired drivers, offenders whose crimes are committed to support drug use, psychopathic offenders,

---

1. Programmes must be based within a clear model of change.
2. Programmes should have clear and justified selection criteria for selection of offenders.
3. Programmes should intervene on a range of dynamic risk factors.
4. Programmes should use effective methods of change.
5. Programmes should encompass skills-orientated targets.
6. The dosage (sequencing, intensity, and duration) of programmes should be outlined and based within research.
7. The programme should be designed as to attend to motivation and engagement issues.
8. The programme should be embedded within coherent sentence planning.
9. The programme should attend to issues of programme integrity.
10. The programme should be designed as to allow for continued evaluation.

Figure 12.6: Correctional services accreditation panel accreditation criteria

female and acquisitive offenders. Additionally there are a number of 'general offending programmes', developed not to address offence specific treatment needs but for the needs of recidivistic offenders who have usually been convicted of a variety of offences.

Whilst the objective of this rigorous process is to ensure quality evidence-based programmes, critics have condemned manualized group work on the basis that it is not tailored to individual needs, is at odds with the theoretical principles of **cognitive behavioural** therapy, and acts to deskill treatment deliverers by removing their ability to practice "clinical artistry" (Wilson, 1996, p. 295). Respondents to these criticisms have suggested the combination of one-to-one and group work intervention allowing more individualized approaches whilst retaining the practical and economic efficiencies of group work (Hollin & Palmer, 2006). Further, it has been proposed that a reduction in clinical artistry, whilst perhaps demoralizing to staff, may not negatively impact on the programme (Hollin, 2006). Hollin has proposed that the limiting of this practice by manualization might indeed protect against threats to the concept of programme integrity.

The term 'programme integrity' refers to the practice of delivering an intervention in line with the programme manual's instructions. If a well designed and evidence-based programme is not delivered as intended, it is likely that the effectiveness of this programme will be undermined. The importance of this concept is demonstrated in its adoption as one of the principles of effective practice (see Figure 12.6). Hollin (1995) has described three potential threats to programme integrity: programme drift (the gradual alteration of the aims and method of delivery of the programme), programme reversal (the undermining of the programme and its delivery due to resistance and opposition to the aims and methods) and programme non-compliance (the programme facilitators tinker with the programme altering the contents, aims, or treatment targets). All three of these threats compromise the programme in some way and could hence render the work as, at best, worthless or, at worst, damaging to the overall aim of reducing recidivism.

A study of the implementation of programmes within community settings in England and Wales discovered that practitioners were often confused about the perceived conflict between maintaining programme integrity and the need to ensure the Andrews & Bonta (1994) principle of responsivity (Hollin *et al.*, 2002). As mentioned earlier in this chapter, responsivity refers to the matching of the style and methods of delivery to the learning styles of the programme participants to ensure offender engagement with the intervention. On the one hand, therefore, practitioners understand that their practice should not deviate from the programme manual but, on the other hand, often feel the need to do so to be responsive to the needs of the programme participants. As such, the success of the programme may lie, in part, in the programme facilitator's ability to do just this. The skills required to undertake this work successfully should not therefore be underestimated.

GENERAL OFFENDING BEHAVIOUR PROGRAMMES

The general offending behaviour programmes draw on the theory of cognitive social learning (Bandura, 1977, 2001) which proposes that an individual does not require direct experience of an event in order to learn from it. Instead learning can occur indirectly through the observation of an event happening to some other person. Moreover, this observational learning, or 'vicarious reinforcement', is thought to explain how people acquire and maintain certain behavioural patterns. Bandura proposed that there are three classes of people from whom the individual may learn: family members, peer groups, and figurative models viewed, for example, through the media. General offending behaviour programmes, therefore, promote the reduction of offending behaviour, through the acquisition of new skills. Using reinforcement strategies, offenders are encouraged to improve their problem-solving skills to enable the selection of alternatives to criminal behaviour. Furthermore general offending behaviour programmes promote the acquisition of self-management and social interaction skills.

The three group-based general offending programmes accredited for use within Prisons and Probation Services in England and Wales are the Enhanced Thinking Skills (ETS), the Think First, and the Reasoning and Rehabilitation (R&R) programmes. The R&R programme was first of these programmes to appear on the correctional scene. This programme was developed in Canada and, to date, has been implemented within 17 different countries (Antonowicz, 2005). This programme, the longest of the general offending behaviour programmes at 38 two-hour sessions, was first manualized in 1985 after a long period of development, piloting and revision and then further revised at the turn of the century (Porporino & Fabiano, 2000; Ross & Fabiano, 1985a). The R&R programme comprises a range of components which promote the acquisition and rehearsal of new skills. These components are: interpersonal cognitive problem-solving skills, social skills, self-control, emotional management, creative thinking, critical reasoning, values enhancement, and meta-cognition. This curriculum is delivered using a combination of direct tutoring and more interactive learning, with the main focus being on the latter, more 'Socratic', method of provision. Within this, programme deliverers utilize role plays, guided discussion, group exercises, and small group work.

As discussed earlier in this chapter, the risk principle purports that the level of intervention should match the risk level of those required to attend. On the basis of this principle, the intensive R&R programme has been designated as the programme of choice of higher risk offenders. The ETS programme was developed to complement the R&R programme and to fill the gap in provision for lower risk offenders within the Prison Service of England and Wales. The focus of this programme, similar to R&R, is on the provision of interpersonal problem solving, social, and moral reasoning skills through interactive programme delivery (Clark, 2000). The programme also heavily promotes the use of 'pro-social modelling' whereby the facilitators model positive behaviours and interaction.

The Think First programme (McGuire, 2000) differs from the two previous general offending behaviour programmes in that, in addition to the social cognitive components of problem solving, self-management and social skills training, it is also offence focused. As such, the programme provides for an analysis of the offender's own criminal behaviour with the intention of enabling behaviour modification. Through the use of the '5-WH' exercises, programme participants break down their offences and analyse in detail what happened, who was involved, when it happened, where it happened, and why it occurred. The repetition of this exercise, focusing on the offender's series of crimes, allows for the emergence of patterns of behaviour and highlights contributory factors. Avoidance strategies are then developed to prevent the repetition of the problem behaviours.

The Think First programme is available in two different forms. The community-based version of the programme comprises a mix of individual pre- and post- group sessions and 22 two-hour group sessions. The total contact time of this programme is thus 54 hours. In contrast, the prison-based version of Think First is comprised of 30 two-hour group sessions only.

These general offending behaviour programmes have been subject to a steadily increasing number of evaluations of their effectiveness. A recent meta-analytic review of the R&R programme in Canada, the US, the UK and Sweden concluded that programme attendees were 14% less likely to reoffend than the control group participants (Tong & Farrington, 2006). Evaluations of the Think First programme have also concluded that the programme produces positive changes on psychometrics tests (McGuire & Hatcher, 2001; Steele, 2002a), and in relation to reconviction (Roberts 2004; Steele, 2002b). Indeed a national evaluation of all three programmes delivered within community settings concluded that all three programmes produced significant reductions in reconviction amongst the programme-completer group comparative to the controls

CASE STUDY

John

John is a 22-year-old man who has just been convicted by his local Magistrate's Court of burglary. John has a history of similar criminal behaviour and has also previously breached a community order. John was assessed prior to sentencing as having an OGRS2 score of 64 (medium to high risk of reoffending) and also as being deficient in cognitive skills such as self-control and problem recognition. John's pre-sentence report, therefore, recommended to the Court that John be sentenced to a community penalty with the requirement of attending a general offending behaviour programme. This sentence was passed by the Magistrates. John therefore has to report to his Offender Manager (a probation officer) once a fortnight and attend the Enhanced Thinking Skills (ETS) programme.

During John's supervision meetings with his Offender Manager, John has the opportunity to address those needs, identified by his OASys assessment, which are related to his offending behaviour. His OASys profile has indicated John has offending-related needs in the fields of accommodation and employment. In his supervision meetings with his Offender Manager, John has the opportunity to discuss how his unemployment status results in a lack of money and hence he feels he has no option but to commit burglary in order to live. He is also able to discuss his accommodation problems and to receive advice on how these might be alleviated.

After a period of four weeks from sentence, John is asked to attend the next ETS programme. John is nervous about doing so as he had particularly bad experiences at school and consequently does not have very good literacy skills. Once

(Continued)

he starts the programme, however, John quickly realizes that the programme is quite different from school: although is it challenging in that it makes him think about how his own thoughts, feelings and behaviours interact with each other, it is more relaxed, and the tutors are less authoritarian than his old school teachers. Despite this, there are clear and strict rules about attendance – if he misses sessions he will be sent back to court.

Eleven weeks later, John and his programme colleagues complete the ETS programme. This process has not been easy but there were six group members who got to the end of the programme. John has also arranged some permanent accommodation and has started to apply for jobs. In conversations with his Offender Manager he states that the ETS programme has made him stop and think about his behaviour and what the consequence might be before acting. John is proud of himself for completing the programme (he has even received a certificate!) and is hopeful that with his new skills he can resist offending again in the future.

(Hollin *et al.*, 2004; Hollin *et al.*, 2008; Palmer *et al.*, 2007). A comparison of the three programmes showed that across the three programmes, Think First outperformed ETS and R&R in relation to attrition and reconviction rates (Palmer *et al.*, 2007).

VIOLENT OFFENDING BEHAVIOUR PROGRAMMES

Interventions for violent offenders serve two distinct types of offending behaviour: intimate partner violence and general violent offending. Polaschek (2006) has remarked that such programmes currently reside within the "underdeveloped corner of offender rehabilitation" (p. 145) and argues that the majority of violent offending programmes are yet to develop a rationale which draws multi-factorial aetiological theory to inform the treatment targets of the programme.

Interventions serving intimate partner, or domestic, violence tend to be grounded within single-factor theoretical models, such as feminist (Pence & Paymar, 1993), social learning (Bandura, 1973), or family systems theory (Stith, Rosen & McCollum, 2002). The most prominent of the intimate partner violence programmes are those based within the 'Duluth model' (Pence & Paymar, 1993). The original Duluth project, established in the 1980s, provided a comprehensive, coordinated community response to domestic violence. Within this feminist and psycho-educational model, the violent perpetrator is viewed as entirely responsible for their own behaviour which serves to assert power and control over their partner. The response to this behaviour within the Duluth context involves the multitude of community agencies that typically respond to domestic violence, for example, the police, courts, victim, correctional, and social services. The model encourages multi-agency working in the pursuit of justice, the provision of practical and emotional support to the victim(s), and the prevention of future domestic violence. The latter of these aims is addressed within a perpetrator programme that uses cognitive-behavioural and psycho-educational methods to challenge the attitudes and beliefs supportive of intimate partner violence, whilst also promoting social skills, and enhancing victim empathy. The Duluth model has since been adopted within the correctional services of North America and Europe. Research outcome studies, which are methodologically challenging due in part to the nature of the violence and the offence-recording practices, are yet to deliver anything more than modest effect sizes (Babcock, Green & Robie, 2004; Gondolf, 2001; Jones *et al.*, 2004). One reason for this might relate to process factors: research investigating the implementation of the perpetrator programme within England and Wales has called for greater emphasis on generating the community response and more available support for the victims of intimate partner violence (Bilby & Hatcher, 2004).

The Aggression Replacement Training programme (ART: Goldstein & Glick, 1987; Goldstein, Glick & Gibbs, 1998) is perhaps the most widely available programme for generally violent offenders. Developed originally for aggressive youths, the programme is now also available in a revised format for adult violent offenders (Hatcher *et al.*, in press). Goldstein *et al.* (1998) argue that an aggressive act derives from multiple causes. They propose that the internal influences on an individual's aggressive behaviour can be traced to three factors: first, to a general shortfall in personal, interpersonal, and social-cognitive skills, the combination of which usually ensure pro-social behaviour; second, to the overuse of impulsive and aggressive behaviour coupled with a low level of anger control; third, to an immature, egocentric, and concrete style of moral reasoning. The ART programme, therefore, aims to tackle these three factors through skillstreaming, anger control, and moral reasoning training. The behavioural skillstreaming component draws on social learning theory in the identification, development, and practice of social skills which form pro-social behaviour. These skills are developed further through role play, discussion, and performance feedback. Anger control training draws on the early anger control work of Novaco (1975) and Miechenbaum (1977). This emotion-oriented component aims to equip the individual with the ability to manage their anger and aggression. These self-control sessions identify personal triggers and the likely consequences of anger and aggression. The increased self-awareness gained from such exercises is then used to develop alternative pro-social coping strategies, such as, negotiation, self-talk, or even avoidance of the situations that trigger anger. The moral reasoning component addresses concrete and egocentric thinking typically seen in those who display aggressive behaviour (Antonowicz & Ross, 2005; Barriga & Gibbs, 1996; Liau, Barriga & Gibbs, 1998; Ross & Fabiano, 1985b). Thus, this component aims to enhance the offenders' moral reasoning which is associated with increased pro-social behaviour.

The ART programme has been evaluated across different client groups, settings, and outcomes, resulting in a body of evidence which suggests that ART can be an effective intervention (for a review, see Goldstein, 2004). A recent evaluation of the community-based adult version of ART (Hatcher *et al.*, in press) concluded that being allocated to the ART programme resulted in a 13.3% reduction in reconviction compared to matched controls, whilst completers of the programme performed even better and demonstrated a 15.5% reduction in reconviction.

SEX OFFENDING BEHAVIOUR PROGRAMMES

There is a multiplicity of theories that aim to explain sex-offending behaviour (see Chapter 2 for a discussion of these theories). Treatment programmes for sex offenders have drawn on these theories in the identification dynamic criminogenic needs to be targeted by treatment. These dynamic risk factors can be classified into four domains (Craissati & Beech, 2003; Thornton, 2002):

- deviant sexual interests
- distorted attitudes that are supportive of and justify sex offending
- interpersonal deficits such as problems with intimacy, self-esteem, anxiety, feelings of inadequacy or emotional loneliness, and
- self-management problems that limit the capability to plan, solve problems and control life events.

Modern treatment programmes for sex offenders use cognitive-behavioural methods to target these dynamic needs through goal-oriented and structured exercises, role play, and the non-aggressive challenging of offence supportive attitudes. The Sex Offender Treatment Programme has been delivered within the England and Wales Prison Service since 1992. The original programme, termed the Core programme, is suitable for medium risk offenders and requires the commitment of approximately 170 hours of group treatment. High-risk sex offenders are required to attend the Core programme plus the 140 hours of group and 20 hours of individual treatment which comprise the Extended programme. Further versions of the programme are available for low-risk sex offenders (the Rolling programme: 80–100 hours), those who have learning difficulties or social functioning problems (the Adapted programme: 140 hours) and those who have completed the Core programme but require additional input prior to release (the Better Lives Booster programme: 60 hours). Similar programmes are also available within community settings; for example, the Community Sex Offender Groupwork Programme (C-SOGP) has been accredited for delivery within the Probation Service in England and Wales since 2000. This programme has an initial 50-hour induction module, which can then either be followed by a 50-hour **relapse prevention** block for low/medium risk and low deviancy offenders or a longer 150-hour full programme for high risk or medium/high deviancy offenders (West Midlands Probation Service, 2000).

The evaluation evidence relating to treatment programmes for sex offenders has been mixed in its conclusions. An evaluation of California's Sex Offender Treatment and Evaluation Project (SOTEP: Marques, 1999) reported limited affects of programme attendance in relation to reconviction: 13% of programme completers had been arrested for further sex crimes compared to 13.8% of untreated controls. Friendship, Mann & Beech (2003), in an evaluation of a prison-based sex offender treatment programme, reported sexual and violent reconviction rates of 4.6% and 8.1% for the treatment and untreated comparison groups respectively. The comparison of purely sexual reconviction rates, however, showed that there was minimal impact in this regard (2.6% treatment group versus 2.8% comparison group). Further analysis revealed that the programme had the strongest impact on those in the medium risk bracket. For example, those programme attendees assessed to be medium–low risk were reconvicted at a rate of 2.7% as compared to 13.5% of the untreated comparisons. The reductions in reconviction for the low- and high-risk offenders were by no means as high (0.7% and 2.1% respectively). This research serves as a reminder that manualized treatment is not a 'one-size-fits-all' solution and calls for targeting practices to ensure appropriate allocation of offenders to treatment.

SUMMARY

Evidence-based offending behaviour programmes, such as those described within this chapter, are now commonplace within correctional services throughout the Western world. The number of offenders who completed a programme in the year 2006–2007 in England and Wales alone reached 19 875 (Hill, 2007). Despite this prolific use, there is still a great deal to learn about how these programmes impact on the lives of those who are subject to them. We can be confident, from the results of meta-analytical research, that these programmes can reduce the recidivistic behaviour of offenders who complete them. We have still to gain answers to more specific questions however, such as why people drop-out from programmes, how offenders can be motivated to increase their engagement, and how organizational factors may impact on programme effectiveness. It is only through the conduct of good quality research that these questions can be answered and correctional provision further enhanced.

ESSAY/DISCUSSION QUESTIONS

1. Compare actuarial and clinical risk assessment methods. What are the limitations of these methods when they are used to assess the likelihood of an individual reoffending in the future?

2. Discuss the potential consequences of failing to conduct a comprehensive risk assessment on an offender. How might this impact on the offender, other individuals and society?

3. How effective is the 'one-size-fits-all' approach to offender rehabilitation? Has programme accreditation been successful in the aim of reducing recidivist behaviour?

4. What are the methodological problems with evaluating offending behaviour programmes? What methodology would you use to test whether such programmes reduce recidivism?

REFERENCES

Andrews, D.A. (1982). *The Level of Supervision Inventory (LSI): The first follow-up*. Toronto: Ontario Ministry of Correctional Services.

Andrews, D.A. & Bonta, J. (1994). *The psychology of criminal conduct*. Cincinnati, OH: Anderson Publishing.

Andrews, D.A. & Bonta, J. (1995). *The Level of Service Inventory – Revised manual*. Toronto: Multi-Health Systems.

Andrews, D.A., Zinger, I., Hoge, R.D., Bonta, J., Gendreau, P., & Cullen, F.T. (1990). 'Does correctional treatment work? A clinically relevant and psychologically informed meta-analysis'. *Criminology, 28*, 369–404.

Antonowicz, D.H. (2005). The Reasoning and Rehabilitation Program: Outcome evaluations with offenders. In M. McMurran & J. McGuire (Eds), *Social problem solving and offending: Evidence, evaluation and evolution* (pp. 163–181). Chichester: John Wiley & Sons.

Antonowicz, D.H. & Ross, R.R. (2005). Social problem-solving deficits in offenders. In M. McMurran & J. McGuire (Eds), *Social problem-solving and offending: Evidence, evaluation and evolution* (pp. 91–102). Chichester: John Wiley & Sons.

Babcock, J.C., Green, C.E., & Robie, C. (2004). Does batterers' treatment work? A meta-analytical review of domestic violence treatment. *Clinical Psychiatry Review, 23*, 1023–1053.

Bandura, A. (1973). *Aggression: A social learning analysis*. Englewood Cliffs, NJ: Prentice-Hall.

Bandura, A. (1977). *Social learning theory*. New York: Prentice-Hall.

Bandura, A. (2001). Social cognitive theory: An agentic perspective. *Annual Review of Psychology, 52*, 1–26.

Barriga, A.Q. & Gibbs, J.C. (1996). Measuring cognitive distortion in antisocial youth: Development and preliminary validation of the "How I Think" questionnaire. *Aggressive Behavior, 22*, 333–343.

Bilby, C. & Hatcher, R. (2004). Early stages in the development of the Integrated Domestic Abuse Programme (IDAP): Implementing the Duluth Domestic Violence pathfinder. Home Office Online Report 29/04. London: Home Office. Retrieved 30 April 2007 from: http://www.homeoffice.gov.uk/rds/pdfs04/rdsolr2904.pdf

Bonta, J., Law, M., & Hansen, K. (1998). The prediction of criminal and violent recidivism among mentally disordered offenders: A meta-analysis. *Psychological Bulletin, 123*, 123–142.

Bunton, J. & Morphew, R. (2007). Continuing professional development: Lessons from a European Union twinning project. *Forensic Update, 89*, 25–28.

Clark, D.A. (2000). *Theory manual for Enhanced Thinking Skills*. Prepared for Joint Prison–Probation Accreditation Panel. London: Home Office.

Cleckley, H. (1964). *The mask of sanity*. St Louis, MO: C.V. Mosby.

Coid, J., Yang, M., Ullrich, S., et al. (2007). *Predicting and understanding risk of reoffending: The prisoner cohort study*. Research Summary 6. London: Ministry of Justice.

Cooke, D. (2000). Current risk assessment instruments. In *The report of the committee on serious violent and sexual offenders* (pp. 151–158). Retrieved 30 September 2007 from: http://www.scotland.gov.uk/maclean/docs/svso.pdf

Copas, J.B. & Marshall, P. (1998). The Offender Group Reconviction Scale: the statistical reconviction score for use by probation officers. *Journal of the Royal Statistical Society, Series C 47*, 159–171.

Correctional Services Accreditation Panel (CSAP) (2006). *The Correctional Services Accreditation Panel Report 2005–6*. London: Home Office

Coulson, G., Nutbrown, V., & Giulekas, D. (1993). Using the Level of Supervision Inventory in placing female offenders in rehabilitation programmes or halfway houses. *IARCA Journal, 5*, 12–13.

Craissati, J. & Beech, A. (2003). A review of dynamic risk variables and their relationship to risk prediction in sex offenders. *Journal of Sexual Aggression, 9*, 41–55.

Dingwall, R. (1989). Some problems about predicting child abuse and neglect. In O. Stevenson (Ed.), *Child abuse: Public policy and professional practice* (pp. 28–53). Hemel Hempstead: Harvester Wheatsheaf.

Douglas, K.S., Cox, D.N., & Webster, C.D. (1999). Violence risk assessment: Science and practice. *Legal and Criminological Psychology, 4*, 149–184.

Douglas, K.S., Guy, L.S., & Weir, J. (2006). HCR-20 *violence risk assessment scheme: Overview and annotated bibliography.* Burnaby, Canada: Department of Psychology, Simon Fraser University.

Douglas, K.S. & Webster, C.D. (1999). The HCR-20 violence risk assessment scheme: concurrent validity in a sample of incarcerated offenders. *Criminal Justice and Behavior, 26,*3–19.

Forth, A.E. Hart, S.D., & Hare, R.D. (1990). Assessment of psychopathy in male young offenders. *Psychological Assessment, 2,* 342–344.

Friendship, C. Mann, R., & Beech, A. (2003). *The Prison-based Sex Offender Treatment Programme – An evaluation.* Home Office Research Findings 205.

Goldstein, A.P. (2004). Evaluations of effectiveness. In A.P. Goldstein, R. Nensen, B. Daleflod, & M. Kalt (Eds), *New perspectives on Aggression Replacement Training* (pp. 230–244). Chichester: John Wiley & Sons.

Goldstein, A.P. & Glick, B. (1987). *Aggression Replacement Training: A comprehensive intervention for adolescent youth.* Champaign, IL: Research Press.

Goldstein, A.P., Glick, B., & Gibbs, J.C. (1998). *Aggression Replacement Training* (Revised edn). Champaign, IL: Research Press.

Gondolf, E.W. (2001). Limitations of experimental evaluation of batterer programs. *Trauma, Violence and Abuse, 2,* 79–88.

Grove, W.M. & Meehl, P.E. (1996). Comparative efficiency of informal (subjective, impressionistic) and formal (mechanical, algorithmic) prediction procedures: The clinical–statistical controversy. *Psychology, Public Policy, and Law, 2,* 293–323.

Grubin, D. (1997). Predictors of risk in serious sex offenders. *British Journal of Psychiatry, 170,* s17–s21.

Grubin, D. & Wingate, S. (1996) Sexual offence recidivism: Prediction versus understanding. *Criminal Behaviour and Mental Health, 6,* 349–359.

Hanson, R.K. & Thornton, D. (1999). *Static 99: Improving the predictive accuracy of actuarial risk assessments for sex offenders.* Ottawa: Public Works and Government Services Canada.

Hare, R.D. (1980). A research scale for the assessment of psychopathy in criminal populations. *Personality and Individual Differences, 1,* 111–119.

Hare, R.D. (1991). *The Hare Psychopathy Checklist – Revised.* Toronto, Ontario: Multi-Health Systems.

Hart, S.D., Hare, R.D., & Forth, A.E. (1994). Psychopathy as a risk marker for violence: Development and validation of a screening version of the Revised Psychopathy Checklist. In J. Monahan & J. Steadman (Eds), *Violence and mental disorder: Developments in risk assessment* (pp. 81–98). Chicago: The University of Chicago Press.

Hatcher, R.M., Palmer, E.J., McGuire, J., Hounsome, J.C., Bilby, C.A.L., & Hollin, C.R. (in press). Aggression Replacement Training with adult male offenders within community settings: A reconviction analysis. *Journal of Forensic Psychiatry and Psychology.*

Hill, R. (2007). *National Probation Service: Performance Report 24.* Retrieved 10 October 2007 from: http://http://www.probation.homeoffice.gov.uk/output/page34.asp

Hollin, C.R. (1995). The meaning and implications of 'programme integrity'. In J. McGuire (Ed.), *What works: Reducing reoffending* (pp. 195–208). Chichester: John Wiley & Sons.

Hollin, C.R. (2006). Offending behaviour programmes and contention: Evidence-based practice, manuals, and programme evaluation. In C.R. Hollin & E.J. Palmer (Eds), *Offending behaviour programmes: Development, application, and controversies.* (pp. 33–67) Chichester: John Wiley & Sons.

Hollin, C.R., McGuire, J., Hounsome, J., Hatcher, R.M, Bilby, C.A.L., & Palmer, E.J., (2008). Cognitive skills offending behaviour programmes in the community: A reconviction analysis. *Criminal Justice and Behavior, 35,* 269–283.

Hollin, C.R., McGuire, J., Palmer, E.J. *et al.* (2002). *Introducing pathfinder programmes into the probation service: An interim report.* Home Office Research Study 247. London: Home Office Research, Development and Statistics Directorate.

Hollin, C.R. & Palmer, E.J. (2003). Level of Service Inventory-Revised profiles of violent and nonviolent prisoners. *Journal of Interpersonal Violence, 18,* 1075–1086.

Hollin, C.R. & Palmer, E.J. (2006). Offending behaviour programmes: Controversies and resolutions. In C.R. Hollin & E.J. Palmer (Eds), *Offending behaviour programmes: Development, application, and controversies.* (pp. 247–278) Chichester: John Wiley & Sons.

Hollin, C.R., Palmer, E.J., McGuire, J. Hounsome, J., Hatcher, R., & Bilby, C. (2005). *An evaluation of pathfinder programmes in the probation service.* Unpublished research report to the Home Office Research, Development, and Statistics Directorate.

Hollin, C.R., Palmer, E.J., McGuire, J., Hounsome, J., Hatcher, R., Bilby, C., & Clark, C. (2004). *Pathfinder programmes in the probation service: A retrospective analysis.* Home Office Online Report 66/04. Retrieved 6 October 2007, from: http://www.probation.homeoffice.gov.uk/output/page34.asp

Home Office (2007). *Statistics of mentally disordered offenders 2005.* Home Office Statistical Bulletin 05/07. London: Home Office.

House of Commons (2006). *Report of the Zahid Mubarek inquiry.* London: Her Majesty's Stationery Office.

Howard, P. (2006). *The offender assessment system: An evaluation of the second pilot.* Home Office Research Findings Paper 278. London: Home Office.

Howard, P., Clark, D., & Garnham, N. (2006). *An evaluation of the offender assessment system in three pilots 1999–2001.* London: Home Office.

Howe, E. (1994). Judged person dangerousness as weighted averaging. *Journal of Applied Social Psychology, 24,* 1270–1290.

Howells, K. & Hollin, C.R. (1989). *Clinical approaches to violence.* Chichester: John Wiley & Sons.

Jones, A.S., D'Agostino, R.B., Gondolf, E.W., & Heckert, A. (2004). Assessing the effect of batterer program completion on reassault using propensity scores. *Journal of Interpersonal Violence, 19,* 1002–1020.

Klassen, C. (1999). *Predicting Aggression in psychiatric inpatients using 10 historical factors: Validating the "H" of the HCR-20.* Unpublished thesis. Vancouver: Simon Fraser University.

Klaus, P. (2007). *Crime and the Nation's Households, 2005.* Washington, DC: US Department of Justice.

Liau, A.K., Barriga, A.Q., & Gibbs, J.C. (1998). Relations between self-serving cognitive distortions and overt vs. covert antisocial behavior in adolescents. *Aggressive Behavior, 24,* 335–346.

Limandri, B. & Sheridan, D. (1995). Prediction of interpersonal violence: Fact or fiction. In J.C. Campbell (Ed.), *Assessing dangerousness: Violence by sexual offenders, batterers, and child abusers*. Thousand Oaks, CA: Sage Publications.

Litwack, T.R. (2001). Actuarial versus clinical assessments of dangerousness. *Psychology, Public Policy and Law, 7*, 409–443.

Marques, J.K. (1999). How to answer the question "does sex offender treatment work". *Journal of Interpersonal Violence, 14*, 437–451.

McGuire, J. (2000). *Think First: Programme manual*. London: National Probation Service.

McGuire, J. & Hatcher, R. (2001). Offence focused problem solving: Preliminary evaluation of a cognitive skills program. *Criminal Justice and Behaviour, 28*, 564–587.

Mental Health Act 1983. London, UK: Her Majesty's Stationery Office (HMSO).

Miechenbaum, D.M. (1977). *Cognitive behavior modification*. New York: Plenum Press.

Milner, J.S. & Campbell, J.C. (1995). Prediction issues for practitioners. In J. Campbell (Ed.), *Assessing dangerousness: Violence by sexual offenders, batterers, and child abusers*, p. 41–67. Thousand Oaks, CA: Sage Publications.

Moley, S. Taylor, P., Kaiza, P., & Higgins, P. (2007). *Crime in England and Wales: Quarterly update to June 2007*. London: Home Office.

Monahan, J. (1981). *The clinical prediction of violence*. Beverley Hills, CA: Sage.

Moore, R. (2006). The Offender Assessment System (OASys) in England and Wales. *Probation in Europe, 37*, 12–13.

Moore, R. (2007). *Adult offenders' perceptions of their underlying problems: Findings from the OASys self-assessment questionnaire*. Home Office Research Findings 284. London: Home Office.

Morana, H.C.P., Arboleda-Flrez, J., & Câmara, F.P. (2005). Identifying the cut-off score for the PCL-R scale (psychopathy checklist-revised) in a Brazilian forensic population. *Forensic Science International, 147*, 1–8.

National Offender Management Service (2006). *The NOMS Offender Management Model*. London: Home Office.

Novaco, R.W. (1975). *Anger control: The development and evaluation of an experimental treatment*. Lexington, MA: D.C. Heath.

Palmer, E.J., McGuire, J., Hounsome, J.C. *et al.* (2007). Offending behaviour programmes within the community: The effects on reconviction of three programmes with adult male offenders. *Legal and Criminological Psychology, 12*, 251–264.

Pence, E. & Paymar, M. (1993). *Education groups for men who batter: The Duluth model*. New York: Springer.

Polaschek, D.L.L. (2006). Violent offender programmes: Concept, theory, and practice. In C.R. Hollin & E.J. Palmer (Eds), *Offending behaviour programmes*. Chichester: John Wiley & Sons.

Porporino, F.J. & Fabiano, E.A. (2000). *Theory manual for reasoning and rehabilitation* (Revised). Ottawa: T3 Associates.

Quinsey, V.L., Harris, G.T., Rice, M.E., & Cormier, C.A. (1998). *Violent offenders: And managing the risk*. Washington, DC: American Psychological Association.

Quinsey, V.L., Harris, G.T., Rice, M.E., & Cormier, C.A. (2006). *Violent offenders: Appraising and managing risk* (2nd edn). Washington, DC: American Psychological Association.

Quinsey, V.L., Harris, G.T., Rice, M.E., & Lalumiere, M.L. (1993). Assessing treatment efficacy in outcome studies of sex offenders. *Journal of Interpersonal Violence, 8*, 512–523.

Raynor, P. (2007). Risk and need assessment in British probation: the contribution of LSI-R. *Psychology, Crime and Law, 13*, 125–138.

Raynor, P., Kynch, J., Roberts, C., & Merrington, S. (2000). *Risk and Need Assessment in Probation Services: An evaluation.* Home Office Research Study 211. London: Home Office.

Rice, M.E. & Harris, G.T. (1995). Violent recidivism: Assessing predictive validity. *Journal of Consulting and Clinical Psychology, 63*, 737–748.

Roberts, C. (2004). An early evaluation of a cognitive offending behaviour programme (Think First) in probation areas. *Vista: Perspectives on Probation, 8*, 130–136.

Roberts, C., Burnett, R., Kirby, A., & Hamill, H. (1996). *A System for Evaluating Probation Practice.* Probation Studies Unit Report 1. Oxford: University of Oxford Centre for Criminological Research.

Ross, R.R. & Fabiano, E.A. (1985a). *Reasoning and Rehabilitation: Manual.* Ottawa: AIR Training & Associates.

Ross, R.R. & Fabiano, E.A. (1985b). *Time to think: A Cognitive Model of Delinquency Prevention and Offender Rehabilitation.* Johnson City, TN: Institute of Social Sciences and Arts.

Schlager, M.D. & Simourd, D.J. (2007). Validity of the Level of Service Inventory – Revised among African American and Hispanic male offenders. *Criminal Justice and Behavior, 34*, 545–554.

Serin, R.C. (1991). Psychopathy and violence in criminals. *Journal of Interpersonal Violence, 6*, 423–431.

Serin, R.C., Peters, R., & Barbaree, H. (1990). Predictors of psychopathy and release outcomes in a criminal population. *Psychological Assessment, 2*, 419–422.

Shields, I.W. (1993). The use of the Young Offender Level of Service Inventory (YOLSI) with adolescents. *IARCA Journal, 5*, 10–26.

Shields, I.W. & Simourd, D.J. (1991). Predicting predatory behaviour in a population of incarcerated young offenders. *Criminal Justice and Behavior, 18*, 180–194.

Simourd, D.J. & Malcolm, P.B. (1998). Reliability and validity of the Level of Service Inventory-revised among federally incarcerated sex offenders. *Journal of Interpersonal Violence, 13*, 261–274.

Steele, R. (2002a). *Psychometric Features of Think First Participants' Pre and Post Programme.* Research and Information Section, National Probation Service, Merseyside.

Steele, R. (2002b). *Reconviction of Offenders on Think First.* Research and Information Section, National Probation Service, Merseyside.

Stith, S.M., Rosen, K.H., & McCollum, E.E. (2002). Developing a manualized couples treatment for domestic violence: Overcoming challenges. *Journal of Marital and Family Therapy, 30*, 305–318.

Strand, S., Belfrage, H., Fransson, G., & Levander, S. (1999) Clinical and risk management factors in risk prediction of mentally disordered offenders – more important than historical data. *Legal and Criminological Psychology, 4*, 67–76.

Taylor, R. (1999). *Predicting Reconvictions for Sexual and Violent Offences using the Revised Offender Group Reconviction Scale.* Home Office Research Findings 104. London: Home Office.

Thornton, D. (1997). *Structured anchored clinical judgement.* Paper presented at the NOTA Annual Conference, Southampton.

Thornton, D. (2002). Constructing and testing a framework for dynamic risk assessment. *Sexual Abuse: A Journal of Research and Treatment, 14*, 137–151.

Thornton, D., Mann, R., Webster, S., *et al.* (2003). Distinguishing and combining risks for sexual and violent recidivism. In R.A. Prentky, E.S. Janus, & M.C. Seto (Eds), Sexually coercive behavior: Understanding and management. *Annals of the New York Academy of Sciences, 989*, 225–235.

Tong, L.S.J. & Farrington, D.P. (2006). How effective is the 'Reasoning and Rehabilitation' programme in reducing reoffending? A meta-analysis of evaluations in four countries. *Psychology, Crime and Law, 12*, 3–24.

Webster, C.D., Douglas, K.S., Eaves, D., & Hart, S.D. (1997). *HCR-20: Assessing risk for violence*, version 2. Burnaby, British Columbia: Mental Health, Law, & Policy Institute, Simon Fraser University.

Webster, S.D., Mann, R.E., Carter, A.J. *et al.* (2006). Inter-rater reliability of dynamic risk assessment with sexual offenders. *Psychology, Crime and Law, 12*, 439–452.

West Midlands Probation Service (2000). *Sex offender groupwork theory manual.* West Midlands Probation Service: Sex Offender Unit.

Wilson, G.T. (1996). Manual-based treatments: The clinical application of research findings. *Behaviour, Research and Therapy, 34*, 295–314.

Wintrup, A. (1996) *Assessing risk of violence in mentally disordered offenders with the HCR-20.* Vancouver: Simon Fraser University.

ANNOTATED FURTHER READING

Hollin, C.R. (Ed.) (2001). *Handbook of offender assessment and treatment.* Chichester: John Wiley & Sons. *A comprehensive guide to offender assessment and treatment covering issues such as risk assessment, the discussion of theoretical approaches to treatment, and the assessment and treatment of different types of offenders. All chapters are written by experts within each field. Book is also available in a shorter 'essential' handbook.*

Hollin, C.R., & Palmer, E.J. (Eds) (2006). *Offending behaviour programmes: Development, application, and controversies.* Chichester: John Wiley & Sons. *A perfectly readable edited book that introduces offending behaviour programmes for general and offence specific offenders. Provides a detailed view of the current situation relating to offending behaviour programmes, the evaluative evidence for and against them, and the issues and controversies that surround them.*

Marshall, L., Serran, G., Marshall, W.L., & Fernandez, Y. (Eds) (2006). *Sexual offender treatment: Controversial issues.* Chichester: John Wiley & Sons. *An edited book which not only discusses theoretical and practical issues in the treatment of sex offenders but also tackles issues such as diagnostic problems with sex offenders, shame and guilt in child molesters and risk assessment of sex offenders.*

McGuire, J. (Ed.) (1995). *What works: Reducing reoffending: guidelines from research and practice.* Chichester: John Wiley & Sons. *A classic text which stimulated the debate concerning 'What Works' in offender rehabilitation during the mid 1990s and onwards. Covers a discussion of the 'What Works' debate, as well as issues in practice, delivery and implementation of offending behaviour programmes.*

Palmer, E.J., McGuire, J., Hounsome, J.C. *et al.* (2007). Offending behaviour programmes within the community: The effects on reconviction of three programmes with adult male offenders. *Legal and Criminological Psychology, 12,* 251–264. *A recently published national evaluation of three general offending behaviour programmes within community settings in England and Wales.*

GLOSSARY

Absolute judgment: A method of deciding which person in a line-up is the perpetrator that is based on the degree to which their face matches the witness' memory of the perpetrator. An absolute judgment is independent of the other members of the line-up (cf. **relative judgment**).

Accusatorial strategies: see Confrontational process.

Achieving Best Evidence: Current official guidance in England and Wales (from 2001) for all parties (e.g. legal personnel, police officers, social workers) and covering all vulnerable witnesses, from the initial interview through to court appearance.

Actuary: An expert who performs in an actuarial role assesses the relative probabilities of an event or outcome for the court.

Actus reus: Literally 'guilty act'; that a criminal act has occurred.

Adversarial: Arrangements designed to bring out the truth of a matter, through adversarial (conflict-based) techniques such as cross-examination.

Adversarial court system: Frequently referred to as accusatorial. Each side presents a case (prosecution and defence) before a court. The judge gives no help to either side nor participates in the discovering of the truth amid the conflicting accounts.

Aetiology: The science of causation, especially the enquiry into the origin and causes of a disease or condition.

Age-crime curve: A common pattern of criminal behaviour that describes an increase as the adolescent matures, a peak in the late teens and early twenties and then a decrease as age increases.

Algorithm: A mathematical procedure that must be followed in a set order and will derive an overall score.

Amnesia: Loss of memory. Such loss can be selective or global.

Anatomically-correct dolls (ACDs): Realistic dolls, used in CSA cases and therapy, with external male or female genitalia to assist non-verbal expression of sexual activity.

Anatomically-detailed dolls: see Anatomically-correct dolls.

Anchors: Common-sense rules that concern unquestioned assumptions about people, behaviour and ideas.

Anchored narratives: The relating of an ordered sequence of events that occur over time and are embedded in anchors.

Balance of probability: Also known as the 'preponderance of evidence'. The standard is met if the proposition is more likely to be true than not true.

Bias: A distortion of memory that may arise from the effect of personal knowledge, experience or expectation.

Bio-social: The influence, both independently and cumulatively, of biological and social factors in promoting criminal behaviour.

Blended memories: A mix of initial and post-event memory details.

British Crime Survey: An annual survey conducted on behalf of the Home Office which measures the amount of crime in England and Wales by asking a sample of the population about their experiences of crime in the preceding year.

Celerity: In penology, the amount of time that elapses between an offence being committed and an official sanction being imposed.

Central detail: The focus of action or events.

Certainty: In penology, the likelihood of legal punishment as a result of committing a crime, which may be assessed objectively (with reference to official statistics) or subjectively (with reference to the experience of individual offenders).

Change order: Cognitive interview prompt to recall the initial event in a different order (e.g. backwards).

Change perspective: Cognitive interview prompt to recall the initial event from another perspective of an initial event.

Civil: Matters concerning private rights and not offences against the state.

Civil cases: Cases that are concerned with private wrongs, as between one person and another.

Classical conditioning: The process of learning by association in which specific stimuli (e.g. being fed) become associated with a reflex response (e.g. salivation).

Closed questions: Questions that are worded in such a way as to elicit either a 'yes' or 'no' answer, or some other single-word answer.

Coerced-compliant false confession: False confession given in the face of coercion by the investigator but only to appease the investigator and not accepted by the suspect

Coerced-internalized false confession: False confession given in the face of coercion by the investigator, but which becomes fully accepted as the truth by the suspect.

Cognitive-behavioural: A model or approach in psychological therapy and training, derived from a synthesis of concepts from behaviourism and cognitive psychology and focusing on the interconnections of thoughts, feelings and behaviour and how they can be modified over time.

Cognitive mnemonics: Memory-jogging techniques for a cognitive interview.

Cognitive schemata: General conceptual frameworks, or clusters of knowledge, regarding objects, people and situations.

Cognitive script: A type of schema involving behaviour or action.

Cognitive skills training: A method of working with individuals designed to help them acquire or improve capacities for problem solving in everyday activities, particularly with reference to the social domain (social problem-solving training).

Commitment: An effect whereby once a face has been identified by a witness in one procedure, the witness becomes committed to the identification and is likely to identify the same face if seen again in a subsequent procedure. The effect is observed even when the initial judgment is mistaken.

Common law: The form of law that was universal or 'common' in England after unification with the Normans and is based on judicial precedents as opposed to statutory laws.

Compliance: Agreeing to or with the perceived wishes of the experimenter; yielding or submitting to what is seen as the experimenter's expectations.

Concordance: Term used in genetic research for two individuals who both possess or lack some particular trait or characteristic. Rates of concordance may be used to identify the genetic basis of such factors as criminal behaviour, when all other factors are controlled.

Conformity: The tendency for people to adopt the behaviours, attitudes, and values of other members of a reference group.

Confrontation: A term used in Britain to refer to a procedure in which the witness is permitted to view the suspect for the purpose of identification. A confrontation may occur in a police station, although this procedure is rarely used. A street confrontation may be conducted shortly after a crime has been committed if there is insufficient evidence to arrest the suspect in the absence of an identification. In the US this procedure is referred to as a **show-up**.

Confrontational process: Interviewing style that sees a confession as the only satisfactory outcome to an interview with a suspect.

Context reinstatement: Cognitive interview prompt to reinstate mentally the surrounding context of the initial event.

Control Question Test (CQT): A method of polygraph testing. Control questions concern transgressions in the past, designed to force everyone, guilty or otherwise, to give a deceptive response. Reactions to control questions are then compared to questions relevant to the crime under investigation: the guilty person should react more strongly to the relevant questions than to the control questions, while the opposite pattern is expected for innocent people.

Conversation management interview: Technique proposed by Dr Eric Shepherd, which emphasizes the police officer's awareness and management of the interview, both verbally and non-verbally.

Corroboration: Confirmation by other or additional sources.

Covert sensitization: Method developed in behaviour therapy, applying conditioning principles to induce individuals to associate socially or personally unacceptable feelings and behaviour with an experience of disgust and thereby reduce their potency.

Credibility: The quality of being believable or trustworthy.

Criminal cases: Cases that are concerned with offences deemed to be against the public interest.

Criminogenic need: Factors that are intrinsically linked to individual criminal offending behaviour patterns. Examples may include positive attitudes towards criminal behaviour, drug misuse, anti-social personality, problem-solving skills and how hostility/aggression is expressed. An alternative term used to describe *dynamic risk factors* (see below).

Criteria-Based Content Analysis (CBCA): Method for analysing children's statements in terms of indices that are believed to reflect truthfulness; part of Statement Validity Analysis.

Cross-examination: The questioning of a witness for the other side in a case.

Crown Court: The Crown Court deals with all crime committed for trial by Magistrates' Courts. Cases for trial are heard before a judge and jury. The Crown Court also acts as an Appeal Court for cases heard and dealt with by Magistrates. The Crown Court can also deal with some civil and family matters. The Crown Court is divided into tiers, depending on the type of work dealt with.

Cue-dependent theory: Theory that successful retrieval of memories requires access to a cue or prompt encoded contemporaneously with the original event.

Cued recall: The additional information volunteered by a person when prompts or cues are offered to stimulate remembrance.

Culpability: Liability to blame; guilty as charged.

Culprit-description strategy: A method of selecting members of a line-up on the criterion that their appearance matches the attributes mentioned in the witness' description of the culprit.

Default value: An attribute that was not mentioned in a description but is assumed to take a default value. For example, a witness may not mention that a perpetrator was not wearing glasses. The default value would be that he was not.

Deterrence: One of the objectives of sentencing, based on the premise that adverse consequences (punishment) will make recurrence of offending (criminal recidivism) less likely.

Deterrence theory: In penology, the doctrine that the costs of committing crimes will have a suppressant effect on the frequency or severity of criminal activity. *General deterrence* refers to the effect of visible punishments on the population as a whole. *Specific deterrence* refers to the impact on the subsequent behaviour of individuals convicted and sentenced.

Developmental criminology: The differing forms of deviant behaviour exhibited by offenders as their criminal career evolves.

Directed masturbation: Also called masturbatory reconditioning, a behaviour therapy technique, based on conditioning principles, employed to help individuals with inappropriate sexual urges or attractions to divert their interests in more socially acceptable or less harmful ways.

Disinhibition: Lowering of inhibitions due to another factor.

Disassociation: A defensive disruption in the normally occurring connection among feelings, thoughts, behaviours and memories, consciously or unconsciously invoked, to reduce psychological distress during or after traumatic episodes.

Distribution: The range and frequency of scores of any group of participants under test. While the means of two tested groups may differ significantly, the range of scores of the two groups may overlap.

Dizygotic twins: Twins who have only half of their genes in common, e.g. fraternal (sororal) twins on average have the same degree of genetic similarity as siblings.

DNA: Deoxyribonucleic acid: the material inside the nucleus of cells that carries genetic information. Each individual possesses a unique profile and this has become a powerful tool in the detection of offenders where genetic material has been left at a crime scene.

Dock identification: A procedure used for formal identification, particularly under Scottish Law. A witness in a court is asked whether they can see the perpetrator present in the court. The expectation is that the witness will identify the prisoner in the dock.

Documentary evidence: Material that includes, photographs, plans, documentary hearsay, affidavits, videotapes, etc.

Ecological validity: The degree to which experimental conditions reproduce accurately real-life situations. Ecological validity is closely related to external validity.

Effect size: A statistic used to compare the magnitude of the effect of an independent variable across different studies. In meta-analysis, statistics of this kind are combined across several studies to produce a *mean effect size*.

Either-way offence: An offence for which the accused may elect the case to be dealt with either summarily by the magistrates or by committal to the Crown Court to be tried by jury.

Elaboration: Creating a relationship between two items in memory.

Electroencephalogram (EEG): Procedure in which changes in the electrical potential of the brain are recorded.

Emotional events: Incidents, both naturally occurring and contrived, which give rise to strong affect from participants or observers.

Encoding: Initial stage of memory resulting from external information being perceived by the observer.

Encoding specificity principle: The principle that the probability of an item is being retrieved from memory is proportional to the overlap of cues present at encoding and at **retrieval**.

Episodic: Relating to a specific episode or event.

Estimator variable: A factor that may affect the reliability of eyewitness memory, which is not under the control of the criminal justice system. The influence of estimator variables may serve to estimate the probability of accurate memory in the relevant circumstances. The time for which the witness was able to view the perpetrator is an example of an estimator variable (cf. **system variable**).

Ethical interviewing: Method of interview advocated by Shepherd (1991), emphasizing the importance of the interviewer showing human feeling towards suspects.

Evidence: Information presented in testimony or in documents that is used to persuade the fact finder (judge or jury) to decide the case for one side or the other.

Examination-in-Chief: That examination which is made of a witness by a party calling him or her.

Expert evidence: Person employed to give evidence on a subject who by training, knowledge and experience is qualified to express a professional opinion. The law defines an opinion as a statement not expressing a direct perception.

Explicit: A memory of which the person remembering is aware and is able to use to generate a response (e.g. a verbal description or a positive identification at a line-up.)

Eyewitness memory: The study of memory and its problems from the perspective of an eyewitness to crime.

Factual approach: The disclosure by the interviewer of all available evidence to the suspect, sometimes even false information, with the presumption that this will to lead to a quick confession, as the suspect believes that further resistance is useless.

False confessions: Any confession or any admission to a criminal act that the confessor did not commit.

Familiarity: A feeling that a detail has been previously experienced in the absence of contextual details.

Foil: A person who appears in a live, video or photographs line-up. The foils are volunteers who are not suspects. They are also referred to as distracters, fillers or line-up members in the research literature. In the English legal context they are usually referred to as volunteers and in Scotland as stand-ins.

fMRI: Functional magnetic resonance imagery. Technique of imaging activity with widespread uses in psychology, including searching for neural correlates of deception.

Free recall: The information volunteered by a person in answer to the single prompt 'What happened?'

Functional analysis: An approach to understanding behaviour that focuses on determining its function for the individual.

Fuzzy-trace theory: A dual-process model of memory proposed by Brainerd and Reyna whereby verbatim and gist traces are encoded for each detail.

Grooming: Attempting to befriend a child with the intention of gaining their trust (and possibly that of the child's carers) with the intent of having sexual contact with the child. This behaviour was deemed a criminal offence in England and Wales by the Sexual Offences Act 2003.

Ground truth: The reality of what actually occurred in a given event; sometimes impossible to establish in criminal investigations on the basis of witness' statements alone.

Groupthink: The tendency of a decision-making group to filter out undesirable input so that a consensus may be reached, especially if it is in line with the leader's viewpoint.

Guilt-presumptive process: Style of interviewing which assumes the guilt of the suspect.

Guilty Knowledge Test (GKT): A method of polygraph testing. Suspects are given multiple-choice questions concerning details of the crime containing one correct alternative which only a guilty person might be expected to know. The guilty suspect should experience more physiological arousal to the correct alterative compared to the others, while an innocent suspect will react similarly to all alternatives.

Heuristics: Cognitive strategies or 'rules of thumb', often used as short cuts in solving a complex inferential task.

High-stake lies: Lies, the effectiveness of which are critical to the liar; typically lies told by a suspect during a police interview.

Homogenization: The view that victims and offenders are uniform in composition and can be treated as mutually exclusive groups.

Hypermnesia: Memory that actually increases rather than decreases in strength and detail over time.

Iatrogenic: A medical or psychological condition caused by the form of treatment. The allegation that false memories are caused by inappropriate psychotherapeutic techniques would be an example.

Identity parade: The term used in Britain to refer to a live line-up of people for the purpose of allowing the witness to attempt to make an identification.

Implant memories: To create a false memory in a person through misleading questioning or other suggestive means.

Implicit: An effect of memory that exerts an influence on behaviour of which the person remembering is unaware. For example, innocent suspects may be mistakenly identified because they have been seen on a prior occasion of which the witness has no conscious **recollection**.

Incapacitation: An objective of sentencing; use of criminal justice intervention to reduce criminality by removing offenders from crime opportunities.

Informational social influence: The need to conform to sources of information other than our own because we believe others' interpretations are more accurate than our own.

Information-gathering strategies: Style of interview where the interview seeks to establish facts about a crime from the suspect rather than immediately assuming his or her guilt.

Information-processing theories: A set of theories that explain memory in terms of encoding, storage, and retrieval processes.

Inquisitorial court system: A type of judicial trial common to most European countries whereby the court judges play an active role in assembling the case material and questioning all witnesses. After hearing the evidence, the court judges apply their own reasoning to determine where the truth lies.

Integrity: The extent to which an intervention is delivered as planned and in accordance with the model of change on which it is based; sometimes called fidelity, programme integrity, treatment integrity.

Intentional explanations: Explanations in terms of meaning and intentions may be required for human behaviour because of the causality inherent in biological systems that have inbuilt and acquired goals, aims and objectives. This type of explanation is frequently contrasted with the causality (cause leading to effect) found in physical systems.

Intermediaries: One of the special measures permitted by the YJCE Act 1999. An intermediary assists by communicating to the witness questions put to him or her, and then communicating the witness' response back to the questioner. The intermediary must be approved, and can act in court, or assist in making of video-recorded evidence-in-chief.

Interpersonal skills training: A method of working with individuals designed to help them acquire new skills, or improve their skills, for interaction with others; also known as social skills training.

Interrogation manuals: Books, memorandums or other printed recommendations principally written by police officers, detectives, or former staff members of scientific crime laboratories.

Interviewer bias: An interviewer who shapes the course of the interview to maximize disclosures that are consistent with what he/she believes a child witnessed or experienced.

Interviewer's behaviour: Behaviour that may be based on different grounds (e.g. a presumption of guilt or genuine empathy), which has an influence on how the interviewer act in the interviewing situation.

Investigative interviewing: A broader term than interrogation, implying a fair, dualistic, and open-minded communication to obtain accurate and reliable information conducted in the frame of the national law and the UN Human, Civil and Political Rights agreements.

Lateralization: The way in which certain functions are associated with the left or right hemisphere of the brain.

Lawyerese: see Legalese.

Layered Voice Analysis (LVA): Lie detection technique based on highly sophisticated technology that uses a computer program to analyse speech errors occurring when a raw signal (sound) is digitized. Such errors are very difficult for the human ear to detect, but it is argued that these can be measured by more refined methods.

Leading questions: Questions worded in such a way as to suggest or imply the answer that is being sought.

Learning disabilities: Developmental difficulties in learning, language and general cognition.

Legalese: Refers to lexically and syntactically complicated language that has developed to meet the needs of the legal profession and often deployed in questions to witnesses at court.

Level of processing: The degree (or depth) to which an item is cognitively processed. Deep processing that involves a complex semantic association (e.g. judging the personality of somebody from their face) tends to result in a better memory than shallow processing (e.g. judging the face to be male).

Level of Service/Case Management Inventory: A specially constructed assessment instrument, developed by Canadian researchers, for combining a range of information about an individual to estimate risk of future offending, factors likely to influence it, and to design a plan of supervision or management accordingly.

Line-up: American term for an identification parade.

Linguistic Inquiry and Word Count (LIWC): A computer-based technique that creates linguistic profiles by means of categorizing words into different classes.

Live link: One of the special measures permitted by the YJCE Act 1999.

Long-term memory: Memories for details that have been stored in a long-term store.

Low-stake lies: Lies which have trivial consequences: typically the lies told by participants in laboratory studies of deception.

Magistrates' Court: A Court where criminal proceedings are commenced before lay magistrates (called 'Justices of the Peace' in the UK) who examine the evidence/statements and either deal with the case themselves or commit to the Crown Court for trial or sentence. Also has jurisdiction in a range of civil matters.

Malleable: Capable of being shaped by extraneous forces, such as other witnesses, questioners, or self-reflection.

Memorandum of Good Practice: Original official guidance (introduced in 1992) for police officers and social workers in England and Wales conducting video-recorded investigative interviews with child witnesses for possible criminal proceedings. Now superseded by *Achieving Best Evidence* (2001).

Memory strategies: Deliberate mental activities used to hold details in working memory, to store information, and to transfer information to long-term memory and existing knowledge.

Mens rea: Literally 'guilty mind'; that there is criminal intent/responsibility.

Meta-analysis: A method of integrating the quantitative findings from a number of primary studies, using statistical analysis to detect trends amongst the results obtained.

Misinformation effect: Social (acquiescence) and psychological (memory) factors that affect participant's encoding, storage, retrieval, and reporting of events.

Misinformation paradigm: Three-phased paradigm for testing misinformation effect developed by Elizabeth Loftus.

Mock crime: Technique much used in forensic psychology in which unsuspecting observers are exposed to a realistic but contrived criminal act.

Mock witness: A person who was not present at a crime (or staged event) but is used to evaluate the fairness of an identification procedure. A mock witness serves to model a real witness who has no memory of the original event other than any information provided by the experimenter at the identification procedure.

Modelling: Learning of behaviour by observing another individual performing that behaviour and then copying it.

Monozygotic twins: Twins who share the same genotypes, for example identical twins.

Mugshot: Photographs of convicted criminals kept by the police. Mugshot albums (or witness albums) are shown to witnesses when the police do not know the identity of a suspect. A witness may be shown an album of photographs of people who have been convicted of similar offences. The procedure differs from a line-up because all of the people in a mugshot album are suspects.

Multimodal: A term used to describe intervention programmes that have more than one target of change or employ more than one method of achieving it.

National Offender Management Service (NOMS): NOMS is a directorate of the Ministry of Justice within England and Wales tasked with reducing reoffending and protecting the public. NOMS encompassed the Prison and Probation Services and aims to 'bridge the divide between custody and community'.

Need principle: Developed by Andrews and colleagues alongside the risk and responsivity principles, the need principle states that interventions should target only those needs (or risk factors), which contribute to offending behaviour. Such factors have been termed 'criminogenic' needs.

Negative feedback: Question strategies that imply the interviewees' first answer may be incorrect.

Neuropsychological: The area of psychology that focuses on the relationships between neurological processes and behaviour.

Offender Group Reconviction Scale: A prediction instrument for use in estimating the likely recidivism rate of a sample of offenders over a two-year period, based on static risk indicators; derived from statistical analysis of a large database of criminal records, conducted by the Research, Development and Statistics Directorate of the UK Ministry of Justice.

Offending behaviour programme: A specially designed and structured sequence of methods and exercises, usually guided by a manual, for direct work with offenders with the objective of the reducing criminal recidivism/offending behaviour.

Olfactory aversive conditioning: A behaviour therapy technique, based on conditioning principles, employed with individuals who have committed sexual offences as a result of socially unacceptable patterns of sexual arousal and associated behaviour.

Operant behaviour: Behaviour that is learnt as a result of the reinforcing or punishing environmental consequences it produces.

Oral testimony: Evidence given to a court, verbally rather than in writing.

Organization: Storage of details to-be-recalled at a later time.

PACE: see Police and Criminal Evidence Act (1984).

Paradigm: The approach taken to investigation based on the values, beliefs, philosophy of knowledge and tested explanations of the researcher. Different researchers operate under different paradigms.

PEACE model of interviewing: Mnemonic denoting the following phases of the interview *Planning and preparation, Engage and explain, Account, clarification and challenge, Closure and Evaluation.*

Penology: The study of legal punishment and of how it is administered.

Peripheral detail: Details which lie outside the central focus of actions or events.

Photo-spread: A line-up of photographs normally consisting of one photograph of the suspect presented amongst foils. The procedure is widely used in the US for formal identification by eyewitnesses.

Plaintiff: One who commences a law suit against another.

Polarization: After deliberating with one another, people are likely to move towards a more extreme point in the direction to which they were previously inclined.

Police and Criminal Evidence Act: Act originally introduced in England and Wales in 1984 governing the conduct of police investigations and interactions with suspects and subject to periodic revision.

Polygraph: Sometimes called the 'lie detector'; a machine that measures typically, galvanic skin response, cardiovascular activity and breathing patterns in suspects under questioning.

Post-event information: Information that a witness may acquire after the relevant incident has occurred. Post-event information may affect a witness' testimony. Misleading post-event information may result in memory distortion.

Powerful speech: Style of speech characterized as forceful, authoritative and confident. Contrast with powerless speech.

Powerless speech: Style of speech characterized as hesitant, faltering and lacking in confidence. Contrast with powerful speech.

Preparation: Activities concerned with assessing the needs of the witness, providing support, liaising and communicating on the witness' behalf, and preparing the witness for the trial (e.g. providing information, court visit).

Presumption of innocence: Legal philosophy that all suspects are innocent until proven guilty.

Presupposition: What is implicitly involved in making an assertion; a presupposition is a necessary condition for either the truth or the falsity of the statement that presupposes it.

Prima facie: On the first view; at first glance/sight; on the face of it.

Probative: Helpful to the court; serving as proof.

Programme: A structured sequence of learning opportunities, with objectives and contents planned in advance, designed to support and encourage change; usually accompanied by a manual or other materials to allow it to be reproduced on successive occasions. See *Offending Behaviour Programme*.

Proof beyond reasonable doubt: The standard in a criminal case requiring that the jury be satisfied to a moral certainty that every element of a crime has been proven by the prosecution. This standard of proof does not require that the state establish absolute certainty by eliminating all doubt, but it does require that the evidence be so conclusive that all reasonable doubts are removed from the mind of the ordinary person.

Psychodynamic: Theories deriving from Sigmund Freud's work.

Psychological Stress Evaluator (PSE): Alternative name for Voice Stress Analysis.

Psychosocial: Relating to the psychological and social factors which independently and cumulatively influence the development of criminal behaviour.

Punishment: Aversive stimuli that result from a specific behaviour, and so leads to a decrease in that behaviour.

Rapport: Interview instruction to development a friendly relationship between an interviewer and an interviewee.

Real evidence: Diverse material forms that enable inference through senses.

Reality monitoring: The process by which people distinguish memories of real events from memories of imagined events. The distinction is based on such considerations as contextual information concerning time and place, semantic information, cognitive operations, and the presence of perceptual features.

Recall: Remembering an item seen or heard previously. Free recall refers to a witness' own self-generated account. Recall can be cued, for example, by asking questions.

Recognition: A judgment that an item presented during a test has been previously seen or heard, as in a line-up procedure.

Recollection: The act of recalling a specific episode. The term is often used to distinguish the subjective experience of conscious recollection of a memory from recall of an attribute that is not accompanied by a conscious recollection of experience of seeing or hearing it.

Rehabilitation: An objective of sentencing, and of allied criminal justice initiatives, concerned with constructive efforts to provide education, training, or other services to enable offenders to become re-integrated in society, with the conjoint aim of reducing recidivism.

Rehearsal: Repetition of to-be-remembered details.

Reinforcement: Rewarding stimuli that result from a specific behaviour and so lead to an increase in that behaviour.

Relapse prevention: Originally conceptualized for the treatment of addictive behaviours such as alcoholism, relapse prevention is a self-control programme designed to help people from relapsing into episodes of problem behaviour. Often used in the treatment of sex offenders, relapse prevention attempts to provide the offender with a set of personalized skills which help the offender maintain a positive change in their problem behaviour.

Relative judgment: A judgment of which item from a set of alternatives is most likely to have been seen before. Often used to refer to a judgment by an eyewitness of which line-up member is most like the person seen (cf. **absolute judgment**).

Report all: cognitive interview prompt to tell everything.

Representativeness: The degree to which a sample of jurors represents the characteristics of the population as a whole.

Responsivity: A design feature that contributes to effectiveness of intervention programmes with offenders.

Responsivity principle: Developed by Andrews and colleagues alongside the principles of risk and need, the responsivity principle proposes that the method delivery of an intervention should match those to whom it is delivered. *General responsivity* refers to an overall approach in which activities have clear objectives and structure, and entail active engagement of participants in processes focused on behavioural or attitudinal change. *Specific responsivity* requires taking into account factors that reflect diversity amongst participants in terms of age, gender, ethnicity, language, ability level, or learning style.

Restorative justice: A relatively recent departure in criminal justice in several countries, entailing services through which offenders make reparations to victims for the harm they have done, sometimes through a carefully managed negotiation and reconciliation process involving a range of 'stakeholders'.

Retribution: One of the objectives of sentencing, and influential theory of the sentencing process, based on the proposal that the harm done by offenders requires society to rectify an imbalance so created, by punishing the offender appropriately.

Retrieval: The process of accessing a memory. Retrieval might involve **recall, recognition** or facilitation on an indirect test of memory.

Retrieval environment: External and internal (to the observer) conditions existing at the time an attempt is made to retrieve a given memory.

Retrieval interference: Condition when access to the memory trace of an initially experienced event is blocked by subsequent misinformation.

Right-thinking persons' test: Principle that a person, knowing all the facts, [would] feel that the passing of any sentence other than a custodial one would not have done justice.

Risk assessment: A set of procedures and methods for estimating the likelihood of future offending by an individual or the level of harm that might be caused by it and for identifying the factors associated with it.

Risk factor: An individual or environmental variable that has been shown through empirical research to be associated with greater likelihood of involvement in criminal activity (or other type of problem). *Static* risk factors are historically set by past events (e.g. age at first conviction); *dynamic* risk factors are more immediate influences on offending behaviour, are likely to vary over short- or medium-term periods, and are potentially susceptible to change through intervention efforts.

Risk management: System of arrangements or interventions put in place to contain or reduce the likelihood of recurrence of harmful behaviour, alongside procedures for monitoring this over time.

Risk-needs-responsivity model (RNR): An evidence-based approach to working with those who have broken the law, and engaging in constructive work with them, based on research concerning the likelihood of re-offending, the factors likely to influence it, and aspects of the manner in which interventions are designed and delivered.

Risk principle: Developed by Andrews and colleagues alongside the principles of need and responsivity, the risk principle states that the level of intervention received by an offender should match the level of risk that the offender poses. Higher risk individuals should receive a higher level of intervention than lower risk individuals.

Rules of evidence: Standards governing whether evidence in a civil or criminal case is admissible.

Safeguarding: The process of protecting individuals from abuse or neglect, preventing impairment of their health and development, and promoting their welfare and life chances.

Scientific Content Analysis (SCAN): Technique originally developed by Sapir, based on the assumption that a statement based on memory of an actual experience differs in content from a statement based on invention.

Screens: One of the special measures permitted by the YJCE Act 1999.

Script: A representation of the typical format of repeated everyday events, such as buying goods in a shop, eating a meal in restaurant etc.

Self-management: A form of cognitive behavioural intervention designed to increase individuals' capacities for exercising internalized control over aspects of their thoughts, feelings of behaviour that are causing difficulty or distress.

Self-manipulations: Hand/finger and leg/foot movements popularly believed to be associated with deception.

Self-reinforcement: Learning to behave in a certain way as a result of self-approval.

Sentence, sentencing: The penalty imposed on an individual found guilty of an offence in a court of law; the process through which this is decided.

Sentencing Reasons Form: A document completed by magistrates that states the main aims of the sentence imposed.

Sequential line-ups or identification parades: Each parade member is shown or presented one at a time.

Severity: In penology, the magnitude of a punishment or the estimated amount of pain or discomfort a convicted offender would be likely to endure.

Show-up: see Confrontation.

Simulated amnesia: Attempt to evade responsibility for a crime by pretending to have no memory for the event in question.

Simultaneous line-ups: All parade members are shown or presented together.

Social Impact Theory: The likelihood that a person will respond to social influence increases with *strength, immediacy, and number*.

Social loafing: The phenomenon that persons make less effort to achieve a goal when they work in a group than when they work alone.

Social schema and scripts: Cognitive frameworks that guide individual's behaviour by providing organizational structures for new experiences/social cues.

Source attribution: The attribution of a memory to a specific source or episode. A source attribution error refers to a situation when a memory is mistakenly attributed to the incorrect source or episode.

Source-monitoring error: Term associated with Marcia Johnson to describe incorrect attribution of the source of a memory.

Special measures: The measures specified in the YJCE Act 1999, which may be ordered for eligible witnesses by means of a special measures direction. They include: screens; live link; video-recorded evidence-in-chief; intermediaries and aids to communication.

Staged theft: Technique in forensic research involving the theft of an object in front of a participant who believes the theft to be genuine.

Standards of proof: Indicates the degree to which the point must be proven. In a civil case, the burden of proof rests with the plaintiff, who must establish his or her case by such standards of proof as a 'preponderance of evidence' or 'clear and convincing evidence'.

Statement Validity Analysis (SVA): A method of assessing the veracity of child witness statements in trials for sexual offences. SVA is used extensively in Sweden, Germany and the Netherlands. The basis of the technique is a belief that truthful, reality-based verbal statements differ significantly from unfounded, falsified or distorted verbal statements – and these differences can be detected. The overall SVA procedure involves (a) a semi-structured interview; (b) a criterion-based content analysis (CBCA) of the statements made; and (c) an evaluation of the CBCA outcome. The CBCA itself comprises 19 criteria, broken down into three General Characteristics criteria, ten Specific Content criteria, five Motivation-related Content criteria, and one Offence-specific Element criterion.

Stereotype: A generalized belief about an entity, or a group of people that is often over-simplified and does not take account of individual differences or other variation in everyday situations.

Storage: The process by which a memory is maintained over time. Storage can be subject to decay or interference from similar memories.

Story model: Holistic judgments based on causal relations between evidence.

Street identification: A street identification may be conducted shortly after a crime has been committed if there is insufficient evidence to arrest the suspect in the absence of an identification. A street identification may consist of allowing the witness to view an informal group, driving the witness around the area to see if they recognize the culprit, or a **confrontation** with a person already detained, perhaps in response to a description broadcast on a police radio.

Suggestibility: Degree to which an individual may be unduly influenced by forms of questioning or the power of the questioner to give the answer the questioner desires.

Suggestion: Distortion of memory that arises from misleading **post-event information**.

Suggestiveness: Distortions of perception or memory that can arise from deliberate or incidental contextual influences.

Summary offences: A criminal offence that is triable only by a Magistrates' Court.

Suspect-resemblance strategy: A method of selecting members of a line-up on the criterion that their appearance is similar to the appearance of the suspect (cf. **culprit-description strategy**).

Symptomology: The study of symptoms and syndromes associated with a particular condition or phenomenon.

System variables: Aspects of a criminal investigation over which investigators have control, e.g. the instructions at an identification parade (cf. **estimator variable**).

Tertiary prevention: Systematic attempt to reduce further offence recidivism by work with convicted offenders within the criminal justice system; contrasted with primary prevention (which has a long-term developmental focus, e.g. work with families in deprived neighbourhoods) and secondary prevention (work with individuals or groups at risk of involvement in delinquency, e.g. children involved in bullying, or truanting from school).

Therapeutic jurisprudence: A perspective that sees the law (rules of law, legal procedures, and roles of legal actors) itself as a social force that often produces therapeutic or anti-therapeutic consequences, which means the law's impact on emotional life and psychological well-being.

Trace-alteration: Misinformation which overwrites/alters the memory trace of an initially experienced event (Elizabeth Loftus).

Transcript: The formal official record of an interview.

Transfer of control: Cognitive interview instruction to pass the control of an interview to the interviewee.

UnDeutsch Hypothesis: Hypothesis, first enunciated by Udo UnDeutsch, that if a child's statement is based on the memory of an actual experience, it will differ in content and quality from a statement based on fabrication.

Validity checklist: Final stage of Statement Validity Analysis in which alternative hypotheses are considered concerning a child's statement.

Vicarious reinforcement/learning: Learning to behave in a certain way as a result of observing the reinforcing and punishing consequences of that behaviour for other people.

Video identification: A procedure of conducting a line-up in which the witness views successive video clips of the line-up members. This procedure is used for the overwhelming majority of formal identification procedures in England and Wales, replacing the use of live line-ups.

Video-recorded evidence-in-chief: 'Video recording' refers to any recording on any medium, from which a moving image (with sound) may be produced. Video-recorded evidence-in-chief is usually an early investigative interview with a vulnerable witness that has been conducted by a trained practitioner (e.g. police officer) and recorded. First introduced by the Criminal Justice Act 1991 and one of the special measures permitted by the YJCE Act 1999.

Voice Stress Analysis: Belief that by measuring the activity in the muscles responsible for producing speech it may be possible to infer the speaker's mental state (e.g., experiences of stress).

Voir dire: Jury selection process of questioning prospective jurors.

Voluntary false confession: False confession offered by the suspect without any coercion from the investigator.

Voyeurism: A practice within which people derive sexual pleasure from observing other individuals. Non-consensual voyeurism is deemed to be an illegal act in England and Wales under section 67 of Sexual Offences Act 2003.

Vulnerable witnesses: Witnesses may be vulnerable due to their youth, incapacity or circumstances. This encompasses children, the elderly, individuals with learning difficulties, or physical impairments, victims of sexual offences, individuals with mental health problems and all persons where there is a risk that the quality of their evidence at trial may be diminished by reason of fear or distress.

Weapon focus: Phenomenon displayed by victims of crime to focus on the weapon employed to the detriment of detail concerning the appearance of the offender.

Working memory: Term developed by Baddeley to describe the stage of memory where incoming information is actively related to existing information stored in long-term memory.

INDEX